THEORIES OF PREACHING
Selected Readings in the Homiletical Tradition

Richard Lischer

THE LABYRINTH PRESS
Durham, North Carolina

Library of Congress Cataloging in Publication Data

Theories of preaching.

Includes index.

    1. Preaching. I. Lischer, Richard.
    BV4222.T48   1987   251   87-3504
    ISBN 0-939464-46-2
    ISBN 0-939464-45-4 (pbk.)

Printed in the United States of America

THEORIES OF PREACHING

To
Adam Lischer
courage, humor, grace

CONTENTS

PREFACE

Theories of Preaching is organized into eight divisions with between four and nine selections under each division. I have provided a brief orientation to each selection and maintained a conversation between the positions represented in the various selections. As a help to the reader, matters of spelling, capitalization, punctuation, and the like have been made uniform. Omissions are marked by an ellipsis. In some cases footnotes have been placed in brackets in the text; for the sake of clarity and brevity many other footnotes have been eliminated.

A theological and historical cross-section of the church's homiletics offers an exciting depth of riches, but also several painful limitations. One such limit is the foreshortened perspective on preaching that in most selections restricts that office to males. At times the "manliness" of preaching, as it is represented in some authors, may be oppressive to the reader, whether female or male. It is my judgment that to change the language is to tamper with matters over which I have no jurisdiction and, ultimately, to rewrite history. Thus in every case the authors' language stands.

The titles after each author's name are usually my own distillation of the material, though in some cases I have used the exact chapter titles or subheadings in the original work. At the end of each introduction the source and original title of the selection is indicated as precisely as possible and, where applicable, according to the directions of the publisher holding the copyright. In the page references I have not tried to account for the occasional paragraph or page that has been elided from the selection.

Much of the material used in *Theories of Preaching* lies in the public domain, but the book would not have been possible without the permission granted by the holders of copyright material. Some of the publishers, most notably Fortress Press, have been exceptionally generous with their permissions, and I am grateful to them.

PREFACE

I also wish to thank several individuals for their invaluable assistance: Harriet Leonard of the Duke Divinity School Library, Emerson Ford of Perkins Library of Duke University, and Ted Campbell of the Divinity School. Grant Wacker of the University of North Carolina led me to the right selection on Pentecostalism. Susan Harsh translated the Rudolf Bohren selection from the German, and my colleague, Teresa Berger, assisted in its revision. The most critical and therefore the most helpful suggestions were offered by Elizabeth Achtemeier of Union Theological Seminary, Richmond, Virginia. Her careful assessment of the section on biblical interpretation in particular lent strength and coherence to the whole work.

The Association of Theological Schools and the Duke University Research Council furthered my research with generous grants. The Duke Divinity School supported the preparation of the manuscript in a number of ways. I am especially grateful to our Director of Communications, Christopher Walters-Bugbee, and to Judy Owens, for their cooperation and expertise.

David Steinmetz of Labyrinth Press first encouraged me to start this project and later, just as valuably, enjoined me to stop and hand over the finished product. To David and Virginia Steinmetz I owe a great debt of gratitude for their editorial guidance, encouragement, and friendship.

Richard Lischer
The Divinity School
Duke University

INTRODUCTION
THE PROMISE OF RENEWAL

This book is designed to make available to the student and practicing pastor a generous and systematic sampling of the church's reflection on its central activity, the proclamation of the word of God. In the practice of ministry, even theological students may forget to ask theological questions about the nature of the skills they are learning. Preaching may appear to be a practical relief from academic preparations for ministry; it may seem that homiletics can avoid theological issues and move directly to sermon-design and delivery. If students do wish to learn more of the homiletical tradition than is found in current textbooks, the relevant materials are scattered and inaccessible to them. The result is that homiletics for seminary students has a two-dimensional quality. They suspect that there is more depth there than meets the eye, but in the absence of the theological and historical sources they are left to formulate their own theories and to find their own contexts for preaching. Later, when these same students have assumed local pulpits, the pressure of performance will militate against serious reflection on preaching, and questions such as, "For what purpose do we preach?" or "By what authority?" will go unanswered.

The word "theories" in the book's title might well be "theologies," for the main criterion for a selection's inclusion is its contribution to a clearer theological understanding of preaching. Much could be chosen from the fields of literary criticism, rhetoric, communications, cultural anthropology, and history, but to do so would be to create a very different kind of book, one that focuses on preaching's satellites rather than the integrated act of preaching itself. Thus I have limited myself to selections either directly related to preaching or, in a few cases, prefatory to it. With

1

these limits in mind, it quickly becomes apparent how few theologies of preaching the church has produced in the past 1900 years.

There are many frustrations in assembling what little there is: some of the greatest theologians and preachers never wrote a sustained reflection on the art of preaching. Foundational thinkers like Thomas Aquinas, Tauler, Luther, Knox, Schleiermacher, and Tillich, valued preaching highly and were gifted preachers but for the most part contributed only passing comments and flashes of insight on the subject. Their "theology of preaching" can only be inferred from their general positions and their sermons. Today we have no lack of books on preaching, but too many are satisfied with inspirational advice and make no critical connections with the church's theological tradition.

In this book the church's wisdom on preaching is organized around the following themes: (1) What is Preaching? (2) The Preacher, (3) The Event, (4) Biblical Interpretation, (5) Rhetoric, (6) The Hearer, (7) The Holy Spirit, (8) Theology, Word and Sacrament. The matter of definition is not as sterile as it first appears. How one defines any activity will dictate one's attitude toward the task and its execution. Since preaching presents an eternal triangle of message, speaker, and audience, the choice of a point of departure for its definition—e.g., the gospel, the preacher's character, or the needs of the congregation—determines the shape and purpose of the sermon. Indeed, almost all the succeeding categories are implicitly contained in the definition of preaching.

Unavoidably, there is overlap between categories. Preaching is a unified event that takes place in the fusion of elements represented by these categories and others not named. It can be divided and scrutinized only conceptually. For example, one might wish a separate category for the content of the gospel and another for the delivery of the sermon. But it is precisely in the *act* of preaching that these two components are unified, with the result that preaching is a rhetorical act of transmission rather than a body of data. Hence the category, "The Event." The reader should also be aware of the implicit dialogue between such categories as "Rhetoric" and "The Holy Spirit." Both are essential to preaching, but neither Augustine nor Barth was able to separate out rhetorical skills from the work of the Holy Spirit. A similar partnership exists between the highly divergent worldviews represented by the earlier selections on "Biblical Interpretation" (Augustine, Bonaventure, Luther) and contemporary studies of hermeneutics, the latter partaking of the historicist and critical spirit of the last 150 years. Nevertheless, each selection insists on wrestling with a text in preparation for preaching, and each dwells on the relationship of the interpreter to that which is interpreted. The

2

final category, "Theology, Word and Sacrament," recognizes that preaching, dogmatics, and worship are each the church's language about or to God. This final section inquires after the relationship of word and sacrament, preaching and worship. How do preaching and dogmatics differ? How do they serve one another?

A thematic and historical collection such as this offers a fascinating portrait of continuity and discontinuity in theology. On some issues the church's theologians once spoke continuously; now they are silent. Some controversies the church actually resolved, buried, and from them moved on to new challenges. Others were temporarily arrested only to break free in new forms in new generations.

The person of the preacher is a good example of a topic that was once of great importance to the medieval church but is now seldom discussed in homiletics. Most homiletical treatises after Augustine and through the Middle Ages (e.g., Alan of Lille and Guibert of Nogent) deal with the authority, formation, and holiness of the one who is appointed to preach. The same concerns are evident in seventeenth, eighteenth, and nineteenth century classics on the ministry, whether by Baxter, Herbert, Spener, or Schleiermacher. Despite the wave of interest in spirituality in the church today, one discerns no revival of the classical concern for the holiness of the preacher. The book on the preacher's holiness (aside from a chapter or two in Forsyth's *Positive Preaching and Modern Mind*) has not been written. The recent rediscovery of "my story" as a major element in what is sometimes called autobiographical preaching is not a substitute for Christian character, without which the sermon is only words.

The practice of allegory in interpretation and preaching is an example of an issue which appears to have been resolved by the church, first in the struggle of the Reformation, and later in the literary and historical theories of biblical interpretation. The debate over "meaning" in texts remains a contested issue for theoreticians of hermeneutics, but the church's reliance on and enjoyment of allegory appears to have disappeared for good.

For more than a millennium it appeared that Augustine had relieved the church's agony over the use of secular rhetoric, but something like that original concern surfaced again in Puritanism's insistence on "plain and perspicuous" English, and now in our own era of emerging communications techniques, the issue, like Halley's Comet, has returned. This time, in addition to the debate over emotional and manipulative oratory which occupied Augustine, or the "airy dews of effeminate Rhetorick" which offended Puritanism, contemporary Christianity is confronted with media technology that can fabricate or simulate "church" in the

3

family rooms of millions of television viewers. How is this modern communications technique—and the preaching it conveys—to be evaluated over against traditional ecclesiology, which presupposes the fellowship of word and table?

Another, final, issue whose colors have changed has to do with the human versus the divine operation in the effectiveness of preaching. For Puritans such as Jonathan Edwards the sermon was related to the sovereignty of God and a specific, sensationalist anthropology. In such a scheme, what skill could the preacher possibly exert and what freedom could the listener possibly enjoy? Theologically, the 19th-century revivalists and "pulpit princes" overwhelmed Puritan qualms about freedom and determinism. 20th-century thinking in theology as well as the social sciences appears to have tabled the question indefinitely.

On the other hand, some questions have not gone away. One of these, the relation of law and gospel in preaching, is represented in several sections of this book. Luther's passion for the gospel ignited the discussion, and the abiding danger of moralism keeps it alive. The law-gospel debate was taken up by Wesley, Edwards, Finney, Barth, and many others who attempted to formulate the proportions of the relation between law and gospel in the sermon. The debate continues less explicitly in the work of Bultmann, Ebeling, and the New Hermeneutic school. No one in the discussion doubted the importance of the gospel, however it was defined; what continues to be debated is the theological propriety of exposing sin with the law and, after applying the comfort of the gospel, using that same law as a guide in the reformation of the hearer's morals and habits. The word of God promises results, and preachers have always wanted to see them with their own eyes. What then is the most appropriate response to the preached word? Is it the life of Christian freedom (in service) enjoyed by one who, said Luther, is *semper justificandi*, always under the necessity of being justified? Is it sanctification and the pursuit of perfection, as Wesley preached, or the solution of one's personal problems, as counseled by Fosdick? Or are the results of preaching more immediately and dramatically manifest in the terrors to the affections induced by the Puritan sermon, the mass conversions of a Finney revival, or the ecstasy of a Pentecostalist meeting? Or is the goal of the sermon more modest (or more profound), namely, as Geoffrey Wainwright argues, the interpretation of the eucharist for those who would be Christ's body in the world?

Whatever the answers proposed, many of the selections in this book breathe a longing for the renewal of preaching. From every era of the church's history we hear voices decrying the corruption of preaching and

4

calling for its reformation. If the church is to achieve that renewal of preaching, it will find it where it has always found it, in the reappropriation of the gospel. Most every reform movement in the church, whether the Franciscan, Dominican, Lollard, Brethren, Lutheran, Presbyterian, or Methodist, has meant not only a revival of preaching but a re-forming of its method of presentation. But in no case did the redesign work precede the theological earthquake that made it necessary. Neither the New Testament Evangelists, nor Augustine, Luther, or Wesley created new forms of preaching for rhetorically motivated reasons. The notion of *ars gratia artis* is as foreign to the great preachers as it is to the New Testament. "The new utterance," as Amos Wilder calls the gospel, and its renewal in preaching, has always depended on its own inner logic to give formal direction to its expression. The many books on form and design which have dominated our generation's homiletical thinking cannot produce the renewal promised by the gospel. Instead of seeking a device by which to clothe and communicate a religious idea, preachers will eventually ask the more integrated, theological question: What is it about the *gospel* that demands this particular expression? It is this question—and our ability to answer it—that holds the promise of the renewal of preaching.

I
WHAT IS PREACHING?

ALAN OF LILLE

The Seventh Rung

The universal association of preaching with the Christian faith has not
led to a uniform definition of the task. Some theologians have begun
their definition from the nature of the message, others from the character
or holiness of the preacher. The Cistercian scholar and religious, Alan of
Lille (c. 1128–1202), forsakes one key element in the classical definition
of oratory, namely, persuasion, and instead speaks pastorally of "formation" as the goal of Christian preaching. Persuasion indicates a
sudden change of attitude; formation implies a lifelong process which
the author compares to climbing a ladder. Alan is an influential figure
in the so-called Renaissance of the 12th century as well as in the whole
history of preaching. Not for 800 years—since Augustine—had a Christian author attempted a systematic treatment of homiletics. According to
James J. Murphy, the definition of preaching with which Alan begins his
Compendium marks "the first formal definition in the 1200-year history of
the church" (*Rhetoric in the Middle Ages*, Berkeley, 1974, p. 307). From that
definition, reprinted below, Alan elaborates forty-seven sermonettes
exemplifying the various purposes and audiences of preaching. These he
concludes with a humorous message directed "To Sleepyheads (*Ad
somnolentes*)." Alan did not invent the complex "university sermon," nor
did he insist on specific rules of sermon construction. Yet his work does
reveal his century's interest in the logical *division* of ideas (usually into
threes) and its overwhelming reliance on the biblical *authorities* in homiletics and preaching. Within twenty years of Alan the traits suggested by
his treatise had become a torrent of technical manuals on preaching,
representing nothing less than a homiletical and rhetorical "revolution"
in Europe (see Murphy, p. 310).

Alan of Lille, *The Art of Preaching*, Cistercian Fathers Series, Number 23,
trans. Gilian R. Evans (Kalamazoo: Cistercian Publications, 1981),
pp. 15–22. © Cistercian Fathers. Used by permission.

Jacob beheld a ladder reaching from earth to heaven, on which angels were ascending and descending. The ladder represents the progress of the catholic man in his ascent from the beginning of faith to the full development of the perfect man. The first rung of this ladder is confession; the second, prayer; the third, thanksgiving; the fourth, the careful study of the Scriptures; the fifth, to inquire of someone more experienced if one comes upon any point in Scripture which is not clear; the sixth, the expounding of Scripture; the seventh, preaching.

The man who repents his sin then should first set his foot on the first rung of this ladder by confessing his sin. He should mount to the second rung by praying to God that grace may be bestowed on him. The third rung is reached through thanksgiving for the grace which is given. The ascent to the fourth rung is made by studying Scripture so as to preserve the gift of grace—for Holy Scripture teaches how grace, once given, may be held fast. In this way the fifth rung is seen in sight when a doubtful point arises, and the reader asks someone senior to help him understand it. The sixth rung is reached when the reader himself expounds Holy Scripture to others. He climbs the seventh rung when he preaches in public what he has learned from Scripture.

Various writers have composed treatises on the other "rungs," how and when one must "mount" them. Little has been said up to now about preaching: its nature, by whom and to whom it should be delivered, on what subjects and in what manner, at what time or in what place. We have thought it worthwhile to compile a treatise on the subject, for the edification of our "neighbors."

First, then, we must see what preaching is, what form it should take—in the surface aspects of its words, and in the weight of its thoughts—and how many kinds of preaching there are. Secondly, we must consider who the preachers should be; thirdly, to whom the sermon should be delivered; fourthly, for what reasons, and fifthly, in what place.

Preaching is an open and public instruction in faith and behavior, whose purpose is the forming of men; it derives from the path of reason and from the fountainhead of the "authorities." Preaching should be public, because it must be delivered openly. That is why Christ says: "What I say to you in your ear, preach upon the housetops." For if preaching were hidden, it would be suspect; it would seem to smell of heretical dogmas. The heretics preach secretly in their assemblies, so that they may the more easily deceive others. Preaching should be public because it must be delivered not to one, but to many; if it were given to a single man, it would not be preaching but teaching—for that is where the distinction lies between preaching, teaching, prophecy and public speaking. Preaching is that instruction which is offered to many, in public, and for their edification. Teaching is that which is given to one or to many, to add to their knowledge. Prophecy gives warning of what is to come, through the revelation of future events. Public speaking is the admonishing of the people to maintain the well-being of the community. By means of what is called "preaching"–instruction in matters of faith and behavior–two aspects of theology may be introduced: that which appeals to the reason and deals with the knowledge of spiritual matters, and the ethical, which offers teaching on the living of a good life. For preaching sometimes teaches about holy things, sometimes about conduct. This is what is meant by the angels ascending and descending. Preachers are the "angels," who "ascend" when they preach about heavenly matters, and "descend" when they bend themselves to earthly things in speaking of behavior.

In the remainder of our definition, the ultimate reason for preaching– the benefit it brings–is implied in: "whose purpose is the forming of men." Because preaching must be dependent on reasoning and corroborated by authoritative texts, we have: "it derives from the path of reason and from the fountainhead of the 'authorities.'"

Preaching should not contain jesting words, or childish remarks, or that melodiousness and harmony which result from the use of rhythm or metrical lines; these are better fitted to delight the ear than to edify the soul. Such preaching is theatrical and full of buffoonery, and in every way to be condemned. Of such preaching the prophet says: "Your innkeepers mix water with the wine." Water is mingled with wine in the preaching in which childish and mocking words–what we may call "effeminacies"–are put into the minds of the listeners. Preaching should not glitter with verbal trappings, with purple patches, nor should it be too much enervated by the use of colorless words: the blessed keep to a middle way. If it were too heavily-embroidered [the sermon] would seem to have been contrived with excessive care, and elaborated to win the admiration of man, rather than for the benefit of our neighbors, and so it would move less the hearts of those who heard it. Those who preach in this way are to be compared with the pharisees, who made the tassels of their garments long, and wore large phylacteries. Such preaching may be said to be suspect, yet it is not to be wholly condemned, but rather tolerated. For St. Paul says: "On whatever occasion Christ is preached, I rejoice in it and shall rejoice." It serves no purpose to interpolate at intervals the phrase: "to the greater glory of Christ," for Christ is no less angered by false praise than by a denial of the truth. Such–as a rule–is the teaching of heretics, who propound truths and introduce falsehoods among them. It is said of them: "even jackals bare their breasts and feed their young." These jackals have the faces of young girls, but the feet of horses. Horses' hooves are not cloven, but stand squarely on the ground. By "jackals," therefore, we should understand "heretics," who have the faces of young girls, but whose bodies end in the scorpion's sting. For first they propound the truth and then they draw false conclusions from it. They have indeed the feet of horses, for they do not divide their hearts' desire between the love of God and the love of their neighbor, but they set all their desires on earthly pleasures. Such preaching must be wholly rejected, because it is full of vices and dangers. There should be some weight in the thought of a good sermon, so that it may move the spirits of its hearers, stir up the mind, and encourage repentance. Let the sermon rain down doctrines, thunder forth admonitions, soothe with praises, and so in every way work for the good of our neighbors. There are some who make earthly gain the motive for their preaching, but their preaching is extravagant; such are rather merchants than preachers, and so their preaching is to be heard and endured. That is why the Lord says: "Do what they tell you to do, but do not follow the example they set."

There are three kinds of preaching: that which is by the spoken word, of which it is said: "Go, preach the gospel to every creature." Another is by means of the written word, as when the Apostle says that he has "preached" to the Corinthians because he has written them a letter. The third is by deed, as it is said: "Every work of Christ is our instruction."

This should be the form of preaching: it should develop from, as it were, its own proper foundation, from a theological authority—especially a text from the Gospels, the Psalms, the Epistles of Paul, or the Books of Solomon, for in these, in particular, edifying instruction resounds. Texts should also be taken from other books of Holy Writ if necessary, and if they have a bearing on the theme in hand.

And so the preacher must win the goodwill of his audience through the humility he shows in his own person, and through the profitableness of his subject-matter. He must say that he propounds the word of God to his listeners so that it may bring forth fruit in their minds, not for any earthly gain, but to set them on their way and to help them make progress. He must make it clear that the sermon is not designed to arouse the foolish acclaim of the mob, nor tempered to win popular favor, nor shaped to evoke applause, as in a theater. It is composed to instruct the souls of the listeners, so that they may concentrate, not on who is speaking to them, but on what he is saying. It is not the sharpness of the thorn that we should dwell on, but the sweetness of the rose.

Honey can be sucked from the broken reed, and fire may be struck from a stone. Thus, if he is committed to his task, [the preacher] should show how profitable it is to hear the word of God.

He should also assure his listeners that he will speak briefly and to their profit, and that he has been led to speak only by his love for his listeners; that he does not speak as one greater in knowledge or in wisdom, or as one who lives a better life, but because things are sometimes revealed to the little ones which are not shown to the great; and at such a time, the great ought to be silent. And because sometimes the great do not wish to preach, it is not surprising if lesser men then prattle. For if the learned are silent, the very stones will speak and cry out. So the preacher should come to the exposition of the proposed text, and bend everything he says to the edification of the listener. Let him not begin with a text which is too obscure or too difficult, in case his listeners are put off by it and so listen less attentively. Nor, in the expounding of his authority, should he move too quickly away from his text, in case the beginning should be out of keeping with the middle and the middle with the end. He should also bring in other authorities to corroborate the first, especially those which are relevant to his subject. He may also, on occasion, insert sayings of the pagan writers—just as the Apostle Paul sometimes introduces quotations from the philosophers into his epistles, for he will make an apt point if he provides a fresh illumination by such a skillful juxtaposition. He may also introduce moving words which soften hearts and encourage tears. But let the sermon be brief, in case prolixity should cause boredom. When the preacher sees that his hearers' minds are moved, and that they weep freely, and that their expressions are downcast, he should hold back a little, but not too much, for, as Lucretius says: "Nothing dries up faster than a tear." Finally, he should make use of examples to prove what he says, because teaching by means of examples is a familiar method.

PHILLIPS BROOKS

The Two Elements in Preaching

The most durable of all definitions of preaching was given by Phillips
Brooks (1835–1893) in his Beecher Lectures at Yale in 1877. "Truth through
personality" was the logical extension of Bushnell's theory of Christian
experience as the authority for truth. The phrase was epigraph to an era
of Christian liberalism exemplified by the urban and urbane ministry of
Brooks himself. His sympathy for personality—"manliness" is a frequent
term in Brooks—as well as his sensitivity to the needs of the listener, take
him well out of the orbit of Calvinism. But his intellectual confidence in
"the truth" is even further removed from the psycho-spiritual manipu-
lations of nineteenth century revivalism. If the successes of his contemporary Dwight Moody threatened him, he never said so. Brooks' *Lectures*
have traveled the century more effectively than any nineteenth century
treatise on preaching, perhaps because the temper of his times and
personality is so much like our own. At the time of the lectures Brooks
was Rector of Trinity Church, Boston. When he died as Bishop of
Massachusetts, the Boston Stock Exchange closed and 20,000 people
came to mourn America's most influential preacher.

Phillips Brooks, *Lectures on Preaching* (New York: E. P. Dutton &
Company, 1907 [1877]), pp. 5–26.

Preaching is the communication of truth by man to men. It has in it
two essential elements, truth and personality. Neither of those can it
spare and still be preaching. The truest truth, the most authoritative
statement of God's will, communicated in any other way than through
the personality of brother man to men is not preached truth. Suppose
it written on the sky, suppose it embodied in a book which has been so
long held in reverence as the direct utterance of God that the vivid

personality of the men who wrote its pages has well-nigh faded out of it; in neither of these cases is there any preaching. And on the other hand, if men speak to other men that which they do not claim for truth, if they use their powers of persuasion or of entertainment to make other men listen to their speculations, or do their will, or applaud their cleverness, that is not preaching either. The first lacks personality. The second lacks truth. And preaching is the bringing of truth through personality. It must have both elements. It is in the different proportion in which the two are mingled that the difference between two great classes of sermons and preaching lies. It is in the defect of one or the other element that every sermon and preacher falls short of the perfect standard. It is in the absence of one or the other element that a discourse ceases to be a sermon, and a man ceases to be a preacher altogether. . . .

This was the method by which Christ chose that his gospel should be spread through the world. It was a method that might have been applied to the dissemination of any truth, but we can see why it was especially adapted to the truth of Christianity. For that truth is preeminently personal. However the gospel may be capable of statement in dogmatic form, its truest statement we know is not in dogma but in personal life. Christianity is Christ; and we can easily understand how a truth which is of such peculiar character that a person can stand forth and say of it, "I am the truth," must always be best conveyed through, must indeed be almost incapable of being perfectly conveyed except through personality. And so some form of preaching must be essential to the prevalence and spread of the knowledge of Christ among men. There seems to be some such meaning as this in the words of Jesus when he said to his disciples, "As my Father has sent me into the world even so have I sent you into the world." It was the continuation, out to the minutest ramifications of the new system of influence, of that personal method which the Incarnation itself had involved.

If this be true, then, it establishes the first of all principles concerning the ministry and preparation for the ministry. Truth through personality is our description of real preaching. The truth must come really through the person, not merely over his lips, not merely into his understanding and out through his pen. It must come through his character, his affections, his whole intellectual and moral being. It must come genuinely through him. I think that, granting equal intelligence and study, here is the great difference which we feel between two preachers of the word. The gospel has come *over* one of them and reaches us tinged and flavored with his superficial characteristics, belittled with his littleness. The gospel has come *through* the other, and we receive it impressed and winged with all the earnestness and strength that there is in him. In the first case the man has been but a printing machine or a trumpet. In the other case he has been a true man and a real messenger of God. . . .

Let us look now for a few moments at these two elements of preaching—truth and personality; the one universal and invariable, the other special and always different. There are a few suggestions that I should like to make to you about each.

And first with regard to the truth. It is strange how impossible it is to separate it and consider it wholly by itself. The personalness will cling to it. There are two aspects of the minister's work, which we are constantly meeting in the New Testament. They are really embodied in two words, one of which is "message," and the other is "witness." "This is the message which we have heard of him and declare unto you," says St. John in his first Epistle. "We are his witnesses of these things," says St. Peter before the council at Jerusalem. In these two words together, I think, we have the fundamental conception of the matter of all Christian preaching. It is to be a message given to us for transmission, but yet a message which we cannot transmit until it has entered into our own experience, and we can give our own testimony of its spiritual power. The minister who keeps the word "message" always written before him, as he prepares his sermon in his study, or utters it from his pulpit, is saved from the tendency to wanton and wild speculation, and from the mere passion of originality. He who never forgets that word "witness," is saved from the unreality of repeating by rote mere forms of statement which he has learned as orthodox, but never realized as true. If you and I can always carry this double consciousness, that we are messengers, and that we are witnesses, we shall have in our preaching all the authority and independence of assured truth, and yet all the appeal and convincingness of personal belief. It will not be we that speak, but the spirit of our Father that speaketh in us, and yet our sonship shall give the Father's voice its utterance and interpretation to his other children.

I think that nothing is more needed to correct the peculiar vices of preaching which belong to our time, than a new prevalence among preachers of this first conception of the truth which they have to tell as a message. I am sure that one great source of the weakness of the pulpit is the feeling among the people that these men who stand up before them every Sunday have been making up trains of thought, and thinking how they should "treat their subject," as the phrase runs. There is the first ground of the vicious habit that our congregations have of talking about the preacher more than they think about the truth. The minstrel who sings before you to show his skill, will be praised for his wit, and rhymes, and voice. But the courier who hurries in, breathless, to bring you a message, will be forgotten in the message that he brings. . . .

Whatever else you count yourself in the ministry, never lose this fundamental idea of yourself as a messenger. As to the way in which one shall best keep that idea, it would not be hard to state; but it would involve the whole story of the Christian life. Here is the primary necessity that the Christian preacher should be a Christian first, that he should be deeply cognizant of God's authority, and of the absoluteness of Christ's truth. That was one of the first principles which I ventured to assume as I began my lecture. But without entering so wide a field, let me say one thing about this conception of preaching as the telling of a message which constantly impresses me. I think that it would give to our preaching just the quality which it appears to me to most lack now. That quality is breadth. I do not mean liberality of thought, not tolerance of opinion, nor anything of that kind. I mean largeness of movement, the great utterance of great truths, the great enforcement of great duties, as distinct from the minute, and subtle, and ingenious treatment of little topics, side issues of the soul's life, bits of anatomy, the bric-a-brac of theology. . . .

And then another result of this conception of preaching as the telling of a message is that it puts us into right relations with all historic Christianity. The message never can be told as if we were the first to tell it. It is the same message which the church has told in all the ages. He who tells it today is backed by all the multitude who have told it in the past. He is companied by all those who are telling it now. The message is his witness; but a part of the assurance with which he has received it, comes from the fact of its being the identical message which has come down from the beginning. Men find on both sides how difficult it is to preserve the true poise and proportion between the corporate and the individual conceptions of the Christian life. But all will own today the need of both. The identity of the church in all times consists in the identity of the message which she has always had to carry from her Lord to men. All outward utterances of the perpetual identity of the church are valuable only as they assert this real identity. There is the real meaning of the perpetuation of old ceremonies, the use of ancient liturgies, and the clinging to what seem to be apostolic types of government. The heretic in all times has been not the errorist as such, but the self-willed man, whether his judgments were right or wrong. "A man may be a heretic in the truth," says Milton. He is the man who, taking his ideas not as a message from God, but as his own discoveries, has cut himself off from the message-bearing church of all the ages. I am sure that the more fully you come to count your preaching the telling of a message, the more valuable and real the church will become to you, the more true will seem to you your brotherhood with all messengers of that same message in all strange dresses and in all strange tongues.

I should like to mention, with reference to the truth which the preacher has to preach, two tendencies which I am sure that you will recognize as very characteristic of our time. One is the tendency of criticism, and the other is the tendency of mechanism. Both tendencies are bad. By the tendency of criticism I mean the disposition that prevails everywhere to deal with things from outside, discussing their relations, examining their nature, and not putting ourselves into their power. Preaching in every age follows, to a certain extent, the changes which come to all literature and life. The age in which we live is strangely fond of criticism. It takes all things to pieces for the mere pleasure of examining their nature. It studies forces, not in order to obey them, but in order to understand them. It talks about things for the pure pleasure of discussion. Much of the poetry and prose about nature and her wonders, much of the investigation of the country's genius and institutions, much of the subtle analysis of human nature is of this sort. It is all good; but it is something distinct from the cordial sympathy by which one becomes a willing servant of any of these powers, a real lover of nature, or a faithful citizen, or a true friend. Now it would be strange if this critical tendency did not take possession of the preaching of the day. And it does. The disposition to watch ideas in their working, and to talk about their relations and their influence on one another, simply as problems, in which the mind may find pleasure without any real entrance of the soul into the ideas themselves, this, which is the critical tendency, invades the pulpit, and the result is an immense amount of preaching which must be called preaching about Christ as distinct from preaching Christ. There are many preachers who seem to do nothing else, always discussing Christianity as a problem instead of announcing Christianity as a message, and proclaiming Christ as Savior. I do not undervalue their discussions. But I think we ought always to feel that such discussions are not the type or ideal of preaching. They may be necessities of the time, but they are not the work which the great apostolic preachers did, or which the true preacher will always most desire. Definers and defenders of the faith are always needed, but it is bad for a church, when its ministers count it their true work to define and defend the faith rather than to preach the gospel. Beware of the tendency to preach about Christianity, and try to preach Christ. To discuss the relations of Christianity and science, Christianity and society, Christianity and politics, is good. To set Christ forth to men so that they shall know him, and in gratitude and love become his, that is far better. It is good to be a Herschel who describes the sun; but it is better to be a Prometheus who brings the sun's fire to the earth.

I called the other tendency the tendency of mechanism. It is the disposition of the preacher to forget that the gospel of Christ is primarily addressed to individuals, and that its ultimate purpose is the salvation of multitudes of men. Between the time when it first speaks to a man's soul, and the time when that man's soul is gathered into heaven, with the whole host of the redeemed, the gospel uses a great many machineries which are more or less impersonal. The church, with all its instrumentalities, comes in. The preacher works by them. But if the preacher ever for a moment counts them the purpose of his working, if he takes his eye off the single soul as the prize he is to win, he falls from his highest function and loses his best power. All successful preaching, I more and more believe, talks to individuals. The church is for the soul. . . .

Of the second element in preaching, namely, the preacher's personality, there will be a great deal to say, especially in the next lecture. But there are two or three fundamental things which I wish to say today.

The first is this, that the principle of personality once admitted involves the individuality of every preacher. The same considerations which make it good that the gospel should not be written on the sky, or committed merely to an almost impersonal book, make it also most desirable that every preacher should utter the truth in his own way, and according to his own nature. It must come not only through man but through men. If you monotonize men you lose their human power to a large degree. If you could make all men think alike it would be very much as if no man thought at all, as when the whole earth moves together with all that is upon it, everything seems still. Now the deep sense of the solemnity of the minister's work has often a tendency to repress the free individuality of the preacher and his tolerance of other preachers' individualities. His own way of doing his work is with him a matter of conscience, not of taste, and the conscience when it is thoroughly awake is more intolerant than the taste is. Or, working just the other way, his conscience tells him that it is not for him to let his personal peculiarities intrude in such a solemn work, and so he tries to bind himself to the ways of working which the most successful preachers of the word have followed. I have seen both these kinds of ministers: those whose consciences made them obstinate, and those whose consciences made them pliable; those whose consciences hardened them to steel or softened them to wax. However it comes about, there is an unmistakable tendency to the repression of the individuality of the preacher. It is seen in little things: in the uniform which preachers wear, and the disposition to a uniformity of language. It is seen in great things: in the disposition which all ages have witnessed to draw a line of orthodoxy inside the lines of truth. Wisely and soberly let us set ourselves against this influence. The God who sent men to preach the gospel of his Son in their humanity, sent each man distinctively to preach it in his humanity. Be yourself by all means, but let that good result come not by cultivating merely superficial peculiarities and oddities. Let it be by winning a true self full of your own faith and your own love. The deep originality is noble, but the surface originality is miserable. It is so easy to be a John the Baptist, as far as the desert and camel's hair and locusts and wild honey go. But the devoted heart to speak from, and the fiery words to speak, are other things.

Again, we never can forget in thinking of the preacher's personality that he is one who lives in constant familiarity with thoughts and words which to other men are occasional and rare, and which preserve their sacredness mainly by their rarity. That fact must always come in when we try to estimate the influences of a preacher's life. What will the power of that fact be? I am sure that often it weakens the minister. I am sure that many men who, if they came to preach once in a great while in the midst of other occupations, would preach with reality and fire, are deadened to their sacred work by their constant intercourse with sacred things. Their constant dealing with the truth makes them less powerful to bear the truth to others, as a pipe through which the water always flows collects its sediment, and is less fit to let more water through. And besides this, it ministers to self-deception and to an exaggeration or distortion of our own history. The man who constantly talks of certain experiences, and urges other men to enter into them, must come in time, by very force of describing those experiences, to think that he has undergone them. You beg men to repent, and you grow so familiar with the whole theory of repentance that it is hard for you to know that you yourself have not repented. You exhort to patience till you have no eyes or ears for your own impatience. It is the way in which the man who starts the trains at the railroad station must come in time to feel as if he himself had been to all the towns along the road whose names he has always been shouting in the passengers' ears, and to which he has for years sold them their tickets, when perhaps he has not left his own little way-station all the time. I know that all this is so, and yet certainly the fault is in the man, not in the truth. The remedy certainly is not to make the truth less familiar. There is a truer relation to preaching, in which the constancy of it shall help instead of harming the reality and earnestness with which you do it. The more that you urge other people to holiness the more intense may be the hungering and thirsting after holiness in your own heart. Familiarity does not breed contempt except of contemptible things or in contemptible people. The adage, that no man is a hero to his *valet de chambre*, is sufficiently answered by saying that it is only to a *valet de chambre* that a truly great man is unheroic. You must get the impulse, the delight, and the growing sacredness of your life out of your familiar work. You are lost as a preacher if its familiarity deadens and encrusts, instead of vitalizing and opening your powers. And it will all depend upon whether you do your work for your Master and his people or for yourself. The last kind of labor slowly kills, the first gives life more and more.

C. H. DODD

The Primitive Preaching

Soon after its publication in 1936 *The Apostolic Preaching and Its Developments* was recognized as a seminal work in the field of biblical studies and homiletics. At a time when the academic world had begun dissecting the Bible by means of form and source criticism, C. H. Dodd (1884–1973), the consummate British scholar and theologian, announced the unity of the church's proclamation, its *kerygma*. Dodd sharply distinguished *kerygma* or missionary preaching from *didache* or instruction, asserting that only the former belonged to the preaching of the primitive church. His ideas drew fire from many quarters. Many biblical scholars disputed his absolute distinction between preaching and teaching, as well as his dogmatic insistence upon "realized eschatology" as the exclusive position of the first church. Liberals, for whom the timeless teachings of Jesus represented the essence of Christianity, were offended by the eschatological strangeness of the message Dodd delineated. What optimists remained after the Great War were also dismayed by the subsidiary place of ethics in Dodd's *kerygma*. Finally, preachers of succeeding decades have been sobered and challenged by Dodd's admonition: "Much of our preaching in church at the present day would not have been recognized by the early Christians as *kerygma*." Like no other statement this century *The Apostolic Preaching* forced preachers to examine their own work and to ask, What is preaching?

C. H. Dodd, *The Apostolic Preaching and Its Developments*, pp. 13, 17, 74–78. Reprinted 1980 by Baker Book House. Used by permission.

The Pauline *kerygma*, therefore, is a proclamation of the facts of the death and resurrection of Christ in an eschatological setting which gives significance to the facts. They mark the transition from "this evil age" to the "age to come." The "age to come" is the age of fulfilment. Hence the importance of the statement that Christ died and rose "according to the Scriptures." Whatever events the Old Testament prophets may indicate as impending, these events are for them significant as elements in the coming of "the day of the Lord." Thus the fulfilment of prophecy means that the day of the Lord has dawned: the age to come has begun. The death and resurrection of Christ are the crucial fulfilment of prophecy. By virtue of them believers are already delivered out of this present evil age. The new age is here, of which Christ, again by virtue of his death and resurrection, is Lord. He will come to exercise his lordship both as judge and as savior at the consummation of the age. . . .

It is true that the *kerygma* as we have recovered it from the Pauline epistles is fragmentary. No complete statement of it is, in the nature of the case, available. But we may restore it in outline somewhat after this fashion:

The prophecies are fulfilled, and the new Age is inaugurated by the coming of Christ.
He was born of the seed of David.
He died according to the Scriptures, to deliver us out of the present evil age.
He was buried.
He rose on the third day according to the Scriptures. He is exalted at the right hand of God, as Son of God and Lord of quick and dead.
He will come again as judge and savior of men.

The apostolic preaching as adopted by Paul may have contained, almost certainly did contain, more than this. Comparison with other forms of the *kerygma* may enable us to expand the outline with probability; but so much of its content can be demonstrated from the epistles, and the evidence they afford is of primary value. . . .

In this survey of the apostolic preaching and its developments two facts have come into view: first, that within the New Testament there is an immense range of variety in the interpretation that is given to the *kerygma*; and, secondly, that in all such interpretation the essential elements of the original *kerygma* are steadily kept in view. Indeed, the farther we move from the primitive modes of expression, the more decisively is the central purport of it affirmed. With all the diversity of the New Testament writings, they form a unity in their proclamation of the one gospel. At a former stage of criticism, the study of the New Testament was vitalized by the recognition of the individuality of its various writers and their teachings. The results of this analytical stage of criticism are of permanent value. With these results in mind, we can now do fuller justice to the rich many-sidedness of the central gospel which is expressed in the whole. The present task of the New Testament criticism, as it seems to me, is the task of synthesis. Perhaps, however, "synthesis" is not quite the right word, for it may imply the creation of unity out of originally diverse elements. But in the New Testament the unity is original. We have to explore, by a comparative study of the several writings, the common faith which evoked them, and which they aimed at interpreting to an ever-widening public. . . .

There is one further part of the task, to which in these lectures I have done no more than allude, and that is, to ascertain the relation between the apostolic preaching and that of Jesus Christ himself. I have said something about it elsewhere. I will here only state my belief that it will be found that the primitive *kerygma* arises directly out of the teaching of Jesus about the kingdom of God and all that hangs upon it; but that it does only partial justice to the range and depth of his teaching, and needs the Pauline and Johannine interpretations before it fully rises to the height of the great argument. It is in the Fourth Gospel, which in form and expression, as probably in date, stands farthest from the original tradition of the teaching, that we have the most penetrating exposition of its central meaning.

In conclusion, I would offer some brief reflections upon the relation of this discussion to the preaching of Christianity in our own time.

What do we mean by preaching the gospel? At various times and in different circles the gospel has been identified with this or that element in the general complex of ideas broadly called Christian; with the promise of immortality, with a particular theory of the Atonement, with the idea of "the fatherhood of God and the brotherhood of man," and so forth. What the gospel was, historically speaking, at the beginning, and during the New Testament period, I hope these lectures have in some measure defined. No Christian of the first century had any doubt what it was, or any doubt of its relevance to human need. How far can it be preached in the twentieth century?

A well-known New Testament scholar has expressed the opinion that "the modern man does not believe in any form of salvation known to ancient Christianity" [Kirsopp Lake, *Landmarks of Early Christianity*, p. 77]. It is indeed clear that the primitive formulation of the gospel in eschatological terms is as strange as it could well be to our minds. It is no wonder that it has taken a long time, and stirred up much controversy, to reach the frank conclusion that the preaching of the early church, and of Jesus himself, had its being in this strange world of thought. For many years we strove against this conclusion. We tried to believe that criticism could prune away from the New Testament those elements in it which seemed to us fantastic, and leave us with an original "essence of Christianity," to which the modern man could say, "This is what I have always thought." But the attempt has failed. At the center of it all lies this alien, eschatological gospel, completely out of touch, as it seems, with our ways of thought.

But perhaps it was not much less out of touch with the thought of the Hellenistic world to which the earliest missionaries appealed. Paul at least found that the gospel had in it an element of "foolishness" and "scandal" for his public. But he and others succeeded in reinterpreting it to their contemporaries in terms which made its essential relevance and truth clear to their minds. It is this process of reinterpretation that we have been studying. Some similar process is clearly demanded of the preachers of the gospel in our time. If the primitive "eschatological" gospel is remote from our thought, there is much in Paul and John which as it stands is almost equally remote, and their reinterpretations, profound and conclusive though they are, do not absolve us from our task.

But the attempt at reinterpretation is always in danger of becoming something quite different; that which Paul called, "preaching another Jesus and another gospel." We have seen that the great thinkers of the New Testament period, while they worked out bold, even daring ways of restating the original gospel, were so possessed by its fundamental convictions that their restatements are true to its first intention. Under all variations of form, they continued to affirm that in the events out of which the Christian church arose there was a conclusive act of God, who in them visited and redeemed his people; and that in the corporate experience of the church itself there was revealed a new quality of life, arising out of what God had done, which in turn corroborated the value set upon the facts.

The real problem for the student of the New Testament is not whether this or that incident in the life of Jesus is credibly reported, this or that saying rightly attributed to him; nor yet whether such and such a doctrine in Paul or John can be derived from Judaism or the "mystery-religions." It is, whether the fundamental affirmations of the apostolic preaching are true and relevant. We cannot answer this question without understanding the preaching, nor understand it without painstaking study of material which in some of its forms is strange and elusive; but without answering this question, we cannot confidently claim the name of Christian for that which we preach. To select from the New Testament certain passages which seem to have a "modern" ring, and to declare that these represent the "permanent element" in it, is not necessarily to preach the gospel. It is, moreover, easy to be mistaken, on a superficial reading, about the true meaning of passages which may strike us as congenial. Some of them may not be as "modern" as they sound. The discipline of confronting the gospel of primitive Christianity, in those forms of statement which are least congenial to the modern mind, compels us to re-think, not only the gospel, but our own prepossessions.

It is for this reason that I conceive the study of the New Testament, from the standpoint I have indicated, to be of extreme importance just now. I do not suggest that the crude early formulation of the gospel is our exclusive standard. It is only in the light of its development all through the New Testament that we learn how much is implied in it. But I would urge that the study of the Synoptic Gospels should be more than an exercise in the historical critic's art of fixing the irreducible minimum of bare fact in the record; and that the study of Paul and John should be more than either a problem in comparative religion or the first chapter in a history of dogma. Gospels and epistles alike offer a field of study in which the labor of criticism and interpretation may initiate us into the "many-sided wisdom" which was contained in the apostolic preaching, and make us free to declare it in contemporary terms to our own age.

DIETRICH BONHOEFFER

The Proclaimed Word

At about the same time C. H. Dodd was lecturing at King's College, London, Dietrich Bonhoeffer (1906–1945) was directing the tiny Confessing Church seminary at Finkenwalde and offering a course in homiletics. Seminary life included daily worship and Bonhoeffer's active participation in the hearing and critiquing of sermons. *Hearing* the word of God even in the most unaccomplished effort was as important as artful proclamation. At Finkenwalde Bonhoeffer reassessed the ground of homiletics, moving from ecclesiology to radical Christology. The sermon neither contains the word of God nor points to the Lord. In its entirety it *is* the incarnate yet often hidden Christ and is thus clothed in Christ's own humility and power. Such a word cannot be *made* relevant or validated by the preacher's experience. Given his radical view of the Incarnation (and preaching) in 1937, Bonhoeffer's shift to so-called religionless language in 1944–45 is far from abrupt. His *Homiletics* of 1937 prepared the way for the following prediction in a sermon written from prison in 1944: "It is not for us to prophesy the day (though the day will come) when men will once more be called so to utter the word of God that the world will be changed and renewed by it. It will be a new language, perhaps quite non-religious, but liberating and redeeming — as was Jesus' language; it will shock people and yet overcome them by its power; it will be the language of a new righteousness and truth, proclaiming God's peace with men and the coming of his kingdom" (*Letters and Papers from Prison*, New York: Macmillan, 1953, p. 300).

Dietrich Bonhoeffer, *Worldly Preaching*, ed. Clyde E. Fant (Nashville and New York: Thomas Nelson Inc., 1975), pp. 126–130. © Clyde E. Fant. Used by permission.

The proclaimed word has its origin in the Incarnation of Jesus Christ. It neither originates from a truth once perceived nor from personal experience. It is not the reproduction of a specific set of feelings. Nor is the word of the sermon the outward form for the substance which lies behind it. The proclaimed word is the incarnate Christ himself. As little as the Incarnation is the outward shape of God, just so little does the proclaimed word present the outward form of a reality; rather, it is the thing itself. The preached Christ is both the Historical One and the Present One. (Kähler: the preached Christ is the so-called historical Jesus.) He is the access to the historical Jesus. Therefore the proclaimed word is not a medium of expression for something else, something which lies behind it, but rather it is the Christ himself walking through his congregation as the Word.

In the Incarnation the Word became flesh. God, the Son, took on human form. So he accepts all of mankind and bears it in himself, in that he is fleshly. He embraces the whole of humanity with its genuinely sinful nature. That he wears this humanness is the whole mystery of the Gospels. It is not enough to say that he suffers with mankind—he actually takes mankind upon himself. It is false to say that the Logos accepted, that is, adopted, man; instead, he has taken on human nature, my nature and your nature. His flesh is our flesh and our flesh is his flesh. This also means that in the Incarnation the new mankind is established. Mankind has become one through the Incarnation. The congregation is already present in the embodied Christ; his body is "we ourselves." The church is included in the Incarnation as the *sanctorum communio*.

The proclaimed word is the Christ bearing human nature. This word is no new Incarnation, but the Incarnate One who bears the sins of the world. Through the Holy Spirit this word becomes the actualization of his acceptance and sustenance. The word of the sermon intends to accept mankind, nothing else. It wants to bear the whole of human nature. In the congregation all sins should be cast upon the Word. Preaching must be so done that the hearer places all of his needs, cares, fears, and sins upon the Word. The Word accepts all of these things. When preaching is done in this way, it is the proclamation of Christ. This proclamation of the Christ does not regard its primary responsibility to be giving advice, arousing emotions, or stimulating the will—it will do these things, too—but its intention is to sustain us. The Word is there that burdens might be laid upon it. We are all borne up by the word of Christ. Because it does so, it creates fellowship. Because the Word includes us into itself, it makes of us members of the body of Christ. As such we share in the responsibility of upholding one another. Thus the word of Christ also presupposes Christian brotherhood. The Word intends that no one should remain alone, for in him no one remains alone. The Word makes individuals part of one body.

Word and congregation. Because the word conveys the new humanity, by its very nature it is always directed toward the congregation. It seeks community, it needs community, because it is already laden with humanity. At this point it is significant to notice that the word produces its own momentum. It proceeds from itself toward the congregation in order to sustain it. The preacher does not therefore accomplish the application of the word; he is not the one who shapes it and forms it to suit the congregation. With the introduction of the biblical word the text begins moving among the congregation. Likewise the word arises out of the Bible, takes shape as the sermon, and enters into the congregation in order to bear it up. This self-movement of the word to the congregation should not be hindered by the preacher, but rather he should acknowledge it. He should not allow his own efforts to get in its way. If we attempt to give impetus to the word, then it becomes distorted into words of instruction or education or experience. As such it can no longer uphold the congregation nor sustain it. Upon Christ, however, who is the proclaimed Word, should fall all of the need, the sin and death of the congregation.

The form of the proclaimed word. The form of the preached word is different from every other form of speech. Other speeches are structured so that they have some truth which they wish to communicate either behind them or beneath them or over them, or else they are arranged so as to express an emotion or teach a concept. These human words communicate something else besides what they are of themselves. They become means to an end. The meaning of the proclaimed word, however, does not lie outside of itself; it is the thing itself. It does not transmit anything else, it does not express anything else, it has no external objectives — rather, it communicates that it is itself: the historical Jesus Christ, who bears humanity upon himself with all of its sorrows and its guilt. The sustaining Christ is the dimension of the preached word. The biblical content of the proclaimed word makes clear this distinction from all other forms of speech. Cultic expressions only make it unclear. How can our words again become the proclaimed word in this original sense?

The unique dignity of the word. The promise to be able to accept men and sustain them has been given to the spoken word. Nothing is equal in dignity to the spoken word. As the Logos has adopted human nature, so the spoken word actualizes our adoption. It is *that* word which the

Logos honors, not some magical transaction. Therefore our adoption is not a matter of some kind of psychi-magical act through which we are adopted and included into Christ. What really happens is that we are accepted through the clearly heard and understood word of Christ. Cult and liturgy can therefore only serve as adoration, celebration, and praise of the clearly spoken word of God. Proclamation, therefore, in the strictest sense, does not issue from cultic ritual but from the testimony of the word. Liturgy and cultic acts serve proclamation. In the proclaimed word, according to the promise, Christ enters into his congregation which in its liturgy adores him, calls unto him, and awaits him. In the proclaimed word Christ is alive as the Word of the Father. In the proclaimed word he receives the congregation unto himself. Through the Word the world was created. The Word became incarnate. The incarnate Word continues to exist for us in the Scripture. Through the Holy Spirit, the incarnate Word comes to us from the Scripture in the sermon. And it is one and the same Word: the Word of creation, the Word of the Incarnation, the Word of the Holy Scripture, the Word of the sermon. It is the creating, accepting, and reconciling Word of God, for whose sake the world exists.

Because we were created by the Word and are daily kept by it, because we have been reconciled through the Word before we knew it, therefore only through this Word are we able to recognize God. Through this Word we find certainty. This Word alone affects our will. Only this Word keeps on being clear to us in its accusations and its promises. Only this Word makes us without excuse. Music and symbols (as the Berneuchen movement believed) do not make us without excuse; they are not unequivocal and do not break down the will! Music and symbols do not create the *anthropos pneumatikos*, but likely the *pseukikos*. The word, however, conveys the Spirit and does accomplish this. With cultic endeavors we are in danger of wanting to add something to the preached word, of attempting to lend a particular style of expression to it. But it may not be and does not need to be so undergirded. The word of the sermon is not one species of the genus "word," but rather it is just the opposite: all of our words are species of the one, original Word of God which both creates and sustains the world.

For the sake of the proclaimed word the world exists with all of its words. In the sermon the foundation for a new world is laid. Here the original word becomes audible. There is no evading or getting away from the spoken word of the sermon; nothing releases us from the necessity of this witness, not even cult or liturgy. Everything revolves about the accepting and sustaining witness of Christ. This is the way we must learn to look at the sermon again.

While the Word accepts and sustains us, there is nevertheless no fusion of God's being with ours, no identification of the godly nature with human nature. The Word accept us and bears us in that he forgives sin and keeps us in the commandments of God. The relationship of the Word to us is one of providing forgiveness and assurance along the pathways of our lives. There is no mystical metamorphosis which occurs, but rather faith and sanctification.

The sacrament of the word (*Sacramentum verbi*). Because the Word is the Christ accepting men, it is full of grace but also full of judgment. Either we will let ourselves be accepted and be forgiven and be borne up by Christ, or we remain unaccepted. If we ignore the spoken word of the sermon, then we ignore the living Christ. There is a sacrament of the word.

Therefore the preacher needs to approach the sermon with the utmost certainty. The word of Scripture is certain, clear, and plain. The preacher should be assured that Christ enters the congregation through those words which he proclaims from the Scripture. Luther could say that the preacher did not have to pray the fifth request of the Lord's Prayer after his sermon ["Forgive us our trespasses"]. The sermon should not leave the preacher despairing and perplexed, but rather it should make him joyful and certain.

CARL MICHALSON

On the Gospel

Carl Michalson (1915–1965) was professor of systematic theology in the Theological School of Drew University where he maintained a lively interest in preaching. He was not concerned with practical mechanics but with preaching as the essential bearer of Christian meaning. He came to this "high" view of preaching by way of his own radically historical theology with its universal, biblical, existential, and eschatological dimensions. Michalson believed that the only language capable of bringing coherence to these is the language of Jesus, the Word made flesh and the "hinge of history." The only clue to the nature of preaching is the nature of Christ's gospel. Contemporary preaching, then,—without simple recital or repristination—must strive to reactivate the language of the gospel in such a way that preaching may once again be true to history in all its dimensions. Michalson owed much to Luther, Kierkegaard, Bultmann, and the existentialists, but, with regard to the *language* of the gospel, his work was begun by the prisoner, Bonhoeffer.

Carl Michalson, "Communicating the Gospel," *Theology Today*, Vol. XIV, No. 3 (October, 1957), 321–333. Reprinted by permission.

The gospel is the story of God's turning to man in Jesus of Nazareth. In a single report it tells us to whom we really belong and saves us from being lost. Part of the gospel is the good news that God has appointed a people called the church for the purpose of enjoying the story and telling it to others. It is as if Christians have witnessed a mysterious event. God has turned to man in Jesus of Nazareth, and Christians are those who have seen that this is what Jesus was about. From now on, what others will know about that event depends on whether or not some witness is willing to testify. A Christian is one who acknowledges that

God has turned to man in Jesus and who takes upon himself the responsibility of turning to the world with that report. Hence, to be a Christian is to be involved in the problem of the communication of the gospel.

How, then, shall we turn to the world? The best answers to that question are to be found in the nature of the message itself. One appeals in vain to methods of communication if they are not enlightened by the message. Public relations bureaus can catalogue every soft spot in the public's sales resistance and never have a positive suggestion for Christian communication. Writers may know every literary strategy from Aeschylus to Yeats and yet be powerless to evoke an act of Christian faith. Artists may be able to see beneath the surface of ordinary affairs to the turbulence and formlessness beneath, yet lack the authority to say, "Peace, be still," or the one perspective that makes "all things cohere." Before the physicist Helmholtz could arrive at the nature of vision, he had to do more than study the human eye. He had to study the properties of light. Similarly, the clue to the strategy of Christian communication is best found in the nature of the message itself.

The gospel is the good news about who God is and to whom therefore we belong. As such it speaks to our needs and longing from out of the ultimate depth of reality. It is easy to be misled about the meaning of the gospel by the fact that the first four books of the New Testament are named "Gospels." The four Gospels appear to be narrations of the history of Jesus' life and teachings, so that the word "gospel" takes on the connotation of a short historical narrative. The Gospels are not so much histories, however, as they are propaganda contrived to elicit faith in Jesus as the revealer of God. They engage in evangelism, not biography. "These are written that you may believe that Jesus is the Christ, the Son of God, and that believing you may have life in his name" (John 20:31).

The communication of the gospel is not directed, then, to just any old question people happen to be asking. It is directed to the question about the ultimate meaning of life and a man's relation to it. As Gabriel Marcel has observed, one can spend a whole day in an art museum and appreciate nothing if he has asked the wrong questions. "Will I recognize these paintings when I see them again?" "Is this a profitable experience I am having?" The realm of beauty and meaning is dumb before such queries. A school-boy may simply study the answers at the back of his book, as Kierkegaard points out. But he should know that in the process he will never learn to solve a problem.

People who are confronting the message of Christianity with questions which the gospel is not really attempting to answer, or digging out answers to questions which they themselves have not yet asked, violate a basic condition for Christian communication: namely, the truth about God and the truth about man involve each other.

But human questions which do not pertain to the mystery of man's ultimate significance will never open the way for the coming of the divine answers. Cervantes' Don Quixote may not be any nearer the kingdom of heaven simply by virtue of his painful sense of being a stranger in this world, nor Dostoevsky's Ivan by virtue of his burdening sense of guilt. But at least the gospel can be addressed to such questions. The gospel is God's answer to questions of a certain quality. "What must I do to be saved?" "Who will deliver me from the body of this death?" "Why am I something and not nothing?"

It would be sheer vanity, then, to attempt to accommodate the gospel answer to other kinds of questions. It would be roughly parallel to attempting to solve lessons in French grammar by solutions at the back of an algebra text. Christians can be made to feel needlessly stupid by their quandary in the presence of the kinds of questions others raise. "Can you prove it?" "What makes you think it's better than other faiths?" "How could God create the world in six days?" "Is the Bible the inspired word of God?" "Is a belief in bodily resurrection something we can hold today?" Christians can invent answers to any of these questions. But the answers are usually not gospel, for they do not communicate the knowledge of who God is and to whom therefore man belongs.

Not all questions are equally deserving of answers. Questions asked from mere curiosity or intellectual acquisitiveness are not the questions which draw upon the wisdom of the Christian message. Some answer to such questions should probably be given, if only in the interests of fair play. However, both parties of the dialogue should know to what extent they are putting off the real issue. The gospel is the answer to the question men ought to be asking because of their destiny as men. And as Kierkegaard has said, it is untrue to answer a question in a medium in which it has not been asked. How ironical, then, for a Christian to prepare himself as a debater in the interests of the promulgation of the Christian faith, only to discover his vocation to be more that of the town crier. Or consider the irony of training the Christian witness in the arts of persuasion, only to discover it is the task of the witness not to convince his hearers but to "transport them out of themselves" (Longinus).

The gospel is the good news about God and man which comes in a certain form, the form of proclamation. Now proclamation is basically an auditory phenomenon. The witness or the preaching is an appeal more to the ear than to the eye. It was the Apostle Paul who laid down this formula. "How are they to believe in him of whom they have never heard? . . . So faith comes from what is heard, and what is heard comes by the preaching of Christ" (Rom. 10:14 and 17). Or, as Luther says it in his commentary on this passage, "Faith is an acoustical affair." Peter verified the method when he claimed that it was *"by my mouth* the Gentiles should hear the word of the gospel and believe." . . .

What, then, does one proclaim when he communicates the gospel? The New Testament does not leave us in doubt about that. Everywhere the apostles were saying substantially the same thing. They were uttering short, terse, summary statements about the significance of the appearance of Jesus of Nazareth as the Christ. "The God of our fathers raised Jesus whom you killed by hanging him on a tree. God exalted him at his right hand as leader and savior, to give repentance to Israel and forgiveness of sins. And we are witness to these things, and so is the Holy Spirit whom God has given to those who obey him" (Acts 5:30-32). The rather extensive history of the short life of Jesus was summarized in just such pithy proclamations, called in the Greek language, *kerygma*.

By now the meaning of the Christian faith extends itself into vast and voluminous accounts which occupy great lengths of shelf space. Yet it is known that the rudiments of communication are present in these early reductions. The task of the theologian is to sift through the voluminous account for the authentic kerygma. The task of the witness is to proclaim the kerygma.

Such an emphasis on the summation of the gospel in short sentences could, of course, convey a false impression. While the witness of the church took the form of propositions, with acoustical concomitants, essentially the communication was not the spoken word but the event of speaking the word. The revelation of God came originally in the event of Jesus of Nazareth preaching himself as the revelation of God. Judged by any ordinary standard, Jesus was not different from anyone else. But Jesus himself provided the standard by which to judge who he was, for example, Luke 4:18 and 21. Jesus came preaching himself as the preacher, as the revealer, as the truth. Jesus came as the event in which God turns decisively to his people. His words are a part of that larger but more significant event which is Jesus as the Word of God. Everything recorded in the Gospels is a reflection of this basic gospel, as dew-drops on grass record the simplicity of the rising sun. It is possible to read the Gospels and to become enamored of the details of Jesus' amazing life. But that could be to miss the synoptic event which is his very significance as revealer of God.

When the friends and followers of Francis Xavier sorted through his letters with the intention of collecting them in a single memorial volume, they hit upon a device reminiscent of the apostolic preaching. They cut the letters in pieces and arranged them in the form of a cross. In this same way, embracing the events and sayings of the life and ministry of Jesus there is the single event of his witness to the truth that in him God was turning decisively to man. The Bible catches this event in short phrases which, when sounded through God's vocal apparatus in the church, renew the event. "Jesus is Lord!" "Christ died for our sins." "The word became flesh and dwelt among us full of grace and truth." "God was in Christ reconciling the world unto himself." . . .

There is more communication of the gospel in the event of the witness to the lordship of Christ than in theories about Christ's nature. There is more communication of the gospel in the act of preaching than in the content of the sermon. The gospel is communicated more efficiently in the fact of the church's existence than in statements about the nature of the church. And there is more gospel in the phenomenon of a Bible than in the defense of its authority.

Some one recently gave my son a compass. I see it almost anywhere around the house amid the rest of our clutter. Nothing in our house seems to stay in the same place, not even that compass. But the compass always seems to know where it is. Every time I see it, it is pointing in the same direction. This is the impressive thing about the Christian witness. In a world of voluminous accounts and miscellaneous directions it is the event which, wherever it occurs, signifies the polar event in the destiny of man. No man is irremediably lost so long as there is a Christian witness. And now that there is, men who seek God through other media "are like mariners who voyaged before the invention of the compass" (John Donne).

What is being suggested here is that there is more communication of the gospel in the steady, faithful witness of the worshipping community—in its reading of the Scriptures, its conduct of the sacraments, and its unending chain of prayer—than there is in the effort to establish beachheads for the Christian message on the soil of alien faiths and philosophies. There is more justification for such a position than has yet met the eye. For the Christian gospel is not simply good news which must be proclaimed to be heard. It is *new* news. The gospel is a *new testament*, related to the old not as something more recent but as something *different*. If it were simply more recent chronologically, there would scarcely be any point at this late date in considering it as something new. However, the gospel still remains new, in the sense of shockingly different. The gospel should still be expected to meet with the reaction it evoked in its earliest form: the sense of scandal, paradox, enmity, and mystery. . . .

The gospel itself provides for the possibility of its own understanding. Therefore, one does not testify to others with the expectation that their prior acquaintance with the subject will help them understand. One rather testifies with the expectation that what he is saying is providing the conditions for the very understanding of the truth.

What if others still do not understand? Here the temptations are perilously distressing. In desperation or, what is worse, embarrassment, you panic and step outside the language of your faith for the explanation of your faith. In the act, you lose the very hope one has of understanding you. What do you do if you have just played your original composition and no one understands it? Do you give a lecture on modern music? If you are communicatively efficient, you will simply play it again—not in despair, but joyfully, for you know that the hope for its understanding is in the playing of it, not in abstract explanations. . . . The communication of the Christian gospel continually waits upon the breaking in of illumination where darkness formerly prevailed. And every time it happens, it is a miracle of the moment.

The gospel, which is the good news proclaimed by Christians as something new every day, is at the same time the once-for-all news (Rom. 6:10, Heb. 7:27). It is the *final* edition. One who hears it should have the same sensations once felt when hearing the voice of a newsboy cracking the night with the latest headline on the war, the elections, or the fights.

If the once-for-all character of the Christian gospel were tied to the sheer fact of a happening in the past, it would be a bit difficult for the Christian communication to sound up-to-the-minute. The truth is, as Luther said, that the gospel is not historical in the sense of a picture which hangs on the wall. It is more like what is known in Marcel Proust's *Remembrance of Things Past* as the "metaphoric memory." It does for time what time does for space: transcends it. Time is telescoped in such a way as to make the event of God's turning to us in Christ a reality of the present moment. The gospel, then, is once-for-all, not in the sense of being located in the irrevocable and irrecoverable past, not in the sense that it can never be repeated. It is final in the sense that it is so full and complete that it can never be rivalled or superseded.

It is fortunate for the Christian witness that this is so. For the event of the witness depends to a great extent on the use of words, and words suffer by the passage of time. Take, for instance, Hegel's illustration. At this moment I jot down the sentence, "Now it is night!" How does this sentence sound when read tomorrow morning? The meaning of the sentence has suffered by the passage of time. But then how do the once-for-all passages in the New Testament sound when put to the same test? "Now is the accepted time!" "I *am* the way, the truth, and the life." To say that the gospel is the final news is to say that time never stales this event. It is historical in a very unusual sense: not that it is done for, once for all, in the past; it is the repeatable event *par excellence*.

But if the gospel is final in this sense, its language is cast less in the matrix of chronological history and more in the dynamics of present address. The event of God's turning to us in Christ, when expressed propositionally, would sound less like "Washington crossed the Delaware" and more like "I love you." The gospel is the final news in the sense in which a wedding ceremony is final: you date it, as you date Washington's crossing the Delaware; but you commit your future, as in the marriage covenant, and you keep the commitment up-to-date by the repetition of the covenant in daily whispers of self-surrender.

Nor is the gospel final in the sense of being the last truth, as if one thereafter need not seek further for truth. It is not all the news there is; it is simply the best news, the saving truth. For it is the beginning of all truth. It is the perspective that redeems all other truth for us. It is the source and orientation of the meaning of the other truths we hold. Hence, a Christian is not one who deliberately blinds his eyes to the existence of other truths because he has the once-for-all truth. The finality of the Christian truth is rather to him as a lens by which all other truth comes into meaningful focus and coherence. The Christian student does not abandon the university library because he has the truth. The truth in Christ becomes a reading-glass which brings the deceptively fragmentary perspectives of a university library into a single focus.

The net results of witnessing to the final news will be the evoking of decision. The preaching of the gospel requires decision (Rom. 10:16). When this news is heard, filibuster is ruled out and the time for decision is at hand. In the presence of the sudden illumination of the gospel one cannot respond as a character in a Chekhov play, longing wistfully but never acting. "No one who puts his hand to the plow and looks back is fit for the kingdom of God" (Luke 9:62). . . .

Finally, the gospel to which Christians witness is official news. It is not invented out of the top of the head and it does not spring from the current situation. It is as venerable as the apostolic witness. The history of the living church is the history of the will to maintain continuity with that witness. When one is called to witness to the gospel, he is called into a community of interpretation which presupposes an entire history of Christian witness. And at the source of this history is the apostolic tradition, the official news, whose mark and authority resides in the way in which it recognizes that the good news is the event of God's turning to us in Jesus of Nazareth.

The meaning of this for Christian communication is not always fully appreciated. It is simply that Christians, for whom witness is an essential part of their lives, are called upon to witness not to their particular experience of the gospel, and least of all to their private opinions about what constitutes the truth. They are called upon in announcing Jesus as Lord to mingle their voices with the prophets and apostles.

II
THE PREACHER

JOHN CHRYSOSTOM

The Temptations of Greatness

The classical ideal of oratory was that of "the good man speaking well." Preaching in the post-classical age was also concerned with the person of the speaker—not merely in the Aristotelian sense of *ethos*, which is the speaker's character as perceived by the audience, but with holiness and the conformity of the preacher's life to his message. John (surnamed) Chrysostom (347–407) epitomizes the church's ambivalence toward classical rhetoric. As a speaker he was without peer, the greatest preacher and biblical commentator of the Greek Church. Yet he warned against the public acclaim sought by every great orator and insisted that preachers should be "trained in the indifference to praise." Such training he understands to be essential in the spiritual formation of the preacher, especially in a rhetorical culture like his own with its "passion for sermons." As preacher, bishop, and apologist, Chrysostom spent his life in the pursuit of holiness. Before becoming Archbishop of Constantinople he ruled for many years from the pulpit of the church in Antioch. There he passionately rebuked the private and public immorality for which the city was infamous. In addition to his prowess as a rhetorician and lawyer, Chrysostom brought to his preaching a keenness of moral, historical, and psychological insight by which he recreated the "world" of the biblical text with such power that the contemporary reader may still be moved by his sermons. Shining through his sermons is Chrysostom's uncompromising asceticism, an aggressive, outspoken holiness which neither the capital city nor its empress, Eudoxia, could tolerate. He died in his second exile in 407. One biographer has called him both a "prince" and a "martyr of the pulpit," for the boldness of his preaching both made his fame and bought him trouble. Ironically, the one whose oratory moved congregations to wild applause was persecuted for his criticism of the megalomania of public officials and preachers. In the *Paradisio*

43

Dante places Chrysostom between Nathan, who rebuked the sins of the court, and Anselm, who suffered exile for his convictions.

John Chrysostom, *Treatise Concerning the Christian Priesthood*, Book V, 1–6, trans. W. R. W. Stephens, *A Select Library of the Nicene and Post-Nicene Fathers of the Christian Church*, ed. Philip Schaff, Vol. IX (New York: The Christian Literature Company, 1889), pp. 70–73.

How great is the skill required for the teacher in contending earnestly for the truth, has been sufficiently set forth by us. But I have to mention one more matter beside this, which is a cause of numberless dangers, though for my own part I should rather say that the thing itself is not the cause, but they who know not how to use it rightly, since it is of itself a help to salvation and to much good besides, whenever thou findest that earnest and good men have the management of it. What then, do I mean by this? The expenditure of great labor upon the preparation of discourses to be delivered in public. For to begin with, the majority of those who are under the preachers' charge are not minded to behave towards them as towards teachers, but disdaining the part of learners, they assume instead the attitude of those who sit and look on at the public games; and just as the multitude there is separated into parties, and some attach themselves to one, and some to another, so here also men are divided, and become the partisans now of this teacher, now of that, listening to them with a view to favor or spite. And not only is there this hardship, but another quite as great. For if it has occurred to any preacher to weave into his sermons any part of other men's works, he is exposed to greater disgrace than those who steal money. Nay, often where he has not even borrowed anything from any one, but is only suspected, he has suffered the fate of a thief. And why do I speak of the works of others when it is not permitted to him to use his own resource without variety? For the public are accustomed to listen not for profit, but for pleasure, sitting like critics of tragedies, and of musical entertainments, and that facility of speech against which we declaimed just now, in this case becomes desirable, even more than in the case of barristers, where they are obliged to contend one against the other. A preacher then should have loftiness of mind, far exceeding my own littleness of spirit, that he may correct this disorderly and unprofitable pleasure on the part of the multitude, and be able to lead them over to a more useful way of hearing, that his people may follow and yield to him, and that he may not be led away by their own humors, and this it is not possible to arrive at, except by two means: indifference to their praise, and the power of preaching well.

For if either of these be lacking, the remaining one becomes useless, owing to its divorce from the other, for if a preacher be indifferent to praise, and yet cannot produce the doctrine "which is with grace seasoned with salt," he becomes despised by the multitude, while he gains nothing from his own nobleness of mind; and if on the other hand he is successful as a preacher, and is overcome by the thought of applause, harm is equally done in turn, both to himself and the multitude, because in his desire for praise he is careful to speak rather with a view to please than to profit. And as he who neither lets good opinion influence him, nor is skillful in speaking, does not yield to the pleasure of the multitude, and is unable to do them any good worth mentioning, because he has nothing to say, so he who is carried away with desire for praise, though he is able to render the multitude better service, rather provides in place of this such food as will suit their taste, because he purchases thereby the tumult of acclamation.

The best kind of bishop must, therefore, be strong in both these points, so that neither may supplant the other. For if when he stands up in the congregation and speaks words calculated to make the careless wince, he then stumbles, and stops short, and is forced to blush at his failure, the good of what he has spoken is immediately wasted. For they who are rebuked, being galled by what has been told them, and unable to avenge themselves on him otherwise, taunt him, with jeers at this ignorance of his, thinking to screen their own reproach thereby. Wherefore he ought, like some very good charioteer, to come to an accurate judgment about both these good things, in order that he may be able to deal with both as he may have need; for when he is irreproachable in the eyes of all, then he will be able, with just so much authority as he wishes, both to correct and to remit from correction all those who are under his rule. But without this it will not be easy for him to do so. But this nobleness of soul should be shown not only up to the limit of indifference to praise, but should go further in order that the gain thus gotten may not in its turn be fruitless.

To what else ought he then to be indifferent? Slander and envy. Unseasonable evil speaking, however (for of course the bishop undergoes some groundless censure), it is well that he should neither fear nor tremble at excessively, nor entirely pass over; but we ought, though it happen to be false, or to be brought against us by the common herd, to try and extinguish it immediately. For nothing so magnifies both an evil and a good report as the undisciplined mob. For accustomed to hear and to speak without stopping to make inquiry, they repeat at random everything which comes in their way, without any regard to the truth of it. Therefore the bishop ought not to be unconcerned about the multitude, but straightway to nip their evil surmisings in the bud; persuading his accusers, even if they be the most unreasonable of all men, and to omit nothing which is able to dispel an ill-favored report. But if, when we do all this, they who blame us will not be persuaded, thenceforward we should give them no concern. Since if any one be too quick to be dejected by these accidents, he will not be able at any time to produce anything noble and admirable. For despondency and constant cares are mighty for destroying the powers of the mind, and for reducing it to extreme weakness. Thus then must the priest behave towards those in his charge, as a father would behave to his very young children; and as such are not disturbed either by their insults or their blows, or their lamentations, nor even if they laugh and rejoice with us, do we take much account of it; so should we neither be puffed up by the promises of these persons nor cast down at their censure, when it comes from them unseasonably. But this is hard, my good friend; and perhaps, methinks, even impossible. For I know not whether any man ever succeeded in the effort not to be pleased when he is praised, and the man who is pleased at this is likely also to desire to enjoy it, and the man who desires to enjoy it will, of necessity, be altogether vexed and beside himself whenever he misses it. For as they who revel in being rich, when they fall into poverty are grieved, and they who have been used to live luxuriously cannot bear to live shabbily; so, too, they who long for applause, not only when they are blamed without a cause, but when they are not constantly being praised, become, as by some famine, wasted in soul, particularly when they happen themselves to have been used to praise, or if they hear others being praised. He who enters upon the trial of preaching with desires of this kind, how many annoyances and how many pangs dost thou think that he has? It is no more possible for the sea to be without waves than that man to be without cares and grief.

For though the preacher may have great ability (and this one would only find in a few), not even in this case is he released from perpetual toil. For since preaching does not come by nature, but by study, suppose a man to reach a high standard of it, this will then forsake him if he does not cultivate his power by constant application and exercise. So that there is greater labor for the wiser than for the unlearned. For there is not the same degree of loss attending negligence on the part of the one and the other, but the loss is in exact proportion to the difference between the two possessions. For the latter [the unlearned] no one would blame, as they furnish nothing worth regarding. But the former, unless they are constantly producing matter beyond the reputation in which all hold them, great censure attends on all hands; and besides these things, the latter would meet with considerable praise, even for small performances, while the efforts of the former, unless they be specially wonderful and startling, not only fail to win applause, but meet with many fault-finders. For the audience set themselves to be critics, not so much in judgment of what is said as of the reputation of the speaker, so that whenever any one excels all others in oratorical powers, then especially of all others does he need laborious study. For this man is not allowed to avail himself of the usual plea which human nature urges, that one cannot succeed in everything; but if his sermons do not throughout correspond to the greatness of the expectations formed, he will go away without having gained anything but countless jeers and censures; and no one takes this into consideration about him, that dejection and pain, and anxiety, and often anger, may step in, and dim the clearness of his thoughts and prevent his productions from coming from him unalloyed, and that on the whole being but a man, he cannot be constantly the same, nor at all times acquit himself successfully, but naturally must sometimes fall short of the mark, and appear on a lower level of ability than usual. None of these things, as I said, are they willing to take into consideration, but charge him with faults as if they were sitting in judgment on an angel; though in other cases, too, a man is apt to overlook the good performances of his neighbor, though they be many and great, and if anywhere a defect appears, even if it be accidental, even if it only occur at long intervals, it is quickly perceived, and always remembered, and thus small and trifling matters have often lessened the glory of many and great doings.

Thou seest, my excellent friend, that the man who is powerful in preaching has peculiar need of greater study than others; and besides study, of forbearance also greater than what is needed by all those whom I have already mentioned. For thus are many constantly springing up against him, in a vain and senseless spirit, and having no fault to find with him, but that he is generally approved of, hate him; and he must bear their bitter malice nobly, for as they are not able to hide this cursed hatred, which they so unreasonably entertain, they both revile, and censure, and slander in private, and defame in public, and the mind which has begun to be pained and exasperated, on every one of these occasions, will not escape being corrupted by grief. For they will not only revenge themselves upon him by their own acts, but will try to do so by means of others, and often having chosen some one of those who are unable to speak a word, will extol him with their praises and admire him beyond his worth. Some do this through ignorance alone, some through ignorance and envy, in order that they may ruin the reputation of the other, not that they may prove the man to be wonderful who is not so, and the noble-minded man has not only to struggle against these, but often against the ignorance of the whole multitude; for since it is not possible that all those who come together should consist of learned men, but the chances are that the larger part of the congregation is composed of unlearned people, and that even the rest, who are clearer headed than they, fall as far short of being able to criticize sermons as the remainder again fall short of them; so that only one or two are seated there who possess this power; it follows, of necessity, that he who preaches better than others carries away less applause, and possibly goes home without being praised at all, and he must be prepared to meet such anomalies nobly, and to pardon those who commit them in ignorance, and to weep for those who acquiesce in them on account of envy as wretched and pitiable creatures, and not to consider that his powers have become less on either of these accounts. For if a man, being a pre-eminently good painter, and superior to all in his art, sees the portrait which he has drawn with great accuracy held up to ridicule, he ought not to be dejected, and to consider the picture poor, because of the judgment of the ignorant; as he would not consider the drawing that is really poor to be something wonderful and lovely, because of the astonishment of the inartistic.

For let the best artificer be himself the critic of his own designs, and let his performances be determined to be good or poor, according as the mind which designed them gives sentence upon them. But let him not even consider the opinion, so erroneous and inartistic, of the outside world. Let, therefore, the man who undertakes the strain of teaching never give heed to the good opinion of the outside world, nor be dejected in soul on account of such persons; but laboring at his sermons so that he may please God, (For let this alone be his rule and determination, in discharging this best kind of workmanship, not acclamation, nor good opinions,) if, indeed, he be praised by men, let him not repudiate their applause, and when his hearers do not offer this, let him not seek it, let him not be grieved. For a sufficient consolation in his labors, and one greater than all, is when he is able to be conscious of arranging and ordering his teaching with a view to pleasing God.

For if he be first carried away with the desire for indiscriminate praise, he will reap no advantage from his labors, or from his power in preaching, for the mind being unable to bear the senseless censures of the multitude is dispirited, and casts aside all earnestness about preaching. Therefore it is especially necessary to be trained to be indifferent to all kinds of praise. For to know how to preach is not enough for the preservation of that power, if this be not added: and if any one would examine accurately the man who is destitute of this art, he will find that he needs to be indifferent to praise no less than the other, for he will be forced to do many wrong things in placing himself under the control of popular opinion. For not having the energy to equal those who are in repute for the quality of their preaching, he will not refrain from forming ill designs against them, from envying them, and from blaming them without reason, and from many such discreditable practices, but will venture everything, even if it be needful to ruin his own soul, for the sake of bringing down their fame to the level of his own insignificance. And in addition to this, he will leave off his exertions about his work; a kind of numbness, as it were, spreading itself over his mind. For much toil, rewarded by scanty praise, is sufficient to cast down a man who cannot despise praise, and put him into a deep lethargy, since the husbandman even when he spends time over some sorry piece of land, and is forced to till a rock, quickly desists from his work, unless he is possessed of much earnestness about the matter, or has a fear of famine impending over him. For if they who are able to speak with considerable power, need such constant exercise for the preservation of their talent, he who collects no materials at all, but is forced in the midst of his efforts to meditate; what difficulty, what confusion, what trouble will he experience, in order that he may be able at great labor to collect a few ideas! and if any of those clergy who are under his authority, and who are placed in the inferior order, be able in that position to appear to better advantage than he; what a divine mind must he have, so as not to be seized with envy or cast down by despondency. For, for one to be placed in a station of higher dignity, and to be surpassed by his inferior in rank, and to bear this nobly, would not be the part of any ordinary mind, nor of such as my own, but of one as hard as adamant; and if, indeed, the man who is in greater repute be very forbearing and modest, the suffering becomes so much the more easily borne. But if he is bold and boastful and vainglorious, a daily death would be desirable for the other; he will so embitter his life, insulting him to his face, and laughing at him behind his back, wresting much of his authority from him, and wishing to be everything himself. But he is possessed of the greatest security, in all these circumstances, who has fluency in preaching, and the earnest attention of the multitude about him, and the affection of all those who are under his charge. Dost not thou know what a passion for sermons has burst in upon the minds of Christians now-a-days? and that they who practice themselves in preaching are in especial honor, not only among the heathen, but among them of the household of the faith? How then could any one bear such disgrace as to find that all are mute when he is preaching, and think that they are oppressed, and wait for the end of the sermon, as for some release from work; while they listen to another with eagerness though he preach long, and are sorry when he is about to conclude; and almost angry when it is his purpose to be silent. If these matters seem to thee to be small, and easily to be despised, it is because of thine inexperience. They are truly enough to quench zeal, and to paralyze the powers of the mind, unless a man withdraw himself from all human passions, and study to frame his conduct after the pattern of those incorporeal powers, who are neither pursued by envy nor by longing for fame, nor by any other morbid feeling. If then there be any man so constituted as to be able to subdue this wild beast, so difficult to capture, so unconquerable, so fierce; that is to say, public fame, and to cut off its many heads, or rather to forbid their growth altogether; he will easily be able to repel these many violent assaults, and to enjoy a kind of quiet haven of rest.

GEORGE HERBERT

The Parson Preaching

Seventeenth century Anglican spirituality is exemplified in the life of George Herbert (1593–1633), one-term member of Parliament, country rector, and England's greatest religious poet. The true center of Herbert's universe was neither the political world of London nor his obscure village of Bemerton, but the church and its ministry. Herbert's spirituality strikes a perfect balance between the ascetic and the mundane service of God and between the soul's inner devotion and the community's corporate worship. The church's liturgy, calendar, and architecture form the organizing principle of his collection of poems, *The Temple*. The church's calling to ordinary, daily holiness is the central message of his prose classic, *The Country Parson*, written not to memorialize his own brief ministry but, as Herbert put it, "that I may have a Mark to aim at." Testimonies to Herbert's saintliness abound but perhaps none so eloquent as the poet's own description of every preacher's calling to be a "window" of grace:

> Lord, how can man preach thy eternal word?
>   He is a brittle crazy glass:
> Yet in thy temple thou dost him afford
>   This glorious and transcendent place,
>   To be a window, through thy grace.

George Herbert, *The Temple and the Country Parson* (Boston: James B. Dow, 1842 [1652]), pp. 296–300, 368–369.

The country parson preacheth constantly. The pulpit is his joy and his throne. If he at any time intermit [is absent], it is either for want of health; or against some festival, that he may the better celebrate it; or for

51

the variety of the hearers, that he may be heard at his return more attentively. When he intermits, he is ever very well supplied by some able
man; who treads in his steps, and will not throw down what he hath
built; whom also he entreats to press some point that he himself hath
often urged with no great success, that "so in the mouth of two or three
witnesses the truth may be more established."

When he preacheth, he procures attention by all possible art: both by
earnestness of speech; it being natural to men to think, that where is
much earnestness, there is somewhat worth hearing: and by a diligent
and busy cast of his eye on his auditors, with letting them know that he
marks who observes, and who not: and with particularizing of his
speech now to the younger sort, then to the elder, now to the poor, and
now to the rich—"This is for you, and this is for you;"—for particulars ever
touch, and awake, more than generals. Herein also he serves himself of
the judgments of God: as of those of ancient times, so especially of the
late ones; and those most, which are nearest to his parish; for people are
very attentive at such discourses, and think it behooves them to be so,
when God is so near them, and even over their heads. Sometimes he
tells them stories and sayings of others, according as his text invites him:
for them also men heed, and remember better than exhortations; which,
though earnest, yet often die with the sermon, especially with country
people; which are thick, and heavy, and hard to raise to a point of zeal
and fervency, and need a mountain of fire to kindle them; but stories and
sayings they will well remember. He often tells them, that sermons are
dangerous things; that none goes out of church as he came in, but either
better or worse; that none is careless before his Judge; and that the word
of God shall judge us.

By these and other means the parson procures attention; but the
character of his sermon is *holiness*. He is not witty, or learned, or eloquent, but *holy*:—a character that Hermogenes never dreamed of, and
therefore he could give no precepts thereof. But it is gained,—First, by
choosing texts of devotion, not controversy; moving and ravishing texts,
whereof the scriptures are full.—Secondly, by dipping and seasoning
all our words and sentences in our hearts before they come into our
mouths; truly affecting, and cordially expressing all that we say: so that
the auditors may plainly perceive that every word is heart-deep.—
Thirdly, by turning often, and making many apostrophes to God; as, "O
Lord! bless my people, and teach them this point!" or, "O my Master, on
whose errand I come, let me hold my peace, and do thou speak thyself;
for thou art love; and when thou teachest, all are scholars." Some such

irradiations scatteringly in the sermon, carry great holiness in them. The prophets are admirable in this. So Isa. 64; "Oh, thou that wouldest rend the heavens, that thou wouldest come down," etc. And Jeremy (chapter 10), after he had complained of the desolation of Israel, turns to God suddenly, "O Lord! I know that the way of man is not in himself," etc.—Fourthly, by frequent wishes of the people's good, and joying therein; though he himself were, with St. Paul, "even sacrificed upon the service of their faith." For there is no greater sign of holiness, than the procuring and rejoicing in another's good. And herein St. Paul excelled, in all his epistles. How did he put the Romans "in all his prayers" (Rom. 1:9); and "ceased not to give thanks" for the Ephesians (Eph. 1:16); and for the Corinthians (1 Cor. 1:4); and for the Philippians "made request with joy" (Phil. 1:4); and is in contention for them whether to live or die, be with them or Christ (ver. 23); which, setting aside his care of his flock, were a madness to doubt of. What an admirable epistle is the second to the Corinthians! How full of affections! He joys, and he is sorry; he grieves, and he glories! Never was there such a care of a flock expressed, save in the great Shepherd of the fold, who first shed tears over Jerusalem, and afterwards blood. Therefore this care may be learned there, and then woven into sermons; which will make them appear exceeding reverend and holy.—Lastly, by an often urging of the presence and majesty of God; by these, or such like speeches—"Oh, let us take heed what we do! God sees us; he sees whether I speak as I ought, or you hear as you ought; he sees hearts, as we see faces. He is among us; for if we be here, he must be here; since we are here by him, and without him could not be here." Then, turning the discourse to his majesty,—"and he is a great God, and terrible; as great in mercy, so great in judgment! There are but two devouring elements, fire and water; he hath both in him. 'His voice is as the sound of many waters,' (Rev. 1); and he himself is 'a consuming fire.'" (Heb. 12)—Such discourses shew very holy.

The parson's method in handling of a text consists of two parts:—First, a plain and evident declaration of the meaning of the text;—and secondly, some choice observations, drawn out of the whole text, as it lies entire and unbroken in the scripture itself. This he thinks natural, and sweet, and grave. Whereas the other way, of crumbling a text into small parts, (as, the person speaking or spoken to, the subject, and object, and the like,) hath neither in it sweetness, nor gravity, nor variety; since the words apart are not scripture, but a dictionary, and may be considered alike in all the scripture.

The parson exceeds not an hour in preaching, because all ages have thought that a competency: and he that profits not in that time, will less afterwards; the same affection which made him not profit before, making him then weary; and so he grows from not relishing, to loathing.

A Prayer After Sermon

Blessed be God, and the Father of all mercy, who continueth to pour his benefits upon us. Thou hast elected us, thou hast called us, thou hast justified us, sanctified, and glorified us. Thou wast born for us, and thou livedst and diedst for us. Thou hast given us the blessings of this life, and of a better. O Lord! thy blessings hang in clusters; they come trooping upon us; they break forth like mighty waters on every side. And now, Lord, thou hast fed us with the bread of life. "So man did eat angel's food." O Lord, bless it! O Lord, make it health and strength to us!—still striving and prospering so long within us, until our obedience reach the measure of thy love, who hast done for us as much as may be. Grant this, dear Father, for thy Son's sake, our only Savior: to whom, with thee and the Holy Ghost,—three persons, but one most glorious, incomprehensible God,—be ascribed all honor, and glory, and praise, ever. Amen.

RICHARD BAXTER

On the Making of the Preacher

The Reformed Pastor by Richard Baxter (1615–1691) appeared only four
years after Herbert's *The Country Parson* and immediately established
itself as a trustworthy guide to pastoral theology and spirituality. Baxter's
is a larger work and less introspective than Herbert's. It betrays a sense
of emergency born of chaotic conditions in the churches and among the
clergy during the interregnum. Baxter developed the book out of the
famous Worcester *Agreement* signed by more than fifty ministers in
Worcester. The clerics pledge to redress the "sins of the ministry" and to
promote the restoration of holiness in the churches, with special attention given to the personal instruction of lapsed Christians and the spiritual renewal of preaching. The influence of *The Reformed Pastor* has extended through the centuries, touching established and non-conforming
Christians alike, including Philip Jacob Spener, Philip Doddridge, the
Wesleys, Thomas Chalmers, C. H. Spurgeon, and countless others.

Richard Baxter, *The Reformed Pastor* (New York: T. Mason and G. Lane,
1837 [1656]), pp. 172–180.

It is the common danger and calamity of the church to have unregener-
ate and inexperienced pastors; and to have men become preachers before
they are Christians; to be sanctified by dedication to the altar, as God's
priests, before they are sanctified by hearty dedication to Christ as his
disciples; and so to worship an unknown God, and to preach an unknown Christ, an unknown Spirit, an unknown state of holiness and
communion with God, and a glory that is unknown, and likely to be
unknown to them for ever. He is likely to be but a heartless preacher who
has not the Christ and grace that he preaches in his heart. O that all our
students in the university would well consider this! What a poor busi-

ness it is to themselves to spend their time in knowing some little of the works of God, and some of those names that the divided tongues of the nations have imposed on them, and not to know the Lord himself, exalt him in their hearts, nor to be acquainted with that one renewing work that should make them happy. They do but walk in a vain show, and spend their lives like dreaming men, while they busy their wits and tongues about abundance of names and notions, and are strangers to God and the life of saints. If ever God awaken them by his grace, they will have cogitations and employments so much more serious than their unsanctified studies and disputations were, that they will confess they did but dream before. A world of business they make themselves about *nothing*, while they are willful strangers to the primitive, independent, necessary Being, who is all in all. Nothing can be rightly known, if God be not known; nor is any study well managed, nor to any great purpose, where God is not studied. We know but little of the creature, till we know it as it stands in its order and respect to God: single letters and syllables unconnected are nonsense. He who overlooks the Alpha and Omega, and sees not the beginning and end, and him in all, who is the *all* of all, sees nothing at all. All creatures are, as such, broken syllables: they signify nothing as separated from God. Were they separated actually, they would cease to be, and the separation would be an annihilation; and when we separate them in our fancies, we make nothing of them to ourselves. It is one thing to know the creatures as Aristotle, and another thing to know them as a Christian. None but a Christian can read one line of his physics, so as to understand it rightly. . . . I hope you perceive what I aim at in all this, viz., that to see God in his creatures, to love him, and converse with him, was the employment of man in his upright state; that this is so far from ceasing to be our duty, that it is the work of Christ to bring us back to it; and, therefore, the most holy men are the most excellent students of God's works, and none but the holy can rightly study or know them. His works are great, sought out of all them that have pleasure therein; but not for themselves, but for him that made them. Your study of physics and other sciences is not worth a rush if it be not God by them that you seek after. To see and admire, to reverence and adore, to love and delight in God appearing to us in his works, and purposely to peruse them for the knowledge of God, this is the true and only philosophy, and the contrary is mere folly, and is called so again and again by God himself. This is the sanctification of your studies, when they are devoted to God, and when he is the life of them all, and they are directed to him as their end and principal object.

Therefore, I shall presume to tell you by the way, that it is a grand error, and of dangerous consequence in the Christian academies, (pardon the censure from one so unfit for it, seeing the necessity of the case commands it,) that they study the creature before the Redeemer, and set themselves to physics, and metaphysics, and mathematics, before they set themselves to theology; whereas no man who has not the vitals of theology is capable of going beyond a fool in philosophy; and all that such do is but doting about questions and opposition of sciences, falsely so called. And as by affecting a separated creature-knowledge Adam fell from God, so they who mind these profane, empty babblings, and oppositions of science, falsely so called, miss the end of all right study; they err concerning the faith; while they will needs prefer these, they miss that faith which they pretend to aim at. Their pretense is, that theology, being the end, and the most perfect branch, must be the last, and all the subservient sciences must go before it. . . .

It is evident therefore that theology must lay the ground and lead the way in all our studies, when we are once so far acquainted with words and things as is needful to our understanding the sense of its principles. If God must be searched after in our search of the creatures, and we must affect no separated knowledge of them, then tutors must read God to their pupils in all; and divinity must be the beginning, the middle, the end, the life, the all of their studies; and our physics and metaphysics must be reduced to theology, and nature must be read as one of God's books, which is purposely written for the revelation of himself. The Holy Scripture is the easiest book. When you have first learned God and his will there, in the necessary things, address yourselves cheerfully to the study of his works, that you may see there the creature itself as your alphabet, and their order as the connection of syllables, words, and sentences, and God as the subject matter of all, and their respect to him as the sense or signification; and then carry on both together, and never more play the mere scriveners; stick no more in your letters and words, but read every creature as a Christian or a divine. If you see not yourselves and all things as living, and moving, and having being in God, you see nothing, whatever you think you see. If you perceive not in your perusals of the creatures, that God is all, and in all, you may think perhaps that you know something, but you know nothing as you ought to know. He who sees and loves God in the creature, the same is known and loved of him. Think not so basely of the works of God and your physics as that they are only preparatory studies for boys. It is a most high and noble part of holiness to search after, behold, admire, and love the great Creator in all his works. How much have the saints of God been employed in it! The beginning of Genesis, the books of Job and the Psalms, may acquaint us that our physics are not so little akin to theology as some suppose. I do therefore, in zeal to the good of the church, and their own success in their most necessary labors, propound it to the consideration of all pious tutors, whether they should not as early and as diligently read to their pupils, or cause them to read, the chief parts of practical divinity (and there is no other) as any of the sciences; and whether they should not go together from the very first? It is well that they hear sermons; but that is not enough. If they have need of private help in philosophy besides public lectures, how much more in theology! If tutors would make it their principal business to acquaint their pupils with the doctrine of life, and labor to set it home upon their hearts, that all might be received according to its weight, and read to their hearts as well as to their heads, and so carry on the rest of their instructions, that it might appear they made them but subservient to this, and that their pupils may feel what they drive at in all, and so that they would teach all their philosophy *in habitu theologico*, this might be a happy means to make happy souls, a happy church and commonwealth. The same I mean also respecting schoolmasters to their scholars. But when languages and philosophy have almost all their time and diligence, and instead of reading philosophy like divines, they read divinity like philosophers, as if it were a thing of no more moment than a lesson of music or arithmetic, and not the doctrine of everlasting life; this is what blasts so many in the bud, and pesters the church with unsanctified teachers. Hence it is that we have so many worldlings to preach of the invisible felicity, and so many carnal men to declare the mysteries of the Spirit; and I would I had not cause to say, so many infidels to preach Christ, or so many atheists to preach the living God; and when they are taught philosophy before or without religion, what wonder if their philosophy be all, or most of their religion; if they grow up into admirations of their unprofitable fancies, and deify their own deluded brains, when they know no other God; and if they reduce all their theology to their philosophy, as some have done.

Again: I address myself to all those who have the education of youth, especially in order to prepare them for the ministry. You who are schoolmasters and tutors, begin and end with the things of God. Speak daily to the hearts of your scholars those things which must be wrought into their hearts, or else they will be undone. Let some piercing words fall frequently from your mouths, of God, the state of their souls, and the life to come. Do not say they are too young to understand and entertain them. You little know what impressions they may make which you discern not. Not only the soul of that boy, but a congregation, or many souls therein, may have cause to bless God for your zeal and diligence, yea, for one such seasonable word. You have a great advantage above others to do them good. You have them before they are grown to the worst, and they will hear you when they will not hear another. If they are destined to the ministry, you are preparing them for the special service of God; and should they not first have the knowledge of him whom they must serve? O think with yourselves what a sad thing it will be to their own souls, and what a wrong to the church of God, if they come out from you with carnal hearts to so holy, spiritual, and great a work! Of a hundred students that are in one of your colleges, how many may there be who are serious, experienced, godly men: some talk of too small a number. If you should send one half of them on a work that they are unfit for, what bloody work will they make in the church! Whereas if you be the means of their thorough sanctification, how many souls may bless you, and what greater good can you possibly do the church! When their hearts are once savingly affected with the doctrine which they study and preach, they will study it heartily, and preach it heartily. . . .

Content not yourselves to have the main work of grace; but be also very careful . . . that you preach to yourselves the sermons you study before you preach them to others. . . . When I let my heart grow cold, my preaching is cold; and when it is confused, my preaching is so too: and I can observe the same frequently in the best of my hearers, that, when I have a while grown cold in preaching, they have cooled accordingly; and the next prayers that I have heard from them have been too much like my preaching. We are the nurses of Christ's little ones. If we forbear our food we shall famish them; they will quickly find it in the want of milk, and we may quickly see it again in them in the cold and dull discharge of their several duties. If we let our love go down, we are not likely to raise theirs up. If we abate our holy care and fear, it will appear in our doctrine. If the matter show it not, the manner will. If we feed on unwholesome food, either errors or fruitless controversies, our hearers are likely to fare the worse for it. Whereas if we abound in faith, love, and zeal, how will it overflow to the refreshing of our congregations, and how will it appear in the increase of the same graces in others.

PHILIP JACOB SPENER

The Reform of Preaching

Like George Herbert and Richard Baxter, who reacted to deplorable conditions in the church and among its clergy, Philip Jacob Spener (1635–1705) was also moved to protest the formalism and bureaucracy of his church, the Lutheran church in Germany. As supervisor of the ministerium in Frankfurt am Main he strengthened the catechizing of the young, instituted home meetings for the cultivation of holiness (known as the *collegia pietatis*), encouraged lay participation in worship, and urged the reform of preaching and homiletical training. He objected to the aridity of orthodoxist scholasticism and its unedifying influence on preaching. Much of German Pietism has a familiar ring to contemporary Christians, especially Spener's criticism of the lectionary and the monologic sermon, as well as his advocacy of small-group discussion of Christian issues. In all his proposals Spener's concern was practical, for example: "that *sermons* be so prepared by all that their purpose (faith and its fruits) may be achieved in the hearers to the greatest possible degree." The aim of his program for preaching was not a new homiletical technique, but the re-formation of the "inner man," a transformation which, if it is to be effected in the congregation, must begin in the soul of the preacher. (For another Pietist view of preaching see "A Letter to a Friend Concerning the Most Useful Way of Preaching" by August Hermann Francke in *Pietists*, ed. Peter C. Erb [New York: Paulist Press, 1983], pp. 117–127).

Philip Jacob Spener, *Pia Desideria*, trans. and ed. Theodore G. Tappert (Philadelphia: Fortress Press, 1964), pp. 87–91, 115–117. Copyright © by Fortress Press 1964. Used by permission.

Thought should be given to a more extensive use of the word of God among us. We know that by nature we have no good in us. If there is to be any good in us, it must be brought about by God. To this end the word of God is the powerful means, since faith must be enkindled through the gospel, and the law provides the rules for good works and many wonderful impulses to attain them. The more at home the word of God is among us, the more we shall bring about faith and its fruits.

It may appear that the word of God has sufficiently free course among us inasmuch as at various places (as in this city) there is daily or frequent preaching from the pulpit. When we reflect further on the matter, however, we shall find that with respect to this first proposal, more is needed. I do not at all disapprove of the preaching of sermons in which a Christian congregation is instructed by the reading and exposition of a certain text, for I myself do this. But I find that this is not enough. In the first place, we know that "all scripture is inspired by God and profitable for teaching, for reproof, for correction, and for training in righteousness" (II Tim. 3:16). Accordingly *all* scripture, without exception, should be known by the congregation if we are all to receive the necessary benefit. If we put together all the passages of the Bible which in the course of many years are read to a congregation in one place, they will comprise only a very small part of the Scriptures which have been given to us. The remainder is not heard by the congregation at all, or is heard only insofar as one or another verse is quoted or alluded to in sermons, without, however, offering any understanding of the entire context, which is nevertheless of the greatest importance. In the second place, the people have little opportunity to grasp the meaning of the Scriptures except on the basis of those passages which may have been expounded to them, and even less do they have opportunity to become as practiced in them as edification requires. Meanwhile, although solitary reading of the Bible at home is in itself a splendid and praiseworthy thing, it does not accomplish enough for most people.

It should therefore be considered whether the church would not be well advised to introduce the people to Scripture in still other ways than through the customary sermons on the appointed lessons.

This might be done, first of all, by diligent reading of the Holy Scriptures, especially of the New Testament. It would not be difficult for every housefather to keep a Bible, or at least a New Testament, handy and read from it every day or, if he cannot read, to have somebody else read. . . .

Then a second thing would be desirable in order to encourage people to read privately, namely, that where the practice can be introduced the books of the Bible be read one after another, at specified times in the public service, without further comment (unless one wished to add brief summaries). This would be intended for the edification of all, but especially of those who cannot read at all, or cannot read easily or well, or of those who do not own a copy of the Bible.

For a third thing it would perhaps not be inexpedient (and I set this down for further and more mature reflection) to reintroduce the ancient and apostolic kind of church meetings. In addition to our customary services with preaching, other assemblies would also be held in the manner in which Paul describes them in I Corinthians 14:26-40. One person would not rise to preach (although this practice would be continued at other times), but others who have been blessed with gifts and knowledge would also speak and present their pious opinions on the proposed subject to the judgment of the rest, doing all this in such a way as to avoid disorder and strife. This might conveniently be done by having several ministers (in places where a number of them live in a town) meet together or by having several members of a congregation who have a fair knowledge of God or desire to increase their knowledge meet under the leadership of a minister, take up the Holy Scriptures, read aloud from them, and fraternally discuss each verse in order to discover its simple meaning and whatever may be useful for the edification of all. Anybody who is not satisfied with his understanding of a matter should be permitted to express his doubts and seek further explanation. On the other hand, those (including the ministers) who have made more progress should be allowed the freedom to state how they understand each passage. Then all that has been contributed, insofar as it accords with the sense of the Holy Spirit in the Scriptures, should be carefully considered by the rest, especially by the ordained ministers, and applied to the edification of the whole meeting. Everything should be arranged with an eye to the glory of God, to the spiritual growth of the participants, and therefore also to their limitations. Any threat of meddlesomeness, quarrelsomeness, self-seeking, or something else of this sort should be guarded against and tactfully cut off especially by the preachers who retain leadership in these meetings.

Not a little benefit is to be hoped for from such an arrangement. Preachers would learn to know the members of their own congregations and their weakness or growth in doctrine and piety, and a bond of confidence would be established between preachers and people which would serve the best interests of both. At the same time the people would have a splendid opportunity to exercise their diligence with respect to the word of God and modestly to ask their questions (which they do not always have the courage to discuss with their minister in private) and get answers to them. In a short time they would experience personal growth and would also become capable of giving better religious instruction to their children and servants at home. In the absence of such exercises, sermons which are delivered in continually flowing speech are not always fully and adequately comprehended because there is no time for reflection in between or because, when one does stop to reflect, much of what follows is missed (which does not happen in a discussion). On the other hand, private reading of the Bible or reading in the household, where nobody is present who may from time to time help point out the meaning and purpose of each verse, cannot provide the reader with a sufficient explanation of all that he would like to know. What is lacking in both of these instances (in public preaching and private reading) would be supplied by the proposed exercises. It would not be a great burden either to the preachers or to the people, and much would be done to fulfill the admonition of Paul in Colossians 3:16, "Let the word of Christ dwell in you richly, as you teach and admonish one another in all wisdom, and as you sing psalms and hymns and spiritual songs." In fact, such songs may be used in the proposed meetings for the praise of God and the inspiration of the participants.

This much is certain: the diligent use of the word of God, which consists not only of listening to sermons but also of reading, meditating, and discussing (Ps. 1:2), must be the chief means for reforming something, whether this occurs in the proposed fashion or in some other appropriate way. The word of God remains the seed from which all that is good in us must grow. If we succeed in getting the people to seek eagerly and diligently in the book of life for their joy, their spiritual life will be wonderfully strengthened and they will become altogether different people.

There are probably few places in our church in which there is such want that not enough sermons are preached. But many godly persons find that not a little is wanting in many sermons. There are preachers who fill most of their sermons with things that give the impression that the preachers are learned men, although the hearers understand nothing of this. Often many foreign languages are quoted, although probably not one person in the church understands a word of them. Many preachers are more concerned to have the introduction shape up well and the transitions be effective, to have an outline that is artful and yet sufficiently concealed, and to have all the parts handled precisely according to the rules of oratory and suitably embellished, than they are concerned that the materials be chosen and by God's grace be developed in such a way that the hearers may profit from the sermon in life and death. This ought not to be so. The pulpit is not the place for an ostentatious display of one's skill. It is rather the place to preach the word of the Lord plainly but powerfully. Preaching should be the divine means to save the people, and so it is proper that everything be directed to this end. Ordinary people, who make up the largest part of a congregation, are always to be kept in view more than the few learned people, insofar as such are present at all.

As the Catechism contains the primary rudiments of Christianity, and all people have originally learned their faith from it, so it should continue to be used even more diligently (according to its meaning rather than its words) in the instruction of children, and also of adults if one can have these in attendance. A preacher should not grow weary of this. In fact, if he has opportunity, he would do well to tell the people again and again in his sermons what they once learned, and he should not be ashamed of so doing.

I shall here gladly pass over additional observations that might well be made about sermons, but I regard this as the principal thing: Our whole Christian religion consists of the inner man or the new man, whose soul is faith and whose expressions are the fruits of life, and all sermons should be aimed at this. On the one hand, the precious benefactions of God, which are directed toward this inner man, should be presented in such a way that faith, and hence the inner man, may ever be strengthened more and more. On the other hand, works should be so set in motion that we may by no means be content merely to have the people refrain from outward vices and practice outward virtues and thus be concerned only with the outward man, which the ethics of the heathen can also accomplish, but that we lay the right foundation in the heart, show that what does not proceed from this foundation is mere hypocrisy, and hence accustom the people first to work on what is inward (awaken love of God and neighbor through suitable means) and only then to act accordingly.

One should therefore emphasize that the divine means of word and sacrament are concerned with the inner man. Hence it is not enough that we hear the word with our outward ear, but we must let it penetrate to our heart, so that we may hear the Holy Spirit speak there, that is, with vibrant emotion and comfort feel the sealing of the Spirit and the power of the word. Nor is it enough to be baptized, but the inner man, where we have put on Christ in baptism, must also keep Christ on and bear witness to him in our outward life. Nor is it enough to have received the Lord's Supper externally, but the inner man must truly be fed with that blessed food. Nor is it enough to pray outwardly with our mouth, but true prayer, and the best prayer, occurs in the inner man, and it either breaks forth in words or remains in the soul, yet God will find and hit upon it. Nor, again, is it enough to worship God in an external temple, but the inner man worships God best in his own temple, whether or not he is in an external temple at the time. So one could go on.

Since the real power of all Christianity consists of this, it would be proper if sermons, on the whole, were pointed in such a direction. If this were to happen, much more edification would surely result than is presently the case.

PHOEBE PALMER

The Great Army of Preaching Women

"Do not be startled, dear reader. We do not intend to discuss the question of 'Women's Rights' . . . " So begins *The Promise of the Father* by Phoebe Palmer (1807–1874), American Methodist evangelist and spiritual leader. True to her word, Palmer did not devote her books to the feminist cause, but her uncompromising pursuit of holiness or, in Wesleyan terms, "perfect love," led her to radical positions such as abolition, temperance, and the encouragement of women to the preaching office. Behind her stood not only the perfectionism of Wesley but also the pietism of Spener and others who wished to purify and sanctify the church. Before her lay the endless controversies concerning the Second and Third Blessings which would eventually splinter one wing of American Methodism into an array of Holiness and Pentecostal groups. Phoebe Palmer's belief in the perfectibility of the Christian well accorded with the optimistic spirit of mid-nineteenth-century America. The "Tuesday Meetings for the Promotion of Holiness" held in her New York home drew visitors from around the world and continued even after her death. With her husband Walter C. Palmer she led evangelistic meetings in America and Europe. Her detractors questioned whether her emphasis on personal faith effectively excluded the work of the Holy Spirit, but her influence among American Methodists and Holiness groups remained strong into the 1880's. In this chapter Palmer offers a closely reasoned argument from Scripture on behalf of woman's right to preach. To this she appends "A Life Picture" which graphically depicts the exclusion of women from the pulpit as a waste of resources and an offense to Jesus Christ.

Phoebe Palmer, *The Promise of the Father* (New York: W. C. Palmer, Jr., 1872), pp. 21–33.

Did the tongue of fire descend alike upon God's daughters as upon his sons, and was the effect similar in each?

And did all these waiting disciples, who thus, with one accord, continued in prayer, receive the grace for which they supplicated? It was, as we observe, the gift of the Holy Ghost that had been promised. And was this promise of the Father as truly made to the daughters of the Lord Almighty as to his sons? See Joel 2:28-29: "And it shall come to pass afterward, that I will pour out my Spirit upon all flesh; and your sons and your daughters shall prophesy, your old men shall dream dreams, your young men shall see visions. And also upon the servants and upon the handmaids in those days will I pour out my Spirit." When the Spirit was poured out in answer to the united prayers of God's sons and daughters, did the tongue of fire descend alike upon the women as upon the men? How emphatic is the answer to this question! "And there appeared unto them cloven tongues, like as of fire, and it sat upon *each of them*." Was the effect similar upon God's daughters as upon his sons? Mark it, O ye who have restrained the workings of this gift of power in the church. "And they were *all* filled with the Holy Ghost, and began to speak as the Spirit gave utterance." Doubtless it was a well nigh impelling power, which was thus poured out upon these sons and daughters of the Lord Almighty, moving their lips to most earnest, persuasive, convincing utterances. Not alone only did Peter proclaim a crucified risen Savior, but each one, as the Spirit gave utterance, assisted in spreading the good news; and the result of these united ministrations of the Spirit, through human agency, was that three thousand were in one day pricked to the heart. Unquestionably, the whole of this newly baptized company of one hundred and twenty disciples, male and female, hastened in every direction, under the mighty constrainings of that perfect love that casteth out fear, and great was the company of them that believed.

And now, in the name of the Head of the church, let us ask, Was it designed that these demonstrations of power should cease with the day of Pentecost? If the Spirit of prophecy fell upon God's daughters, alike as upon his sons in that day, and they spake in the midst of that assembled multitude, as the Spirit gave utterance, on what authority do the angels of the churches restrain the use of that gift now? Has the minister of Christ, now reading these lines, never encouraged open female testimony, in the charge which he represents? Let us ask, What account will you render to the Head of the church, for restricting the use of this endowment of power? Who can tell how wonderful the achievements of the cross might have been, if this gift of prophecy, in woman, had continued in use, as in apostolic days? Who can tell but long since the gospel might have been preached to every creature? Evidently this was a *speciality* of the last days, as set forth by the prophecy of Joel. Under the old dispensation, though there was a Miriam, a Deborah, a Huldah, and an Anna, who were prophetesses, the special outpouring of the Spirit upon God's daughters as upon his sons, seems to have been reserved as a characteristic of the last days. This, says Peter, as the wondering multitude beheld these extraordinary endowments of the Spirit, falling alike on all the disciples, – this is that which was spoken by the prophet Joel, "And also upon my servants and upon my handmaidens will I pour out my Spirit."

And this gift of prophecy, bestowed upon all, was continued and recognized in all the early ages of Christianity. The ministry of the word was not confined to the apostles. No, they had a laity for the times. When, by the cruel persecutions of Saul, all the infant church were driven away from Jerusalem, except the apostles, these scattered men and women of the laity "went everywhere *preaching the word,*" that is, proclaiming a crucified, risen Savior. And the effect was, that the enemies of the cross, by scattering these men and women, who had been saved by its virtues, were made subservient to the yet more extensive proclamation of saving grace.

Impelled by the indwelling power within, these Spirit-baptized men and women, driven by the fury of the enemy in cruel haste from place to place, made all their scatterings the occasion of preaching the gospel everywhere, and believers were every where multiplied, and daily were there added to the church such as should be saved.

Says the Rev. Dr. Taft, "If the nature of society, its good and prosperity, in which women are jointly and equally concerned with men, if in *many cases*, their fitness and capacity for instructors being admitted to be equal to the other sex, be not reasons sufficient to convince the candid reader of woman's teaching and preaching, because of two texts in Paul's Epistles (1 Cor. 14:34; 1 Tim. 2:12) let him consult the paraphrase of Locke, where he has proved to a demonstration that the apostle, in these texts, never intended to prohibit women from praying and preaching in the church, provided they were dressed as became women professing godliness, and were qualified for the sacred office. Nor is it likely that he would, in one part of his Epistle, give directions how a woman, as well as a man, should pray and prophesy in public, and presently after, in the very same Epistle, forbid women, endowed with the gifts of prayer and prophecy, from speaking in the church, when, according to his own explication of prophecy, it is 'speaking unto others for edification, exhortation, and comfort.' Besides, the apostle, in the Epistle to the church at Corinth, says, 'Follow after charity, and desire spiritual gifts, but rather that ye may prophesy.' Again, 'I would that ye all spake with tongues, but rather that ye prophesied.' Here the apostle speaks to the church in general; and the word *all* must comprehend every individual member; and since he had just before given directions about a woman's praying and prophesying, we conclude that his desire extended to women as well as to men. Certainly the word *all* includes both men and women; otherwise the mind of Paul 'who was made a minister of the Spirit,' would have been more narrow than that of Moses, who was only a minister of the law; for when Joshua came and told Moses that Eldad and Medad prophesied in the camp, and desired him to forbid them, Moses said unto him, 'Enviest thou for my sake? Would God that all the Lord's people were prophets, and that he would put his Spirit upon them.' Now, all the Lord's people must certainly comprehend the Miriams and Deborahs in the camp, as well as the Eldads and Medads."

Dr. Clarke says (Rom. 16:12), " 'Salute Tryphena and Tryphosa, who labored in the Lord. Salute the beloved Persis, who labored much in the Lord'—two holy women, who, it seems, were assistants to the apostle in his work, probably by exhorting, visiting the sick, etc. Persis was another woman who, it seems, excelled the preceding; for of her it is said, she *labored much in the Lord*. We learn from this, that Christian *women*, as well as *men*, labored in the ministry of the word. In those times of simplicity all persons, whether men or women, who had received the knowledge of the truth, believed it to be their duty to propagate it to the utmost of their power.

"Many have spent much useless labor in endeavoring to prove that these women did not *preach*. That there were some *prophetesses*, as well as *prophets*, in the Christian church, we learn; and that *woman* might pray or prophesy, provided she had her head covered, we know; and that whoever prophesied, spoke unto others to edification, exhortation, and comfort, St. Paul declares, 1 Cor. 14:3. That no preacher can do more, every person must acknowledge because to edify, exhort, and comfort, are the prime ends of the gospel ministry. If women thus prophesied, then women preached."

Chrysostom and Theophilact take great notice of Junia, mentioned in the apostle's salutations. In our translation (Rom. 16:7) it is, "Salute Andronicus and Junia, my kinsmen, and my fellow-prisoners, who are of note among the apostles." By the word *kinsmen* one would take Junia not to have been a woman, but a man. But Chrysostom and Theophilact were both Greeks; consequently, they knew their mother tongue better than our translators, and they say it was a woman. It should, therefore, have been translated, "Salute Andronicus and Junia, my kinsfolk." The apostle salutes other *women* who were of note among them, particularly Tryphena and Tryphosa, who labored in the Lord, and Persis, who labored much in the Lord.

Again, if we look into ecclesiastical history, we shall find women very eminent in the church long after the days of the apostles; I say women who were distinguished for their piety, their usefulness, and their sufferings. Witness the story of Perpetua and Felicitas, martyrs for the Christian faith, which contains traits that touch the most insensible, and cannot be read without a tear. Eusebius speaks of Potominia Ammias, a prophetess in Philadelphia, and others, who were equally distinguished by their zeal for the love which they bore to Jesus Christ.

Justin Martyr, who lived till about A.D. 150, says in his Dialogue with Trypho, the Jew, "that both *women* and *men* were seen among them who had the gifts of the Spirit of God, according as Joel the prophet had foretold, by which he endeavored to convince the Jew that the *latter days* were come; for by that expression, Manassah Ben Israel tells us, all their wise men understood the times of Messias."

Dodwell, in his Dissertations on Irenaeus, says, "that the extraordinary gift of the spirit of prophecy was given to others besides the apostles, and that not only in the *first* and *second*, but in the *third* century, even to the time of Constantine, men of all sorts and ranks had these gifts — yea, and *women* too." Therefore we may certainly conclude that the prophetic saying of the Psalmist 68:11 was verified: "The Lord gave the word, and great was the company of those that published it." In the original Hebrew it is, "Great was the company of women publishers, or women evangelists." Grotius explains Ps. 68:11, "*Dominus dabat sermonem, id est, materiam loquendi uberem, nempe ut feminarum praedicantium (victorias) multum agmen diceret, scilicet, eaquae sequuntur*"—"The Lord shall give the word, that is, plentiful matter of speaking; so that he would call those which follow the great army of preaching women, viz., victories, or female conquerors."

A Supposition

Suppose one of the brethren who had received the baptism of fire on the day of Pentecost, now numbered among those who were scattered everywhere preaching the word, had met a female disciple who had also received the same endowment of power. He finds her proclaiming Jesus to an astonished company of male and female listeners. And now imagine he interferes and withstands her testimony by questioning whether women have a right to testify of Christ before a mixed assembly. Would not such an interference look worse than unmanly? And were her testimony, through this interference, restrained, or rendered less effectual, would it not, in the eye of the Head of the church, involve guilt? Yet we do not say but a person may err after the same similitude and be sincere, on the same principle that Saul was sincere when he withstood the cruel havoc of the church. He verily thought he was doing God service. But when his mind was enlightened to see that, in persecuting these men and women, he was withstanding God, and rejecting the divinely ordained instrumentalities by which the world was to be saved, he could no longer have been sincere unless he had taken every possible pains to make his refutal of error as far reaching as had been his wrong. And how the heart of that beloved disciple of the Savior would have been grieved, and her hands weakened, by one whom she would have a right to look to for aid against the common enemy, and for sympathy in her work!

A large proportion of the most intelligent, courageous, and self-sacrificing disciples of Christ are females. "Many women followed the Savior" when on earth; and, compared with the fewness of male disciples, many women follow him still. Were the women who followed the incarnate Savior earnest, intelligently pious, and intrepid, willing to sacrifice that which cost them something, in ministering to him of their substance? In like manner, there are many women in the present day, earnest, intelligent, intrepid, and self-sacrificing, who, were they permitted or encouraged to open their lips in the assemblies of the pious in prayer, or speaking as the Spirit gives utterance, might be instrumental in winning many an erring one to Christ. We say, were they permitted and encouraged; yes, encouragement may now be needful. So long has this endowment of power been withheld from use by the dissuasive sentiments of the pulpit, press, and church officials, that it will now need the combined aid of these to give the public mind a proper direction, and undo a wrong introduced by the man of sin centuries ago.

But more especially do we look to the ministry for the correction of this wrong. Few, perhaps, have really intended to do wrong; but little do they know the embarrassment to which they have subjected a large portion of the church of Christ by their unscriptural position in relation to this matter. The Lord our God is one Lord. The same indwelling spirit of might which fell upon Mary and the other women on the glorious day that ushered in the present dispensation still falls upon God's daughters.

Not a few of the daughters of the Lord Almighty have, in obedience to the command of the Savior, tarried at Jerusalem; and, the endowment from on high having fallen upon them, the same impelling power which constrained Mary and the other women to speak as the Spirit gave utterance impels them to testify of Christ.

"The testimony of Jesus is the spirit of prophecy." And how do these divinely baptized disciples stand ready to obey these impelling influences? Answer, ye thousands of Heaven-touched lips, whose testimonies have so long been repressed in the assemblies of the pious! Yes, answer, ye thousands of female disciples, of every Christian land, whose pent-up voices have so long, under the pressure of these man-made restraints, been uttered in groanings before God.

But let us conceive what would have been the effect, had either of the male disciples interfered with the utterances of the Spirit through Mary or any of those many women who received the baptism of fire on the day of Pentecost. Suppose Peter, James, or John had questioned their right to speak as the Spirit gave utterance before the assembly, asserting that it were unseemly, and out of the sphere of woman, to proclaim a risen Jesus, in view of the fact that there were *men* commingling in that multitude. How do you think that He who gave woman her commission on the morning of the resurrection, saying, "Go, tell my brethren," would have been pleased with an interference of this sort?

But are there not doings singularly similar to these being transacted now? We know that it is even so. However unseemly on the part of brethren, and revolting to our finer sensibilities, such occurrences may appear, we have occasion to know that they are not at all unusual in religious circles. We will refer to a Christian lady of more than ordinary intellectual endowments, of refined sensibilities, and whose literary culture and tastes were calculated to constitute her a star in the galaxy of this world.

A Life Picture

I have seen a lovely female turn her eye away from the things of time, and fix it on the world to come. Jesus, the altogether lovely, had revealed himself to her, and the vision of her mind was absorbingly entranced with his infinite loveliness, and she longed to reveal him to others. She went to the assembly of the pious. Out of the abundance of her heart she would fain have spoken, so greatly did her heart desire to win others over to love the object of her adoration. Had she been in a worldly assembly, and wished to attract others with an object of admiration, she would not have hesitated to have brought out the theme in conversation, and attracted listeners would have taken her more closely to their hearts, and been won with the object of her love. But she is now in the assembly of the pious. It is true many of them are her brothers and sisters, but cruel custom sealed her lips. Again and again she goes to the assembly for social prayer and the conference meeting, feeling the presence and power of an indwelling Savior enthroned uppermost in her heart, and assured that he would have her testify of him. At last she ventures to obey God rather than man. And what is the result? A committee is appointed to wait on her, and assure her that she must do so no more. Whisperings are heard in every direction that she has lost her senses; and, instead of sympathizing looks of love, she meets averted glances and heart repulses. This is not a fancy sketch; no, it is a life picture. Ye who have aided in bringing about this state of things, how does this life picture strike you?

Who Was Rejected?

Think of the feelings of the Christian lady, who has thrown herself in the bosom of your church community, in order that she may enjoy the sympathies of Christian love and fellowship. Has grace divested her of refined sensibilities? No! grace has only turned those refined sensibilities into a sanctified channel, and given her a yet more refined perception of everything pure, and lovely, and of good report. What must be the sufferings of that richly endowed, gentle, loving heart? But was it not her loving, gentle, indwelling Savior that would fain have had her testify for *him*? and in rejecting her testimony for Jesus, did not Jesus, the Head of the church, take it as done unto himself?

P. T. FORSYTH

The Authority of the Preacher

The word "prophetic" is often associated with the message of the great
Scottish Congregationalist Peter Taylor Forsyth (1848–1921). His "posi-
tive" theology opposed the shallow liberalism of culture-Christianity
decades before Barth and the later crisis-theology (a term coined by
Forsyth). He focused on the *kerygma* as the principle of unity in the New
Testament long before Dodd brought such thinking into vogue. Before
Dibelius and Bultmann introduced the academy to Gospel criticism, the
Evangelical Forsyth wrote, "The New Testament (the Gospels even), is a
direct transcript, not of Christ, but of the preaching of Christ." No one
since Luther had so firm a grasp of the kerygmatic nature of the New
Testament, and no one in this century has translated that insight into
homiletical theology with more vigor than P. T. Forsyth. Toward the end
of his 25-year pastorate, before becoming Principal of Hackney College
in London, Forsyth apparently underwent a spiritual reconversion that
completely reoriented his life and thought. His theology was now gov-
erned by the holiness of God and the centrality of the cross, which are
mediated to humanity in a moral relationship with God. He sketched the
vision in his famous sermon "Holy Father" and later in many books,
including *The Person and the Place of Jesus Christ, The Work of Christ*, and
in 1907 his Beecher Lectures at Yale, *Positive Preaching and Modern Mind*.

P. T. Forsyth, *Positive Preaching and Modern Mind* (New York: A. C.
Armstrong, 1907), pp. 3–5, 41–50.

It is, perhaps, an overbold beginning, but I will venture to say that with
its preaching Christianity stands or falls. That is surely so, at least in
those sections of Christendom which rest less upon the church than
upon the Bible. Wherever the Bible has the primacy which is given it

in Protestantism, there preaching is the most distinctive feature of worship. . . .

Preaching (I have said) is the most distinctive institution in Christianity. It is quite different from oratory. The pulpit is another place, and another kind of place, from the platform. Many succeed in the one, and yet are failures on the other. The Christian preacher is not the successor of the Greek orator, but of the Hebrew prophet. The orator comes with but an inspiration, the prophet comes with a revelation. In so far as the preacher and prophet had an analogue in Greece it was the dramatist, with his urgent sense of life's guilty tragedy, its inevitable ethic, its unseen moral powers, and their atoning purifying note. Moreover, where you have the passion for oratory you are not unlikely to have an impaired style and standard of preaching. Where your object is to secure your audience, rather than your gospel, preaching is sure to suffer. I will not speak of the oratory which is but rhetoric, tickling the audience. I will take both at their best. It is one thing to have to rouse or persuade people to do something, to put themselves into something; it is another to have to induce them to trust somebody and renounce themselves for him. The one is the political region of work, the other is the religious region of faith. And wherever a people is swallowed up in politics, the preacher is apt to be neglected; unless he imperil his preaching by adjusting himself to political or social methods of address. The orator, speaking generally, has for his business to make real and urgent the present world and its crises, the preacher a world unseen, and the whole crisis of the two worlds. The present world of the orator may be the world of action, or of art. He may speak of affairs, of nature, or of imagination. In the pulpit he may be what is called a practical preacher, or a poet–preacher. But the only business of the apostolic preacher is to make men practically realize a world unseen and spiritual; he has to rouse them not against a common enemy but against their common selves; not against natural obstacles but against spiritual foes; and he has to call out not natural resources but supernatural aids. Indeed, he has to tell men that their natural resources are so inadequate for the last purposes of life and its worst foes that they need from the supernatural much more than aid. They need deliverance, not a helper merely but a Savior. The note of the preacher is the gospel of a Savior. The orator stirs men to rally, the preacher invites them to be redeemed. . . . With preaching Christianity stands or falls because it is the declaration of a gospel. Nay more—far more—it is the gospel prolonging and declaring itself.

I venture here to state at once what I will go on to explain, that the preacher is the organ of the only real and final authority for mankind.

He is its organ, and even its steward; but he is not its vicar, except at Rome.

The question of the ultimate authority for mankind is the greatest of all the questions which meet the West, since the Catholic Church lost its place in the sixteenth century, and since criticism no longer allows the Bible to occupy that place. Yet the gospel of the future must come with the note of authority. Every challenge of authority but develops the need of it. And that note must sound in whatever is the supreme utterance of the church, in polity, pulpit, or creed. It seems clear, indeed, unless the whole modern movement is to be simply undone, that the church must draw in the range of its authority, and even Catholicism must be modified if it is to survive. But the church can never part with the tone of authority, nor with the claim that, however it may be defined, the authority of its message is supreme. That is the very genius of an evangelical religion; for it declares that that which saves the world shall also judge the world, and it preaches the absolute right over us of the Christ who bought us—the active supremacy in conscience of our moral redemption. It is the absence of the note of authority that is the central weakness of so many of the churches; and it is the source of their failure to impress society with their message for the practical ends of the kingdom of God. It is useless to preach the kingdom when we do not carry into the center of life the control of a King. The first duty of every soul is to find not its freedom but its Master. And the first charge of every church is to offer, nay to mediate, him.

The authority of the preacher was once supreme. He bearded kings, and bent senates to his word. He determined policies, ruled fashions, and prescribed thought. And yet he has proved unable to maintain the position he was so able to take. He could not insure against the reaction which has now set in as severely as his authority once did. That reaction has long been in force; and today, however great may be his vogue as a personality, his opinion has so little authority that it is not only ignored but ridiculed. In that respect the pulpit resembles the press, whose circulation may be enormous, while elections, and such like events, show that the influence of its opinions is almost nil.

But between the press and the pulpit there is this mighty difference. The pulpit has a Word, the press has none. The pulpit has a common message and, on the strength of it, a claim, while the press has no claim to anything but external freedom of opinion and expression. The one has a gospel which is the source of its liberty, the other has no gospel but liberty, which in itself is no gospel at all. Liberty is only opportunity for a gospel. The true Gospels not only claim it, they create it. But, in itself, it is either the product of a gospel, or a means thereto; it is not an end. It is no more an end than evolution is, which is only the process of working out an end that the mere process itself does not give. Liberty in itself is not an end; and it has only the worth of its end. The chief object of the liberty of the press is facts. It must be free to publish facts. But the pulpit has not merely a fact but a Word. The press is there for information, or for suggestion at most, it is not there for authority; but the pulpit is there with authority; and the news it brings is brought for the sake of the authority. The press may offer an opinion as to how the public should act, but the pulpit is there with a message as to whom the acting public must obey and trust. The press is an adviser, but the pulpit is a prophet; the press may have a thought, the pulpit must have a gospel, nay a command. . . .

Therefore, the pulpit has an authority. If it have not, it is but a chair and not a pulpit. It may discourse, but it does not preach. But preach it must. It speaks with authority. Yet the authority is not that of the preacher's person; it is not mere authoritativeness. For us that goes without saying. What does not go unsaid, what needs saying is, that the preacher's authority is not the authority even of his truth. In the region of mere truth there is no authority. Mere truth is intellectual, and authority is a moral idea bearing not upon belief but upon will and faith, decision and committal. It is not statements that the preacher calls on us to believe. It is no scheme of statements. It is not views. It is not a creed or a theology. It is a religion, it is a gospel, it is an urgent God. In the region of mere theology we may be bold to say there is no authority; the authority is all in the region of religion. The creed of the church catholic should have great prestige, but not authority in the proper sense. Belief, in the region of theology, is a matter of truth or truths; it is science, simple or complex. And science knows no authority. But in the region of religion belief is faith. It is a personal relation. It is belief in a person by a person. It is self committal to him. With the heart man believeth unto salvation. It is a personal act towards a person. It is trust in that person, and response to the power of his act. . . . It is a moral relation of obedience and authority.

The authority of the pulpit is thus a personal authority. Yet it is not the authority of the preacher's person, or even of his office. His office may demand much more respect than the fanatics of freedom allow, but it cannot claim authority in the strict sense. The personal authority of the pulpit is the authority of the divine person who is its burthen. It is an external authority, but it is the authority of an inward objective, living, saving God, before whose visitation the prophet fades like an ebbing voice, and the soul of the martyr cries invisible from under the altar of the cross. . . .

For the soul, and conscience, the words higher or lower mean authority or they mean nothing. Even in the celestial time when the soul shall be in complete harmony with God the relation must always be worship, and therefore authority and obedience. The supreme thing is not a weight that lies on us but a crown that governs us and lifts us up for ever. Unless we frankly adopt the positivist position, where humanity is to itself not only a law but an object of worship, there must be an authority both for man and men. And as for the externality of it—surely if there be an authority it must be external. It must come to us, and not rise out of us. It must come down on man and not proceed from him. It is a word to our race, not from it. The content of our conscience descends on us, it is no projection of ours. It were less than conscience if it were; for the law that we made we could unmake and the order we issued we could recall. Treat the autonomy of conscience as you will, but do not remove the accent from the *nomos* to the *autos*. If it be a *nomos* it is a product of more than ourselves, more than man—it is of God. Otherwise it would be but a self-imposed condition, from which at any time we might be self-released. And it could bind none, even while it remained binding, but him who had imposed it on himself. And then it would not be conscience but earnest whim.

But then, it is asked, is it not one of the greatest and surest results of modern progress that, if there be an authority, it must be inward, it must be in the soul, it must be by consent? Yes, indeed, that is one of the greatest and best blessings of the modern time. But do you realize what that means? Surely the more inward it is the more is it external. The more we retire to our inner castle the more we feel the pressure of the not-ourselves, and the presence of our Overlord. The more spiritual we are the more we are under law to another. To internalize the authority is to subtilize it, and therefore to emphasize it; for it is the subtler realities that bear upon us with the most persistent, ubiquitous, and effective pressure. The more inward we go the more external the authority becomes, just because it becomes more of an authority, and more unmistakably, irresistibly so.

If we were not so Philistine that the most accurate words seem pedantic, the proper word would be not external but objective. Because external has come, for the man in the street, to mean outside his own body, or his own family, or his own self-will, his own individuality; while what we are really concerned with is outside our own soul, our own personality. What we are suffering from is not mere externality but unconquered inwardness, subjectivism, individualism, ending in egotism. It is our subjectivism which gives externals their enslaving power over us. If within us we find nothing over us we succumb to what is around us. It is a cure for our subjectivism that we need, a cure for our egotism. And that is to be found in nothing physically external, nothing institutionally so, but only in an objective, moral and spiritual, congenial yet antithetic, in an objective to the ego, yea to the race, which objective alone gives morality any meaning. . . .

By all means then the divine authority must be inward—if we are sure what we mean, if we do not come to mean that we are our own authority—which I am afraid is the popular version with which the preacher has to contend. The authority must be inward, it is true. The modern preacher must accept that principle, and correct all its risks of perversion and debasement. His message must be more and more inward. But it must be *searchingly* inward. That is to say, it must be inward with the right of search, as an authority; and not simply as a servant, a suppliant, an influence, an impression, a sensibility. It must be above all else a moral authority, having right and not mere influence or prestige, demanding action, obedience and sacrifice, and not merely echo, appreciation, stirrings, and thrills.

Thus when we move the authority from an external church or book to the forum of the conscience, when in the face of humanity or society we claim to call our soul our own, we have not ended the strife; we have but begun one more serious on another plane. And, in many cases, we have but opened the gates of confusion, and let loose the floods of inner tumult. The recognition of the inwardness, in many cases, seems to destroy the authority. Perhaps it does so in most cases at first. We are too full of ourselves to desire another to rule over us. And even when we desire it there are few who are so familiar with their inner selves as to be able to distinguish with any certainty the shepherd's voice, amid the gusts or sighings or their own fitful selves.

HANS VAN DER GEEST

The Personality of the Preacher

The theological application of modern theories of personality has brought homiletics full circle to classical rhetoric's concern with *character* and medieval Christianity's emphasis on the *formation* of the preacher. Although psychological assessments of preaching lack the moral and theological depth of Chrysostom, Baxter, or Spener, they offer insights into the effectiveness of the preacher and the responsiveness of congregations. The research of Hans van der Geest (1933–) focuses on the importance of trust between preacher and listener. He concludes that this relationship cannot be effected by homiletical technique alone, but is reflective of the strength (or ineffectiveness) of the preacher's personality. Van der Geest suggests a clinical model for the training of preachers that would take into account the unique gifts and needs of each preacher. The wealth of theological and practical wisdom in his book emerges from an empirical base of 200 worship services and interviews with parishioners, most of which took place under the auspices of the Center for Clinical Pastoral Education in Zollikerberg, Switzerland, where the author is Supervisor. *Presence in the Pulpit*, the original title of which is *Du hast mich angesprochen* (You have spoken to me), is the only book available that is rigorously restricted to the sermon's (and the preacher's) *effect* on the listener. On the basis of his research van der Geest isolates three dimensions of effective preaching as it is perceived by the listener: (1) the hearer's trust of the preacher, derived in large measure from the wholeness of the preacher's personality; (2) deliverance, which is the sermon's power to make God's new reality present; (3) nurture of Christians for life in the world. *Presence in the Pulpit* bears obvious resemblances to Brooks' emphasis on personality and Spener's cell-group approach to ministerial formation, the difference lying in van der Geest's clinical documentation and his use of psychological categories to assess the health or sickness of modern preaching.

Hans van der Geest, *Presence in the Pulpit*, trans. Douglas W. Stott (Atlanta: John Knox Press), pp. 143–153. English translation copyright John Knox Press, 1981. Used by permission.

In the previous chapters I have followed the listener reactions to worship services and sermons. Three dimensions of experience in that worship service became visible, as well as continually new aspects of the reactions to what was offered in worship services. My impression is that this procedure has not left very much of fundamental homiletics untouched.

An unambiguous discovery in each analysis of worship service and sermon concerns the close relationship between the preacher's concrete modes of behavior and his or her personality. It is no accident when a preacher says "I" often, too often, or seldom, or if a preacher speaks extemporaneously, preaches legalistically or speaks graphically. These visible and audible elements are all deeply rooted in the personality. Anyone wishing to change them must not only change the externally perceivable facts, but must also take into consideration the invisible roots.

An adequate fundamental posture for the preacher has emerged in fairly clear outline from the presentation of listener reactions and my accompanying reflections. I wish to summarize this now, although it may seem presumptuous to attempt a definition of the "correct" preacher. It could imply that one expects the miracle of the worship service from the preacher and not from God, but I don't think this kind of distortion is a temptation for me. Those suspecting presumptuousness here have probably brought it themselves. The "correct" preacher is a standard for measurement which does not actually exist, and I personally do not claim to do justice to this image myself at all times and in all aspects. One needs a great deal of humor, a bit of the ability to laugh at oneself, and a great deal of trust in God's far-reaching activity in order to write and read about the ideal of the correct preacher. Otherwise it will just be discouraging. So the image is meant as a point of orientation and as an aid. It helps those who believe one's entire vocational life is also a kind of atonement, and it may frighten off those who indeed are conducting worship services and preaching, but who should not be. Being a preacher is not for everyone.

I will list the aspects in which that basic posture of the preacher has emerged from the dimensions already discussed. (I will draw some parallels to Fritz Riemann, *Der Prediger aus tiefenpsychologischer Sicht*. Riemann describes four main types of preachers with their respective good and bad character traits, but that's too systematized and construed for my way of thinking. In reality the personalities of preachers cannot be divided into these main types, since most people exhibit strong characteristics from various types. Nonetheless I find it good that Riemann has directed attention to the preacher's personality.)

A Sense of Calling

When God wishes his word to be proclaimed, this does not exclude the possibility that the person doing the proclaiming genuinely wants to do it. Considered theologically, this calling is the connection between the two. For the preacher's experience this means he or she feels personally spoken to and engaged by the gospel and called to proclaim it to others. A preacher would be crippled without a consciousness of being called. The feeling of being touched inwardly by the gospel, and the conviction that others should also experience that in their own ways, give the inner motivation to fulfill various preconditions necessary for conducting a worship service properly. The preacher will speak clearly to the congregation and thus come across personally, something indispensable for awakening trust in the listeners. This attitude will show that being spoken to cannot come just from the preacher, but in a decisive way from God; this expectation will become clear in prayers and in other ways. If the preacher personally feels spoken to and engaged, he or she will be able to convey the astonishment resulting from that and will awaken among the listeners a similar astonishment in the face of the gospel. Being engaged will produce the courage to proclaim that gospel, to say things that cannot be rationally supported.

The fact that the preacher feels addressed by God will also have consequences for the content. Fate will not be granted too much respect, but neither will the claim be made that the church proclamation has the answers to the world's riddles. That personal feeling of being spoken to gives access to the substance of sermon and prayer, and leads to that total seriousness with which the preacher's work is performed. The worshippers will be captivated by that seriousness.

In this feeling of being spoken to and of being called, the preacher is not basically different from any other Christian. The calling pertains to the *imitatio Christi*, not necessarily to the office of the pastor. Personal, social and other factors give this calling a form which for some people means choosing the vocation of the pastor, though the same calling is realized by others in other forms. In a broad sense it can be said that every Christian is called to proclaim; this common task becomes most clearly visible in the preacher.

One of the most terrible agonies a preacher can experience is becoming inwardly unsure about whether to preach or not. The spiritual energy for this task is given by a feeling—perhaps even deeply hidden or unconscious—of being called inwardly to the work of preaching. If this feeling is missing, the sensitive preacher has a sense of being placed in an impossible situation. Externally this may show up perhaps as a missing address of God or in lifeless prayers.

As far as I can see there are basically two spiritual situations in which this agony arises. First, there are men and women who too rashly choose a vocation requiring them to preach. This is an especially sad situation for pastors, since the foundation of their entire vocational existence is missing if they are not personally engaged. Their training offers them almost no alternative work possibilities, and who wants or can start all over again if one already has a family and an established lifestyle? The solution of preaching in spite of the uncertainty is more than questionable. Church authorities have no real way of finding out whether young theologians are personally spoken to and engaged by the gospel. This would require a more intensive acquaintance with the students instead of an examining commission. As long as that remains an unrealistic wish, the agony will come up again and again: preachers without inner motivation.

The second situation, one that occurs much more frequently, is that of an alienation from oneself. The bad part of it is that it's too much trouble for many people to talk with young theologians about being engaged by God. In formal training the word "objective" is quickly equated with "avoidance of existential areas." Faith can quickly be reduced to theology, and thus life to a theory, and for young theologians this often means they lose contact with the roots of their vocational choice. They would be ashamed to refer to inner processes not discussed in learned texts. However, in pastoral training situations with students and young pastors it has become clear to me that beneath that normal skepticism concerning one's calling there is often a discarded consciousness of a very great inner involvement, a *vocatio interna*. This consciousness only dares come forth a bit in a personal atmosphere of acceptance and understanding.

Only very rarely, I believe, can one find absolute certainty concerning the calling to the pastorate. Indeed, it would even be a very questionable certainty. The heritage of pietism, with its overemphasis of a calling as only an inner and thus irrational experience, still affects theologians in that they have a bad conscience if they have not had this experience. However, the question is legitimate whether a preacher is personally engaged by the gospel. This engagement is fundamentally synonymous with the *vocatio interna*. The path to the pastorate is for many preachers simply the social framework of their faith, and as soon as they find this access to their faith again the former joy in their vocation awakens again. Preachers must be able to speak about this deepest root of their pastoral existence. It is a matter of their relationship to the Lord they are to proclaim, and they are crippled before they begin if there is no clarity about this.

A Feeling of Responsibility

In a harmonious growth process people not only learn how to become independent themselves, but also how to accept responsibility for others. Accepting responsibility involves more and is more difficult than being independent, just as being a father or mother is more than just being an adult. Only a person willing and able to support others will be able to take on an authoritative function. A supporting, caring attitude is indispensable for awakening trust, though today this is not one of the most popular roles. To the extent that a preacher has schizoid tendencies, he or she will have difficulty at precisely this point. A merciless manner will sooner shock than awaken trust. Hysterical characteristics also make it difficult to be involved and carry responsibility. In the chapters on security and deliverance I have tried to show how difficult it is for young preachers as soon as they discover they are an authority figure in the traditional worship service. The external structure of the worship service requires a preacher able to find the proper stance as an authority.

The content structure of the proclamation also demands this feeling of responsibility; otherwise, the realm of humility and obedience, of law and of involvement in faith disappears from view with the consequences described in the third chapter. That feeling of responsibility guards against a naïve, unrealistic avoidance of problems and opens one's eyes to the complexity of life. The responsible preacher will try to discover clearly the structure of the biblical message and not just be given over uncritically to flights of fancy. He or she seeks words which will show people clearly where the proclamation wants to speak to them. Neither does the preacher make things too easy for the listeners, but rather shows them the realistic ways to go, even if there is accompanying pain. In this way the preacher is dependable and can awaken feelings of security.

Seeking Contact with Oneself

Human life offers the somewhat unnerving possibility of taking over the values of others and thus losing contact with oneself. Those whose values and traditions I take over are then so important to me that I basically forget myself. I am only a mouthpiece, and no longer a person, and I love myself only to the extent that I correspond to those ideal standards; I don't love myself for what I essentially am. In such a situation, however, I cannot really feel love for others; there is no longer an "I" capable of love, but ony a mouthpiece, a copy. I am able to preach personally if I accept myself; only then will I dare show myself and be open.

I will awaken deep experiences in others to the extent that I am able to reach myself. If I overplay feelings of revenge because they are indeed terrifying, or if I rationalize a pious faith in order to agree with a theological theory, then I am closing myself off, and in the worship service I am drawing from a well which is going dry. That level of yearning and security is reached only by preachers who also seek access to their own interior, an interior which at first glance normally appears comical, childish, and not really ready to be shown in public. Preachers with compulsive tendencies become so afraid that it's painful for them to find that path to themselves.

Contact with oneself is of decisive importance while preparing a sermon. The idea for the sermon emerges only in a creative restlessness, when the preacher dares ignore those constricting thoughts acquired elsewhere, thoughts that will be needed again only when it is time to examine the ideas.

I have shown how poorly preachers come across when they overplay themselves. Precisely the thing they are suppressing inside ends up having an effect on the listeners, and that is what is tragic about suppression. It has an effect on others without our wanting it to, and does so much more strongly than we think is possible. That suppressed element becomes autonomous, slips from our control and takes on a demonic power. Everyone has problems and confusing forces inside; that's not so bad, it's a part of life. Disturbances in communication don't begin in life's problems, on the contrary, difficulties can bring people close together. Disturbances arise where we don't admit to them. Preachers not willing to admit their insecurity will preach so securely that the listeners will in the first place not be able to identify with them, and will in the second place be aggravated with their style. Their insecurity, on the other hand, would create a link wherever they brought it in. Instead of preaching human security, they would preach God's promise, which comes to the aid of those of us who are insecure. Persons finding no contact with themselves will offer something foreign which may be right, but also boring.

The question of to what extent preachers should reveal themselves cannot be answered with simple rules. Not all openness is useful, but a façade certainly does very little for communication. Emotional openness invites participation, and extemporaneous speech is generally a decisive step towards such openness.

Preachers must also find access to themselves as an aid to vividness, an element decisively important in the dimension of understanding. Real vividness emerges in communication only if the preachers see inwardly; those not seeking access to themselves will hide behind the images of others or behind abstractions.

Preachers sometimes invent an audience which actually is not even present. This, too, is a direct result of not being in contact with oneself. If I don't recognize the strife inside myself, I will preach against strife and thus only be addressing myself instead of the actual participants in the worship service. The preacher's suppression then shows itself as legalistic demands which are mercilessly laid on the congregation. This legalism quite possibly betrays an unresolved problem within the preacher, who may simply be unconsciously dealing with that problem.

Persons in contact with themselves and liking themselves will have no trouble recognizing the emotional realm of the worship service and then speaking to the worshippers in this realm.

Giving of Oneself

Anyone seeking community with others is self-giving toward these people, and this is also true for a preacher conducting a worship service. Some people have a great deal of trouble with this act of giving of oneself. It's probably most difficult for people with a compulsive or schizoid attitude toward life. The danger is then too much reserve, and the preacher will not be fulfilling all the conditions necessary for a worship service. Intellectualism is a notorious form of reserve. One speaks to others only rationally; there is little risk because the trained pastor is intellectually fairly superior. In this way few mistakes are possible, since the pastor puts a stop to any self-giving. The people in the worship service, however, are disappointed because they are not fully spoken to or addressed.

Only very few preachers give much thought to the relationship between theology and faith. Far too many consider them to be the same thing, something I find scandalous. Theology is a rational undertaking; its justification, power, and limits all reside in the intellectual realm. Faith is an existential act encompassing the entire person. Theology belongs in the sermon preparation and examination of ideas, but has no business whatever in the pulpit. "Only a person who has already dealt with theology and become a total person again with theology's rich yield is able to come up with a sermon structure capable of speaking directly to people" [Otto Haendler, *Die Predigt*, p. 238]. Cooking pots don't belong on the festively decorated table. In the pulpit a believing—and again and again unbelieving—Christian proclaims Christ the Lord, from whom a miracle is expected. That is not a theological undertaking, but rather an existential communicative act. It is the parallel to the appearance of Jesus, who did not teach as the scribes, but as one who had authority (Mark 1:22). Proclamation often leads to one-sidedness and exaggerations not allowed in theology. Theology lacks the concrete reference to time and place, and should thus be more balanced and generalized than the individual sermon. Proclamation requires of the preacher not thinking, but first of all self-giving, which includes speaking extemporaneously. Without this kind of involvement there will be none of that feeling of consecration and intimacy so essential for a worship service characterized by encounter. Of course, the Lord himself can make up for the preacher's inadequacy, but it's unreasonable to expect too much, even from God.

Intense involvement is a part of faith. God's promise requires surrender and a trust in his capacity to make things right. Rigidness and legalism arise if there is no carefree joy. Richard Riess maintains that a legalistic sermon always points to a compulsive personality. That is not confirmed by the analyses presented in this book. One finds legalism in other personality types as well. The preacher who gives of self will be able to come across vividly and narrate well because he or she is not held back by the fear of being misunderstood. The joy found in surrender will eliminate precisely that pressure sometimes caused by the feeling of responsibility.

87

The Preacher

Standing in Belief and Unbelief

It will be hard to decide which is more difficult to cope with — belief or unbelief. The step into faith in Christ means an existential surrender and is paid for with the loss of many old and secure habits. Consciously admitting unbelief — something which for better or worse is invariably recurring in every person — means becoming insecure as regards that ultimate trust. Neither is very easy, but both are necessary for preachers. With no relationship to their own unbelief they do not take seriously the resistance of others to God's commandments and promises, the result being a harmless proclamation. Preachers with what Fritz Riemann calls hysterical tendencies are most likely to make this mistake. Riemann also mentions depressive characteristics which lead to this kind of harmless proclamation. The listeners are not able to integrate the temptation they experience into the worship service, and those for whom this is important are not spoken to. Preachers holding their ground in that tension between belief and unbelief will speak to the listeners' aggravation with God, their complaints and accusations and their apathy because the preachers are able to see those things in themselves as well. They do not identify with the biblical text; rather, they examine the reality of experience to see just what reactions God's word elicits in people. Only then can temptation be overcome. The preacher then represents the congregation as a questioning listener and is its credible counterpart when he or she finds peace in the midst of that questioning.

Both Leading and Letting Alone

Concerning good contact, it's of decisive importance for anyone in a leadership position to find the proper rhythm between leading and letting alone. Someone who only leads will become a despot. Someone who only lets alone will become uninvolved. Leadership is promising only in a balanced relationship between these two contrasting positions. It's probably not easy for anyone to find this balanced relationship. Compulsive preachers are inclined to lead too strongly. This is already of significance in the question of being genuine. A person who is *only* genuine quickly becomes an exhibitionist. Distance and respect for one's counterpart are both also a part of proper sincerity. A preacher who is too personal does not leave the listeners enough free space, but if there is not *enough* leadership, then the listener feels neither taken seriously nor spoken to.

The art of narration presupposes that the preacher not only presents, but also leaves some things open to conjecture. The preacher should portray accurately enough to be vivid, and vaguely enough for the listener to become activated inwardly. A person who leads too gladly will tend to narrate too thoroughly and become theatrical. A person who does not gladly lead will tend to narrate unclearly.

Performing the Task Decisively and Without Presumption

In a worship service we are dealing with existential matters in which there is no hierarchy among people. Over against God they are all equally small. Nonetheless, the preacher conducts the worship service and the listeners are led. This means the preacher will come into a tension in which all stand *primi inter pares* [first among equals]: the polarity between the normal worshipper and the official.

Today a balanced relationship between these two roles leads to an execution of authority from the perspective of the adult ego, not of the parent ego. A lack of involvement threatens whenever a preacher does not want to be that *primus*, and presumptuousness threatens whenever one no longer experiences oneself as being among *pares*. Even more so than for listeners, it's important for the preacher's feeling of identity to find the proper balance here. Depressive tendencies sometimes hold back proper decisiveness, hysterical ones the proper modesty.

The danger of presumptuousness arises when preachers identify too strongly with the biblical text, as if the gospel is no longer scandalous for them. An abuse of the pulpit also threatens wherever they overestimate their own function. Political sermons are especially vulnerable to this temptation. Finally, we need to mention hidden attacks on certain groups or persons sometimes found in sermons. They don't seem structured in an authoritarian way, but an aggressive undertone betrays the preacher's desire to push a personal opinion through from the pulpit. One might even maintain that hostility and aggression are the most obvious characteristics of pastoral emotion.

In these seven dispositions I have now summarized the basic posture a preacher must strive for in order to give the listeners in a traditional worship service what they expect. This summary is a model which is unlikely ever to be fully realized in a single individual, but the capacity to be totally realized is no prerequisite for a valid model. It serves as a point of orientation, and a preacher should know at which points of the model to exercise caution. It's likely that some kind of effort is required at one point or another just to stay in motion, which means that it would not really be favorable if the preacher were indeed able to realize the optimum posture.

If a preacher is able to make the worship service participants feel truly spoken to and engaged, it's a basic posture rendering that possible, not the technique used and not the content of the words spoken. The *relationship* between preacher and listener is the place where the decisive element in the worship service takes place. To be sure, factors other than merely the preacher do play a role, but the personality of this man or this woman is so determinative that if it comes across negatively, there is almost no hope that the listener will feel spoken to. A preacher's positive self-presentation enables that homiletical technique and the meaning of the spoken words to have a promising effect. . . .

The Competency of the Preacher

In the ideal preacher one can find a unity between personal self-presentation and liturgical and homiletical technique. Whenever this preacher says "I," it's not because of trying to fulfill the most current homiletical rules, but because it comes out spontaneously. By speaking vividly, this preacher is telling what has been seen with the inner eye and not just what has been read in a book. An agreement reigns between visible and audible behavior and inner attitude. The ability to conduct a worship service has a twofold structure. First, the preacher has a facility with language, with the liturgical progression, and with spatial relationships. On the other hand, he or she stands behind what is said and does so with the whole person, with enthusiasm, and with seriousness. The preacher's work is a simultaneous occurrence of physically perceivable forms of expressions and intuitively noticeable inner participation.

What I am calling the twofold structure is in reality a unity, though a separation is necessary for theory and reflection. Our culture lacks a system of thought which does justice to the human being's psychosomatic unity, which is not particularly tragic as long as we do not forget that the separation is actually unrealistic.

That twofold structure of competence requires that the preacher's training run along two tracks, encompassing technical and methodical aspects—more general factors—as well as the personal or individual element. Each preacher's training should be tailor-made because each is unique and because this uniqueness is essential for the sermon. As soon as the training becomes one-tracked, things don't look as promising. Homiletical books, including this one, don't really contribute to the actual structuring of worship services and sermons; at best they may make extremely small contributions. They serve rather the scholarly discussion *concerning* the sermon and are accordingly read by the more learned among the preachers. But one cannot necessarily say that these more learned pastors engage their congregations better or speak to them more fully. All the objective, universal aids concerning what one should say in the sermon do not help the preacher enough because his or her own uniqueness is not taken into consideration. Although I generally value very highly the work of Manfred Josuttis, it's for this reason that I think he underestimates the difficulties when he expects better sermons if preachers will just prepare themselves better on a critical and exegetical level and take reformation theology more seriously. The same applies to Gert Otto, who looks for the cause of ineffective sermons not in poor theology, but in the "linguistic disinterestedness and incapacity of many preachers."

This does not mean to say the homiletical essays and publications are meaningless. In the first place the theoretical discussion is not super-fluous, and in the second the technical, i.e., exegetical, systematic, and rhetorical suggestions are meaningful in and for themselves. It's just that they must be complemented by something tuned in to the personality of the preacher.

The other aspect, if isolated, is just as unpromising. One can work with the personality within a good group therapy or in individual dis-cussion with competent psychiatrists, or one can do it in the circle of one's own friends, relatives and colleagues. Who would dare doubt the value of this work in and for itself? It's just that it does not aid the train-ing of a preacher, or at most only makes a very small contribution.

All this training is effective only when the two work structures en-counter one another; homiletical and liturgical training emerges within that tension between theological and rhetorical guides on the one hand, and the concern for the personality on the other. Only the vocational problems touch the preacher's personality at a place where this work with that personality becomes fruitful for the sermon. It's like building a tunnel—one must dig and put up supports at the same time. First dig a bit, then erect some more supports; one activity without the other would be meaningless. The same is the case in a preacher's training. As soon as someone conducts a worship service and thus realizes all the theological and rhetorical suggestions and advice, one also shows one's personality. The listener reactions do not only show clearly which theological rules have or have not been kept; they also show which basic stance or posture of personality is coming across. There is then work to be done on two fronts.

For homiletical and liturgical training this means one must pay much closer attention to the preachers and theology students personally, since there is certainly no dearth of technical, theological, and rhetorical advice and the production of further editions will no doubt go on. But the personal interest in the men and women preparing for conducting worship services must be expanded with continual reference to the problems of content of exegetical and systematic theology. The analyses of worship services and sermons show how much influence the preacher's entire person has, and even someone who regrets that should for the sake of reality recognize that this person deserves attention.

In the experience of most pastors it becomes clear how strongly their worship services, and particularly their sermons, as far as their own feelings are concerned, are tied in with their own personality. Almost all preachers are basically very sensitive to criticism and—even more significant—embarrassed and defensive when listeners enthusiastically thank them for what the preacher has given to the listener through the sermon. In the last century Christian Palmer said, "the sermon is the full manifestation of the personality." Even people who theoretically argue against this or deny it also perceive this to be true. Many pastors gain their identity precisely as preachers. On the average, pastors spend more than thirteen hours a week in preparation for sermon and official duties. This expenditure of time also makes it clear why preaching is experienced as an expression of personality. It is only traditional homiletical theory, not the congregation or the preacher's own perception, which overlooks the enormous significance of the preacher's personality.

Two fundamental questions arise as soon as the training of preachers becomes serious about the personality. First: Who is to conduct this training? Second: Do all preachers want to have personality taken into consideration during training?

The development of personalities should never be put into the hands of only one person, because every person has blind spots, weaknesses, and prejudices. That is not so bad in and for itself, but it is reason enough to delegate such development to several people. Within the framework of clinical pastoral education, which is able to make a small contribution to homiletical and liturgical training, this problem is solved by having the preacher's accompaniment to be a circle of colleagues under the supervision of a leader.

III
THE EVENT

MARTIN LUTHER

Proclamation Versus Moralism

Preaching is an event in which one person engages others with the gospel of God. The word accomplishes its mission when it is proclaimed in the assembly of believers and truly heard by the congregation. In preaching, the message, its articulation, and its reception are fused into a single transaction. Perhaps no one better understood the eventfulness of the preached word than Martin Luther (1483–1546), who once said, "Faith is an acoustical affair." In a clear and irenic preface to a collection of his sermons, Luther reminds his readers that there is one gospel found in many forms in both the Old and New Testaments. Luther well understood the oral, sermonic basis of the New Testament and regularly used "gospel," "word," "kerygma," and "preaching" interchangeably. By these terms he meant an oral proclamation of the good news of God in Jesus Christ by which Christ himself is made available *pro nobis* (for us). "For the preaching of the gospel is nothing else than Christ coming to us, or we being brought to him." In the following selection Luther contrasts preaching that offers Christ as a gift with moralism, or the preaching of Christ-as-example. The saving benefit of Christ, he says, is not his example but his grace. The one who receives that grace, in turn, becomes a gift and example or, as Luther says elsewhere, a "little Christ" to the neighbor.

Martin Luther, *A Brief Instruction on What to Look for and Expect in the Gospels*, trans. E. Theodore Bachmann, *Luther's Works*, Vol. 35, ed. E. Theodore Bachmann and Helmut Lehmann (Philadelphia: Fortress Press, 1960 [1521]), pp. 117–123. Copyright © 1960, Fortress Press. Used by permission.

One should thus realize that there is only one gospel, but that it is described by many apostles. Every single epistle of Paul and of Peter, as well as the Acts of the Apostles by Luke, is a gospel, even though they do not record all the works and words of Christ, but one is shorter and includes less than another. There is not one of the four major Gospels anyway that includes all the words and works of Christ; nor is this necessary. Gospel is and should be nothing else than a discourse or story about Christ, just as happens among men when one writes a book about a king or a prince, telling what he did, said, and suffered in his day. Such a story can be told in various ways; one spins it out, and the other is brief. Thus the gospel is and should be nothing else than a chronicle, a story, a narrative about Christ, telling who he is, what he did, said, and suffered—a subject which one describes briefly, another more fully, one this way, another that way.

For at its briefest, the gospel is a discourse about Christ, that he is the Son of God and became man for us, that he died and was raised, that he has been established as a Lord over all things. This much St. Paul takes in hand and spins out in his epistles. He bypasses all the miracles and incidents [in Christ's ministry] which are set forth in the four Gospels, yet he includes the whole gospel adequately and abundantly. This may be seen clearly and well in his greeting to the Romans, where he says what the gospel is, and declares, "Paul, a servant of Jesus Christ, called to be an apostle, set apart for the gospel of God which he promised beforehand through his prophets in the holy scriptures, the gospel concerning his Son, who was descended from David according to the flesh and designated Son of God in power according to the Spirit of holiness by his resurrection from the dead, Jesus Christ our Lord," etc.

There you have it. The gospel is a story about Christ, God's and David's Son, who died and was raised and is established as Lord. This is the gospel in a nutshell. Just as there is no more than one Christ, so there is and may be no more than one gospel. Since Paul and Peter too teach nothing but Christ, in the way we have just described, so their epistles can be nothing but the gospel.

Yes even the teaching of the prophets, in those places where they speak of Christ, is nothing but the true, pure, and proper gospel—just as if Luke or Matthew had described it. For the prophets have proclaimed the gospel and spoken of Christ, as St. Paul here reports and as everyone indeed knows. Thus when Isaiah in chapter fifty-three says how Christ should die for us and bear our sins, he has written the pure gospel. And I assure you, if a person fails to grasp this understanding of the gospel, he will never be able to be illuminated in the Scripture nor will he receive the right foundation.

Be sure, moreover, that you do not make Christ into a Moses, as if Christ did nothing more than teach and provide examples as the other saints do, as if the gospel were simply a textbook of teachings or laws. Therefore you should grasp Christ, his words, works, and sufferings, in a twofold manner. First as an example that is presented to you, which you should follow and imitate. As St. Peter says in I Peter 4, "Christ suffered for us, thereby leaving us an example." Thus when you see how he prays, fasts, helps people, and shows them love, so also you should do, both for yourself and for your neighbor. However this is the smallest part of the gospel, on the basis of which it cannot yet even be called gospel. For on this level Christ is of no more help to you than some other saint. His life remains his own and does not as yet contribute anything to you. In short this mode [of understanding Christ as simply an example] does not make Christians but only hypocrites. You must grasp Christ at a much higher level. Even though this higher level has for a long time been the very best, the preaching of it has been something rare. The chief article and foundation of the gospel is that before you take Christ as an example, you accept and recognize him as a gift, as a present that God has given you and that is your own. This means that when you see or hear of Christ doing or suffering something, you do not doubt that Christ himself, with his deeds and suffering, belongs to you. On this you may depend as surely as if you had done it yourself; indeed as if you were Christ himself. See, this is what it means to have a proper grasp of the gospel, that is, of the overwhelming goodness of God, which neither prophet, nor apostle, nor angel was ever able fully to express, and which no heart could adequately fathom or marvel at. This is the great fire of the love of God for us, whereby the heart and conscience become happy, secure, and content. This is what preaching the Christian faith means. This is why such preaching is called gospel, which in German means a joyful, good and comforting "message"; and this is why the apostles are called the "twelve messengers." . . .

See, when you lay hold of Christ as a gift which is given you for your very own and have no doubt about it, you are a Christian. Faith redeems you from sin, death, and hell and enables you to overcome all things. O no one can speak enough about this. It is a pity that this kind of preaching has been silenced in the world, and yet boast is made daily of the gospel.

Now when you have Christ as the foundation and chief blessing of your salvation, then the other part follows: that you take him as your example, giving yourself in service to your neighbor just as you see that Christ has given himself for you. See, there faith and love move forward, God's commandment is fulfilled, and a person is happy and fearless to do and to suffer all things. Therefore make note of this, that Christ as a gift nourishes your faith and makes you a Christian. But Christ as an example exercises your works. These do not make you a Christian. Actually they come forth from you because you have already been made a Christian. As widely as a gift differs from an example, so widely does faith differ from works, for faith possesses nothing of its own, only the deeds and life of Christ. Works have something of your own in them, yet they should not belong to you but to your neighbor. . . .

When you open the book containing the Gospels and read or hear how Christ comes here or there, or how someone is brought to him, you should therein perceive the sermon or the gospel through which he is coming to you, or you are being brought to him. For the preaching of the gospel is nothing else than Christ coming to us, or we being brought to him. When you see how he works, however, and how he helps everyone to whom he comes or who is brought to him, then rest assured that faith is accomplishing this in you and that he is offering your soul exactly the same sort of help and favor through the gospel. If you pause here and let him do you good, that is, if you believe that he benefits and helps you, then you really have it. Then Christ is yours, presented to you as a gift.

After that it is necessary that you turn this into an example and deal with your neighbor in the very same way, be given also to him as a gift and an example. . . .

What a sin and shame it is that we Christians have come to be so neglectful of the gospel that we not only fail to understand it, but even have to be shown by other books and commentaries what to look for and what to expect in it. Now the Gospels and epistles of the apostles were written for this very purpose. They want themselves to be our guides, to direct us to the writings of the prophets and of Moses in the Old Testament so that we might there read and see for ourselves how Christ is wrapped in swaddling cloths and laid in the manger [Luke 2:7], that is, how he is comprehended [*Vorfassett*] in the writings of the prophets. It is there that people like us should read and study, drill ourselves, and see what Christ is, for what purpose he has been given, how he was promised, and how all Scripture tends toward him. For he himself says in John 5 [:46], "If you believed Moses, you would also believe me, for he wrote of me." Again [John 5:39], "Search and look up the Scriptures, for it is they that bear witness to me." . . .

Therefore also Luke, in his last chapter, says that Christ opened the minds of the apostles to understand the Scriptures. And Christ, in John 10, declares that he is the door by which one must enter, and whoever enters by him, to him the gatekeeper (the Holy Spirit) opens in order that he might find pasture and blessedness. Thus it is ultimately true that the gospel itself is our guide and instructor in the Scriptures, just as with this foreword I would gladly give instruction and point you to the gospel.

But what a fine lot of tender and pious children we are! In order that we might not have to study in the Scriptures and learn Christ there, we simply regard the entire Old Testament as of no account, as done for and no longer valid. Yet it alone bears the name of Holy Scripture. And the gospel should really not be something written, but a spoken word which brought forth the Scriptures, as Christ and the apostles have done. This is why Christ himself did not write anything but only spoke. He called his teaching not Scripture but gospel, meaning good news or a proclamation that is spread not by pen but by word of mouth.

JONATHAN EDWARDS

Preaching the Terrors

Jonathan Edwards (1703–1758) was Colonial America's foremost theologian, revivalist, philosopher, and psychologist. During the 1730's and 40's he found himself under constant obligation to defend the spiritual authenticity of the waves of revival sweeping New England and his own parish in Northampton, Massachusetts. Edwards buttressed his defense of old-fashioned Puritanism with the new psychology of John Locke. The groanings and distress of those "under awakenings," i.e., whose consciences have been aroused, are to be understood as empirical manifestations of God's intervention and not as self-generated impulses. Theologically, such terrors to "the affections" are necessary in order to prepare the listeners to embrace the gospel. The preacher is not unlike the surgeon who thrusts his lance to the "core of the wound" in order to effect complete healing. The writer's observations on suicide as a potential consequence of the preaching of the law give the modern reader some inkling of the deadly seriousness with which the Puritan mind approached the Sunday sermon. Edwards was not so much a preacher of hellfire as a remorseless clinician of the predicament of the human race, which in his most famous sermon he likened to a spider dangling above a flame.

Jonathan Edwards, *Thoughts on the Revival of Religion in New England, 1740 to which is prefixed A Narrative of the Surprising Work of God in Northampton, Mass., 1735* (New York: American Tract Society, n.d.), pp. 244–252.

Another thing that some ministers have been greatly blamed for, and I think unjustly, is *speaking terror to them that are already under great terrors,* instead of comforting them. Indeed if ministers in such a case go about to terrify persons with that which is not true, or to affright them by

100

representing their case worse than it is, or in any respect otherwise than it is, they are to be condemned; but if they terrify them only by still holding forth more light to them, and giving them to understand more of the truth of their case, they are altogether to be justified. When sinners' consciences are greatly awakened by the Spirit of God, it is by light imparted to the conscience, enabling them to see their case to be, in some measure, as it is; and if more light be let in, it will terrify them still more: but ministers are not therefore to be blamed because they endeavor to hold forth more light to the conscience, and do not rather alleviate the pain they are under, by intercepting and obstructing that light that shines already.

To say anything to those who have never believed in the Lord Jesus Christ, which represents their case any otherwise than exceeding terrible, is not to preach the word of God to them; for the word of God reveals nothing but truth, but this is to delude them. Why should we be afraid to let persons that are in an infinitely miserable condition know the truth, or to bring them into the light for fear it should terrify them? It is light that must convert them, if ever they are converted. The more we bring sinners into the light while they are miserable and the light is terrible to them, the more likely it is that by and by the light will be joyful to them. The ease, peace and comfort that natural men enjoy, have their foundation in darkness and blindness; therefore as that darkness vanishes and light comes in, their peace vanishes and they are terrified: but that is no good argument why we should endeavor to bring back their darkness that we may promote their present comfort.

The truth is, that as long as men reject Christ and do not savingly believe in him, however they may be awakened, and however strict and conscientious and laborious they may be in religion, they have the wrath of God abiding on them, they are his enemies and the children of the devil, (as the Scripture calls all that be not savingly converted, Matt. 13:38; 1 John, 3:10) and it is uncertain whether they shall ever obtain mercy. God is under no obligation to show them mercy, nor will he be if they fast and pray and cry never so much; and they are then especially provoking God under those terrors, in that they stand it out against Christ, and will not accept of an offered Savior, though they see so much need of him; and seeing this is the truth, they should be told so, that they may be sensible what their case indeed be.

To blame a minister for thus declaring the truth to those who are under awakenings, and not immediately administering comfort to them, is like blaming a surgeon because, when he has begun to thrust in his lance, whereby he has already put his patient to great pain, and he shrieks and cries out with anguish, he is so cruel that he will not stay his hand, but goes on to thrust it in further, until he comes to the core of the wound. Such a compassionate physician, who, as soon as his patient began to flinch, should withdraw his hand and go about immediately to apply a plaster to skin over the wound and leave the core untouched, would be one that would heal the hurt slightly, crying "peace, peace, when there is no peace."

Indeed something else besides terror is to be preached to them whose consciences are awakened. "The gospel" is to be preached to them: they are to be told that there is a Savior provided, that is excellent and glorious, who has shed his precious blood for sinners, and is every way sufficient to save them; that stands ready to receive them, if they will heartily embrace him; for this is also the truth, as well as that they now are in an infinitely dreadful condition: this is the word of God. Sinners, at the same time that they are told how miserable their case is, should be earnestly invited to come and accept of a Savior, and yield their hearts to him, with all the winning, encouraging arguments for them so to do that the gospel affords. But this is to induce them to *escape* from the misery of the condition that they are now in; but not to make them think their present condition less miserable than it is, or at all to abate their uneasiness and distress while they are in it. That would be the way to quiet them and fasten them in it, and not to excite them to fly from it.

Comfort, in one sense, is to be held forth to sinners under awakenings of conscience, that is, comfort is to be offered to them in Christ, on condition of their flying *from their present miserable state* to him: but comfort is not to be administered to them *in their present state*, as any thing that they have now any title to while out of Christ. No comfort is to be administered to them from any thing *in them*, any of their qualifications, prayers or other performances, past, present, or future; but ministers should, in such cases, strive to their utmost to take all such comforts from them, though it greatly increases their terror. A person that sees himself ready to sink into hell is ready to strive, some way or other, to lay God under some obligation to him; but he is to be beat off from every thing of that nature, though it greatly increases his terror to see himself wholly destitute, on every side, of any refuge, or any thing of his own to lay hold of; as a man that sees himself in danger of drowning is in terror and endeavors to catch hold on every twig within his reach, and he that pulls away those twigs from him increases his terror; yet if they are insufficient to save him, and by being in his way prevent his looking to that which will save him, to pull them away is necessary to save his life. . . .

I am not afraid to tell sinners that are most sensible of their misery, that their case is indeed as miserable as they think it to be, and a thousand times more so; for this is the truth. Some may be ready to say, that though it be the truth, yet the truth is not to be spoken at all times, and seems not to be seasonable then; but, it seems to me, such truth is never more seasonable than at such a time, when Christ is beginning to open the eyes of conscience. Ministers ought to act as co-workers with him: to take that opportunity, and to the utmost to improve that advantage and strike while the iron is hot; and when the light has begun to shine, then to remove all obstacles, and use all proper means that it may come in more fully, and the work be done thoroughly then. And experience abundantly shows that to take this course is not of a hurtful tendency, but very much the contrary. I have seen, in very many instances, the happy effects of it, and often times a very speedy happy issue, and never knew any ill consequence in case of real conviction, and when distress has been only from thence.

I know of but one case wherein the truth ought to be withheld from sinners in distress of conscience, and that is the case of *melancholy*: and it is not to be withheld from them then because the truth tends to do them hurt, but because if we speak the truth to them, sometimes they will be deceived and led into error by it through the strange disposition there is in them to take things wrong; so that that which as it is spoken is truth, as it is heard, and received, and applied by them is falsehood; and the truth will be thus misapplied by them, unless it be spoken with abundance of caution and prudence, and consideration of their disposition and circumstances.

But the most awful truths of God's word ought not to be withheld from a *public congregation* because it may happen that some such melancholic persons may be in it, any more than the Bible is to be withheld from the Christian world because it is manifest that there are a great many melancholic persons in Christendom that exceedingly abuse the awful things contained in the Scripture to their own wounding. Nor do I think that to be of weight which is made use of by some as a great and dreadful objection against the terrifying preaching that has of late been in New England, namely, that there have been some instances of melancholic persons that have so abused it that the issue has been the murder of themselves. The objection from hence is no stronger against awakening preaching, than it is against the Bible itself; hundreds, and probably thousands of instances might be produced of persons that have murdered themselves under religious melancholy; and these murders probably never would have been if it had not been for the Bible, or if the world had remained in a state of heathenish darkness. The Bible has not only been the occasion of these sad effects, but of thousands and I suppose millions of other cruel murders that have been committed, in the persecutions that have been raised, that never would have been if it had not been for the Bible: many whole countries have been, as it were, deluged with innocent blood, which would not have been if the gospel never had been preached in the world. It is not a good objection against any kind of preaching, that some men abuse it greatly to their hurt.

It has been acknowledged by all divines as a thing common in all ages and all Christian countries, that a very great part of those that sit under the gospel do so abuse it that it only proves an occasion of their far more aggravated damnation, and so of men's eternally murdering their souls, which is an effect infinitely more terrible than the murder of their bodies. It is as unjust to lay the blame of these self-murders to those ministers who have declared the awful truths of God's word in the most lively and affecting manner they were capable of, as it would be to lay the blame of hardening men's hearts and blinding their eyes, and their more dreadful eternal damnation, to the prophet Isaiah, or Jesus Christ, because this was the consequence of their preaching with respect to many of their hearers. Isaiah, 6:10; John, 9:39; Matt. 13:14. Though a very few have abused the late awakening preaching to so sad an effect as to be the cause of their own temporal death, yet it may be, to one such instance there have been hundreds, yea, thousands that have been saved by this means from eternal death.

What has more especially given offense to many, and raised a loud cry against some preachers, as though their conduct were intolerable, is their *frighting poor innocent children* with talk of hell-fire and eternal damnation. But if those that complain so loudly of this really believe, what is the general profession of the country, that all are by nature the children of wrath and heirs of hell; and that every one that has not been born again, whether he be young or old, is exposed every moment to eternal destruction under the wrath of Almighty God; I say, if they really believe this, then such a complaint and cry as this betrays a great deal of weakness and inconsideration. As innocent as children seem to us to be, yet if they are out of Christ they are not so in God's sight, but are in a most miserable condition as well as grown persons; they are naturally very senseless and stupid, being *born as the wild ass' colt*, and need much to awaken them. Why should we conceal the truth from them?

Will those children, that have been dealt so tenderly with as to hide from them their sin, and that have lived and died insensible of their misery until they come to feel it in hell, ever thank parents and others for their tenderness in not letting them know what they were in danger of? If parents' love towards their children was not blind, it would affect them much more to see their children every day exposed to eternal burnings, and yet senseless, than to see them suffer the distress of that awakening that is necessary in order to their escape from them, and that tends to their being eternally happy as the children of God. A child that has a dangerous wound may need the painful lance as well as grown persons; and that would be a foolish pity, in such a case, that should hold back the lance and throw away the life. I have seen the happy effects of dealing plainly and thoroughly with children in the concerns of their souls, without sparing them at all in many instances, and never knew any ill consequences of it in any one instance.

JOHN WESLEY

Mixing Law and Gospel

When accused of being a "legal preacher," John Wesley (1703–1791) responded with a brief justification of his homiletical method, including his use of the law in Christian assemblies. As for Luther and Edwards, so also for Wesley, the authentic practice of preaching depends upon the theological understanding of the relationship of law and gospel. Wesley advocates the "mixing" of law and gospel, but not their confusion in the order of salvation. Unlike Luther, who contraposed law and gospel as implacable foes, Wesley situates them on a continuum of God's good will toward humanity and is thus able to speak of the "comfort" of the law. Whereas Luther dwelt upon the convicting authority of the law over the sinner, Wesley expands the law's uses to the enlightenment and sustenance of the believing soul on its quest for holiness. In another place Wesley offers his famous "general method of preaching," which is "to invite, to convince, to offer Christ, to build up—and to do this in some measure in every sermon." The law plays a key role in the building up of one who has received Christ. Karl Barth's later formula—"the law is nothing else than the necessary form of the gospel, whose content is grace"—is congruent with Wesley's use of the law in service of the gospel.

John Wesley, "Letter on Preaching Christ," December 20, 1751, *The Works of the Rev. John Wesley, A.M.*, Vol. XI, Third ed. (London: John Mason, 1830), pp. 480–486.

The point you speak of in your letter of September 21, is of a very important nature. I have had many serious thoughts concerning it, particularly for some months last past; therefore, I was not willing to speak hastily or slightly of it, but rather delayed till I could consider it thoroughly.

I mean by *preaching the gospel*, preaching the love of God to sinners, preaching the life, death, resurrection, and intercession of Christ, with all the blessings which, in consequence thereof, are freely given to true believers.

By *preaching the law*, I mean, explaining and enforcing the commands of Christ, briefly comprised in the Sermon on the Mount.

Now, it is certain, preaching the gospel to penitent sinners "begets faith"; that it "sustains and increases spiritual life in true believers."

Nay, sometimes it "teaches and guides" them that believe; yea, and "convinces them that believe not."

So far all are agreed. But what is the stated means of feeding and comforting believers? What is the means, as of begetting spiritual life where it is not, so of sustaining and increasing it where it is?

Here they divide. Some think, preaching the law only; others, preaching the gospel only. I think, neither the one nor the other; but duly mixing both, in every place, if not in every sermon.

I think, the right method of preaching is this: At our first beginning to preach at any place, after a general declaration of the love of God to sinners, and his willingness that they should be saved, to preach the law, in the strongest, the closest, the most searching manner possible; only intermixing the gospel here and there, and showing it, as it were, afar off.

After more and more persons are convinced of sin, we may mix more and more of the gospel, in order to "beget faith," to raise into spiritual life those whom the law hath slain: but this is not to be done too hastily neither. Therefore, it is not expedient wholly to omit the law; not only because we may well suppose that many of our hearers are still unconvinced; but because otherwise there is danger, that many who are convinced will heal their own wounds slightly; therefore, it is only in private converse with a thoroughly convinced sinner, that we should preach nothing but the gospel.

If, indeed, we could suppose a whole congregation to be thus convinced, we should need to preach only the gospel: And the same we might do, if our whole congregation were supposed to be newly justified. But when these grow in grace, and in the knowledge of Christ, a wise builder would preach the law to them again; only taking particular care to place every part of it in a gospel light, as not only a command, but a privilege also, as a branch of the glorious liberty of the sons of God. He would take equal care to remind them, that this is not the cause, but the fruit, of their acceptance with God; that other cause, "other foundation can no man lay, than that which is laid, even Jesus Christ;" that we are still forgiven and accepted, only for the sake of what he hath done and suffered for us; and that all true obedience springs from love to him, grounded on his first loving us. He would labor, therefore, in preaching any part of the law, to keep the love of Christ continually before their eyes; that thence they might draw fresh life, vigor, and strength, to run the way of his commandments.

Thus would he preach the law even to those who were pressing on to the mark. But to those who were careless, or drawing back, he would preach it in another manner, nearly as he did before they were convinced of sin. To those, meanwhile, who were earnest, but feeble-minded, he would preach the gospel chiefly; yet variously intermixing more or less of the law, according to their various necessities.

By preaching the law in the manner above described, he would teach them how to walk in him whom they had received. Yea, and the same means (the main point wherein, it seems, your mistake lies) would both sustain and increase their spiritual life. For the commands are food, as well as the promises; food equally wholesome, equally substantial. These, also, duly applied, not only direct, but likewise nourish and strengthen, the soul.

Of this you appear not to have the least conception; therefore, I will endeavor to explain it. I ask, then, Do not all the children of God experience, that when God gives them to see deeper into his blessed law, whenever he gives a new degree of light, he gives, likewise, a new degree of strength? Now I see, he that loves me, bids me do this; and now I feel I can do it, through Christ strengthening me.

Thus light and strength are given by the same means, and frequently in the same moment; although sometimes there is a space between. For instance: I hear the command, "Let your communication be always in grace, meet to minister grace to the hearers." God gives me more light into this command. I see the exceeding height and depth of it. At the same time I see (by the same light from above) how far I have fallen short. I am ashamed; I am humbled before God. I earnestly desire to keep it better; I pray to him that hath loved me for more strength, and I have the petition I ask of him. Thus the law not only convicts the unbeliever, and enlightens the believing soul, but also conveys food to a believer; sustains and increases his spiritual life and strength.

And if it increases his spiritual life and strength, it cannot but increase his comfort also. For, doubtless, the more we are alive to God, the more we shall rejoice in him; the greater measure of his strength we receive, the greater will be our consolation also.

And all this, I conceive, is clearly declared in one single passage of Scripture: —

"The law of the Lord is perfect, converting the soul; the testimony of the Lord is sure, making wise the simple; the statutes of the Lord are right, rejoicing the heart; the commandment of the Lord is pure, enlightening the eyes. More to be desired are they than gold, yea, than much fine gold; sweeter also than honey, and the honey-comb." They are both food and medicine; they both refresh, strengthen, and nourish the soul.

Not that I would advise to preach the law without the gospel, any more than the gospel without the law. Undoubtedly, both should be preached in their turns; yea, both at once, or both in one: All the conditional promises are instances of this. They are law and gospel mixed together.

According to this model, I should advise every preacher continually to preach the law; the law grafted upon, tempered by, and animated with, the spirit of the gospel. I advise him to declare, explain, and enforce every command of God; but, meantime, to declare, in every sermon, (and the more explicitly the better,) that the first and great command to a Christian is, "Believe in the Lord Jesus Christ;" that Christ is all in all, our "wisdom, righteousness, sanctification, and redemption;" that all life, love, strength, are from him alone, and all freely given to us through faith. And it will ever be found, that the law thus preached both enlightens and strengthens the soul; that it both nourishes and teaches; that it is the guide, "food, medicine, and stay," of the believing soul. . . .

In this manner John Downes, John Bennet, John Haughton, and all the other Methodists, preached, till James Wheatly came among them, who never was clear, perhaps not sound, in the faith. According to his understanding was his preaching; an unconnected rhapsody of unmeaning words, like Sir John Suckling's—Verses, smooth and soft as cream, In which was neither depth nor stream.

Yet (to the utter reproach of the Methodist congregations) this man became a most popular preacher. He was admired more and more wherever he went, till he went over the second time into Ireland, and conversed more intimately than before with some of the Moravian preachers.

The consequence was that he leaned more and more both to their doctrine and manner of preaching. At first, several of our preachers complained of this; but, in the space of a few months, (so incredible is the force of soft words,) he, by slow and imperceptible degrees, brought almost all the preachers then in the kingdom to think and speak like himself.

These, returning to England, spread the contagion to some others of their brethren. But still the far greater part of the Methodist preachers thought and spoke as they had done from the beginning.

This is the plain fact. As to the fruit of this new manner of preaching, (entirely new to the Methodists,) speaking much of the promises, little of the commands; (even to unbelievers, and still less to believers;) you think it has done great good; I think it has done great harm.

I think it has done great harm to the preachers; not only to James Wheatly himself, but to those who have learned of him,—David Trathen, Thomas Webb, Robert Swindells, and John Maddern: I fear to others also; all of whom are but shadows of what they were; most of them have exalted themselves above measure, as if they only "preached Christ, preached the gospel." And as highly as they have exalted themselves, so deeply have they despised their brethren; calling them, "legal preachers, legal wretches;" and (by a cant name) "Doctors," or "Doctors of Divinity." They have not a little despised their ministers also, for "countenancing the Doctors," as they termed them. They have made their faults (real or supposed) common topics of conversation; hereby cherishing in themselves the very spirit of Ham; yea, of Korah, Dathan, and Abiram.

I think it has likewise done great harm to their hearers; diffusing among them their own prejudice against the other preachers; against their ministers, me in particular, (of which you have been an undeniable instance,) against the scriptural, Methodist manner of preaching Christ, so that they could no longer bear sound doctrine; they could no longer hear the plain old truth with profit or pleasure, nay, hardly with patience.

After hearing such preachers for a time, you yourself (need we further witnesses?) could find in my preaching no food for your soul; nothing to strengthen you in the way; no inward experience of a believer; it was all barren and dry; that is, you had no taste for mine or John Nelson's preaching; it neither refreshed nor nourished you.

Why, this is the very thing I assert: That the gospel preachers, so called, corrupt their hearers; they vitiate their taste, so that they cannot relish sound doctrine; and spoil their appetite, so that they cannot turn it into nourishment; they, as it were, feed them with sweetmeats, till the genuine wine of the kingdom seems quite insipid to them. They give them cordial upon cordial, which make them all life and spirit for the present; but, meantime, their appetite is destroyed, so that they can neither retain nor digest the pure milk of the word.

Hence it is, that (according to the constant observation I have made, in all parts both of England and Ireland) preachers of this kind (though quite the contrary appears at first) spread death, not life, among their hearers. As soon as that flow of spirits goes off, they are without life, without power, without any strength or vigor of soul; and it is extremely difficult to recover them, because they still cry out, "Cordials! Cordials!" of which they have had too much already, and have no taste for the food which is convenient for them. Nay, they have an utter aversion to it, and that confirmed by principle, having been taught to call it husks, if not poison: How much more to those bitters which are previously needful to restore their decayed appetite!

This was the very case when I went last into the north. For sometime before my coming, John Downes had scarce been able to preach at all; the three others in the round were such as styled themselves gospel preachers. When I came to review the societies, with great expectation of finding a vast increase, I found most of them lessened by one-third; one entirely broken up. That of Newcastle itself was less by a hundred members than when I visited it before. And of those that remained, the far greater number in every place were cold, weary, heartless, dead. Such were the blessed effects of this gospel preaching! of this new method of preaching Christ!

On the other hand, when, in my return, I took an account of the societies in Yorkshire, chiefly under the care of John Nelson, one of the old way, in whose preaching you could find no life, no food, I found them all alive, strong, and vigorous of soul, believing, loving, and praising God their Savior; and increased in number from eighteen or nineteen hundred, to upwards of three thousand. These had been continually fed with that wholesome food which you could neither relish nor digest. From the beginning they had been taught both the law and the gospel. "God loves you; therefore, love and obey him. Christ died for you; therefore, die to sin. Christ is risen; therefore, rise in the image of God. Christ liveth evermore; therefore live to God, till you live with him in glory."

So we preached; and so you believed. This is the scriptural way, the Methodist way, the true way. God grant we may never turn therefrom, to the right hand or to the left!

CHARLES GRANDISON FINNEY

Preaching for Conversion

Charles G. Finney (1792–1875) is known as the Father of Modern Revivalism. After his conversion, he left his law practice in Adams, N.Y. and,
without formal theological training, sparked a series of revivals that
helped prolong the Second Great Awakening in America. Finney
brought to his preaching the rhetoric of the courtroom and the drama of
the stage and was regularly accused of "demeaning the pulpit." In his
Memoirs he describes his preaching: "The Lord let me loose upon them
in a wonderful manner" and "the congregation began to fall from their
seats in every direction and cry for mercy. . . ." Under his leadership
revivalism became a pragmatic science of mass persuasion with the
Lectures being its textbook. One hundred years after Edwards waited
mightily on the Holy Spirit to work a revival, Finney wrote, "[Revival]
is not a miracle, or dependent on a miracle, in any sense. It is a purely
philosophical [i.e., technical] result of the right use of the constituted
means. . . ." In the following selection, Finney has lifted the story about
Niagara Falls from his sermon, "Sinners Bound to Change Their Own
Hearts." It was this sermon that exposed his Arminianism and his theological distance from the Calvinist orthodoxy of Jonathan Edwards.

Charles G. Finney, "How to Preach the Gospel" in *Lectures on Revivals of
Religion* (New York and London: Fleming H. Revell Company, 1868),
pp. 186–210.

The Scriptures ascribe the conversion of a sinner to four different
agencies—to *men*, to *God*, to the *truth*, and to the *sinner himself*. The
passages which ascribe it to the truth are the largest class. That men
should ever have overlooked this distinction, and should have regarded
conversion as a work performed exclusively by God, is surprising. . . .

In the conversion of a sinner, it is true that God gives the truth efficiency to turn the sinner to God. He is an active, voluntary, powerful agent in changing the mind. But he is not the only agent. The one that brings the truth to his notice is also an agent. We are apt to speak of ministers and other men as only *instruments* in converting sinners. This is not exactly correct. Man is something more than an instrument. Truth is the mere unconscious instrument. But man is more, he is a voluntary, responsible agent in the business. In my printed sermon, No. 1, which some of you may have seen, I have illustrated this idea by the case of an individual standing on the banks of Niagara.

"Suppose yourself to be standing on the banks of the Falls of Niagara. As you stand upon the verge of the precipice, you behold a man lost in deep reverie, approaching its verge unconscious of his danger. He approaches nearer and nearer, until he actually lifts his foot to take the final step that shall plunge him in destruction. At this moment you lift your warning voice above the roar of the foaming waters, and cry out, *Stop*. The voice pierces his ear, and breaks the charm that binds him; he turns instantly upon his heel; all pale and aghast he retires, quivering, from the verge of death. He reels and almost swoons with horror; turns and walks slowly to the public house; you follow him; the manifest agitation in his countenance calls numbers around him; and on *your* approach, he points to you, and says, That man saved my life. Here he ascribes the work to you; and certainly there is a sense in which you had saved him. But, on being further questioned, he says, *Stop*! how that *word* rings in my ears. Oh, that was to me the word of life! Here he ascribes it to the word that aroused him, and caused him to turn. But, on conversing still further, he says, Had I not turned at that instant, I should have been a dead man. Here he speaks of it, and truly, as his own act; but directly you hear him say, Oh the mercy of God! if God had not interposed, I should have been lost. Now the only defect in this illustration is this: In the case supposed, the only interference on the part of God, was a *providential* one; and the only sense in which the saving of the man's life is ascribed to him, is in a providential sense. But in the conversion of a sinner, there is something more than the providence of God employed; for here not only does the providence of God so order it, that the preacher cries, *Stop*, but the Spirit of God urges the truth home upon him with such tremendous power as to induce him to turn."

Not only does the preacher cry, *Stop*, but through the living voice of the preacher the Spirit cries, *Stop*. The preacher cries, "Turn ye, why will ye die." The Spirit pours the expostulation home with such power, that the sinner turns. Now in speaking of this change, it is perfectly proper to say, that the Spirit turned him, just as you would say of a man, who had persuaded another to change his mind on the subject of politics, that he had converted him, and brought him over. It is also proper to say that the truth converted him; as in a case when the political sentiments of a man were changed by a certain argument, we should say that argument brought him over. So also with perfect propriety may we ascribe the change to the living preacher, or to him who had presented the motives; just as we should say of a lawyer who had prevailed in his argument with a jury; he has got his case, he has converted the jury. It is also with the same propriety ascribed to the individual himself whose heart is changed; we should say he had changed his mind, he has come over, he has repented. Now it is strictly true, and true in the most absolute and highest sense; the act is his own act, the turning is his own turning, while God by the truth has induced him to turn; still it is strictly true that he has turned and has done it himself. Thus you see the sense in which it is the work of God, and also the sense in which it is the sinner's own work. The Spirit of God, by the truth, influences the sinner to change, and in this sense is the efficient cause of the change. But the sinner actually changes, and is therefore himself, in the most proper sense, the author of the change. There are some who, on reading their Bibles, fasten their eyes upon those passages that ascribe the work to the Spirit of God, and seem to overlook those that ascribe it to man, and speak of it as the sinner's own act. When they have quoted Scripture to prove it is the work of God, they seem to think they have proved that it is that in which man is passive, and that it can in no sense be the work of man. Some months since a tract was written, the title of which was, "Regeneration, the effect of Divine Power." The writer goes on to prove that the work is wrought by the Spirit of God, and there stops. Now it had been just as true, just as philosophical, and just as scriptural, if he had said that conversion was the work of man. It was easy to prove that it was the work of God, in the sense in which I have explained it. The writer, therefore, tells the truth, so far as he goes; but he has told only half the truth. For while there is a sense in which it is the work of God, as he has shown, there is also a sense in which it is the work of man, as we have just seen. The very title to this tract is a stumbling block. It tells the truth, but it does not tell the whole truth. And a tract might be written upon this proposition, that *"Conversion or regeneration is the work of man"*; which would be just as true, just as scriptural, and just as philosophical, as the one to which I have alluded. Thus the writer, in his zeal to recognize and honor God as concerned in this work, by leaving out the fact that a change of heart is the sinner's *own act*, has left the

114

sinner strongly intrenched, with his weapons in his rebellious hands, stoutly resisting the claims of his Maker, and waiting passively for God to make him a new heart. Thus you see the consistency between the requirement of the text, and the declared fact that God is the author of the new heart. God commands you to make you a new heart, expects you to do it, and if it ever is done, you must do it. . . .

Preaching should be direct. The gospel should be preached *to* men, and not *about* them. The minister must address his hearers. He must preach *to* them *about themselves*, and not leave the impression that he is preaching to them about others. He will never do them any good, farther than he succeeds in convincing each individual that he means him. Many preachers seem very much afraid of making the impression that they mean anybody in particular. They are preaching against certain *sins*, not that have anything to do with the *sinner*. It is the *sin*, and not the *sinner*, that they are rebuking; and they would by no means speak as if they supposed any of *their hearers* were guilty of these abominable practices. Now this is anything but preaching the gospel. Thus did not the prophets, nor Christ, nor the apostles. Nor do those ministers do this, who are successful in winning souls to Christ. . . .

Another important thing to observe is, that a minister should dwell most on those particular points which are most needed. I will explain what I mean.

Sometimes he may find a people who have been led to place great reliance on their own resolutions. They think they can consult their own convenience, and by and by they will repent, when they get ready, without any concern about the Spirit of God. Let him take up these notions, and show that they are entirely contrary to the Scriptures. Let him show that if the Spirit of God is grieved away, *however able* he may be, it is *certain he never will* repent, and that by and by, when it shall be convenient for him to do it, he will have no inclination. The minister who finds these errors prevailing, should expose them. He should hunt them out, and understand just how they are held, and then preach the class of truths which will show the fallacy, the folly, and the danger of these notions.

So on the other hand. He may find a people who have got such views of election and sovereignty, as to think they have nothing to do but to wait for the moving of the waters. Let him go right over against them, and crowd upon them their ability to obey God, and show their obligation and duty, and press them with that until he brings them to submit and be saved. They have got behind a perverted view of these doctrines, and there is no way to drive them out of the hiding-place but to set them

115

right *on these points*. Wherever a sinner is intrenched, unless you pour light upon him *there*, you will never move him. It is of no use to press him with those truths which he admits, however plainly they may in fact contradict his wrong notions. *He supposes* them to be perfectly consistent, and does not see the inconsistency, and therefore it will not move him, or bring him to repentance.

I have been informed of a minister in New England, who was settled in a congregation which had long enjoyed little else than Arminian preaching, and the congregation themselves were chiefly Arminians. Well, this minister, in his preaching, strongly insisted on the opposite points, the doctrine of election, Divine sovereignty, predestination, etc. The consequence was, as might have been expected where this was done with ability, there was a powerful revival. Some time afterwards this same minister was called to labor in another field, in this State, where the people were all on the other side, and strongly tinctured with Antinomianism. They had got such perverted views of election, and Divine sovereignty, that they were continually saying they had no power to do anything, but must wait God's time. Now, what does this minister do but immediately go to preaching the doctrine of election. And when he was asked, how he could think of preaching the doctrine of election so much to that people, when it was the very thing that lulled them to a deeper slumber, he replied "Why, that's the very class of truths by which I had such a great revival in _____;" not considering the difference in the views of the people. And if I am correctly informed, there he is to this day, preaching away at the doctrine of election, and wondering that it does not produce as powerful a revival as it did in the other place. Probably those sinners never will be converted. You must take things as they are, find out where sinners lie, and pour in truth upon them *there*, and start them out from their refuges of lies. It is of vast importance that a minister should find out where the congregation are, and preach accordingly. . . .

When I entered the ministry, there had been so much said about the doctrine of election and sovereignty, that I found it was the universal hiding place, both of sinners and of the church, that they could not do anything, or could not obey the gospel. And wherever I went, I found it indispensable to demolish these refuges of lies. And a revival would in no way be produced or carried on, but by dwelling on that class of truths, which holds up man's ability, and obligation, and responsibility. This was the only class of truths that would bring sinners to submission.

It was not so in the days when President Edwards and Whitefield

116

labored. Then the churches in New England had enjoyed little else than Arminian preaching, and were all resting in themselves and their own strength. These bold and devoted servants of God came out and declared those particular doctrines of grace, divine sovereignty, and election, and they were greatly blessed. They did not dwell on these doctrines exclusively, but they preached them very fully. The consequence was, that because *in those circumstances* revivals followed from such preaching, the ministers who followed, *continued to preach these doctrines almost exclusively*. And they dwelt on them so long, that the church and the world got intrenched behind them, waiting for God to come and do what he required *them* to do, and so revivals ceased for many years.

Now, and for years past, ministers have been engaged in hunting them out from these refuges. And here it is all important for the ministers of this day to bear in mind, that if they dwell exclusively on ability and obligation, they will get their hearers back on the old Arminian ground, and then they will cease to promote revivals. Here a body of ministers who have preached a great deal of truth, and have had great revivals, under God. Now let it be known and remarked, that the reason is, they have hunted sinners out from their hiding places. But if they continue to dwell on the same class of truths till sinners hide themselves behind their preaching, another class of truths must be preached. And then if they do not change their mode, another pall will hang over the church, until another class of ministers shall arise and hunt sinners out of those new retreats. . . .

It is of great importance that the sinner should be made to feel his guilt, and not left to the impression that he is unfortunate. I think this is a very prevailing fault, particularly with printed books on the subject. They are calculated to make the sinner think more of his sorrows than of his sins, and feel that his state is rather unfortunate than criminal. Perhaps most of you have seen a very lovely little book recently published, entitled "Todd's Lectures to Children." It is very fine, exquisitely fine, and happy in some of its illustrations of truths. But it has one very serious fault. Many of its illustrations, I may say most of them, are not calculated to make a correct impression respecting the guilt of sinners, or to make them feel how much they have been to blame. This is very unfortunate. If the writer had guarded his illustrations on this point, so as to make them impress sinners with a sense of their guilt, I do not see how a child could read through that book and not be converted. . . .

Sinners ought to be made to feel that they have something to do, and that is to repent; that it is something which no other being can do for them, neither God nor man, and something which they can do, and do it now. Religion is something to do, not something to wait for. And they must do now, or they are in danger of eternal death.

Ministers should never rest satisfied, until they have annihilated every excuse of sinners. The plea of "inability" is the worst of all excuses. It slanders God so, charging him with infinite tyranny, in commanding men to do that which they have no power to do. Make the sinner see and feel that this is the very nature of his excuse. Make the sinner see that all pleas in excuse for not submitting to God, are an act of rebellion against him. Tear away the last LIE which he grasps in his hand, and make him feel that he is absolutely condemned before God. . . .

I wish now, secondly, to make a few remarks on the manner of preaching.

It should be conversational. Preaching, to be understood, should be colloquial in its style. A minister must preach just as he would talk, if he wishes to be fully understood. Nothing is more calculated to make a sinner feel that religion is some mysterious thing that he cannot understand, than this mouthing, formal, lofty style of speaking, so generally employed in the pulpit. The minister ought to do as the lawyer does when he wants to make a jury understand him perfectly. He uses a style perfectly colloquial. This lofty, swelling style will do no good. The gospel will never produce any great effects, until ministers talk to their hearers, in the pulpit, as they talk in private conversation. . . .

Preaching should be parabolical. That is, illustrations should be constantly used, drawn from incidents, real or supposed. Jesus Christ constantly illustrated his instructions in this way. He would either advance a principle and then illustrate it by a parable, that is, a short story of some event real or imaginary, or else he would bring out the principle in the parable. There are millions of facts that can be used to advantage, and yet very few ministers dare to use them, for fear somebody will reproach them. "Oh," says somebody, "he tells stories." Tells stories! Why, that is the way Jesus Christ preached. And it is the only way to preach. Facts, real or supposed, should be used to show the truth. Truths not illustrated are generally just as well calculated to convert sinners as a mathematical demonstration. Is it always to be so? Shall it always be a matter of reproach that ministers follow the example of Jesus Christ in illustrating truths by facts? Let them do it, and let fools reproach them as storytelling ministers. They have Jesus Christ and common sense on their side. . . .

Preaching should be repetitious. If a minister wishes to preach with effect, he must not be afraid of repeating whatever he sees is not perfectly understood by his hearers. Here is the evil of using notes. The preacher preaches right along just as he has it written down, and cannot observe whether he is understood or not. If he interrupts his reading, and attempts to catch the countenances of his audience, and to explain where he sees they do not understand, he gets lost and confused, and gives it up. If a minister has his eyes on the people he is preaching to, he can commonly tell by their looks whether they understand him. And if he sees they do not understand any particular point, let him stop and illustrate it. If they do not understand one illustration, let him give another, and make it all clear to their minds, before he goes on. But those who write their sermons go right on, in a regular consecutive train, just as in an essay or a book, and do not repeat their thoughts till the audience fully comprehend them.

I was conversing with one of the first advocates in this country. He said the difficulty which preachers find in making themselves understood is that they do not repeat enough. Says he, "In addressing a jury, I always expect that whatever I wish to impress upon their minds, I shall have to repeat at least twice, and often I repeat it three or four times, and even as many times as there are jurymen before me. Otherwise, I do not carry their minds along with me, so that they can feel the force of what comes afterwards." If a jury under oath, called to decide on the common affairs of this world, cannot apprehend an argument unless there is so much repetition, how is it to be expected that men will understand the preaching of the gospel without it. . . .

A minister should aim to convert his congregation. But you will ask, Does not all preaching aim at this? No. A minister always has some aim in preaching, but most sermons were never aimed at converting sinners. And if sinners were converted under them, the preacher himself would be amazed. I once heard a fact on this point. There were two young ministers who had entered the ministry at the same time. One of them had great success in converting sinners, the other none. The latter inquired of the other, one day, what was the reason of this difference. "Why," replied the other, "the reason is, that I aim at a different end from you, in preaching. My object is to convert sinners, but you aim at no such thing. And then you go and lay it to sovereignty in God, that you do not produce the same effect, when you never aim at it. Here, take one of my sermons, and preach it to your people, and see what the effect will be." The man did so, and preached the sermon, and it did produce effect. He was frightened when sinners began to weep; and when one came to him after the meeting to ask what he should do, the minister apologized to him, and said, "I did not aim to wound you, I'm sorry if I have hurt your feelings." Oh, horrible! . . .

It is impossible for a man who writes his sermons to arrange his matter, and turn and choose his thoughts, so as to produce the same effect as when he addresses the people directly, and makes them feel that he means them. Writing sermons had its origin in times of political difficulty. The practice was unknown in the apostles' days. No doubt written sermons have done a great deal of good, but they can never give to the gospel its great power. Perhaps many ministers have been so long trained in the use of notes, that they had better not throw them away. Perhaps they would make bad work without them. The difficulty would not be for the want of mind, but from wrong training. The bad habit is begun with the school boy, who is called to "speak his piece." Instead of being set to express his own thoughts and feelings in his own language, and with his own natural manner, such as nature herself prompts, he is made to commit another person's writing to memory, and then mouths it out in a stiff and formal way. And so when he goes to college, and to the seminary, instead of being trained to *extempore* speaking, he is set to writing his piece, and commit it to memory. I would pursue the opposite course from the beginning. I would give him a subject, and let him first think, and then speak his thoughts. Perhaps he will make mistakes. Very well, that is to be expected—in a beginner. But he will learn. Suppose he is not eloquent, at first. Very well, he can improve. And he is in the very way to improve. This kind of training alone will ever raise up a class of ministers who can convert the world. . . .

All ministers should be revival ministers, and all preaching should be revival preaching; that is, it should be calculated to promote holiness. People say, "It is very well to have some men in the church who are revival preachers and who can go about and promote revivals; but then you must have others to *indoctrinate* the church." Strange! Do they not know that a revival indoctrinates the church faster than anything else? And a minister will never produce a revival, if he does not indoctrinate his hearers. The preaching I have described is full of doctrine, but it is doctrine to be practiced. And that is revival preaching.

There are two objections sometimes brought against the kind of preaching which I have recommended.

That it is letting down the dignity of the pulpit to preach in this collo-quial, lawyer-like style. They are shocked at it. But it is only on account of its novelty, and not for any impropriety there is in the thing itself. I heard a remark made by a leading layman in the center of this state, in regard to the preaching of a certain minister. He said it was the first preaching he ever heard, that he understood, and the first minister he ever heard that spoke as if he believed his own doctrine, or meant what he said. And when he first heard him preach as if he was saying something that he meant, he thought he was crazy. But eventually, he was made to see that it was all true, and he submitted to the truth, as the power of God for the salvation of his soul.

What is the dignity of the pulpit? To see a minister go into the pulpit to sustain its dignity! Alas, alas! During my foreign tour, I heard an English missionary preach exactly in that way. I believe he was a good man, and out of the pulpit he would talk like a man that meant what he said. But no sooner was he in the pulpit, than he appeared like a perfect automaton—swelling, mouthing, and singing, enough to put all the people to sleep. And the difficulty seemed to be that he wanted to maintain the dignity of the pulpit.

It is objected that this preaching is theatrical. The bishop of London once asked Garrick, the celebrated play-actor, why it was that actors in representing a mere fiction, should move an assembly, even to tears, while ministers, in representing the most solemn realities, could scarcely obtain a hearing. The philosophical Garrick well replied, "It is because we represent fiction as reality, and you represent reality as a fiction." This is telling the whole story. Now what is the design of the actor in a theatrical representation? It is so to throw himself into the spirit and meaning of the writer, as to adopt his sentiments, make them his own, feel them, embody them, throw them out upon the audience as living reality. And now, what is the objection to all this in preaching? The actor suits the action to the word, and the word to the action. His looks, his hands, his attitudes, and everything are designed to express the full meaning of the writer. Now this should be the aim of the preacher. And if by "theatrical" be meant the strongest possible representation of the sentiments expressed, then the more theatrical a sermon is, the better. And if ministers are too stiff, and the people too fastidious, to learn even from an actor, or from the stage, the best method of swaying mind, of enforcing sentiment, and diffusing the warmth of burning thought over a congregation, then they must go on with their prosing, and reading, and sanctimonious starch. But let them remember, that while they are thus turning away and decrying the art of the actor, and attempting to support "the dignity of the pulpit," the theaters can be thronged every night. The common-sense people *will be* entertained with that manner of speaking, and sinners will go down to hell.

H. H. FARMER

The I-Thou Encounter

Whether Luther, Wesley, Finney, or Brooks, most great preachers have sensed the eventfulness or immediacy of preaching as a form of encounter. In the Warrack Lectures for 1940, systematic theologian and Presbyterian minister Herbert Farmer (1892–1981) gave lucid homiletical expression to the widely held view of divine truth as God's encounter with humanity. Deeply influenced by Martin Buber and the Christian personalism of his teacher at Cambridge, John Oman, Farmer asserts that God, whom he occasionally calls "the infinite Person," "never enters into *personal* relationship with a man apart from other human persons." When this personal encounter takes the form of preaching, three elements are invariably present: the exercise of will, an articulated claim, and shared meaning. Farmer proposed his theology of the Incarnation and the Christian person in his earlier works, *The World and God, Towards Belief in God,* and subsequently in his Beecher Lectures at Yale, *God and Men* (1946). In 1949 he succeeded C. H. Dodd as Norris-Hulse Professor of Divinity at Cambridge.

H. H. Farmer, *The Servant of the Word* (Philadelphia: Fortress Press, 1964 [1942]), pp. 21–34. Used by permission.

I propose now to develop further the thought that preaching is only to be rightly understood and conducted when it is seen in the context of a Christian understanding of persons and their relationships with one another. It is first, last, and all the time a function of the personal. . . .

I begin with the proposition that God's purpose is such, and he has so made humanity in accordance with that purpose, that he never enters into *personal* relationship with a man apart from other human persons. When he confronts me in the specifically personal I-thou relationship, to use the phraseology referred to in the last lecture, it is always closely bound up with the personal I-thou relationship I have with my fellows. I am related to the personal God in the neighbor, to the neighbor as personal in God. . . .

We might express it by saying that when God created man he *eo facto* created an order or structure of persons in relationship with himself and with one another. This is the ultimate secret of finite personal nature, of specifically human nature. Only as a man is part of, held in, that structure is he distinctively man. If, *per impossibile*, you could lift a man out of it, he would cease to exist as man. It is not that God creates a man and then pops him into the world of persons as a housewife makes a dumpling and pops it into the saucepan, both dumpling and saucepan being capable of existing apart from one another. To come into existence as a man is to be incorporated in this world of the personal, to be in relation to persons—the divine person and human persons—and existence as a man is not possible on any other terms.

It would be easy to interpret what has so far been said to mean that a man stands at one and the same time in *two* relationships which can in principle be separated from one another. On the one hand there is his relationship to the divine person, God, and on the other hand there is his relationship to finite persons, his fellows. Christian thought has not infrequently expressed itself in terms which give countenance to such an idea. The great commandment itself lends color to it—thou shalt love the Lord thy God *and* thy neighbor as thyself. We speak of duties to God *and* of duties to the neighbor. There is Augustine's oft-quoted saying, "Thou hast made us for thyself and our hearts are restless until thy find rest in thee." There is the whole mystical tradition, of which Augustine's words are probably in some measure an echo, that man finds God by withdrawing from the world, including the world of persons. Yet the true Christian understanding is that these two relationships cannot ever be separated from one another. Indeed it would perhaps be better to say that there are not two relationships but only one relationship which is twofold; or, better still, there is one personal continuum with two poles, the infinite personal on the one hand, the finite personal on the other. The individual is related all the time to his neighbor in God and to God in his neighbor, even when he is not aware of it, even when he denies it, and in that relationship his distinctive quality as a human person resides. So that Augustine's saying should be rewritten, "Thou hast made us for thyself and for one another and our hearts are restless until they find rest in thee in one another and in one another in thee." . . .

If now I am asked to say more precisely what is meant by a personal relationship, by an I-thou relationship, to use Buber's terminology, I am in a difficulty just because we are here dealing with an ultimate in the world of being. An ultimate cannot be expressed in terms of anything else; if it could it would not be an ultimate. But seeking to describe what must primarily be identified by each one in the immediacy of experience, it may be said that the heart of the matter is in the relationship of self-conscious, self-directing wills to one another in a situation which is important and significant for both. If you ask me what I mean by a "self-conscious, self-directing will," I cannot say. I can only refer to your own immediate self-awareness. But it is possible to say something about the relationship between such wills which constitutes the specifically "I-thou" world. It is a relationship wherein the activity of one self-conscious, self-directing will is conditioned by that of another in such wise that each remains free. . . .

How then can your will condition mine so that my will remains free? It can do so only by confronting me as an inescapable claim. Both words are important. I am free to reject it—that is why it is claim; if I were not so free, it would be compulsion—but I am not free to escape it, for my rejection of it at once enters into the structure of history, your history, and in varying degree univeral history. If the claim be a right claim, that is, one rooted in the essential nature of the personal world as this has been created by God, the rejection of it can have the most disastrous consequences. Herein, in part, lies the problem of atonement. The problem of atonement is the problem of setting right in a world of inaccessible, "non-manipulatable" wills the rejection of claims which is already part of history and at work in history. It is the restoration of the fabric of the I-thou world when it has been torn.

The idea of a claim, in the sense in which we are here using the term, is, I think, another indefinable. Its impact has to be felt to be known, and it is not analyzable into other notions. It is the basis of the ethical concept of "ought," which is also for that reason unanalyzable, as Sidgwick insists. The ethical is the personal world, the world of history. One thing, however, we can say, and that is that a claim only conditions my will by being understood. I am free to accept or reject it, but I can only accept or reject it by first understanding it. I have not dealt with your claim at all if I have not understood it, if I have not grasped in some measure your world, your point of view, your meaning, and made it my own. This presupposes that though we see things from a different point of view—it is the differences of points of view that make claims possible—yet we are both in the same world and can speak and act in terms of it. This is but to say that reason and self-conscious, self-directing personality go together. By the same argument reasoning *together*, the possibility of, nay the necessity for, a community of insight and understanding, for shared meaning, is an essential part of the personal, the I-thou world.

In the light of these remarks it is possible to see how and why *speech* is so absolutely central and indispensable in the world of personal relationships. In view of what we have to say later about preaching, it is necessary to dwell on this for a little.

What a strange and potent thing speech is! And how the familiarity of it hides from us its strangeness and potency! We sometimes hear debated whether we would rather lose sight or hearing, if we were shut up to such a frightful option. The immediate reaction as a rule is to choose to retain the faculty of sight; the thought of a permanently dark and colorless world affrights us. But I am not sure but what the wiser part would be to choose to retain hearing, for whereas the loss of sight would cut you off from all the loveliness and interest of the world of objects, the loss of hearing would cut you off from the world of persons, and there is no question which is the graver loss, which is the heavier blow at the innermost citadel of our being. The spoken word is right within the core of the I-thou relationship, and the written or printed word is always a poor substitute for it. Mankind seems to have instinctively known this from earliest times. Primitive peoples have a sense of the power of the spoken word which is exaggerated to the point of superstition, but which like many primitive ideas is founded on reality. We used to say in our childhood,

> Sticks and stones may break my bones
> But words will never hurt me!

Nothing could be more false. Words can and do hurt much more penetratingly and destructively than sticks and stones. Perhaps it was because deep down we knew that words can hurt most frightfully that we were so anxious to protest that they did not. The New Testament has a better understanding on the matter: "The tongue is a little member and boasteth great things. Behold how great a matter a little fire kindleth. And the tongue is a fire, a world of iniquity. So is the tongue among our members that it defileth the whole body, and setteth on fire the course of nature, and it is set on fire of hell." The absolute centrality of speech in the world of personal relationships is brought home to you when you are in a foreign country and know nothing of the language and nobody there knows anything of yours. Here you have in effect the frightful situation of both persons being deaf. The sense of utter frustration and loneliness, of alienation and unreality, has to be experienced to be known.

The reason why the spoken word is thus at the very heart of the world of persons in relationship of the I-thou relationship, is that it is supremely that medium of communication wherein the three elements mentioned above, will and claim and shared meaning, are, or can be, at a maximum together in a single, fused unity.

Thus, first, in the spoken word my will objectifies itself for you with such force and immediacy that it and its objectification are one and indissoluble, almost indistinguishable. The word is my will, and my will is the word. This is clumsily and therefore inaccurately expressed, but a single consideration will show what I mean. Precisely at the moment when my will is withdrawn the word ceases as absolutely as annihilation. And it comes into being again just where and when my will ordains it. This is perhaps the nearest we get to the divine activity of creation out of nothing, and of preservation—pure creative and sustaining will. It is this immediate dependence of the spoken word on the will that gives it its superiority over the printed word as a medium of personal relationship. What seems, what indeed from one point of view is, the advantage of the printed word, is that it can be listened to again and again whenever *I* choose—I have only to take the book down from my shelves and read it, and it can stay on my shelves a score or more years and not perish. This is precisely its disadvantage from the point of view of personal relationship; for the essence of the personal relationship is in the activity of *your* will bringing the word into being and giving it the only being it possesses, not in the activity of my will. . . .

Second, and to be taken inseparably with what has just been said, in the spoken word you have in a maximal form the element of claim. When I speak to you my will claims yours. Speech is full of claim.

To begin with, I claim your attention. I should not speak if I did not want you to listen. By speech I ask you to listen. If you will not listen, I waste my breath, as the saying is. Sometimes when I have had occasion to rebuke one of my children, he stuffs his fingers into his ears. The result is a feeling of frustration and impotence in me which is not merely injured parental dignity and *amour propre*. It is as though the child had temporarily vanished, as though a thick wall, infinitely thicker than his puny little fingers, had come down between us. It is not that he has gone deaf, though that would be bad enough. He has *willed* to go deaf. He has repudiated my claim. That stopping of the ears symbolizes, as nothing else can, the awful fact of freedom which lies at the heart of the personal world. And dare we speculate that God gave us no lids for our ears as he did for our eyes, precisely that we might always be open to one another and to the word?

Then, further, by my speech I claim your answer. My word, containing my will, is addressed to your will, and asks your answer containing yours, even if it be only the answer of a nod or a shake of the head. I want response. It is a knock on the door—a call for attention which is also a call for an answer.

Then, again, there is implicit in my speech the claim of truth. Thus there is within it, as there is in all personal dealings, the germ at least of the ethical. Even when I speak to deceive you I rest upon the claim of truth to your allegiance; my lies must have verisimilitude. If neither of us acknowledges the claim of truth, personal intercourse is in so far forth as impossible as if we were both stone deaf. Yet the fact that lies and deception are possible at all shows that we are in the region of claim and not of mechanical necessitation.

This, however, has already involved us in the third point, not to be separated from the other two, that the distinctive *raison d'être* of speech is to convey reasoned meaning, or meaning to reason and understanding. It is the supreme and distinctive vehicle of ideas, propositions, judgments, of truth in a form in which it can be, so to say, held at arm's length and considered. It may include other things in its intention as well, of course. Speech may be designed to excite feeling, or to create an aesthetic impression, or even, as in an advertising slogan, to affect, by repetition and sheer suggestive force, a man's actions almost without his knowing it, but in none of these things does its unique quality appear. Music can evoke feeling, a landscape or a flower can make an aesthetic impression, a forceful gesture or example can act as a powerful suggestion, without speech entering in at all. Speech is nonessential to these things. The unique function of speech is that of conveying in the most explicit way possible the judgment of one self-conscious awareness to another in such wise that both are brought directly and inescapably under the claim of truth. If it does, or seeks to do, any of these other things that we have mentioned—to stimulate feeling, to create aesthetic impression, to influence the will by force of suggestion—*without* doing this, it has not fulfilled its distinctive and noblest function, which, I repeat, is to convey truth in the form of an appeal from one personal insight to another under a common obligation to the truth.

HENRY H. MITCHELL

Preaching as Celebration

One of the most insightful contemporary interpreters of black preaching is the Baptist minister and lecturer, Henry H. Mitchell (1919–). In several books and articles he has explored the genius of black preaching in light of its African heritage and the political, cultural, and religious experience of black people in America. He combines his appreciation of the freedom and cathartic drama of black preaching with a vigorous critique of the white, middle-class pulpit, which he characterizes as "cerebral" and life-less. In the following selection, which supplements his Beecher Lectures given in 1974, he explains how celebration or "climax" in the black sermon lifts both preacher and congregation to the joyous, self-affirming, yet self-forgetting enjoyment of God. By his reference to "the transconscious," a term borrowed from the historian of religions, Mircea Eliade, Mitchell means to describe (in Eliade's words) the "result of immemorial existential situations" now embedded in the black tradition of worship and preaching.

Henry H. Mitchell, *The Recovery of Preaching* (San Francisco: Harper and Row, 1977), pp. 54–62. Copyright © by Henry H. Mitchell. Reprinted by permission of Harper & Row, Publishers, Inc.

The best of gospel preaching is at once proclamation and celebration. Let us agree then as to what we mean by the term celebration. For our purposes celebration is both the literal and the symbolic or ritual expression of praise or joy. It may be in regard to an event or a person, historical or legendary, past or present; or it may relate to an object or a belief. A part of the genius of Black preaching has been its capacity to generate this very kind of celebration, despite the hardest of circumstances. This genius for celebration is partly responsible for the fact that enslaved and otherwise oppressed Blacks have survived the seemingly unbearable. When the oppressor thought they were too ignorant or insensitive to pain to know the depth of their plight, they were in fact well aware of it, but also involved in a vital tradition which literally sustained them by engaging them in praise of God—the dramatic expression of a world view affirming creation and Creator and the ineradicable value of the gift of life.

Preaching *without* celebration is a de facto denial of the good news, in *any* culture. Stated positively, what I propose is that preaching *with* celebration greatly enhances the transconscious retention and the true understanding and application of the gospel. It is my purpose here to spell out the meaning and the supporting rationale of these perhaps sweeping statements.

As I have already indicated in the second chapter, the African folk/oral tradition was so accurately communicated from generation unto generation because of rites which were celebrative. The massive corpus was inculcated in the minds of the young under circumstances which were joyous for the most part. That is to say, most of the folk gatherings were around the happy themes of birth, marriage, planting, harvest, and the advancement of the young through the stages of life. Even the feasts about death were not without joy. The result was a well-remembered corpus of proverbs and rites, with many ordinary folk capable of meticulous recall. More importantly, this tradition was so impressed upon the total transconscious that the life decisions of folk were heavily conditioned if not absolutely controlled by traditional belief. The importance of celebration in this cultural forebear of the Black religious tradition is inescapable. The joy and celebration which characterize Black worship even now are very important in the explanation of miraculous survival of this beauty and richness under the shadows of the oppressed ghetto.

Lest somebody get the notion that this is just the tenacity of a traditional "trip" of Black folks, let us look at the role or function of joy, fun, ecstasy, or celebration in worship, particularly preaching. In the first place, that which is joyously given, received, and celebrated is well nigh unforgettable. The emotional/intellectual tape or script is well cut by the etching agent of ecstasy. The transconscious data bank of the soul can much more readily be depended upon to recall that which was recorded in the midst of such pleasant associations. And when in the dark night of the soul it seems impossible to recapture the joy of the celebration, there is a higher signal which may draw it forth from the data pool even so. The first function of celebration in preaching is reinforcement for retention and availability.

The very title of George Leonard's book, *Education and Ecstasy*, indicates how important joy is to real learning even in the public schools. That importance is still greater in the learning of spiritual values and foundations. In a volume entitled *How Churches Teach* I once declared:

> Shouting may, at times, be put on or manipulated. But at its best it *teaches* "Aunt Jane" and all the rest that the presence of God is sheer ecstasy—that before God we can be absolutely free and uninhibited—and that God freely accepts and loves the real person that we have to hide almost everywhere else. The ecstasy of being somebody-to-the-hilt for even five minutes, *teaches* enough faith to keep an oppressed and despised Black man courageous and creative for another week.

Ecstasy teaches *and* reinforces teaching. It does not always express itself in shouting in Black tradition, but it does always involve deep feelings. Such feelings generate deep trust levels and inscribe the faith indelibly on the transconscious.

A second function of celebration is its fulfillment and affirmation of personhood and identity by means of free expression, which is accepted in the religiocultural context. This has been mentioned already in the quote above, where the shouting Christian is accepted by God while expressing his or her real feelings. This acceptance by God is mediated by the congregation, whose cultural expectations place high value on the shouting evidence of the presence of the Holy Spirit. If the congregation were to view shouting in a different light, it would be hard to sense the acceptance of God counterculturally. Celebration, therefore, provides a supportive structure in which persons are free to pour forth their deepest feelings and to celebrate their own personhood in the midst of celebrating the goodness of God.

Some time ago I was crushed in an Amanuel Day crowd of thousands, stretched as far as eye could see in all directions from Amanuel Church in Addis Ababa. They were celebrating Ethiopian Orthodox Christmas Eve. As the procession bearing the symbolic Ark of the Covenant passed round and round the church, shouts of great joy arose from wave after wave in a sea of literally happy faces. They were a terribly poverty-stricken lot for the most part, and Marx would have called this joy an opiate of the people. But I know that the religious forefathers of these same folk have survived the onslaughts of European and Arab invasion time and again. In the barren wastes to which they have had to retreat to live, they have survived more by an abundance of spiritual feast days than of physical food. Amanuel Day is only one of the nine *minor* feasts, but those thousands were gathered because their chants and cheers, their waving and dancing had meaning there which gave *them* meaning and fulfillment also. The owners of those voices and hands and feet were affirmed as persons while praising God, despite the vastness of their numbers and their great physical need by American standards.

This vast crowd also illustrates a third function of celebration, that of drawing people into community. Celebration is best achieved in the group relationship. It is good, of course, to praise God in solitude, but the enjoyment of God's goodness is multiplied by the sharing of the news. It binds together the host of those who affirm the goodness of God, who are affirmed in his praise, and who joyously affirm others as recipients of that same goodness. The celebrating community may not be personally acquainted, but the group tradition nevertheless provides a supportive context for the expression of the most personal feelings. In turn, the free expression binds the ritual congregation into a warm and emotionally permissive symbolic community.

A fourth facet or function of celebration is that of defining a habitable "living space"—the establishment of a celebrative island of consciousness in an ocean of oppression and deprivation. It might be thought of as roughly equivalent to the Western concept of the power of positive thinking. But it is far more than a wishful and naive attempt to exercise some fancied power of mind over matter. Rather, it couples a realistic facing of the hardest aspects of existence with a firm determination to fix consciousness on whatsoever things exist for which there can be praise to God. The spiritual puts it, "Nobody knows the trouble I see, Glory Hallelujah!"

Preaching which authentically celebrates the goodness of God and of life provides not only ideas but total experiences for the recall of the hearer. The celebration event as event and not just as comforting thought may then be "rerun" by the person in the oppressed audience, as a means of transcending the discouragement of later circumstances. In so doing one elects to live amidst and to focus consciousness on the joyous elements in past experience, as opposed to the perhaps vast majority of painful elements—the horror story of which one is the chief character and which one is, for the time, powerless to change. A spiritual expressed the process of focus of consciousness thus: "Woke up this mornin' with my mind stayed on Jesus, Hallelu, Hallelu, Hallelujah!" Preaching which celebrates the goodness of God equips hearers to stay their minds and focus their consciousness, choosing their living space and transcending the tragedies of oppressed existence.

The final role of celebration is that fitting climax to a balanced proclamation which has already included exegesis, exposition, explanation,
application, and deeply meaningful illustration. The gospel should have
been proclaimed throughout with joy. But the best reinforcement and
the greatest expression of joy must naturally occur when, so to speak,
the lesson is completed and summarized, and thanks and celebration are
offered for it at the end. All else leads up to this climactic moment, and
whatever follows is inevitably anti-climax. Like a symphony, the theme
is stated majestically and powerfully, with prior elaborations now taken
for granted. Fresh spiritual insight and illumination, joyous recall, and
persons fulfilled in community are celebrated together.

To take all these blessings for granted to the extent of a bland and un-
enthusiastic response would be to give evidence of having failed to
appreciate and benefit from it in the first place. No blessing is ever
enjoyed fully unless and until it is carried from the stage of mere mention
to the stage of grateful praise and celebration. The intensity of the
celebration is the accurate index to the depth of the response. If in fact
the gospel is what we have been saying it is — the power of God unto the
very salvation of persons — how can preacher or people respond other
than in celebration?

The question that haunts all of us is simply how one goes about
the task of preaching in such a way as to make possible the gift of
authentic celebration from time to time, especially as we near the close
of the proclamation.

The first and most penetrating answer to this hard question is that
great celebration is only generated by the treatment of great themes. It
should be obvious enough that clever intellectual technicalities do not
beget great joy among any save their inventors. And even they can't live
by their own noodle nuggets in the storms and crises of life. Black Americans have come through trials and tribulations of suicidal proportions,
and they have kept on living when others would have given up long
since, simply because they have been fed on the great themes of the
culture. These would include the goodness of life in the context of a good
creation, and the justice, mercy, goodness and providence of the Creator.
These have generated celebration by building a world view among
churched and unchurched which upheld a hazardous existence by
means of a transconscious trust. Without such high trust and meaning
levels, life would have been squandered in a struggle for a security which
is otherwise impossible for Blacks in this country and within the gift of
God alone. With the embrace of the affirmations of the faith and culture,

life is free to be abundant, enjoyed, and therefore celebrated, no matter how brutally beset. Great themes and affirmations beget celebration.

It should be equally obvious that celebration is generated by the satisfaction of deep-seated human needs. Gratitude begets celebration, and gratitude flows naturally when the cry of persons has been heard answered from the word of God. This may sound trite or old-fashioned, but it is no small thing when a saintly sister says to the preacher, "Son, you lifted my burden this morning." Such a response is heard all too seldom, because it is so infrequently deserved. The comforts of an automated age have not spread to the *souls* of our parishes. Indeed, the saints we serve are more and more isolated and alienated in the midst of their earthly toys. The suburban people-trap also breeds great spiritual needs. With physical existence so well cared for, there is less and less to divert attention from the pressing claims of the ultimate concerns. Persons are more restless than ever until they gratefully find their rest in the God of the great gospel. It is then altogether appropriate that they should celebrate.

Thirdly, celebration is generated by the fulfillment of persons. In the culture of the Black masses this is joyously accomplished in the dialogic character of the preaching tradition. When a Black preacher says, "Surely, this was the Son of God," or "Surely goodness and mercy shall follow me all the days of my life," he pauses after the "Surely." At that point, all who wish may lend a hand in the proclamation of the certitude by offering their own "Surely's." Or when the preacher cries "Have mercy!" in prayer or sermon, he waits for whosoever will to echo the plaintive and ubiquitous petition. Early morning has ancient importance in Black culture, and when the preacher says that Mary went early or "soon" Easter morning, to the tomb, he places the "early" first in the sentence. Then he pauses for the response—the joyous and predictable participation of persons caught up in a story which they literally help to tell. . . .

My final suggestions as to how to foster authentic celebration in preaching have to do with the sensitive timing of the truths presented, coupled with an adequate medium for summation and celebration. For many this may seem an altogether new consideration in organizing a sermon, but timing seriously affects sequence towards celebration. We usually think of sequence in logical, theological, or even chronological terms, but we seldom think of the timing of impact. What is this timing all about? What has it to do with cogency and power?

By timing we really mean emotional pace. To consider timing is to apply and to take seriously the fact that the gospel must be communicated to the whole person, or transconsciously. This takes time, as we have already seen, but time for truth to "sink in" and reach the deeper, slower moving emotions may not be used indiscriminately. Concern for timing involves the weighing of emotional impact. This input, in turn, is used alongside the various other logics possible in the final determination of the sequence of material. It is, of course, understood that the gospel must make a certain kind of sense, but it must do it transconsciously. Like such other art forms as the symphony, the sermon must avoid erratic movement, emotionally speaking, and it must build up to the final statement/celebration and coda.

There are two obvious extremes in this regard. One is the common practice of utter unawareness of emotional impact. It is the sin of being both overly intellectual and inadequately sensitive to the movements of the feelings of the audience. The other extreme is that of the so-called emotional preacher, whose solid content is conveyed unaware if at all. His chief conscious concern is to move people; and his sole criterion for the little organization he does of his material is that of how it will "slay" the congregation.

In between there is a synthesis which teaches as it moves persons, and moves persons as it teaches. It is my deep conviction that God in his providence will never place his messenger in the predicament of having to choose between the two. In fact, I *know* that he calls on us at all times both to illumine and to inspire. There can never be true learning and growth, without deep involvement of the feelings, nor can there be depth of Christian emotion without real growth. Our challenge as preachers is to be as aware of the one factor as of the other, and to build up to a celebration which is, at one and the same time, appropriately summary and reinforcing, as well as unforgettably satisfying emotionally.

IV
BIBLICAL INTERPRETATION

AUGUSTINE

Literal and Figurative Interpretation

Jesus began his public ministry by preaching on a text from Isaiah which he interpreted as a witness to his own Messianic office. Since the time of Jesus his followers have been people of a book, and his preachers have recognized the Scriptures as the source and norm of their proclamation. Already in the patristic period the rules and methods of discovering the sacred text's meaning were crucial to preaching, so much so that when Augustine of Hippo (354–430) produced the church's first textbook on homiletics, *On Christian Doctrine*, he conceived it as a manual for biblical interpretation. The first three books deal with the relation of *things*, or essential realities such as the Trinity, and *signs*, or language that points beyond itself toward things. Although the abundance of the Bible's figurative signs may pose a problem for the interpreter, there is amidst the complexity of linguistic forms a discernable simplicity: all Scripture unfolds the essence of God's love. Where the essential teaching (*doctrina*) is veiled, as it is in much of the Old Testament, the interpreter must either *penetrate* the veil by means of related, clearer passages or *elevate* the letter by means of allegorical interpretation. Allegorical or figurative interpretation serves a number of functions. It defends the divine authority of the whole Bible; it relentlessly pursues central theological themes, such as grace and love, even where they are not apparent; and it develops the spirituality of the interpreter, to whom direct knowledge of God has been lost in the Fall. Much of Augustine's discussion of biblical interpretation takes as its point of departure the third rule of the Donatist Tyconius, "Of Promise and the Law."

Augustine, *On Christian Doctrine*, Book III, selected paragraphs, trans. J. F. Shaw, *A Select Library of the Nicene and Post-Nicene Fathers of the Christian Church*, ed. Philip Schaff, Vol. II (Buffalo: The Christian Literature Company, 1887), pp. 559–567.

But the ambiguities of metaphorical words, about which I am next to speak, demand no ordinary care and diligence. In the first place, we must beware of taking a figurative expression literally. For the saying of the apostle applies in this case too: "The letter killeth, but the spirit giveth life." For when what is said figuratively is taken as if it were said literally, it is understood in a carnal manner. And nothing is more fittingly called the death of the soul than when that in it which raises it above the brutes, the intelligence namely, is put in subjection to the flesh by a blind adherence to the letter. For he who follows the letter takes figurative words as if they were proper, and does not carry out what is indicated by a proper word into its secondary signification; but, if he hears of the Sabbath, for example, thinks of nothing but the one day out of seven which recurs in constant succession; and when he hears of a sacrifice, does not carry his thoughts beyond the customary offerings of victims from the flock, and of the fruits of the earth. Now it is surely a miserable slavery of the soul to take signs for things, and to be unable to lift the eye of the mind above what is corporeal and created, that it may drink in eternal light.

This bondage, however, in the case of the Jewish people, differed widely from what it was in the case of the other nations; because, though the former were in bondage to temporal things, it was in such a way that in all these the One God was put before their minds. And although they paid attention to the signs of spiritual realities in place of the realities themselves, not knowing to what the signs referred, still they had this conviction rooted in their minds, that in subjecting themselves to such a bondage they were doing the pleasure of the one invisible God of all. And the apostle describes this bondage as being like to that of boys under the guidance of a schoolmaster. And those who clung obstinately to such signs could not endure our Lord's neglect of them when the time for their revelation had come; and hence their leaders brought it as a charge against him that he healed on the Sabbath, and the people, clinging to these signs as if they were realities, could not believe that one who refused to observe them in the way the Jews did was God, or came from God. But those who did believe, from among whom the first church at Jerusalem was formed, showed clearly how great an advantage it had been to be so guided by the schoolmaster that signs, which had been for a season imposed on the obedient, fixed the thoughts of those who observed them on the worship of the One God who made heaven and earth. These men, because they had been very near to spiritual things (for even in the temporal and carnal offerings and types, though they did not clearly apprehend their spiritual meaning, they had learnt to adore

138

the One Eternal God,) were filled with such a measure of the Holy Spirit that they sold all their goods, and laid their price at the apostles' feet to be distributed among the needy, and consecrated themselves wholly to God as a new temple, of which the old temple they were serving was but the earthly type. . . .

Now he is in bondage to a sign who uses, or pays homage to, any significant object without knowing what it signifies: he, on the other hand, who either uses or honors a useful sign divinely appointed, whose force and significance he understands, does not honor the sign which is seen and temporal, but that to which all such signs refer. Now such a man is spiritual and free even at the time of his bondage, when it is not yet expedient to reveal to carnal minds those signs by subjection to which their carnality is to be overcome. To this class of spiritual persons belonged the patriarchs and the prophets, and all those among the people of Israel through whose instrumentality the Holy Spirit ministered unto us the aids and consolations of the Scriptures. But at the present time, after that the proof of our liberty has shone forth so clearly in the resurrection of our Lord, we are not oppressed with the heavy burden of attending even to those signs which we now understand, but our Lord himself, and apostolic practice, have handed down to us a few rites in place of many, and these at once very easy to perform, most majestic in their significance, and most sacred in the observance; such, for example, as the sacrament of baptism, and the celebration of the body and blood of the Lord. And as soon as any one looks upon these observances he knows to what they refer, and so reveres them not in carnal bondage, but in spiritual freedom. Now, as to follow the letter, and to take signs for the things that are signified by them, is a mark of weakness and bondage; so to interpret signs wrongly is the result of being misled by error. He, however, who does not understand what a sign signifies but yet knows that it is a sign, is not in bondage. And it is better even to be in bondage to unknown but useful signs than, by interpreting them wrongly, to draw the neck from under the yoke of bondage only to insert it in the coils of error.

But in addition to the foregoing rule, which guards us against taking a metaphorical form of speech as if it were literal, we must also pay heed to that which tells us not to take a literal form of speech as if it were figurative. In the first place, then, we must show the way to find out whether a phrase is literal or figurative. And the way is certainly as follows: Whatever there is in the word of God that cannot, when taken literally, be referred either to purity of life or soundness of doctrine, you may set down as figurative. Purity of life has reference to the love of God and

139

one's neighbor; soundness of doctrine to the knowledge of God and one's neighbor. Every man, moreover, has hope in his own conscience, so far as he perceives that he has attained to the love and knowledge of God and his neighbor. . . .

But as men are prone to estimate sins, not by reference to their inherent sinfulness, but rather by reference to their own customs, it frequently happens that a man will think nothing blameable except what the men of his own country and time are accustomed to condemn, and nothing worthy of praise or approval except what is sanctioned by the custom of his companions; and thus it comes to pass, that if Scripture either enjoins what is opposed to the customs of the hearers, or condemns what is not so opposed, and if at the same time the authority of the word has a hold upon their minds, they think that the expression is figurative. So Scripture enjoins nothing except charity, and condemns nothing except lust, and in that way fashions the lives of men. In the same way, if an erroneous opinion has taken possession of the mind, men think that whatever Scripture asserts contrary to this must be figurative. Now Scripture asserts nothing but the catholic faith, in regard to things past, future, and present. It is a narrative of the past, a prophecy of the future, and a description of the present. But all these tend to nourish and strengthen charity, and to overcome and root out lust.

I mean by charity that affection of the mind which aims at the enjoyment of God for his own sake, and the enjoyment of one's self and one's neighbor in subordination to God; by lust I mean that affection of the mind which aims at enjoying one's self and one's neighbor, and other corporeal things, without reference to God. Again, what lust, when unsubdued, does towards corrupting one's own soul and body, is called *vice*; but what it does to injure another is called *crime*. And these are the two classes into which all sins may be divided. But the vices come first; for when these have exhausted the soul, and reduced it to a kind of poverty, it easily slides into crimes, in order to remove hindrances to, or to find assistance in, its vices. In the same way, what charity does with a view to one's own advantage is *prudence*; but what it does with a view to a neighbor's advantage is called *benevolence*. And here prudence comes first; because no one can confer an advantage on another which he does not himself possess. Now in proportion as the dominion of lust is pulled down, in the same proportion is that of charity built up.

Every severity, therefore, and apparent cruelty, either in word or deed, that is ascribed in Holy Scripture to God or his saints, avails to the pulling down of the dominion of lust. And if its meaning be clear, we are not to give it some secondary reference, as if it were spoken figuratively.

140

Take, for example, that saying of the apostle: "But, after thy hardness and impenitent heart, treasurest up unto thyself wrath against the day of wrath and revelation of the righteous judgment of God; who will render to every man according to his deeds; to them who, by patient continuance in well-doing, seek for glory, and honor, and immortality, eternal life; but unto them that are contentious, and do not obey the truth, but obey unrighteousness, indignation and wrath, tribulation and anguish, upon every soul of man that doeth evil, of the Jew first, and also of the Gentile." But this is addressed to those who, being unwilling to subdue their lust, are themselves involved in the destruction of their lust. When, however, the dominion of lust is overturned in a man over whom it had held sway, this plain expression is used: "They that are Christ's have crucified the flesh, with the affections and lusts." Only that, even in these instances, some words are used figuratively, as for example, "the wrath of God" and "crucified." But these are not so numerous, nor placed in such a way as to obscure the sense, and make it allegorical or enigmatical, which is the kind of expression properly called *figurative*. But in the saying addressed to Jeremiah, "See, I have this day set thee over the nations, and over the kingdoms, to root out, and to pull down, and to destroy, and to throw down," there is no doubt the whole of the language is figurative, and to be referred to the end I have spoken of.

Those things, again, whether only sayings or whether actual deeds, which appear to the inexperienced to be sinful, and which are ascribed to God, or to men whose holiness is put before us as an example, are wholly figurative, and the hidden kernel of meaning they contain is to be picked out as food for the nourishment of charity. Now, whoever uses transitory objects less freely than is the custom of those among whom he lives, is either temperate or superstitious; whoever, on the other hand, uses them so as to transgress the bounds of the custom of the good men about him, either has a further meaning in what he does, or is sinful. In all such matters it is not the use of the objects, but the lust of the user, that is to blame. . . . Keeping company with a harlot, for example, is one thing when it is the result of abandoned manners, another thing when done in the course of his prophecy by the prophet Hosea. Because it is a shamefully wicked thing to strip the body naked at a banquet among the drunken and licentious, it does not follow that it is a sin to be naked in the baths. . . .

The tyranny of lust being thus overthrown, charity reigns through its supremely just laws of love to God for his own sake, and love to one's self and one's neighbor for God's sake. Accordingly, in regard to figurative expressions, a rule such as the following will be observed, to carefully turn over in our minds and meditate upon what we read till an interpretation be found that tends to establish the reign of love. Now, if when taken literally it at once gives a meaning of this kind, the expression is not to be considered figurative.

If the sentence is one of command, either forbidding a crime or vice, or enjoining an act of prudence or benevolence, it is not figurative. If, however, it seems to enjoin a crime or vice, or to forbid an act of prudence or benevolence, it is figurative. "Except ye eat the flesh of the Son of man," says Christ, "and drink his blood, ye have no life in you." This seems to enjoin a crime or a vice; it is therefore a figure, enjoining that we should have a share in the sufferings of our Lord, and that we should retain a sweet and profitable memory of the fact that his flesh was wounded and crucified for us. Scripture says: "If thine enemy hunger, feed him; if he thirst, give him drink;" and this is beyond doubt a command to do a kindness. But in what follows, "for in so doing thou shalt heap coals of fire on his head," one would think a deed of malevolence was enjoined. Do not doubt, then, that the expression is figurative; and, while it is possible to interpret it in two ways, one pointing to the doing of an injury, the other to a display of superiority, let charity on the contrary call you back to benevolence, and interpret the coals of fire as the burning groans of penitence by which a man's pride is cured who bewails that he has been the enemy of one who came to his assistance in distress. . . .

Again, it often happens that a man who has attained, or thinks he has attained, to a higher grade of spiritual life, thinks that the commands given to those who are still in the lower grades are figurative; for example, if he has embraced a life of celibacy and made himself a eunuch for the kingdom of heaven's sake, he contends that the commands given in Scripture about loving and ruling a wife are not to be taken literally, but figuratively; and if he has determined to keep his virgin unmarried, he tries to put a figurative interpretation on the passage where it is said, "Marry thy daughter, and so shalt thou have performed a weighty matter." Accordingly, another of our rules for understanding the Scriptures will be as follows,—to recognize that some commands are given to all in common, others to particular classes of persons, that the medicine may act not only upon the state of health as a whole, but also upon the special weakness of each member. For that which cannot be raised to a higher state must be cared for in its own state.

We must also be on our guard against supposing that what in the Old Testament, making allowance for the condition of those times, is not a crime or a vice even if we take it literally and not figuratively, can be transferred to the present time as a habit of life. For no one will do this except lust has dominion over him, and endeavors to find support for itself in the very Scriptures which were intended to overthrow it. And the wretched man does not perceive that such matters are recorded with this useful design, that men of good hope may learn the salutary lesson, both that the custom they spurn can be turned to a good use, and that which they embrace can be used to condemnation, if the use of the former be accompanied with charity, and the use of the latter with lust. . . .

Therefore, although all, or nearly all, the transactions recorded in the Old Testament are to be taken not literally only, but figuratively as well, nevertheless even in the case of those which the reader has taken literally, and which, though the authors of them are praised, are repugnant to the habits of the good men who since our Lord's advent are the custodians of the divine commands, let him refer the figure to its interpretation, but let him not transfer the act to his habits of life. For many things which were done as duties at that time, cannot now be done except through lust.

And when he reads of the sins of great men, although he may be able to see and to trace out in them a figure of things to come, let him yet put the literal fact to this use also, to teach him not to dare to vaunt himself in his own good deeds, and in comparison with his own righteousness, to despise others as sinners, when he sees in the case of men so eminent both the storms that are to be avoided and the shipwrecks that are to be wept over. For the sins of these men were recorded to this end, that men might everywhere and always tremble at that saying of the apostle: "Wherefore let him that thinketh he standeth take heed lest he fall." For there is hardly a page of Scripture on which it is not clearly written that God resisteth the proud and giveth grace to the humble.

The chief thing to be inquired into, therefore, in regard to any expression that we are trying to understand is, whether it is literal or figurative. For when it is ascertained to be figurative, it is easy, by an application of the laws of things which we discussed in the first book, to turn it in every way until we arrive at a true interpretation, especially when we bring to our aid experience strengthened by the exercise of piety. Now we find out whether an expression is literal or figurative by attending to the considerations indicated above. . . .

When, again, not some one interpretation, but two or more interpretations are put upon the same words of Scripture, even though the meaning the writer intended remain undiscovered, there is no danger if it can be shown from other passages of Scripture that any of the interpretations put on the words is in harmony with the truth. And if a man in searching the Scriptures endeavors to get at the intention of the author through whom the Holy Spirit spoke, whether he succeeds in this endeavor, or whether he draws a different meaning from the words, but one that is not opposed to sound doctrine, he is free from blame so long as he is supported by the testimony of some other passage of Scripture. For the author perhaps saw that this very meaning lay in the words which we are trying to interpret; and assuredly the Holy Spirit, who through him spoke these words, foresaw that this interpretation would occur to the reader, nay, made provision that it should occur to him, seeing that it too is founded on truth. For what more liberal and more fruitful provision could God have made in regard to the sacred Scriptures than that the same words might be understood in several senses, all of which are sanctioned by the concurring testimony of other passages equally divine?

When, however, a meaning is evolved of such a kind that what is doubtful in it cannot be cleared up by indubitable evidence from Scripture, it remains for us to make it clear by the evidence of reason. But this is a dangerous practice. For it is far safer to walk by the light of Holy Scripture; so that when we wish to examine the passages that are obscured by metaphorical expressions, we may either obtain a meaning about which there is no controversy, or if a controversy arises, may settle it by the application of testimonies sought out in every portion of the same Scripture.

BONAVENTURE

A Vision of Abundant Meanings

To the medieval mind the multiplicity of meanings in the biblical text was less a problem than a sign of God's riches which he freely bestows upon his church. The question for the interpreter, then, is 'By what key may the treasury be unlocked?' A millennium earlier, Origen had already graded the levels of the Bible's meaning according to the dimensions of human nature and its capacity for understanding: *flesh* for the literalist, *soul* for the aspiring, *spirit* for the perfected. In the 13th century the Franciscan scholar, cardinal, and saint Bonaventure (1221–1274) established his principles of sacred interpretation upon an elaborate Trinitarian foundation (as opposed to Origen's anthropological model). Just as the Trinity consists of three persons in one essence, Scripture presents three spiritual meanings beneath the surface of the literal. As the following selection makes clear, the three spiritual senses are but the seeds of an infinite multiplication of meanings. Bonaventure perpetuates the spirit of Origen and the language of John Cassian (d. 435) when he writes of the allegorical, moral (or tropological), and anagogical senses. Cassian had illustrated his terms by means of the word "Jerusalem" which, literally, is a city of the Jews, allegorically, the church of Christ, morally, the human soul, and, anagogically, the heavenly city (see James S. Preus, *From Shadow to Promise*, Cambridge, MA: Harvard U. Press, 1969, pp. 21–22). Immediately following this selection, Bonaventure illustrates the sixteen phases of meaning he has discerned in Ezekiel's vision by tracing the nuances of the word "sun" throughout Scripture.

Bonaventure, *Collations on the Six Days, Thirteenth Collation*, in *The Works of Bonaventure*, Vol. V, trans. José de Vinck (Paterson, N.J.: St. Anthony Guild Press, 1970), pp. 183–195. Reprinted by permission of St. Anthony Guild Press.

"Let the waters below the heavens be gathered into one place and let the dry land appear." And so it was. God called the dry land Earth and the assembled waters seas. And God saw that it was good. Then God said, "Let the earth bring forth vegetation: seed-bearing plants and all kinds of fruit trees that bear fruit containing their seed," etc. Such is the third vision, of understanding instructed by Scriptures, which is figured in the work of the third day. And as in the work of the days, there is added a second to the first and a third to the both of them, so also out of the first and second visions there comes forth a third, and this vision is more noble and greater than the preceding two. And although such adaptation and comparison to the work of the third day may not seem properly fitting since the earth is the lowest of the elements, while the Scriptures are most high, yet the relationship is excellently pointed out: for whatever the heavens contain in any measure of excellence, the earth holds or receives or possesses in some measure of liveliness. Wherefore it receives the influences of heaven and brings forth the most beautiful swarms of beings.

Now this vision is concerned with three things, the spiritual meanings of the senses, that is the "sense," the sacramental symbols, and the manifold interpretations that are drawn from them. All of Scriptures may be reduced to these three.

The first are offered to our understanding by means of the gathering of the waters, that is, the spiritual meanings. The second, that is, the sacramental symbols, are represented by the swarming of beings on earth, in this passage: "Let the earth bring forth vegetation." The third, that is, the manifold interpretations, are signified by the seed, in this passage: ". . . containing their seed," etc.

Who can know the infinity of seeds, when in a single one are contained forests of forests and thence seeds in infinite number? Likewise, out of Scriptures may be drawn an infinite number of interpretations which none but God can comprehend. For as new seeds come forth from plants, so also from Scriptures come forth new interpretations and new meanings, and thereby are sacred Scriptures distinct from everything else. Hence, in relation to the interpretations yet to be drawn, we may compare to a single drop from the sea all those that have been drawn so far. . . .

Ezekiel saw this multiformity more clearly, for he beheld "within . . . figures resembling four living creatures"; and the first had the face of a man, the second that of a lion, the third that of an ox, and the fourth that of an eagle. And each one had four faces. And later there appeared a wheel within another. Then the prophet says that "the appearance of the wheels and the work of them was like the appearance of the sea," and that it was "as it were a wheel in the midst of a wheel." And he continues by saying that he "heard the sound of their wings, like the roaring of mighty waters, like the voice of the Almighty." All agree that the four living creatures represent the writers of sacred Scriptures, mostly the Prophets and the Evangelists. According to Gregory, the two wheels having four faces point to Scripture which has the Old and the New Testaments, the four faces being the four principal interpretations, the literal, the figurative, the moral and the anagogical. Their appearance is like a vision of the sea because of the depth of the spiritual mysteries. The sound of their wings is heard when the minds are prompted; and the voice of the Almighty rings out because all things are from God. Hence, in the Apocalypse: "I heard a voice from heaven like a voice of many waters," because of the great number of possible interpretations; a voice of harpers because of the accord of these interpretations, for they agree in such a marvelous way that the resulting harmony is wonderful.

Scriptures, then, have a number of meanings because the voice of God must be expressed in a manner that is sublime. The other sciences are contained within a single sense, but in this one the sense is manifold, and both the language and the topics have significance. In the other sciences, only the language has meaning, for each area of teaching is determined by the signs proper to it; hence the written words and the language are the signs of the meaning—and the written words are the most important of the two; and since the meanings are proportioned and terminated, so also is the language, so that once a noun has been established with a given sense, it must not be used later in a different sense.

But God is the cause of the soul and of language which is formed by the soul, and also of the things with which language is concerned.

Therefore, the first meaning is the literal. After that, because things themselves have a sense, there are three other meanings. For God manifests himself in every creature in a threefold manner: according to substance, power, and operation. And every creature represents God, who is Trinity, and shows the way to him. And because the way to God is through faith, hope, and love, every creature is a suggestion of what we should believe, expect, and do. And parallel to this, there is a threefold spiritual meaning: the allegorical concerning what we should believe, the anagogical concerning what we should expect, and the moral concerning what we should do, for love leads to action.

The literal meaning resembles a natural face, that of a man, while the others are symbolical. The lion, being magnificent, points to allegory, or what we should believe; the face of an ox, that pulls the plow and furrows the soil for the harvest, points to tropology, or moral obligation; the eagle that flies on high points to anagogy.

The first face, the literal, is open; the second is lifted up on high by magnificence; the third, the tropological, is fruitful; the fourth looks upon the sun almost without flinching.

These four are "like the appearance of the sea" because of the primitive origination, the most profound depth, and the abundantly flowing multiformity of the spiritual meanings. And so, as there are three persons within the single essence, there are three meanings beneath the single surface of the letter.

It should be noted, however, that while the world serves man in his body, it serves him more particularly in his soul; and that if it serves to forward life, it serves more particularly to forward wisdom. It is certain that as long as man stood up, he had the knowledge of created things and through their significance, was carried up to God, to praise, worship, and love him. This is what creatures are for, and this is how they are led back to God. But when man had fallen, since he had lost knowledge, there was no longer any one to lead creatures back to God. Hence this book, the world, became as dead and deleted. And it was necessary that there be another book through which this one would be lighted up, so that it could receive the symbols of things. Such a book is Scripture which establishes the likenesses, the properties, and the symbolism of things written down in the book of the world. And so, Scripture has the power to restore the whole world toward the knowledge, praise, and love of God. Hence, if you ask what is the meaning of the serpent to you, or what is its use—it is more useful to you than the whole world because it teaches you how to be prudent, as the ant teaches you how to be wise. Solomon says: "Go to the ant, O sluggard, study her ways and learn wisdom." And Matthew: "Be therefore wise as serpents."

These four meanings are the four rivers of the sea in Scripture: they derive or originate from the sea, and they return to it. Hence sacred Scripture sheds light on all things and retraces them all back to God, thus restoring the original state of creatures. . . .

Every teaching of the Old Testament is either legal, as that of Moses, or historical as that of the historical books, or sapiential as that of the sapiential books, or prophetical as in the Psalms and the twelve minor and the four major prophets. Likewise the Scriptures in the New Testament are either legal as in the Gospels where commands are established, or historical as in the Acts of the Apostles, or sapiential as in the Epistles of Paul to which should be added the Canonical Letters, or prophetical as in the Apocalypse. Although the Epistles are placed after the Gospels, the Acts of the Apostles follow the Gospels immediately. . . .

The legal books correspond to the lion, because of its magnificence and authority; the historical to the ox who pulls the plow, because of its simplicity, and because it furrows the earth; the sapiential to man; and the prophetical to the face of an eagle.

For Scripture tends to lead back to the first beginning by means of reformation, or it describes eternal things, as in the Laws and Gospels. Hence in the Psalm: "He gave them a duty which shall not pass away." And in Ecclesiasticus: "As everlasting foundations upon a solid rock, so the commandments of God in the heart of a holy woman." This woman is the church. For it is not to be understood that the Law or the Commandments will pass away, but rather that they will be better served in the fatherland. For they are not served in the same manner under the Old Testament and under the New Testament: they are served better under the New Testament, and yet better still in the fatherland. God indeed lives by these very Laws which he himself has given.

But when Scripture deals with temporal matters, it is either of the past, and in this it is historical; or of the present, and in this it is sapiential; or of the future, and in this it is prophetical. Hence, there are commandments, examples, documents, and revelations.

And so, this first meaning has four faces: if we ordain them according to the order of Ezekiel, then we obtain an order which is right in itself; but according to our nature, we must turn our eyes to most important eternal matters.

Anagogy is concerned with things from above; allegory, with that which has been done; tropology, with things yet to be done. According to Hugh of Saint-Victor, anagogy is part of allegory, for it is concerned with matters of faith.

Wherefore in the anagogical sense there are four faces, that is, the eternal Trinity of God, the wisdom of the Exemplar, the loftiness of the angels, and the church triumphant. And so, when Scripture speaks of these things, it is a matter of anagogy.

Likewise, in the allegorical sense, there are four faces, that is, Christ's humanity assumed in the nativity and the passion, which are the principal allegories. Second, Mary the mother of God, for marvelous things are said of her in Scripture, since in all cases she is mentioned in relation to her Son. And as regards what some people ask—"Why is so little said about the Blessed Virgin?"—it is of no import, for, in fact, many things are said, for everywhere there is reference to her, and it is more important that she be referred to everywhere than that a specific treatise be composed about her. Third, there is the church militant or mother church, who receives marvelous praises in Scripture. Fourth, there is sacred Scripture itself which says many things in itself, as is evident as regards the wheels, the table, the Cherubim that looked upon each other, and the lampstand.

Again in the tropological sense, there are four faces. The first is spiritual grace and power and all such effects. The second, spiritual life as active and contemplative, and every manner of living. Third, the spiritual throne, such as that of the teacher, the prelate, and the high priest. Fourth, the spiritual fight, or how battle is to be waged against the devil, the world and the flesh.

These are the four faces quadruplicated in each of the meanings.

MARTIN LUTHER

The Letter and the Spirit

Martin Luther (1483-1546) was not the first to exalt the authority of Scripture over tradition, but he was clearest in his understanding of the symbiotic relationship of church traditions and the allegorical interpretation of the Bible. He therefore repudiated the fourfold interpretation, seeking in its stead the "literal, ordinary, natural sense" of Scripture. He particularly objected to those, such as Origen, who found warrant for a spiritual hermeneutic in II Corinthians 4, a passage Luther interpreted *theologically* in terms of the ministries of law and gospel. What is killing about the Old Testament, said Luther, is not its native, literal sense, but rather the revelation of God's law and wrath. Hence his extra measure of abuse for the "superspiritual" Jerome Emser against whom Luther waged a protracted pamphlet war. Despite his protestations, Luther did not abandon spiritual interpretation. He acknowledged the "hidden sense" or "mysteries" but insisted that any meaning deeper than the ordinary must be signaled by Scripture itself. Luther eventually advanced the "historical" interpretation of Scripture by which he retrojected the history of Christ and the church into the Old Testament's domain of allegory. To use Augustine's terms, Luther's Christ becomes the one essential "thing" amidst an array of biblical "signs." His hermeneutic thus prefigures two radical approaches to biblical interpretation: nineteenth-century historicism and twentieth-century theological existentialism.

Martin Luther, ". . . Answer to the Superchristian, Superspiritual, and Superlearned Book of Goat Emser of Leipzig," *Works of Martin Luther*, Vol. III (Philadelphia: Muhlenberg Press, 1930), pp. 346–360.

St. Paul says, II Corinthians 4: "The letter killeth, but the spirit giveth life." This my Emser explains to mean that the Scriptures have a twofold meaning, an external sense and a secret sense, which he calls the literal and the spiritual. The literal sense is supposed to kill and the spiritual to give life. In this he builds on the teaching of Origen, Dionysius, and some others, and thinks he has hit the mark squarely and does not need even to look at the clear Scriptures, since he has the teachings of men. He would like me to imitate him, to abandon the Scriptures and likewise accept the teachings of men. That is something I will not do, although I, too, labored under that error for a time, and I desire to take this opportunity to show clearly how Origen, Jerome, Dionysius, and some others were in the wrong, and how Emser builds his house on the sand, and that it is always necessary to compare the writings of the fathers with the Scripture, and to judge them according to its light.

In the first place, if their opinion were right, that the spiritual sense giveth life and the literal sense killeth, we should be obliged to confess that all sinners are holy and all the saints are sinners; nay, Christ himself with all the angels must at the same time be both living and dead. This we shall make so clear that even Emser with all his ability to lie shall not be able to contradict it. We will take the passage from St. Paul in Galatians 4, where according to the literal sense, the letter, it is stated that Abraham had two sons, Isaac and Ishmael, by two wives, Sarah and Hagar. This is the sense accepted by Christ, God the Holy Spirit, and all the angels and saints. They hold that what the literal sense conveys here is true. And it is indeed true. Well, Emser, where is your Origen now? If you are really the man who fights not with the scabbard but strikes with the blade, speak up now and say that the letter and the literal sense kill Christ and the Holy Spirit together with all the angels and saints. Can a man say anything more blasphemous than Emser does in his madness, that all the truth in the Scripture kills and destroys?

Again, that Abraham signifies Christ, the two women the two Testaments, the two sons the people of the two Testaments, as St. Paul interprets, this is, as you say, the spiritual meaning. But this meaning is held not only by the saints but also by the worst sinners, yea even by the devils in hell. Come right out into the open, my Emser, strike away with the blade and say that all the devils and knaves are holy and have the life which the spirit giveth. Now be honest and confess that when you take this trick away from Origen, Dionysius, Jerome, and many others there is nothing left of them. Are not the Scriptures clearer on this point than all the fathers? . . .

In this way we must interpret all the Scriptures, even the ancient types.

For instance, the Jews were forbidden to eat swine or hare because neither swine nor hare cheweth the cud. This is the literal sense. Thus it was understood by David, all the holy prophets and by Christ himself, together with his disciples, and if they had not thus understood and observed it, they would have set themselves against God. Why did the letter not kill them? Again, that the swine signify the carnal teachings or whatever other spiritual sense one wishes to apply can be understood even by those who live in mortal sin, and by the devils even more easily. Why does not the spirit give life to them? Where are you, O knight with the mighty Leipzig sword? . . . Truly, you must now see and yourself admit what I have told you, that you do not have an inkling of the meaning of "spirit" and "letter" in the Scriptures. You had better tend to your business and let the Scriptures alone. See how little it helps to quote many writers and to build on what they say.

Furthermore, St. Paul says, Romans 7: "The divine law is spiritual, but I am carnal." He cites one of the ten commandments, namely, the *Non concupisces*, Thou shalt not covet, and in an extended and skillful argument shows how that same spiritual law killeth. What will you do here, my Emser? Where are you, O man of the spear and of the dagger and of the edged sword? St. Paul here says that the spiritual law killeth, but you say that the spiritual sense giveth life. Come, pipe up, show your skill: what is the literal, and what the spiritual sense in this commandment, *Non concupisces*? Surely you cannot deny that no other sense can be taken out of these words than that given by their literal meaning. Paul here speaks of the evil lusts of the flesh and yet he calls this law spiritual and maintains that it killeth. And you say, it were better to read a poet's tale than the literal sense of the Scriptures. This is St. Paul's opinion, and he who finds in this commandment any other sense than this literal sense concerning evil lusts finds no meaning in it at all. How well Emser accords with St. Paul: like a donkey singing a duet with a nightingale. All the commandments of God must be treated in the same way, whether they refer to ceremonies or other matters, small or great. It is plain how pitifully Emser has erred in this thing and has shown that he knows less about the Scriptures than a child.

Besides, his mistaken and wrong interpretation is a dishonor to the entire sacred Scriptures and a disgrace to himself. All the labor and diligence of the teachers have no other object than to find the literal sense which alone they regard as valid, so that Augustine declares: *Figura nihil probat*, that is, Emser's "spiritual sense" is not valid, but the other sense is the highest, best, strongest; in short, it is the whole substance, essence, and foundation of Scripture, so that if the literal sense were taken away, all the Scriptures would be nothing. The spiritual sense, which Emser magnifies, is not valid in any controversy. It does not hold water, nor would it matter if no one knew anything about it, as I proved in my book *On the Papacy*. For even if no one knew that Aaron is a type of Christ, it would not matter, neither can it be proven. We must let Aaron be simply Aaron in the ordinary sense, except where the Spirit himself gives a new interpretation, which is then a new literal sense, as St. Paul, for instance, in the Epistle to the Hebrews makes Aaron to be Christ.

How can you be so bold, Emser, as to make the assertion that this literal sense killeth? You are floundering about in ignorance of the import of your own words, when you prate that it is better to read one of Virgil's poems than to read the literal sense of the Scriptures. Thereby you condemn the entire Scripture and give preference to the lies and fictions of the devil over the holy word of God, which has no other valid meaning than the one you call deadly and teach men to shun. But this is smiting with the blade and a correct Emserian spiritual interpretation; thus must the heretic Luther be struck! Turn the tables, Emser, and you will find that the sense which you call spiritual and life-giving, is the very one—if you cling only to it and let the literal sense go—for which it would be better to exchange the poets' tales, for the spiritual sense is unsafe, and the Scriptures exist without it, but they cannot exist without the literal sense. They were right aforetimes who prohibited the books of Origen, for he paid too much attention to this spiritual sense, which was unnecessary, and he neglected the necessary literal sense. For that means the destruction of Scripture and will never make sound theologians. Such are developed only by the one, true, original, and native sense of the words.

The Holy Spirit is the plainest writer and speaker in heaven and earth, and, therefore, his words cannot have more than one, and that the very simplest, sense, which we call the literal, ordinary, natural sense. That the things indicated by the simple sense of his simple words should signify something further and different, and, therefore, one thing should always signify another, is more than a question of words or of language. For the same is true of all other things outside of the Scriptures, since all of God's works and creatures are living signs and words of God, as St. Augustine and all the teachers declare. But we are not on that account to say that the Scriptures or the word of God have more than one meaning.

A painted picture of a living man signifies a person, without need of a word of explanation. But that does not cause you to say that the word "picture" has a twofold sense, a literal sense, meaning the picture, and a spiritual sense, meaning the living person. Now, although the things described in the Scriptures have a further significance, the Scriptures do not on that account have a twofold sense, but only the one which the words give. Beyond that we can give permission to speculative minds to seek and chase after the various significations of the things mentioned, provided they take care not to go too far or too high, as sometimes happens to the chamois hunters and did happen to Origen. It is much surer and safer to abide by the words in their simple sense; they furnish the real pasture and right dwelling-places for all minds. . . .

Many sensible men have made the mistake of calling the "letter" a figure of speech, Augustine among them. As if I were to say, Emser is a stupid ass, and a simple-minded man hearing these words would understand that Emser were actually an ass with long ears and four legs. The man would have been deceived by the letter, whereas I wanted to convey, through the figure of speech, what a blockhead Emser is. Figures of speech are a subject of study in the schools and are called in Greek *schemata*, and in Latin *figurae*, because they are a decking out of speech, even as you adorn the body with jewels. The Scriptures are full of such figures of speech, particularly the books of the prophets. John and Christ in Luke 3 call the Jews *genimina viperarum*, generation of vipers. St. Paul in Colossians 2 calls them dogs. Psalm 109 says: "The dew of thy children shall come out of the womb of the morning." Again: "God shall send the rod of thy strength out of Zion." That means the children of Christ are born, not physically from a mother's womb, but without the work of man, like the dew from heaven, out of the morning of the Christian church. Further, Christ says, Matthew 5: "Ye are the salt of the earth and the light of the world." But this is not what St. Paul means by the word "letter." This belongs to the study of grammar in the schools.

If you can humble yourself and not despise me altogether, I will do what out of Christian duty I owe to my enemy, and not withhold from you God's gift to me. I will give you better instruction in this matter—I say this without boasting—than any you have received heretofore from any teacher except St. Augustine, if perchance you have read his *De Spiritu et Litera*. None of the others will teach you aright. You will not find a single letter in the whole Bible that agrees with what you, together with Origen and Jerome, call the spiritual sense. St. Paul calls it a mystery, a secret, hidden sense, wherefore the earliest of the fathers called it an anagogical, that is, a more remote sense, a meaning by itself, and sometimes also an allegory, St. Paul himself using the latter term in Galatians 4. But that is not yet the "spirit," although the Spirit has given it as well as the letter and all the gifts, as we see from I Corinthians 14: "The Spirit

155

speaketh mysteries." Some, however, because they did not understand this matter, ascribed a fourfold sense to Scripture, the literal, the allegorical, the anagogical, and the tropological, for which there is no foundation whatever.

It is, therefore, not well named the literal sense, for by letter Paul means something quite different. They do much better who call it the grammatical, historical sense. It would be well to call it the speaking or language sense as St. Paul does in I Corinthians 14, because it is understood by everybody in the sense of the spoken language. He who hears the words that Abraham had two sons by two wives, receives them in that sense and has no further thoughts than those indicated by the language, until the Spirit goes farther and reveals the hidden sense concerning Christ and the two covenants and peoples. Such hidden meanings are then called mysteries, just as St. Paul in Ephesians 5 calls the union of Christ and the church in one body a mystery, although the letter of the Scriptures in Genesis 2 speaks of man and wife. Great care is necessary, however, that not everyone shall of himself invent mysteries, as some have done and still do. The Spirit must do it himself or one must prove them by Scripture, as I said in the treatise *On the Papacy*.

Therefore, the text of St. Paul in II Corinthians 4, "The letter killeth but the spirit giveth life," squares with this twofold sense, the spiritual and the literal, as perfectly as Emser's head squares with philosophy and theology. How and why Origen, Jerome, and some other fathers also turned and twisted this text in the same manner I will not discuss now. It is generally known and can easily be proved that they treated other passages in the same way in order to refute the Jews and the heretics. But we ought to excuse them for that and not follow them here like unclean animals who gulp down everything they find and make no distinctions in the work and teaching of the fathers, until at last we follow them only in those things wherein the beloved fathers — as human beings — erred, and depart from them in the things they did well. I could prove this easily from the teachings and the lives of all who now are considered the very worthiest among them.

Let us now consider the text concerning the letter and the spirit. In that passage St. Paul does not write one iota about these two senses, but declares that there are two kinds of preaching or ministries. One is that of the Old Testament, the other that of the New Testament. The Old Testament preaches the letter, the New Testament the spirit. . . .

We see clearly that St. Paul speaks of two tables and two kinds of preaching. The tables of Moses were of stone, on which the law was inscribed by God's finger, Exodus 20. The tables of Christ, or the epistles of Christ, as he calls them here, are the hearts of Christians, in which are written, not letters as on Moses' tables, but the spirit of God, through the preaching of the gospel and the ministry of the apostles. Now, just what does this mean? The letter is naught else but the divine law and commandment which is given in the Old Testament, through Moses, and is taught and proclaimed through Aaron's priesthood. It is called "letter" because it is written with letters on the tables of stone and in books. A letter it must ever remain; it never gives anything except its command. For no man is made better by the law, but only worse, for the law does not give help or grace; it merely commands and demands that a man do what a man never willingly does, and indeed, cannot do. But the spirit, which is divine grace, gives strength and power to the heart, yea, creates a new man who grows to love God's commandments and does with joy all that he ought to do.

This spirit cannot be contained in any letter, it cannot be written with ink, on stone, or in books, as the law can be, but is written only in the heart, a living writing of the Holy Spirit who uses no means at all. Therefore, St. Paul calls it Christ's epistle, not Moses' tables; it is written not with ink, but with the Spirit of God. By this spirit or grace a man does what the law commands and satisfies it. In this manner he becomes free from the letter that kills him and lives through the grace of the Spirit. Everyone that does not have this grace of the living Spirit is dead, although he makes a fine show in the outward keeping of the whole law. For this reason the apostle says of the law that it kills, that it makes no one alive and would keep one eternally in bondage to death unless grace come to set him free and to give him life.

These, then, are the two ministries. The priests, preachers, and ministries of the Old Testament deal with naught else but the law of God; they have as yet no open proclamation of the spirit and of grace. But in the New Testament all the preaching is of grace and the spirit given to us through Christ. For the preaching of the New Testament is naught else but an offering and presentation of Christ to all men out of the pure mercy of God, in such wise that all who believe in him receive God's grace and the Holy Spirit, by which all sin is forgiven, all law is fulfilled, they become God's children, and have eternal salvation. Therefore, St. Paul here calls the New Testament proclamation *ministerium spiritus*, a ministry of the spirit, i.e., a ministry by which the spirit and grace of God are presented and offered to all who by the law have been burdened, killed, and made to long for grace. The law he calls *ministerium literae*, a ministry of the letter, i.e., a ministry which offers nothing but the letter or the law, that produces no life nor a fulfillment of the law whose demands no man can satisfy. Therefore, it must needs remain a letter, and as a letter it can accomplish nothing more than to kill a man, i.e., it shows him what he ought to do and yet cannot do; this makes him realize that he is in disgrace and dead before God, whose commandments he does not keep and yet must keep. . . .

Here we see how excellently St. Paul teaches us to understand aright, Christ, God's grace, and the New Testament. It is all comprised in the fact that Christ came unto our sin, bore it in his body on the cross, and blotted it out, so that all who believed on him were rid of their sin and received grace henceforth to satisfy God's law and the letter that killeth, and thus were made partakers of eternal life. See, that is what is meant by *ministerium spiritus, non literae,* the preaching of the spirit, the preaching of grace, the preaching of a right indulgence, the preaching of Christ, i.e., the New Testament, of which much could be said if the evil spirit had not blinded the world through the pope, and by man-teaching had led it into the abyss of outermost darkness.

Now we see that all commandments lead unto death, since even divine commandments mean death, for everything that is not spirit or grace means death. It is, therefore, monstrous ignorance to call allegories, tropologies, and the like, spirit. They can all be encompassed in language and do not give life, but grace has no receptacle save the heart. . . .

It is indeed true that where only the law is preached and the letter insisted on, as in the Old Testament, and this is not followed by the preaching of the Spirit, there can be only death without life, sin without grace, anguish without comfort. Such preaching produces wretched and captive consciences, and makes men finally despair and die in their sins, and, through this preaching, be eternally damned. This has been done in our day and still is done by the murderous sophists in their *summa* and *confessionalia,* in which they drive and torment the people with contrition, confession, penance and satisfaction. Then they teach good works and preach good doctrine as they say, but not once do they hold up the Spirit and Christ to the afflicted consciences; so that now Christ is unknown to all the world, the gospel lies in a corner, and the whole ministry of the New Testament is suppressed. . . .

To preach the letter and the spirit gives us more to do than we are equal to, even if we began at the beginning of the world and kept on until doomsday.

RUDOLF BULTMANN

Is Exegesis Without Presuppositions Posssible?

Between Reformation exegesis and the modern era lies a revolution in biblical interpretation. Modern hermeneutics expanded the function of the traditional rules of interpretation to include theological and philosophical questions of *understanding*. Hermeneutics asks how the preacher or interpreter can assist twentieth century people to enter into the world of an ancient text in such a way that the modern reader appropriates what is alien. Rudolf Bultmann (1884–1976) posed this question to New Testament interpreters and devoted his scholarly life to answering it. In 1941 his essay "The New Testament and Mythology" outlined his famous program of demythologizing, which has continued as a focus of theological debate. Bultmann's intention was not to abolish New Testament teaching, as his critics insisted, but by means of philological, literary, and existentialist criticism to isolate its authentic kernel and to reinterpret it for a new age. In this enterprise he used Heidegger's philosophy to establish a preunderstanding of the problematic nature of human existence. Only the kerygma of the Crucified One, however, has the power to rescue humanity from inauthentic existence. Bultmann worked out his existentialist hermeneutic in the hope that it would make modern preaching more intelligible. He had learned from Schleiermacher that absolute objectivity in interpretation is impossible, and from Luther that the interpreter is finally justified by faith and not historical proof.

159

The question whether exegesis without presuppositions is possible must be answered affirmatively if "without presuppositions" means "without presupposing the results of the exegesis." In this sense, exegesis without presuppositions is not only possible but demanded. In another sense, however, *no* exegesis is without presuppositions, inasmuch as the exegete is not a *tabula rasa*, but on the contrary, approaches the text with specific questions or with a specific way of raising questions and thus has a certain idea of the subject matter with which the text is concerned.

The demand that exegesis must be without presuppositions, in the sense that it must not presuppose its results (we can also say that it must be without prejudice), may be clarified only briefly. This demand means, first of all, the rejection of all allegorical interpretation. When Philo finds the Stoic idea of the apathetic wise man in the prescription of the law that the sacrificial animal must be without blemish (*Spec. Neg.* I, 260), then it is clear that he does not hear what the text actually says, but only lets it say what he already knows. And the same thing is true of Paul's exegesis of Deut. 25:4 as a prescription that the preachers of the gospel are to be supported by the congregations (I Cor. 9:9) and of the interpretation in the Letter of Barnabas (9:7f.) of the 318 servants of Abraham (Gen. 14:14) as a prophecy of the cross of Christ.

However, even where allegorical interpretation is renounced, exegesis is frequently guided by prejudices. This is so, for example, when it is presupposed that the evangelists Matthew and John were Jesus' personal disciples and that therefore the narratives and sayings of Jesus that they hand down must be historically true reports. In this case, it must be affirmed, for instance, that the cleansing of the temple, which in Matthew is placed during Jesus' last days just before his passion, but in John stands at the beginning of his ministry, took place twice. The question of an unprejudiced exegesis becomes especially urgent when the problem of Jesus' Messianic consciousness is concerned. May exegesis of the Gospels be guided by the dogmatic presupposition that Jesus was the Messiah and was conscious of being so? Or must it rather leave this question open? The answer should be clear. Any such Messianic consciousness would be a historical fact and could only be exhibited as such by historical research. Were the latter able to make it probable that Jesus knew himself to be the Messiah, this result would have only relative certainty; for historical research can never endow it with absolute validity. All knowledge of a historical kind is subject to discussion, and therefore, the question as to whether Jesus knew himself as Messiah remains open.

Every exegesis that is guided by dogmatic prejudices does not hear what the text says, but only lets the latter say what it wants to hear.

The question of exegesis without presuppositions in the sense of un-prejudiced exegesis must be distinguished from this same question in the other sense in which it can be raised. And in this second sense, we must say that there cannot be any such thing as presuppositionless exegesis. That there is no such exegesis in fact, because every exegete is determined by his own individuality, in the sense of his special biases and habits, his gifts and his weaknesses, has no significance in principle. For in this sense of the word, it is precisely his "individuality" that the exegete ought to eliminate by educating himself to the kind of hearing that is interested in nothing other than the subject matter of which the text speaks. However, the one presupposition that cannot be dismissed is the historical method of interrogating the text. Indeed, exegesis as the interpretation of historical texts is a part of the science of history.

It belongs to the historical method, of course, that a text is interpreted in accordance with the rules of grammar and of the meaning of words. And closely connected with this, historical exegesis also has to inquire about the individual style of the text. The sayings of Jesus in the synoptics, for example, have a different style from the Johannine ones. But with this there is also given another problem with which exegesis is required to deal. Paying attention to the meaning of words, to grammar, and to style soon leads to the observation that every text speaks in the language of its time and of its historical setting. This the exegete must know; therefore, he must know the historical conditions of the language of the period out of which the text that he is to interpret has arisen. This means that for an understanding of the language of the New Testament the acute question is, "Where and to what extent is its Greek determined by the Semitic use of language?" Out of this question grows the demand to study apocalypticism, the rabbinic literature, and the Qumran texts, as well as the history of Hellenistic religion.

Examples at this point are hardly necessary, and I cite only one. The New Testament word *pneuma* is translated in German as "Geist." Thus it is understandable that the exegesis of the nineteenth century (e.g., in the Tübingen school) interpreted the New Testament on the basis of the idealism that goes back to ancient Greece, until Hermann Gunkel pointed out in 1888 that the New Testament *pneuma* meant something entirely different—namely, God's miraculous power and manner of action.

The historical method includes the presupposition that history is a unity in the sense of a closed continuum of effects in which individual events are connected by the succession of cause and effect. This does not mean that the process of history is determined by the casual law and that there are no free decisions of men whose actions determine the course of historical happenings. But even a free decision does not happen without a cause, without a motive; and the task of the historian is to come to know the motives of actions. All decisions and all deeds have their causes and consequences; and the historical method presupposes that it is possible in principle to exhibit these and their connection and thus to understand the whole historical process as a closed unity.

This closedness means that the continuum of historical happenings cannot be rent by the interference of supernatural, transcendent powers and that therefore there is no "miracle" in this sense of the word. Such a miracle would be an event whose cause did not lie within history. While, for example, the Old Testament narrative speaks of an interference by God in history, historical science cannot demonstrate such an act of God, but merely perceives that there are those who believe in it. To be sure, as historical science, it may not assert that such a faith is an illusion and that God has not acted in history. But it itself as science cannot perceive such an act and reckon on the basis of it; it can only leave every man free to determine whether he wants to see an act of God in a historical event that it itself understands in terms of that event's immanent historical causes.

It is in accordance with such a method as this that the science of history goes to work on all historical documents. And there cannot be any exceptions in the case of biblical texts if the latter are at all to be understood historically. Nor can one object that the biblical writings do not intend to be historical documents, but rather affirmations of faith and proclamation. For however certain this may be, if they are ever to be understood as such, they must first of all be interpreted historically, inasmuch as they speak in a strange language in concepts of a faraway time, of a world-picture that is alien to us. Put quite simply, they must be translated, and translation is the task of historical science.

If we speak of translation, however, then the hermeneutical problem at once presents itself. To translate means to make understandable, and this in turn presupposes an understanding. The understanding of history as a continuum of effects presupposes an understanding of the efficient forces that connect the individual historical phenomena. Such forces are economic needs, social exigencies, the political struggle for power, human passions, ideas, and ideals. In the assessment of such factors historians differ; and in every effort to achieve a unified point of view the individual historian is guided by some specific way of raising questions, some specific perspective.

This does not mean a falsification of the historical picture, provided that the perspective that is presupposed is not a prejudice, but a way of raising questions, and that the historian is self-conscious about the fact that his way of asking questions is one-sided and only comes at the phenomenon or the text from the standpoint of a particular perspective. The historical picture is falsified only when a specific way of raising questions is put forward as the only one—when, for example, all history is reduced to economic history. Historical phenomena are many-sided. Events like the Reformation can be observed from the standpoint of church history as well as political history, of economic history as well as the history of philosophy. Mysticism can be viewed from the standpoint of its significance for the history of art, etc. However, some specific way of raising questions is always presupposed if history is at all to be understood.

But even more, the forces that are effective in connecting phenomena are understandable only if the phenomena themselves that are thereby connected are also understood! This means that an understanding of the subject matter itself belongs to historical understanding. For can one understand political history without having a concept of the state and of justice, which by their very nature are not historical products but ideas? Can one understand economic history without having a concept of what economy and society in general mean? Can one understand the history of religion and philosophy without knowing what religion and philosophy are? One cannot understand Luther's posting of the ninety-five theses, for instance, without understanding the actual meaning of protest against the Catholicism of his time. One cannot understand the Communist Manifesto of 1848 without understanding the principles of capitalism and socialism. One cannot understand the decisions of persons who act in history if one does not understand man and his possibilities for action. In short, historical understanding presupposes an understanding of the subject matter of history itself and of the men who act in history.

This is also to say, however, that historical understanding always presupposes a relation of the interpreter to the subject matter that is (directly or indirectly) expressed in the texts. This relation is grounded in the actual life-context in which the interpreter stands. Only he who lives in a state and in a society can understand the political and social phenomena of the past and their history, just as only he who has a relation to music can understand a text that deals with music, etc.

Therefore, a specific understanding of the subject matter of the text, on the basis of a "life-relation" to it, is always presupposed by exegesis; and insofar as this is so no exegesis is without presuppositions. I speak of this

163

understanding as a "preunderstanding." It as little involves prejudice as does the choice of a perspective. For the historical picture is falsified only when the exegete takes his preunderstanding as a definitive understanding. The "life-relation" is a genuine one, however, only when it is vital, i.e., when the subject matter with which the text is concerned also concerns us and is a problem for us. If we approach history alive with our own problems, then it really begins to speak to us. Through discussion the past becomes alive, and in learning to know history we learn to know our own present; historical knowledge is at the same time knowledge of ourselves. To understand history is possible only for one who does not stand over against it as a neutral, nonparticipating spectator, but himself stands in history and shares in responsibility for it. We speak of this encounter with history that grows out of one's own historicity as the *existentiell* encounter. The historian participates in it with his whole existence.

This *existentiell* relation to history is the fundamental presupposition for understanding history. This does not mean that the understanding of history is a "subjective" one in the sense that it depends on the individual pleasure of the historian and thereby loses all objective significance. On the contrary, it means that history precisely in its objective content can only be understood by a subject who is *existentiell* moved and alive. It means that, for historical understanding, the schema of subject and object that has validity for natural science is invalid.

Now what has just been said includes an important insight—namely, that historical knowledge is never a closed or definitive knowledge—any more than is the preunderstanding with which the historian approaches historical phenomena. For if the phenomena of history are not facts that can be neutrally observed, but rather open themselves in their meaning only to one who approaches them alive with questions, then they are always only understandable now in that they actually speak in the present situation. Indeed, the questioning itself grows out of the historical situation, out of the claim of the now, out of the problem that is given in the now. For this reason, historical research is never closed, but rather must always be carried further. Naturally, there are certain items of historical knowledge that can be regarded as definitively known—namely, such items as concern only dates that can be fixed chronologically and locally, as, for example, the assassination of Caesar or Luther's posting of the ninety-five theses. But what these events that can thus be dated mean as historical events cannot be definitively fixed. Hence one must say that a historical event is always first knowable for what it is—precisely as a historical event—in the future. And therefore one can also say that the future of a historical event belongs to that event.

Naturally, items of historical knowledge can be passed on, not as definitively known, but in such a way as to clarify and expand the following generation's preunderstanding. But even so, they are subject to the criticism of that generation. Can we today surmise the meaning of the two world wars? No; for it holds good that what a historical event means always first becomes clear in the future. It can definitively disclose itself only when history has come to an end.

What are the consequences of this analysis for exegesis of the biblical writings? They may be formulated in the following theses:

(1) The exegesis of the biblical writings, like every other interpretation of a text, must be unprejudiced.

(2) However, the exegesis is not without presuppositions, because as historical interpretation it presupposes the method of historical-critical research.

(3) Furthermore, there is presupposed a "life-relation" of the exegete to the subject matter with which the Bible is concerned and, together with this relation, a preunderstanding.

(4) This preunderstanding is not a closed one, but rather is open, so that there can be an *existentiell* encounter with the text and an *existentiell* decision.

(5) The understanding of the text is never a definitive one, but rather remains open because the meaning of the Scriptures discloses itself anew in every future.

In the light of what has already been said, nothing further is required in the way of comment on the first and second theses.

As regards the third thesis, however, we may note that the preunderstanding has its basis in the question concerning God that is alive in human life. Thus it does not mean that the exegete must know everything possible about God, but rather that he is moved by the *existentiell* question for God—regardless of the form that this question actually takes in his consciousness (say, for example, as the question concerning "salvation," or escape from death, or certainty in the face of a constantly shifting destiny, or truth in the midst of a world that is a riddle to him).

With regard to the fourth thesis, we may note that the *existentiell* encounter with the text can lead to a yes as well as to a no, to confessing faith as well as to express unfaith, because in the text the exegete encounters a claim, i.e., is there offered a self-understanding that he can accept (permit to be given to him) or reject, and therefore is faced with the demand for decision. Even in the case of a no, however, the understanding is a legitimate one, i.e., is a genuine answer to the question of the text, which is not to be refuted by argument because it is an *existentiell* decision.

So far as the fifth thesis is concerned, we note simply that because the text speaks to existence it is never understood in a definitive way. The *existentiell* decision out of which the interpretation emerges cannot be passed on, but must always be realized anew. This does not mean, of course, that there cannot be continuity in the exegesis of Scripture. It goes without saying that the results of methodical historical-critical research can be passed on, even if they can only be taken over by constant critical testing. But even with respect to the exegesis that is based *existentiell* there is also continuity, insofar as it provides guidance for the next generation — as has been done, for example, by Luther's understanding of the Pauline doctrine of justification by faith alone. Just as this understanding must constantly be achieved anew in the discussion with Catholic exegesis, so every genuine exegesis that offers itself as a guide is at the same time a question that must always be answered anew and independently. Since the exegete exists historically and must hear the word of Scripture as spoken in his special historical situation, he will always understand the old word anew. Always anew it will tell him who he, man, is and who God is, and he will always have to express this word in a new conceptuality. Thus it is true also of Scripture that it only is what it is with its history and its future.

GERHARD EBELING

Word of God and Hermeneutics

The hermeneutical thought of Gerhard Ebeling (1912–), for many years professor of theology at the University of Zürich, owes much to the influence of his teacher, Rudolf Bultmann, as well as to Bonhoeffer and Luther. Like Bultmann, Ebeling's concern with hermeneutics is directly tied to preaching. Following Bonhoeffer (as well as colleague Ernst Fuchs), he seeks to "translate" biblical language into a nonreligious idiom. With Luther, he is preoccupied with the effectiveness of the word of God to illumine, address, and transform human beings. The term "New Hermeneutic" is often associated with Ebeling. Traditional interpretation sought to get control of the object under investigation, namely, the scriptural text. Ebeling understands the word of God as a dynamic act of transmission. It is not a passive or static entity to be brought under the interpreter's control but is "living and active, sharper than any two-edged sword, . . . discerning the thoughts and intentions of the heart" (Heb. 4:12). The essence of the word is interpretive. The interpreter, then, does not seek to understand the word but to understand human existence by means of the word, a process Paul Ricoeur terms the "archaeology of the subject." Preaching will not content itself with excavating the past and drawing contemporary applications. The traditional sequence of exegesis, exposition, and application is taken up by the new and broadened science of hermeneutics with the result that the interpreter/preacher "executes" the text. The written word is set free and allowed to become what it orginally was—a spoken word of address.

Gerhard Ebeling, *Word and Faith* (Philadelphia: Fortress Press, 1963), pp. 311–318, 327–331. Copyright © Fortress Press. Used by permission.

Whatever precise theological definition may be given to the concept of the word of God, at all events it points us to something that happens, viz. to the movement which leads from the text of holy Scripture to the sermon ("sermon" of course taken in the pregnant sense of proclamation in general). As a first definition of the concept of the word of God the reference to this movement from text to proclamation may suffice. For this is in fact according to Christian tradition the primary place of the concept of the word of God. We here set aside questions that probe behind that—why the holy Scripture that presses for proclamation or the proclamation that takes its stand on holy Scripture should be marked out in particular above other things as word of God; or what form of the word of God to some extent precedes Scripture; and whether the word of God is not found also outside the relation of text and sermon. For according to Christian conviction the answers to all these questions can be truly known only in connection with that movement from the text to the sermon. But it is of decisive importance to choose this movement as the starting-point for the definition of the concept of the word of God. . . .

Now if in the word of God we have a case of the word-event that leads from the text of holy Scripture to the proclamation, then the question is, whether hermeneutics can be expected to help towards that happening rightly. Here doubts arise at once. Can the event of the word of God be served at all by scientific methods? Must the hermeneutic approach as such not at once have a destructive effect on the concept of the word of God, as also on the corresponding concept of the Holy Spirit? But doubts, too, of a less radical kind also call in question the service of hermeneutics here. Can hermeneutics not deal only with an exposition which is subject to scientific criteria? Even then there are, as is well known, already great methodological difficulties. Now in so far as the sermon is preceded by a scientific exposition of the text, hermeneutics may also have significance for it. But then the question remains what the scientific exposition contributes to the sermon and what distinguishes it from the exposition that takes place in the sermon itself; whether it is appropriate to contrast the latter as "practical" exposition with the scientific kind and so withdraw it from the strict standpoint of hermeneutics, or to distinguish it as *applicatio* from the *explicatio* and thereby deny that the sermon in its essential nature is exposition at all, however much it may contain textual exposition. Yet is it not bringing the event of the word of God into dangerous isolation from word-events in general, if we withdraw it from the reach of hermeneutics? Indeed, is it not the case that the concept of the word of God can be used at all only when hermeneutic justification can be given for it? But what does "hermeneutics" then mean? Let us therefore attempt first of all a more precise clarification of the concept hermeneutics.

According to the common view there is a sharp distinction between exegesis as the process of exposition itself and hermeneutics as the theory of exposition. And here indeed it is assumed that verbal statements are the object of exposition, i.e., the thing requiring exposition. According to the several kinds of verbal statement, general hermeneutics may be differentiated into various special hermeneutics, though of course without departing from the comprehensive framework of general hermeneutics.

This customary view of hermeneutics requires correction in various respects.

On the threshold of the Enlightenment the "distinction of general and special hermeneutics" had taken the place of the very differently articulated Orthodox distinction of *hermeneutica sacra* and *hermeneutica profana*. The basic proposition that holy Scripture is not to be differently interpreted from other books seemed, it is true, now to allow of only one single science of hermeneutics and to relieve theology of any special discussion of the hermeneutic problem, indeed even to forbid it. But owing to the colorlessness and abstractness of the proposition of a general hermeneutics, it did not exclude the introduction of various special hermeneutics applied and related to concrete subjects, as long as these various special hermeneutics remained subject to and derived from general hermeneutic criteria. Indeed, modern hermeneutics developed at first almost entirely in the form of special hermeneutics of such kinds, in the construction of which theology played an outstanding part along with classical philology and jurisprudence. It can even be said that the principle of a single science of hermeneutics worked itself out in practice as the principle of an increasing hermeneutic specialization.

For theology this meant in the first instance that, although specifically theological hermeneutics disappeared, there arose within theology various hermeneutics in different degrees of specialization, such as biblical, Old Testament or New Testament hermeneutics, or (the demand for this at all events has already been made) in such a way that each biblical book requires a special hermeneutics. We must not let ourselves be deceived about the real nature of this state of affairs by, say, the fact that such extreme specialization was never realized, and that biblical or Old or New Testament hermeneutics owing to the theological dignity of these books at once gives the impression of theological hermeneutics. Strictly, however, the basic conception is, that there is no such thing as theological hermeneutics. For the differentiation in hermeneutics is held to be justified indeed from the standpoint of different literary complexes, but not on the basis of particular, non-universal epistemological principles such as those of theology. Thus hermeneutics in theology became the methodology of definite individual disciplines—viz. the biblical ones—and therewith at once the boundary separating them from dogmatics, which as such had nothing to do with hermeneutics.

The fact that in contrast to this, historical and systematic theology today join hands in the hermeneutic problem and hermeneutics has expanded to become the methodology no longer merely of individual theological disciplines but of theology as a whole, is to a great extent a distant result of Schleiermacher. For his pioneer view of hermeneutics as the theory of the conditions on which understanding is possible modified the relation of general and special hermeneutics in a twofold way.

First: a special hermeneutics must now take strict account of what can here be *differentia specifica*. The view which Schleiermacher himself here put forward in detail is doubtless obsolete. His basic demand, however, is still valid. The view emphatically advanced today by Bultmann that the difference as to what one is after in the interrogation has differentiating character in the hermeneutic sphere is a first step towards further clarification of this side of the hermeneutic problem—a step that is capable of being developed and certainly also stands in need of further development. This provides, without relapsing into an alleged *hermeneutica sacra*, the possibility of speaking of a hermeneutics related to theology as a whole, which on the basis of the specifically theological approach works out structures and criteria of theological understanding that apply in theology not only to the exegetical but also to the dogmatic understanding. It is absolutely necessary that this should then be done in demonstrable connection with a general theory of understanding. The nature of the connection, however, raises difficult problems.

The other impulse which Schleiermacher gave to the further history of hermeneutics is today discernible above all in a surprisingly extended use of the word "hermeneutics." It is not only that hermeneutics can now be spoken of in sciences in which it was not possible before and which do not have to do with texts at all but with phenomena—for example psychology. Rather, the development from Schleiermacher via Dilthey to Heidegger shows that the idea of a theory of understanding is on the move towards laying the foundation of the humanities, indeed even becomes the essence of philosophy, that hermeneutics now takes the place of the classical epistemological theory, and indeed that fundamental ontology appears as hermeneutics.

Thus outside of theology, too, hermeneutics today is breaking through the old, narrow bounds of philological or historiographical hermeneutics, or is plumbing their depths. For theology the hermeneutic problem is therefore today becoming the place of meeting with philosophy. And that always involves at the same time both community and contrast. This confirms once again that in an approach so radical as this there is point in speaking of theological hermeneutics without in any way refurbishing the division into *hermeneutica sacra* and *profana*.

The customary view that hermeneutics is the theory of the exposition of texts already seemed a moment ago to have undergone correction in that phenomena can also be objects of exposition. If we followed that further, then we should doubtless have to limit it to phenomena in so far as they have to do with the linguisticality of existence, and are thus "texts" in the wider sense. Hermeneutics would then also remain related to the word-event. But what is now to be held against the usual view is something other than that.

It is usually taken for granted that the reason why hermeneutics has to do with the word-event is, that verbal statements pose the problem of understanding. Now however much the need for hermeneutics does in fact arise primarily from difficulties of understanding in the word-event, it is nevertheless completely false to take this situation as the point of orientation for one's basic grasp of the relation between word and understanding and of what is ultimately constitutive for hermeneutics. The superficial view of understanding turns matters upside down and must therefore be completely reversed. The primary phenomenon in the realm of understanding is not understanding OF language, but understanding THROUGH language. The word is not really the object of understanding, and thus the thing that poses the problem of understanding, the solution of which requires exposition and therefore also hermeneutics as the theory of understanding. Rather, the word is what opens up and mediates understanding, i.e., brings something to understanding. The word itself has a hermeneutic function.

This opens up a deeper insight into the nature of the word-event. As communication word is promise. It is most purely promise when it refers to something that is not present but absent — and that, too, in such a way that in the promise the absent thing so to speak presents itself; that is, when in word the speaker pledges and imparts himself to the other and opens a future to him by awakening faith within him. The conjunction of God, word, faith, future as the prime necessity for the good of man's human nature requires to be understood as a single vast coherent complex and not as some sort of chance conglomeration to be accepted on positivist terms.

This word-event takes place, Christians confess, in the gospel. It is savingly related to the word-event which always proceeds from God and strikes the foolish man as the law which kills. But for that reason, too, it is only in the light of the gospel that we can grasp what God's word really means and how far the law is God's word. For God's word must not on any account be reduced to a formal concept which would be indifferent towards any intrinsic definition of the word of God. For God's word is not various things, but one single thing—the word that makes man human by making him a believer, i.e., a man who confesses to God as his future and therefore does not fail his fellowmen in the one absolutely necessary and salutary thing, viz. true word.

There is no need to state here the reasons why the proclamation of the word of God appeals to Scripture, and Scripture thus becomes the text of the sermon. I would merely go on to add in conclusion an explanation of how that happens, in what sense Scripture is the text of the sermon, and thus how text and sermon are related to each other.

We begin with the question: What is the aim of the text? It aims at all events to be preserved, read and handed on—and that, too, in the service of the proclamation. Here of course we should at once have to make differentiations, not only between Old and New Testament texts, but also in both cases between different degrees of explicitness with which the aim is proclamation. The question of the aim of the text could indeed be shifted from the individual text to the biblical canon as such. It would of course be a question whether the original intention of the canon would be done justice to by asserting that it aims at being a collection of sermon texts. But above all in face of the individual text it would be a doubtful proceeding to ignore that text itself where this basic question is concerned. It should not be supposed that any and every text in holy Scripture is in itself a sermon text. What is claimed to be a sermon text must at all events seek to serve the proclamation of the word of God. Yet it would not be right to say: the text seeks to be proclaimed. Apart from the fact that such a direct, authoritative aim is present in relatively few texts, that way of putting it would also be fundamentally wrong. For it is not texts that are to be proclaimed. Rather, it is God's word that is to be proclaimed, and that is one single word, but not words of God, not a variety of different texts.

Indeed, we must put a still sharper point on it: if the word-character of God's word is taken strictly, then it is absurd to designate a transmitted text as God's word. Not out of contempt for its content or for its being written, but rather precisely out of respect for both. It is of course entirely true of sermon texts by and large that they are concerned with proclamation that has taken place, and to that extent—if it was right proclamation—with past occurrence of the word of God. Naturally the form of direct speech on God's part cannot here rank as criterion. It is significant that with Jesus (apart from Christian imitations of the prophets) the stylistic form "Thus saith the Lord" ceases—a fact well worth bearing in mind for the doctrine of the word of God. But if it is a case of proclamation that has taken place, then we shall have to say of the sermon text: its aim is, that there should be further proclamation—and that, too, with an ear open towards the text, in agreement with it and under appeal to it.

The process from text to sermon can therefore be characterized by saying: proclamation that has taken place is to become proclamation that takes place. This transition from text to sermon is a transition from Scripture to the spoken word. Thus the task prescribed here consists in making what is written into spoken word or, as we can now also say, in letting the text become God's word again. That that does not normally happen through recitation, should surely be clear. If the concept of exposition can now be applied to this process, then we should have to say it is a question of interpreting the text *as word*.

But is the application of the concept "exposition" here not questionable? This misgiving is in fact justified. Yet we must be very careful in giving place to it. For it is manifestly true all the same that the movement from the text to the sermon is a hermeneutic process in which, indeed to an eminent degree, it is a case of understanding and bringing to understanding. It would undoubtedly be wrong to assert that this movement from the text to the sermon does not come within the scope of the hermeneutic problem as posed by that text. For if its aim is, that what it has proclaimed should be further proclaimed, then the hermeneutic task prescribed by the text in question is not only not left behind when we turn to the sermon, but is precisely then for the first time brought to its fullest explication. The problem of theological hermeneutics would not be grasped without the inclusion of the task of proclamation; it is not until then that it is brought decisively to a head at all. And that, too, because the biblical texts would not be rightly heard unless they were seen to present us with the task of proclamation. . . .

The sermon as such is in point of fact not *exposition* of the text—whereby exposition here means the concentration on the historical task of understanding. For to understand this text as a text means to understand it in its historical givenness as proclamation that has taken place. Now of course the sermon certainly does presuppose intensive efforts towards such understanding of the text. How could it otherwise appeal to it? And it contains also according to the particular circumstances a greater or less degree of explicit interpretation of the text. But the sermon as a sermon is not exposition of the text as past proclamation, but is itself proclamation in the present—and that means, then, that the sermon is EXECUTION of the text. It carries into execution the aim of the text. It is proclamation of what the text has proclaimed. And with that the hermeneutic sense of direction is so to speak reversed. The text which has attained understanding in the exposition now helps to bring to understanding what is to attain understanding by means of the sermon—which is (we can here state it briefly) the present reality *coram Deo*, and that means, in its radical futurity. Thus the text by means of the sermon becomes a hermeneutic aid in the understanding of present experience. Where that happens radically, there true word is uttered, and that in fact means God's word.

PAUL RICOEUR

The Hermeneutic Question

The thought of Paul Ricoeur (1913–   ) has enriched homiletical theory in many ways. His seminal work on metaphor has helped preaching to a clearer understanding of the difference between the derivative nature of illustration and the creative power of metaphor. His work in narrative and structuralism has undergirded preaching's renewed appreciation of story as a powerful instrument of proclamation. His theory of symbol as that which is rooted in the cosmos has led preaching to seek expression of the archetypal beneath the surface of both doctrine and experience. It is in the field of hermeneutics, however, where Ricoeur's work comes into direct dialogue with homiletical theology. No summary can do justice to the complexities of his hermeneutical philosophy. Like Bultmann, Ricoeur's investigations in hermeneutics include an analysis of the relation of the interpreter to the thing interpreted. As in Bultmann, hermeneutics is nothing less than the science of human understanding, the equivalent of philosophy itself. Both men reject the 19th century's notion of hermeneutics as a quest for the original author's psyche or life-experience. In the final analysis, both Bultmann and Ricoeur subject themselves to the power and authority of *texts*. Ricoeur writes, "The sense of the text is not behind the text, but in front of it. It is not something hidden but something disclosed. What has to be understood is not the initial situation of discourse, but what points towards a possible world" (*Interpretation Theory*, p. 87). The following selection is from his "Preface to Bultmann" in which Ricoeur outlines three ways in which Christianity is concerned with hermeneutics.

Paul Ricoeur, *The Conflict of Interpretations* (Evanston: Northwestern University Press, 1974), pp. 381–388. Copyright © Northwestern University Press. Used by permission.

Although there has always been a hermeneutic problem in Christianity, the hermeneutic question today seems to us a new one. What does this situation mean, and why does it seem marked with this initial paradox?

There has always been a hermeneutic problem in Christianity because Christianity proceeds from a proclamation. It begins with a fundamental preaching that maintains that in Jesus Christ the kingdom has approached us in decisive fashion. But this fundamental preaching, this word, comes to us through writings, through the Scriptures, and these must constantly be restored as the living word if the primitive word that witnessed to the fundamental and founding event is to remain contemporary. If hermeneutics in general is, in Dilthey's phrase, the interpretation of expressions of life fixed in written texts, then hermeneutics deals with the unique relation between the Scriptures and what they refer to, the *kerygma* (the proclamation).

This relation between writing and the word and between the word and the event and its meaning is the crux of the hermeneutic problem. But this relation itself appears only through a series of interpretations. These interpretations constitute the history of the hermeneutic problem and even the history of Christianity itself, to the degree that Christianity is dependent upon its successive readings of Scripture and on its capacity to reconvert this Scripture into the living word. Certain characteristics of what can be called the hermeneutic situation of Christianity have not even been perceived until our time. These traits are what makes the hermeneutic problem a modern problem.

Let us try to chart this hermeneutic situation, in a more systematic than historical way. Three moments can be distinguished here which have developed successively, even though implicitly they are contemporaneous.

The hermeneutic problem first arose from a question which occupied the first Christian generations and which held the fore even to the time of the Reformation. This question is: what is the relation between the two Testaments or between the two Covenants? Here the problem of allegory in the Christian sense was constituted. Indeed, the Christ-event is hermeneutically related to all of Judaic Scripture in the sense that it interprets this Scripture. Hence, before it can be interpreted itself—and there is our hermeneutic problem—the Christ-event is already an interpretation of a preexisting Scripture.

Let us understand this situation well. Originally, there were not, properly speaking, two Testaments, two Scriptures; there was one Scripture and one event. And it is this event that makes the entire Jewish economy appear ancient, like an old letter. But there is a hermeneutic problem because this novelty is not purely and simply substituted for the ancient letter; rather, it remains ambiguously related to it. The novelty abolishes the Scripture and fulfills it. It changes its letter into spirit like water into wine. Hence the Christian fact is itself understood by effecting a mutation of meaning inside the ancient Scripture. The first Christian hermeneutics is this mutation itself. It is entirely contained in the relation between the letter, the history (these words are synonyms), of the old Covenant and the spiritual meaning which the gospel reveals after the event. Hence this relation can be expressed quite well in allegorical terms. It can resemble the allegorizing of the Stoics or that of Philo, or it can adopt the quasi-Platonic language of the opposition between flesh and spirit, between shadow and true reality. But what is at issue here is basically something else. It is a question of the typological value of the events, things, persons, and institutions of the old economy in relation to those of the new. Saint Paul creates this Christian allegory. Everyone knows the interpretation of Hagar and Sarah, the two wives of Abraham, and of their lineage. In their regard the Epistle to the Galatians says: "These things are said allegorically." The word "allegory" here has only a literary resemblance to the allegory of the grammarians, which, Cicero tells us, "consists in saying one thing to make something else understood." Pagan allegory served to reconcile myths with philosophy and consequently to reduce them as myths. But Pauline allegory, together with that of Tertullian and Origen, which depend on it, is inseparable from the mystery of Christ. Stoicism and Platonism will furnish only a language, indeed a compromising and misleading surplus.

Hence there is hermeneutics in the Christian order because the kerygma is the rereading of an ancient Scripture. It is noteworthy that orthodoxy has resisted with all its force the currents, from Marcion to Gnosticism, which wanted to cut the gospel from its hermeneutic bond to the Old Testament. Why? Would it not have been simpler to proclaim the event in its unity and thus to deliver it from the ambiguities of the Old Testament interpretation? Why has Christian preaching chosen to be hermeneutic by binding itself to the rereading of the Old Testament? Essentially to make the event itself appear, not as an irrational irruption, but as the fulfillment of an antecedent meaning which remained in suspense. The event itself receives a temporal density by being inscribed in a signifying relation of "promise" to "fulfillment." By entering in this way into a historical connection, the event enters also into an intelligible liaison. A contrast is set up between the two Testaments, a contrast which at the same time is a harmony by means of a transfer. This signifying relation attests that the kerygma, by this detour through the reinterpretation of an ancient Scripture, enters into a network of intelligibility. The event becomes advent. In taking on time, it takes on meaning. By understanding itself indirectly, in terms of the transfer from the old to the new, the event presents itself as an understanding of relations. Jesus Christ himself, exegesis and exegete of Scripture, is manifested as logos in opening the understanding of the Scriptures.

Such is the fundamental hermeneutics of Christianity. It coincides with the spiritual understanding of the Old Testament. Of course, the spiritual meaning is the New Testament itself; but because of this detour through a deciphering of the Old Testament, "faith is not a cry" but an understanding.

The second root of the hermeneutic problem is also Pauline. This is so even though it did not reach its full growth until very recently and, in certain respects, only with the moderns, specifically with Bultmann. This idea is that the interpretation of the Book and the interpretation of life correspond and are mutually adjusted. Saint Paul creates this second modality of Christian hermeneutics when he invites the hearer of the word to decipher the movement of his own existence in the light of the passion and resurrection of Christ. Hence, the death of the old man and the birth of the new creature are understood under the sign of the cross and the paschal victory. But their hermeneutic relation has a double meaning. Death and resurrection receive a new interpretation through the detour of this exegesis of human existence. The "hermeneutic circle" is already there, between the meaning of Christ and the meaning of existence which mutually decipher each other.

Thanks to the admirable work of de Lubac on the "four meanings" of Scripture—historical, allegorical, moral, anagogical—the breadth of this mutual interpretation of Scripture and existence is known. Beyond this simple reinterpretation of the old Covenant and the typological correlation between the two Testaments, medieval hermeneutics pursued the coincidence between the understanding of the faith in the *lectio divina* and the understanding of reality as a whole, divine and human, historical and physical. The hermeneutic task, then, is to broaden the comprehension of the text on the side of doctrine, of practice, of meditation on the mysteries. And consequently it is to equate the understanding of meaning with a total interpretation of existence and of reality in the system of Christianity. In short, hermeneutics understood this way is coextensive with the entire economy of Christian existence. Scripture appears here as an inexhaustible treasure which stimulates thought about everything, which conceals a total interpretation of the world. It is hermeneutics because the letter serves as foundation, because exegesis is its instrument, and also because the other meanings are related to the first in the way that the hidden is related to the manifest. In this way the understanding of Scripture somehow enrolls all the instruments of culture—literary and rhetorical, philosophical and mystical. To interpret Scripture is at the same time to amplify its meaning as sacred meaning and to incorporate the remains of secular culture in this understanding. It is at this price that Scripture ceases to be a limited cultural object: explication of texts and exploration of mysteries coincide. This is the aim of hermeneutics in this second sense: to make the global sense of mystery coincide with a differentiated and articulated discipline of meaning. It is to equate the *multiplex intellectus* with the *intellectus de mysterio Christi*.

Now, among the "four meanings" of Scripture, the Middle Ages made a place for the "moral meaning," which marks the application of the allegorical meaning to ourselves and our morals. The "moral meaning" shows that hermeneutics is much more than exegesis in the narrow sense. Hermeneutics is the very deciphering of life in the mirror of the text. Although the function of allegory is to manifest the newness of the gospel in the oldness of the letter, this newness vanishes if it is not a daily newness, if it is not new *hic et nunc*. Actually, the function of the moral sense is not to draw morals from Scripture at all, to moralize history, but to assure the correspondence between the Christ-event and the inner man. It is a matter of interiorizing the spiritual meaning, of actualizing it, as Saint Bernard says, of showing that it extends *hodie usque ad nos*, "even to us today." This is why the true role of moral meaning comes after allegory. This correspondence between allegorical meaning and our existence is well expressed by the metaphor of the mirror. It is a matter of deciphering our existence according to its conformity with Christ. We can still speak of interpretation because, on the one hand, the mystery contained in the book is made explicit in our experience and its actuality is confirmed here, and because, on the other hand, we understand ourselves in the mirror of the word. The relation between the text and the mirror—*liber et speculum*—is basic to hermeneutics.

This is the second dimension of Christian hermeneutics.

The third root of the hermeneutic problem in Christianity was not fully recognized and understood until the moderns—until the critical methods borrowed from the secular sciences of history and philology had been applied to the Bible as a whole. Here we return to our initial question: how is it that the hermeneutic problem is so old and so modern? Actually this third root of our problem relates to what can be called the hermeneutic situation itself of Christianity, that is, it is related to the primitive constitution of the Christian kerygma. We must return, in fact, to the witness character of the gospel. The kerygma is not first of all the interpretation of a text; it is the announcement of a person. In this sense, the word of God is, not the Bible, but Jesus Christ. But a problem arises continually from the fact that this kerygma is itself expressed in a witness, in the stories, and soon after in the texts that contain the very first confession of faith of the community. These texts conceal a first level of interpretation. We ourselves are no longer those witnesses who have seen. We are the hearers who listen to the witnesses: *fides ex auditu*. Hence, we can believe only by listening and by interpreting a text which is itself already an interpretation. In short, our relation, not only to the Old Testament, but also to the New Testament itself, is a hermeneutic relation.

This hermeneutic situation is as primitive as the two others because the gospel is presented from the time of the second generation as a writing, as a new letter, a new Scripture, added to the old in the form of a collection of writings which will one day be gathered up and enclosed in a canon, the "Canon of Scriptures." The source of our modern hermeneutic problem, then, is this: the kerygma is also a Testament. To be sure, it is new, as we said above; but it is a Testament, that is, a new Scripture. Hence the New Testament must also be interpreted. It is not simply an interpreting with regard to the Old Testament, and an interpreting for life and for reality as a whole; it is itself a text to be interpreted.

But this third root of the hermeneutic problem, the hermeneutic situation itself, has somehow been masked by the two other functions of hermeneutics in Christianity. So long as the New Testament served to decipher the Old, it was taken as an absolute norm. And it remains an absolute norm as long as its literal meaning serves as an indisputable basis on which all the other levels of meaning—the allegorical, moral, and anagogical—are constructed. But the fact is that the literal meaning is itself a text to be understood, a letter to be interpreted.

Let us reflect on this discovery. At first glance it may seem to be a product of our modernity, that is, something which could have been discovered only recently. This is true, for reasons which will be mentioned later. But these reasons themselves refer us back to a fundamental structure which, despite its having been recently discovered, nonetheless was present from the beginning. This discovery is a product of our modernity in the sense that it expresses the backlash of the critical disciplines—philology and history—on the sacred texts. As soon as the whole Bible is treated like the *Iliad* or the Presocratics, the letter is desacralized and the Bible is made to appear as the word of humans. In the same way, the relation "human word/word of God" is placed, no longer between the New Testament and the rest of the Bible, no longer even between the New Testament and the rest of culture, but at the very heart of the New Testament. For the believer, the New Testament itself conceals a relation that needs deciphering. This relation is between what can be understood and received as word of God and what is heard as human speaking.

This insight is the fruit of the scientific spirit, and in this sense it is a recent acquisition. But reflection brings us to discover in the first hermeneutic situation of the gospel the ancient reason for this later discovery. This situation, we have said, is that the gospel itself has become a text, a letter. As a text, it expresses a difference and a distance, however minimal, from the event that it proclaims. This distance, always increasing with time, is what separates the first witness from the entire line of those who hear the witness. Our modernity means only that the distance is now considerable between the place I myself occupy at the center of a culture and the original site of the first witness. This distance, of course, is not only spatial; it is above all a temporal one. But the distance is given at the beginning. It is the very first distance between the hearer and the witness of the event.

Thus the somehow accidental distance of a twentieth-century man, situated in another, a scientific and historical culture, reveals an original distance which remained concealed because it was so short; yet it was already constitutive of primitive faith itself. This distance has only become more manifest, particularly since the work of the *Formgeschichte* school. This school has made us conscious of the fact that the witnesses gathered in the New Testament are not only individual witnesses—free witnesses, one might say; they are already situated in a believing community, in its cult, its preaching, and the expression of its faith. To decipher Scripture is to decipher the witness of the apostolic community. We are related to the object of its faith through the confession of its faith. Hence, by understanding its witness, I receive equally, in its witness, what is summons, kerygma, "the good news."

I hope this reflection has shown that hermeneutics has for us moderns a sense that it did not have for the Greek or Latin Fathers, for the Middle Ages, or even for the Reformers, that the very development of the word "hermeneutics" indicates a "modern" sense of hermeneutics. This modern meaning of hermeneutics is only the discovery, the manifestation, of the hermeneutic situation which was present from the beginning of the gospel but hidden. It is not paradoxical to defend the thesis that the two ancient forms of hermeneutics we have described have contributed to concealing what was radical in the Christian hermeneutic situation. The meaning and function of our modernity is to unveil, by means of the distance which today separates our culture from ancient culture, what has been unique and extraordinary in this hermeneutic situation since the beginning.

JUAN LUIS SEGUNDO

The Hermeneutic Circle

In the liberation theology of Juan Luis Segundo (1925-   ) the hermeneutical "place" of the interpreter is accorded great importance. Segundo was born in Montevideo and has spent most of his life and ministry in Uruguay. He has not been a university teacher in his native land but has forged his theology under conditions of political repression in Catholic communities of lay people. Segundo enlarges the hermeneutical circle so that it encompasses more than Schleiermacher's psychological affinity with the original author or Bultmann's philosophical and theological preunderstanding. Segundo's circle includes the social and political environment (and its attendant ideologies) in which the interpreter reads the text. It should be no secret by now that such environment has the potential to dictate the "meaning" of a passage of Scripture. The poor read the Bible differently than the rich—an assertion dramatically documented by Ernesto Cardenal in *The Gospel in Solentiname*. This social reality calls forth "ideological suspicion" which in turn scrutinizes both theology and exegesis. The new hermeneutic of suspicion poses several questions to all preachers, regardless of nationality: What cultural biases attend the historical-critical method as received from nineteenth and twentieth century German scholarship? To what extent do our sermons bear a hidden ideological agenda—the prevailing socio-political values of our group? What groups or individuals are thereby excluded or rendered voiceless by these values? Does our preaching adequately reflect the needs of the outsiders or forgotten hearers whose economic status or political values differ from our own?

Juan Luis Segundo, *Liberation of Theology*, trans. John Drury (Maryknoll, N.Y.: Orbis Books, 1976), pp. 7-9. Copyright © Orbis Books. Used by permission.

We cannot start with the chicken and the egg, so let us start with the reality of everyday life and consider whether it is possible to differentiate the attitudes of a liberation theologian from those of some other theologian on that basis.

My past and present experience has taught me that theology, for all the changes that may have taken place, continues to be taught in an autonomous way. And this is true not only with respect to future professors of theology but also with respect to average people who will only use theology vis-à-vis the real-life problems that face ordinary people.

In mentioning this autonomy of theology I am referring to a long tradition in the Christian churches. Christianity is a *biblical* religion. It is the religion of a *book*, of various books if you will, for that is precisely what the word "bible" means. This means that theology for its part cannot swerve from its path in this respect. It must keep going back to its book and reinterpreting it. Theology is not an interpretation of mankind and society, not in the first place at least.

Attached as it is to a book, theology does not assert its independence from the past or from the sciences which help it to understand the past: e.g., general history, the study of ancient languages and cultures, the history of biblical forms, and the history of biblical redaction. On the other hand theology does implicitly or explicitly assert its independence from the sciences that deal with the present.

For example, a theologian as progressive as Schillebeeckx can arrive at the conclusion that theology can never be ideological—in the Marxist sense of the term—because it is nothing but the application of the divine word to present-day reality. He seems to hold the naive belief that the word of God is applied to human realities inside some antiseptic laboratory that is totally immune to the ideological tendencies and struggles of the present day.

Now a liberation theologian is one who starts from the opposite end. His suspicion is that anything and everything involving ideas, including theology, is intimately bound up with the existing social situation in at least an unconscious way.

Thus the fundamental difference between the traditional academic theologian and the liberation theologian is that the latter feels compelled at every step to combine the disciplines that open up the past with the disciplines that help to explain the present. And he feels this necessity precisely in the task of working out and elaborating theology, that is to say, in the task of interpreting the word of God as it is addressed to us here and now.

Without this connection between past and present there is no theology

184

of liberation in the long run. You might get a theology which *deals with* liberation, but its methodological naiveté would prove to be fatal somewhere alone the line. It would eventually be reabsorbed by the deeper mechanisms of oppression – one of these being the tendency to incorporate the idiom of liberation into the prevailing language of the status quo.

In this book I am going to try to show that an approach which attempts to relate past and present in dealing with the word of God has to have its own special methodology. I shall give this special methodology a pretentious name and call it the *hermeneutic circle*. Here is a preliminary definition of the hermeneutic circle: it is the continuing change in our interpretation of the Bible which is dictated by the continuing changes in our present-day reality, both individual and societal. "Hermeneutic" means "having to do with interpretation." And the circular nature of this interpretation stems from the fact that each new reality obliges us to interpret the word of God afresh, to change reality accordingly, and then to go back and reinterpret the word of God again, and so on.

The term "hermeneutic circle" is used in a strict sense to designate the method used by Bultmann in interpreting the Scriptures, and the New Testament in particular. At first glance it might seem that my use of the term here is less rigorous. But I hope to show, and the reader will be able to judge this, that my "hermeneutic circle" deserves that designation far more strictly than does Bultmann's. But first I must spell out in greater detail what I am referring to in concrete terms.

I think that two preconditions must be met if we are to have a hermeneutic circle in theology. The first precondition is that the questions rising out of the present be rich enough, general enough, and basic enough to force us to change our customary conceptions of life, death, knowledge, society, politics, and the world in general. Only a change of this sort, or at the very least a pervasive suspicion about our ideas and value judgments concerning these things, will enable us to reach the theological level and force theology to come back down to reality and ask itself new and decisive questions.

The second precondition is intimately bound up with the first. If theology somehow assumes that it can respond to the new questions without changing its customary interpretation of the Scriptures, that immediately terminates the hermeneutic circle. Moreover, if our interpretation of Scripture does not change along with the problems, then the latter will go unanswered; or worse, they will receive old, conservative, unserviceable answers.

It is most important to realize that without a hermeneutic circle, in other words, in those instances where the two aforementioned preconditions are not accepted, theology is always a conservative way of thinking and acting. It is so not so much because of its content but because in such a case it lacks any *here-and-now* criteria for judging our real situation. It thus becomes a pretext for approving the existing situation or for disapproving of it because it does not dovetail with guidelines and canons that are even more ancient and outdated.

It is my feeling that the most progressive theology in Latin America is more interested in *being liberative* than in *talking about liberation*. In other words, liberation deals not so much with content as with the method used to theologize in the face of our real-life situation.

In this chapter I shall present four sample attempts at fashioning a hermeneutic circle. But first I think it would be wise for me to reiterate the two preconditions for such a circle. They are: (1) profound and enriching questions and suspicions about our real situation; (2) a new interpretation of the Bible that is equally profound and enriching. These two preconditions mean that there must in turn be four decisive factors in our circle. Firstly there is our way of experiencing reality, which leads us to ideological suspicion. Secondly there is the application of our ideological suspicion to the whole ideological superstructure in general and to theology in particular. Thirdly there comes a new way of experiencing theological reality that leads us to exegetical suspicion, that is, to the suspicion that the prevailing interpretation of the Bible has not taken important pieces of data into account. Fourthly we have our new hermeneutic, that is, our new way of interpreting the fountainhead of our faith (i.e., Scripture) with the new elements at our disposal.

JAMES A. SANDERS

Contextual Hermeneutics

Recent studies in hermeneutics have reminded preachers of the philosophical, political, ideological, or sexual lens through which the Bible may be interpreted for preaching. James A. Sanders (1927–) does not minimize the importance of the external context of interpretation but, like Ricoeur, encourages preachers to recover the internal hermeneutic at work within the canon itself. Sanders, who is Professor of Intertestamental and Biblical Studies at the School of Theology, Claremont, California, calls attention to the layers of interpretation and reinterpretation in the Bible and cites these as warrant for the church's continuing interpretive activity. When a preacher applies a text to a contemporary situation, he or she is often engaging in a process not unlike the original author's handling of the received tradition. Our continuity with the Bible lies in our participation on the continuum of interpretation which extends from biblical times into the future. The Bible is not a casket of gems, or timeless truths, but a paradigm for faith, life, and interpretation. Two theological principles guide the preacher's interpretation of texts. The first is prophetic critique, which dwells on God's creative freedom, a freedom to be God above all people and institutions. The second he calls constitutive hermeneutics, or the principle of covenantal love, by which God binds himself to a particular people. Although Sanders believes that contemporary culture requires prophetic critique, he makes it clear that both principles are necessary to a faithful explication of God's word. Sanders' terms recall Luther's vocabulary of judgment and promise, law and gospel, and underscore the necessity of a theological framework for preaching from the Bible. The following selection is a part of the author's introduction to a collection of his sermons.

Hermeneutics is of two main sorts. One involves the exegetic tools which have been developed by biblical scholars over the past two centuries in order to recover points originally scored in Bible times by the biblical authors and theologians themselves. These are the "principles, rules, and techniques whereby the interpreter of a text attempts to understand it in its original context." These include all the biblical "criticisms"—text criticism, source criticism, form criticism, tradition criticism, redaction criticism, and canonical criticism—as well as philology and archaeology. These tools have been developed and honed over the past two hundred years and continue to develop. They are focused on both the ancient text and the ancient context.

That meaning, however, is not the one most have in mind when they speak today of hermeneutics. When one hears the term today, outside of such strictly defined Old Testament or New Testament exegetical settings as a seminary class or a meeting of Bible scholars, it usually refers to the second main sort of hermeneutics: those means used to translate a thought or event from one cultural context (from an ancient text) to another (our modern times). This is a sane and sage recognition of the fact that both the ancient writer and the modern interpreter are conditioned by the cultures in which they lived or live. There has to be some kind of conversion key, as it were, to bring the one over into the other if the integrity of the text is to be honored and somehow preserved, and if that text is to be heard at all by the modern listener.

First, then, we try to understand the text in its original context; that requires scientific, exegetic tools of the first sort of hermeneutics. Then we try to understand it in our own context; that is the second sort. The number of people with the expertise to do the former is somewhat limited. But the fruit of their labors is available in books and commentaries published by denominational and secular publishing houses. Part of the reason the churches are asked to support their seminaries in modern times is to support the trained scholars who often teach in those seminaries so that they can do the research and publishing necessary to make that expertise available to the pastors, teachers, and layfolk in the churches.

There are not many people abroad who can engage equally well in both sorts of hermeneutics. Indeed, there is a widespread attitude of dichotomy among both scholars and interpreters which causes people to assume that no one person can do both. . . .

In part because of such dichotomy of thinking Bible scholars have sometimes left the second sort of hermeneutics to folk outside their professional guild. A notable exception has been Rudolf Bultmann, a great New Testament scholar who has spent a great deal of his professional life developing the second sort of hermeneutics. A good many of his students and grand-students have continued his work, agreeing with him and disagreeing with him, trying to work out valid modern enlightenment modes of hermeneutics whereby to render the New Testament messages potent and pertinent today. But aside from such efforts on the part of some Bible scholars most work of the second sort has been done by philosophers and theologians. And all of them tend to import their hermeneutics to the Bible from modern thought forms. There has been some confusion therefore, between hermeneutics – the means of converting ancient thought to contemporary thought forms – and those contemporary thought forms which receive the ancient.

Just as linguists speak of modern "receptor languages" into which ancient texts are translated, so we can speak of modern "receptor thought forms" into which ancient thought forms are rendered by hermeneutics. It is in part the thesis of this book that a valid hermeneutic we might use in interpreting the Bible today can be derived from the biblical experience itself, and not imported from the outside.

The first sort of hermeneutics of which we have spoken, the scholarly tools developed over the past two hundred years which help us recover the points originally scored back in biblical times, has now reached the point in its own development that we are able, to a greater or lesser degree, depending on the passage involved, to recover not only the original points scored but in many cases to recover the hermeneutics used by the biblical thinkers and authors! This was not possible until the development of modern biblical criticism, and even then has become feasible only in very recent times as biblical criticism has improved its tools. Those tools continue to need experimentation and improvement. And at times they fail us. They especially fail us when they become ends in themselves. But they provide us now with the possibility of recovering, in many passages, the hermeneutics used in antiquity when still more ancient traditions were contemporized.

One of the most fruitful newer emphases in biblical study is to begin work on a biblical passage by locating in it citations from or allusions to older traditions which the author called on in advancing his own argument or theme. Sometimes in a New Testament passage there are rather full citations of an Old Testament passage, but often the text has been modified and altered by the New Testament author to suit his or her argument. Sometimes the New Testament author simply used a text of the Old Testament different from those we have, but more often than not the later author actually adapted the older text to the new purposes.

Sometimes the later author simply wove Old Testament traditions into the argument by using familiar Old Testament phrases or themes or ideas. Once such references have been identified, then one begins work on *how* the later author adapted them and made the Old Testament traditions relevant to problems in the early churches. Such re-presentation of older traditions begins of course way back in Old Testament times. Most Jewish literature dating from after the middle of the sixth century B.C.E. was composed in the terms and accents of older traditions. To recover the hermeneutics employed by the biblical author on the tradition cited or alluded to we need to know as much as possible about the ancient context for which the author was writing so as to reconstruct as nearly as possible the concerns of the congregation or community among whom or for whom the author wrote. This is not always possible, and where possible is rarely precise. But there are tools for doing so and they are improving.

The Bible is full of such unrecorded hermeneutics because it is itself so full of re-presented tradition. New Testament study has until recently tended to pay minimal attention to the Old Testament in the New. For some students there seemed to be regret over the amount of good New Testament space taken up and lost in quoting the Old. It was part of the centuries-long Christian conviction in many quarters that the New Testament had superseded the Old. Now we realize what a mine of information can be gained by focusing attention, initially, on the hermeneutic question of an ancient text. A question some of us are asking is whether such unrecorded biblical hermeneutics may not be as important for the churches and synagogues today as anything expressly stated in the Bible. The answer to that question depends in part on one's view of the ontology of the Bible, its nature. If one views the Bible primarily as a source of wisdom, a casket of ancient gems still negotiable today, then the answer is likely to be no. But if one views the Bible primarily as a paradigm, to be applied dynamically to modern idioms and verbs, then the answer is quite likely to be yes, for then we want to learn how they back there, right in the canonical literature itself, dynamically applied their own prior traditions to their day.

The question might arise at this point as to why we should go to all the trouble of recovering the points they scored back then. Is it not the nature of canon, as we say, to be adaptable, and if so why can we not just read it directly for ourselves without bothering to find out how it functioned or what it said specifically back then? There are some very wise and sane people who are saying this today. There is a new group of biblical interpreters who call themselves structuralists. They disdain the use of biblical criticism and focus on the overall structure of a biblical passage no matter when or how it was first composed, or for what purpose. One might rightly point out that the biblical authors themselves did not rehash the original meaning of the traditions or scripture they cited; usually they simply interpreted the tradition quite directly for their own time. There are interesting exceptions, but for the most part the biblical authors sought value in the tradition directly rather than recovering the points it first scored and then applying those points to their time.

It is generally a trait of our post-Enlightenment era to seek original points of traditional material. In fact, it is quite possible to think that biblical criticism has gone too far in its tendency to find authority only in the most primitive meaning of a passage; in this respect it has been a bit antiquarian. Canonical criticism has opened the way to understand the pluralism of how a single tradition may have as many different meanings as there are allusions to it or citations of it in the Bible itself—and how the most primitive is not the only authoritative one.

But neither is the meaning we may discern out of our immediate modern contexts the only authoritative one. On the contrary, unless there are firm exegetic controls applied in reading a text, it is possible that we might never hear what Jeremiah or Jesus said, or what their first hearers understood them to say. The points originally scored by the biblical thinkers and authors gave rise to the very process of preservation of the biblical materials we inherit. No one started out to write a biblical book with such authority that it would be accepted by the several early believing communities. What the original thinker said must have been valuable enough to be remembered and then passed on. We are sophisticated enough to know that what a person intended to communicate and what was heard and understood even by those immediately present may be two quite different things. Then of course the reasons for preserving the material and the reasons the first subsequent generation also found it valuable may have been quite different. What Baruch understood Jeremiah to say in Jerusalem before the Temple fell and what the exiles understood a repetition of his message to mean for them a decade or two later may have been quite different. The factor of context in understanding a text is very important indeed. In fact, recognition of the factor of modern context in reading an ancient text is important if we want to recover the points originally scored. We need to be aware of our own needs and what they do to us when we formulate our questions to pose to an ancient text.

Even scholars, or especially scholars, need to be aware of their own limitations in this regard. A cursory review of the history of biblical criticism in the past two hundred years is informative in this regard. We can now see how the questions which interested scholars in the eighteenth century, or in the nineteenth century, or early in the twentieth, influenced the way they saw a text. Knowledge of such a history of shifting interest and method in scholarly work raises our own consciousness as to what questions we are now asking and makes us aware of the methods we are using. We have only recently been released from the almost unconscious hermeneutic of evolutionism. Interest in this sort of self-criticism has arisen only recently, parallel to the new discipline called the sociology of knowledge. One observation which results from such a review of the past two hundred years is that modern scholarship has lines of continuity with earlier pre-Enlightenment scholarship: We are all human and subject to the Zeitgeist of our times. Another observation such a review affords is that each generation in one way or another felt that it had a special claim on truth, that history was to some degree culminating in its work. With the new sociology of knowledge, and in part because of it, we are in danger of thinking that we are liberated from the earlier tendencies and that we truly have a corner on truth! That is the Catch-22 aspect of intellectual endeavor.

We can all read into a text what we need to find there. Biblical criticism at its best, employed circumspectly, is the best means of avoiding abuse of the Bible. For all our observations that we are all human, scholarship has developed tools over the past two hundred years that can help us recover, to a good degree of probability, the thoughts and understandings of ancient folk. And there is perhaps no field of literary scholarship that is more scrupulously circumspect than biblical criticism. Most folk engaged in it have their identity in some modern denominational form of its traditions (Jewish, Muslim, or Christian), and most of us are extra careful in this regard, more so perhaps than when we work on Ugarit literature or Homer or Herodotus. Indeed, the reaction of some people in the churches and in theology is that we have been too scrupulous: with our methods and tools we have tended to lock the Bible into the past, we have become antiquarian.

Even so the tools developed are very valuable and can now be employed to recover the points originally scored within the biblical orbit (that is, the understandings of a "text" not only when first spoken or written but also in the generations and contexts immediately following, within the range of biblical history). It is only by so doing that we can also recover the hermeneutics of the biblical authors and thinkers themselves. Anytime they contemporized a tradition in their time, they used

192

hermeneutics. The time has now arrived in biblical scholarship to work on those hermeneutics; and we can do so only by using all the tools of biblical scholarship to gauge how the most ancient texts functioned in the less ancient contexts. That requires discerning the ancient contexts and the needs of the earliest believing communities who heard the actual biblical thinkers as much as it requires discerning the ancient texts. We must work not only on biblical literary criticism (source criticism, form criticism, tradition criticism, redaction criticism) but also on biblical historical criticism (philology, archaeology, history of religions, anthropology, secular historiography). We must work not only on text but on context. And if we do so we can then begin to discern these unrecorded hermeneutics latent throughout the Bible. The literature available on internal biblical hermeneutics is not yet very large, but it is growing.

Hermeneutics is theology and theology is hermeneutics. The wisdom of this very old observation is almost immediately and directly applicable to study of biblical or canonical hermeneutics. That is, the deciding light in which one reads a passage is determined by the reader's operative view of God or, to use Dietrich Bonhoeffer's term, of reality, or if one prefers, of truth. And one's view of God tends to emphasize either God's freedom or God's commitment to promises made in a covenantal pact issuing from and out of some great redemptive act (such as the Exodus event or the Christ event). The latter is called divine grace.

On the one hand tradition has always maintained that God is God and hence free to create new factors in the human situation and pull surprises even on his own elect people. John Calvin called this aspect of God's work *opera aliena* (from Isa. 28:21): God is free to follow his own agenda which may surprise even his most faithful adherents. God's freedom is inherent in his role as Creator, which is an ongoing role and was not abandoned after Creation. On the other hand God's function as Redeemer emphasizes God's faithfulness to promises made either to the elect-redeemed or to all creation or to both. God's grace then stresses his reliability and long-suffering.

The hermeneutic of God's freedom as Creator of all the world and of all humankind may be called the hermeneutic of prophetic critique. The hermeneutic of God's grace and commitment to the promises made as the peculiar and particular Redeemer of one ongoing community or group may be called constitutive hermeneutics. The one hermeneutic stresses God's role as Creator of all and the other tends to emphasize God's role as Redeemer of a particular group; the one focuses on the doctrine of creation and the other on the doctrine of redemption. Other doctrines or views tend to be colored by which of these two one stresses, and the history of Christian thought seems to alternate between stress on the one and emphasis on the other. The doctrines of election, ecclesiology, providence, and eschatology may be colored by whether one focuses on God as universal Sovereign of all or on God as Redeemer of a particular group. The one hermeneutic is theocentric, the other christocentric.

Actually, part of the Bible's pluralism is seen in its ability to hold these two emphases in tension. One may employ the most sophisticated tools of biblical criticism to see how Genesis 1 came from one ancient source and Genesis 2 from another. Such an observation helps to understand the apparent contradictions between the two chapters—how, for instance, humanity was created last according to Genesis 1 but was created first according to Genesis 2. So far so good. But it is also very important to observe that some good editor wisely put the two chapters, despite such obvious discrepancies, back to back. And he was supported in that juxtaposition by subsequent believing communities who accepted his work and passed it along as valuable. (This last is a canonical-critical observation.) What then do the two chapters say back to back? They say that God is both majestically transcendent and humbly immanent: neither view of God excludes the other. Traditionally, holding two such opposing views at the same time is called a paradox. But it is very important to observe that the Bible presents these two pictures of God—majestically creating the world by divine fiat *and* calling on Adam and Eve like a pastor—rather constantly throughout. In fact one could say they keep reappearing in alternating cadences.

All efforts to combine the two and mix them so as to view God as a sort of majestic pastor seem to fail. On the contrary the canon as a whole consists of literary units, small and large, some of which almost exclusively stress the one (Ecclesiastes, say) or the other (the Gospel of John). That is the reason the word *paradox* has been used. Other efforts to stress one to the exclusion of the other also fail. To press an exclusivistic christocentric or redemptional view of God runs the danger of denominational hermeneutics: God is our God because he did such and such for us and made us promises he made nobody else, so everybody had best join our church. Or it runs the danger of so stressing divine forgiveness and grace that ethics loses ground altogether. Blessed assurance is absolutely right in Christian doctrine (and Jewish, for that matter); but if it stands alone, out of tension with God's freedom to judge his own people, it becomes cheap grace, or what a student once called sloppy agape. On the other hand to press an inclusivistic theocentric view of God as universal sovereign of all peoples, unfettered by an expectation of how he might

194

act, runs the danger of the view that God is but whimsical and unreliable; ethics loses ground here also.

Holding the two in tension, not attempting either to opt absolutely and always for the one or the other, or to mix them into a neat fifty-fifty formula, seems to be what the Bible does. The reason is that in some contexts or situations in which the believing communities found themselves they needed to hear the challenge of God's freedom, and in other contexts they needed to hear the comfort of God's grace. This is what is meant by the ancient assertion that God's word comforts the afflicted and afflicts the comfortable. Falsehood enters in when a biblical passage or ancient tradition is brought to bear upon a context where it could either comfort cruel people (by stressing God's grace when they needed to hear a challenge) or quench a dimly burning wick (by stressing God's freedom when they needed to hear of comfort and support). Any passage, actually, can be interpreted either way according to the hermeneutic employed—either the hermeneutic of prophetic critique stressing for that context and for that reading God's freedom, or the hermeneutic of constitutive support stressing for that context and for that reading God's grace. . . .

So one of the first hermeneutic techniques we can use to employ prophetic critique in application of a text is dynamic analogy. We should look for the persons and figures in it who might represent different folk today dynamically. Dynamic analogy means we can read a text in different ways by identifying with different people in it. For example if we always identify with Jesus in the passage in Luke 4, his sermon at Nazareth, then we will read the last verse of the pericope (Luke 4:30) wondering how Jesus managed to escape that awful crowd. How marvelous! But if we read the passage again, identifying with the good folk in the synagogue, Jesus' relatives and friends of his hometown, and see how he so sorely offended them that they tried to lynch him, then by the time we get to verse 30 we ask an entirely different question: How did the scoundrel get away?

That is far from blasphemy. In much of his Gospel Luke tries to get us to see why Jesus was crucified—because his sermons and messages were often offensive to the good responsible Presbyterians, I mean Pharisees, of his day. The challenge is then ours. We hear it for ourselves dynamically. We in our day, like them in theirs, presume too much and assume too much of God. We have perhaps domesticated God, made God a sort of guarantor of our agendas, of what we know best. Prophetic critique is full of surprises of this sort (Isa. 28:21). It stresses that besides being the particular Redeemer of Israel, and the God present in Christ, God

195

is the Creator of the whole world and of all peoples, and as such is free to follow his own agenda.

Closely related to the technique of dynamic analogy in reading and interpreting a text for today is the ancient principle from which it comes, that of "memory." In biblical terms the concept of remembering is the concept of recalling traditions about Israel's past in such a way as to identify with those in the story who were our ancestors in the faith. Judaism's annual reading of the complete Torah in the synagogue, parashah by parashah (paragraph) each week, enables Jews to remember who they are. In the opening scene of *Fiddler on the Roof* Tevya sings of the function of tradition in the life of a Jew: by reciting the traditions, especially the basic tradition, Torah, Jews are reminded—no matter where they may be in the world, whether in times of crisis or when tempted to assimilate to the dominant culture, in times of ease when identity so easily slips away—that they are Jews. The Torah story reminds Jews constantly that they are the "people come out of Egypt" (Exod. 1:1); they are the slaves-freed-from-Egypt folk (Exodus 12 and Joshua 24). Down through the centuries it has been the same. The Passover Haggadah stresses it. Memory shapes identity.

In effect, therefore, to remember God's mercies or deeds is to recite the basic Torah story. It is to tell the story of what God has done and said: Creation, election, redemption from Egyptian slavery, guidance in the wilderness, suggestions as to how to shape life and society at Sinai, entrance into the land. The remembrance of God's works tells the faithful who they are, even when the contexts in which they live change, whether they live in or out of Palestine, in this or that culture, under whatever threat, whether in pain or at ease.

So also to remember Christ is to tell what for Christians is the climax of the Torah story, what God did in Christ according to the New Testament. To "do this in remembrance" of him, as Christ commanded the followers at the Last Supper, is to tell the story along with partaking of the bread and the cup. To do so means a sort of breaking down of the barriers of time and space. Just as the Jew experiences time transcended in remembering freedom from slavery and identifies with that first generation of redeemed slaves so that the ancient event is contemporized, so the Christian at the communion table experiences the presence of Christ and the disciples—and indeed of all the saints and martyrs of the church triumphant through the centuries. Not only is time transcended so that the church through the centuries once more knows who it is in the presence of "so great a cloud of witnesses" (Hebrews 12:1), but space is also transcended. The present church militant can experience the transcending of the walls of their meeting houses and cathedrals, and have a contemporary sense of the ecumenical nature of the living body of Christ now. Debates in church history about whether such re-presentation in the Eucharist was effected by transubstantiation (Catholic), "real" presence (Lutheran), or by an immediate act of the Holy Spirit dependent on the faith and intentionality of the participants (left-wing Reformation) all stem from this ancient concept.

In a context of worship and retelling the story remembrance is a powerful tradition, whether at Passover or in the Eucharist. To remember the work of God in Israel and in Christ is to have a renewed sense of who we are, no matter the context into which circumstances have moved us, no matter "where we are." . . .

And this may be done by reading the story not as though it were of events way back there about ancient folk but by reading it dynamically, identifying with those who provide us the best mirrors for our identity. The Bible, except in its Wisdom Literature and traditions, provides very few models of morality. An honest reading of the Bible indicates how many biblical characters were just as limited and full of shortcomings as we today. It would seem that about seventy-five percent of the Bible celebrates the theologem *errore hominum providentia divina*: God's providence works in and through human error and sin. The Bible offers no great or infallible models, no saints in the meaning that word has taken on since biblical times—nearly perfect people. None! It offers indeed very few models to follow at all except the work of God in Creation and in Israel in the Old Testament and the work of God in Christ in the New. Biblical people were just like us! Abraham and Sarah lied when they were scared (Gen. 12:13; 18:15) and laughed (Gen. 17:17; 18:12) when they could not believe their own ears or God either (see chapter 1 below). Jacob, our father, was a liar and supplanter (Gen. 27:19). Joseph was an obnoxious imp (Gen. 37:10). Moses was a murderer and fugitive from justice (Exod. 5:12–15).

The presentation of the disciples in all three synoptic Gospels follows the same theologem: they appear to be incredulous and even rather stupid. Judas's betrayal of Jesus is told in the same scenes as Peter's denial of Jesus and the bickering, sleep, and flight of all the disciples (Luke 22:3–62). When one has come to realize that God can take the selling of our brother Joseph into slavery and turn our evil into our later salvation (Gen. 50:20), then one has also realized that God has taken our selling of Christ to Caesar and made it our salvation. Then one also comes to thank God that Judas too was at the table at the Last Supper and that he also received the bread and the wine, because if he had not been there I could not now come to that table myself. God's greatest grace was manifest in the midst of the drama of betrayal. He gave us the broken bread on the very night we betrayed him.

We need to read the Bible honestly, recognizing that much of it celebrates God's willingness to take our humanity, our frailty, and our limitations and weave them into his purposes. God's grace is not stumped by our limitations, indeed not even by Ramses' need of slave labor nor by Herod's fear of losing his position of power. Did Pharoah's army pursue the fleeing slaves? Did Herod send troops to kill baby boys in Bethlehem? The answer to such questions lies not in "history," but in the theologem that God is not offended by either Pharoah's chariots or Herod's swords. And that is reality. That meets us where we are in history, at whatever point of action, or of reaction to power shifting or threatening to shift from one base to another—and that is on every page of history. What could possibly thwart God's grace at this late date? What can a modern Ramses or Nebuchadnezzar or Herod or Pilate do, qualitatively, that could outreach such freedom or such grace? . . .

Finally, the best way to understand the Bible as the churches' book today is to think of it primarily as a paradigm, not as a box or casket of gems and jewels to be mined. A paradigm is a pattern of function of a noun or verb in any language. The Bible comes to us from a twelve- to fifteen-hundred-year time span covering five different culture eras and reflecting the idioms and metaphors of all those cultures. But as a whole it should be viewed in large part as a paradigm in its function in the believing communities today. A paradigm, first, of the verbs and nouns of God's activities and speech, and then, thereupon, a putative paradigm of the verbs and nouns of our activities and speech in our time and in our contexts. Just as verbs have finite forms and inflections, tenses, modes, and various functions, so the Bible as canon indicates the verbs of God's works, and hence ours in the light thereof. The ontology of the Bible as canon is that of paradigm addressing the faithful in context when they seriously ask the questions, who are we and what are we to do? The answers come in paradigms of faith (identity) and of obedience (lifestyle) appropriate to the contexts in which the questions seek them. There are a number of ways to recite the paradigm in our day and in our contexts—in liturgy, in drama, in dance, in sermons, and most of all by living thoughtfully in its reflection.

PHYLLIS TRIBLE

Feminist Hermeneutics

Phyllis Trible (1932–   ) is Baldwin Professor of Sacred Literature at Union Seminary, New York. With the publication in 1978 of *God and the Rhetoric of Sexuality* she enlarged the concept of the hermeneutics of suspicion to include feminist concerns. Although the Old Testament reflects a patriarchal culture, it also contains a "counterliterature" or submerged witness to the importance of selected women in the tradition and to the feminine characteristics of the Deity, though the latter has been obscured by most translations of the Bible. The feminist hermeneutic does not accept the masculine framework of the Bible as normative for contemporary understanding. But it does more than discard this framework as outdated or primitive. It places Scripture into its historical context and seeks indicators in the text for a direction or movement away from static literalism to the modern appropriation of the message. The feminist hermeneutic, like the hermeneutics of suspicion, "reads between the lines," finding in marginal characters and seemingly incidental events clues to a potentially liberating message buried within the text or the ancient community. Such a dynamic hermeneutical procedure places new and greater demands on the preacher, whose background or social position may only subvert the hidden message of the text.

Born and bred in a land of patriarchy, the Bible abounds in male imagery and language. For centuries interpreters have explored and exploited this male language to articulate theology; to shape the contours and content of the church, synagogue and academy; and to instruct human beings—female and male—in who they are, what roles they should play, and how they should behave. So harmonious has seemed this association of Scripture with sexism, of faith with culture, that only a few have even questioned it.

Within the past decade, however, challenges have come in the name of feminism, and they refuse to go away. As a critique of culture in light of misogyny, feminism is a prophetic movement, examining the status quo, pronouncing judgment and calling for repentance. In various ways this hermeneutical pursuit interacts with the Bible in its remoteness, complexity, diversity and contemporaneity to yield new understandings of both text and interpreter. Accordingly, I shall survey three approaches to the study of women in Scripture. Though these perspectives may also apply to "intertestamental" and New Testament literature, my focus is the Hebrew Scriptures.

When feminists first examined the Bible, emphasis fell upon documenting the case against women. Commentators observed the plight of the female in Israel. Less desirable in the eyes of her parents than a male child, a girl stayed close to her mother, but her father controlled her life until he relinquished her to another man for marriage. If either of these male authorities permitted her to be mistreated, even abused, she had to submit without recourse. Thus, Lot offered his daughters to the men of Sodom to protect a male guest (Gen. 19:8); Jephthah sacrificed his daughter to remain faithful to a foolish vow (Judg. 11:29-40); Amnon raped his half-sister Tamar (II Sam. 13); and the Levite from the hill country of Ephraim participated with other males to bring about the betrayal, rape, murder and dismemberment of his own concubine (Judg. 19). Although not every story involving female and male is so terrifying, the narrative literature nevertheless makes clear that from birth to death the Hebrew woman belonged to men.

What such narratives show, the legal corpus amplifies. Defined as the property of men (Exod. 20:17; Deut. 5:21), women did not control their own bodies. A man expected to marry a virgin, though his own virginity need not be intact. A wife guilty of earlier fornication violated the honor and power of both her father and husband. Death by stoning was the penalty (Deut. 22:13-21). Moreover, a woman had no right to divorce (Deut. 24:1-4) and, most often, no right to own property. Excluded from the priesthood, she was considered far more unclean than the male (Lev. 15). Even her monetary value was less (Lev. 27:1-7).

Clearly, this feminist perspective has uncovered abundant evidence for the inferiority, subordination and abuse of women in Scripture. Yet the approach has led to different conclusions. Some people denounce biblical faith as hopelessly misogynous, although this judgment usually fails to evaluate the evidence in terms of Israelite culture. Some reprehensibly use these data to support anti-Semitic sentiments. Some read the Bible as a historical document devoid of any continuing authority and hence worthy of dismissal. The "Who cares?" question often comes at this point. Others succumb to despair about the ever-present male power that the Bible and its commentators hold over women. And still others, unwilling to let the case against women be the determining word, insist that text and interpreters provide more excellent ways.

The second approach, then, grows out of the first while modifying it. Discerning within Scripture a critique of patriarchy, certain feminists concentrate upon discovering and recovering traditions that challenge the culture. This task involves highlighting neglected texts and reinterpreting familiar ones.

Prominent among neglected passages are portrayals of deity as female. A psalmist declares that God is midwife (Ps. 22:9-10):

> Yet thou art the one who took me from the womb;
>> thou didst keep me safe upon my mother's breast.

In turn, God becomes mother, the one upon whom the child is cast from birth:

> Upon thee was I cast from my birth,
>> and since my mother bore me thou hast been my God.

Although this poem stops short of an exact equation, in it female imagery mirrors divine activity. What the psalmist suggests, Deuteronomy 32:18 makes explicit:

> You were unmindful of the Rock that begot you
>> and you forgot the God who gave you birth.

Though the RSV translates accurately "the God who gave you birth," the rendering is tame. We need to accent the striking portrayal of God as a woman in labor pains, for the Hebrew verb has exclusively this meaning. (How scandalous, then, is the totally incorrect translation in the Jerusalem Bible, "You forgot the God who fathered you.") Yet another instance of female imagery is the metaphor of the womb as given in the Hebrew radicals *rḥm*. In its singular form the word denotes the physical organ unique to the female. In the plural, it connotes the compassion of both human beings and God. God the merciful (*raḥum*) is God the mother. (See, e.g., Jer. 31:15-22.) Over centuries, however, translators and commentators have ignored such female imagery, with disastrous results for God, man and woman. To reclaim the image of God female is to become aware of the male idolatry that has long infested faith.

If traditional interpretations have neglected female imagery for God, they have also neglected females, especially women who counter patriarchal culture. By contrast, feminist hermeneutics accents these figures. A collage of women in Exodus illustrates the emphasis. So eager have scholars been to get Moses born that they pass quickly over the stories that lead to his advent (Exod. 1:8-2:10). Two female slaves are the first to oppose the Pharaoh; they refuse to kill newborn sons. Acting alone, without advice or assistance from males, they thwart the will of the oppressor. Tellingly, memory has preserved the names of these women, Shiphrah and Puah, while obliterating the identity of the king so successfully that he has become the burden of innumerable doctoral dissertations. What these two females begin, other Hebrew women continue.

"A woman conceived and bore a son and when she saw that he was a goodly child she hid him three months. And when she could hide him no longer, she took for him a basket made of bulrushes . . . and she put the child in it and placed it among the reeds at the river's bank. And his sister stood at a distance to know what would be done to him." [Exod. 2:2-4]. In quiet and secret ways the defiance resumes as a mother and daughter scheme to save their baby son and brother, and this action enlarges when the daughter of Pharaoh appears at the riverbank. Instructing her maid to fetch the basket, the princess opens it, sees a crying baby, and takes him to her heart even as she recognizes his Hebrew identity. The daughter of Pharaoh aligns herself with the daughters of Israel. Filial allegiance is broken; class lines crossed; racial and political difference transcended. The sister, seeing it all from a distance, dares to suggest the perfect arrangement: a Hebrew nurse for the baby boy, in reality the child's own mother. From the human side, then, Exodus faith originates as a feminist act. The women who are ignored by theologians are the first to challenge oppressive structures.

Not only does this second approach recover neglected women, but also it reinterprets familiar ones, beginning with the primal woman in the creation story of Genesis 2-3. Contrary to tradition, she is not created the assistant or subordinate of the man. In fact, most often the Hebrew word *'ezer* ("helper") connotes superiority (Ps. 121:2; 124:8; 146:5; Exod. 18:4; Deut. 33:7, 26, 29), thereby posing a rather different problem about this woman. Yet the accompanying phrase "fit for" or "corresponding to" ("a helper corresponding to") tempers the connotation of superiority to specify the mutuality of woman and man.

Further, when the serpent talks with the woman (Gen. 3:1–5), he uses plural verb forms, making her the spokesperson for the human couple – hardly the pattern of a patriarchal culture. She discusses theology intelligently, stating the case for obedience even more strongly than did God: "From the fruit of the tree that is in the midst of the garden, God said, 'You shall not eat from it and you shall not touch it, lest you die.'" If the tree is not touched, then its fruit cannot be eaten. Here the woman builds "a fence around the Torah," a procedure that her rabbinical successors developed fully to protect divine law and ensure obedience.

Speaking with clarity and authority, the first woman is theologian, ethicist, hermeneut and rabbi. Defying the stereotypes of patriarchy, she reverses what the church, synagogue and academy have preached about women. By the same token, the man "who was with her" (many translations omit this crucial phrase) throughout the temptation is not morally superior but rather belly-oriented. Clearly this story presents a couple alien to traditional interpretations. In reclaiming the woman, feminist hermeneutics gives new life to the image of God female.

These and other exciting discoveries of a counterliterature that pertains to women do not, however, eliminate the male bias of Scripture. In other words, this second perspective neither disavows nor neglects the evidence of the first. Instead, it functions as a remnant theology.

The third approach retells biblical stories of terror in memoriam, offering sympathetic readings of abused women. If the first perspective documents misogyny historically and sociologically, this one appropriates such evidence poetically and theologically. At the same time, it continues to look for the remnant in unlikely places.

The betrayal, rape, murder and dismemberment of the concubine in Judges 19 is a striking example. When wicked men of the tribe of Benjamin demand to "know" her master, he instead throws the concubine to them. All night they ravish her; in the morning she returns to her master. Showing no pity, he orders her to get up and go. She does not answer, and the reader is left to wonder if she is dead or alive. At any rate, the master puts her body on a donkey and continues the journey. When the couple arrive home, the master cuts the concubine in pieces, sending them to the tribes of Israel as a call to war against the wrong done to *him* by the men of Benjamin.

At the conclusion of this story, Israel is instructed to "consider, take counsel, and speak" (Judg. 19:30). Indeed, Israel does reply–with unrestrained violence. Mass slaughter follows; the rape, murder and dismemberment of one woman condones similar crimes against hundreds and hundreds of women. The narrator (or editor) responds differently, however, suggesting the political solution of kingship instead of the anarchy of the judges (Judg. 12:25). This solution fails. In the days of David there is a king in Israel, and yet Amnon rapes Tamar. How, then, do we today hear this ancient tale of terror as the imperatives "consider, take counsel and speak" address us? A feminist approach, with attention to reader response, interprets the story on behalf of the concubine as it calls to remembrance her suffering and death.

Similarly, the sacrifice of the daughter of Jephthah documents the powerlessness and abuse of a child in the days of the judges (Judg. 11). No interpretation can save her from the holocaust or mitigate the foolish vow of her father. But we can move through the indictment of the father to claim sisterhood with the daughter. Retelling her story, we emphasize the daughters of Israel to whom she reaches out in the last days of her life (Judg. 11:37). Thus, we underscore the postscript, discovering in the process an alternative translation.

Traditionally, the ending has read, "She [the daughter] had never known man. And *it* became a custom in Israel that the daughters of Israel went year by year to lament the daughter of Jephthah the Gileadite four days in the year" (11:40). Since the verb *become*, however, is a feminine form (Hebrew has no neuter), another reading is likely: "Although she had never known a man, nevertheless *she* became a tradition [custom] in Israel. From year to year the daughters of Israel went to mourn the daughter of Jephthah the Gileadite, four days in the year." By virtue of this translation, we can understand the ancient story in a new way. The unnamed virgin child becomes a tradition in Israel because the women with whom she chooses to spend her last days do not let her pass into oblivion; they establish a living memorial. Interpreting such stories of terror on behalf of women is surely, then, another way of challenging the patriarchy of Scripture.

I have surveyed three feminist approaches to the study of women in Scripture. The first explores the inferiority, subordination and abuse of women in ancient Israel. Within this context, the second pursues the counterliterature that is itself a critique of patriarchy. Utilizing both of these approaches, the third retells sympathetically the stories of terror about woman. Though intertwined, these perspectives are distinguishable. The one stressed depends on the occasion and the talents and interests of the interpreter. Moreover, in its work, feminist hermeneutics embraces a variety of methodologies and disciplines. Archaeology, linguistics, anthropology and literary and historical criticism all have contributions to make. Thereby understanding of the past increases and deepens as it informs the present.

Finally, there are more perspectives on the subject of women in Scripture than are dreamt of in the hermeneutics of this article. For instance, I have barely mentioned the problem of sexist translations which, in fact, is receiving thoughtful attention from many scholars, male and female. But perhaps I have said enough to show that in various and sundry ways feminist hermeneutics is challenging interpretations old and new. In time, perhaps, it will yield a biblical theology of womanhood (not to be subsumed under the label humanity) with roots in the goodness of creation female and male. Meanwhile, the faith of Sarah and Hagar, Naomi and Ruth, the two Tamars and a cloud of other witnesses empowers and sobers the endeavor.

V
RHETORIC

AUGUSTINE

The Uses of Rhetoric

Rhetoric is the theory and practice of purposive discourse. An ancient art, it encompasses the written and the spoken word. The early church agonized over its use of classical rhetoric, encumbered as it was with pagan ideals and associations. Augustine (354–430) helped to relieve the problem by codifying a Christian approach to the rhetoric of preaching. He asked why the sophists should brandish their rhetorical artillery while Christians stand unarmed. His principle of God's (and the church's) ownership of *all* truth, wherever it is to be found, contributed to the foundations of Christian culture and continues still as a principle of Christian liberty. In Book IV of *On Christian Doctrine* Augustine restates broad Ciceronian principles and transposes them into homiletical theory. He addresses standard considerations of audience, diction, rhythm, style, etc. but subjects them all to the unique authority of the Bible, which, in Augustine's treatment, is not only a doctrinal but also a rhetorical textbook for the preacher. He illustrates his comments on the subdued, the temperate, and the majestic styles with detailed rhetorical analyses of texts, e.g. Gal. 4:21–26, Rom. 12:1, and II Cor. 6:2–10 respectively. In both his preaching and his homiletics Augustine steered the western church between the disorganization of the primitive homily and the excesses of the professional oration. He joined his discriminating appreciation of classical rhetoric to the prior claims of Christian truth to produce the church's first and, for nearly a millennium, its only rhetoric of preaching.

Augustine, *On Christian Doctrine*, Book IV, selected paragraphs, trans. J. F. Shaw, *A Selected Library of the Nicene and Post-Nicene Fathers of the Church*, ed. Philip Schaff, Vol. II (Buffalo, 1887), pp. 574–577, 583, 586–587, 593–594.

In the first place, then, I wish by this preamble to put a stop to the expectations of readers who may think that I am about to lay down rules of rhetoric such as I have learnt, and taught too, in the secular schools, and to warn them that they need not look for any such from me. Not that I think such rules of no use, but that whatever use they have is to be learnt elsewhere; and if any good man should happen to have leisure for learning them, he is not to ask me to teach them either in this work or any other.

Now, the art of rhetoric being available for the enforcing either of truth or falsehood, who will dare to say that truth in the person of its defenders is to take its stand unarmed against falsehood? For example, that those who are trying to persuade men of what is false are to know how to introduce their subject, so as to put the hearer into a friendly, or attentive, or teachable frame of mind, while the defenders of the truth shall be ignorant of that art? That the former are to tell their falsehoods briefly, clearly, and plausibly, while the latter shall tell the truth in such a way that it is tedious to listen to, hard to understand, and, in fine, not easy to believe it? That the former are to oppose the truth and defend falsehood with sophistical arguments, while the latter shall be unable either to defend what is true, or to refute what is false? That the former, while imbuing the minds of their hearers with erroneous opinions, are by their power of speech to awe, to melt, to enliven, and to rouse them, while the latter shall in defense of the truth be sluggish, and frigid, and somnolent? Who is such a fool as to think this wisdom? Since, then, the faculty of eloquence is available for both sides, and is of very great service in the enforcing either of wrong or right, why do not good men study to engage it on the side of truth, when bad men use it to obtain the triumph of wicked and worthless causes, and to further injustice and error?

But the theories and rules on this subject (to which, when you add a tongue thoroughly skilled by exercise and habit in the use of many words and many ornaments of speech, you have what is called *eloquence* or *oratory*) may be learnt apart from these writings of mine, if a suitable space of time be set aside for the purpose at a fit and proper age. But only by those who can learn them quickly; for the masters of Roman eloquence themselves did not shrink from saying that any one who cannot learn this art quickly can never thoroughly learn it at all. Whether this be true or not, why need we inquire? For even if this art can occasionally be in the end mastered by men of slower intellect, I do not think it of so much importance as to wish men who have arrived at mature age to spend time in learning it. It is enough that boys should give attention to it; and even of these, not all who are to be fitted for usefulness in the church, but only those who are not yet engaged in any occupation of more urgent necessity, or which ought evidently to take precedence of it. For men of quick intellect and glowing temperament find it easier to become eloquent by reading and listening to eloquent speakers than by following rules for eloquence. And even outside the canon, which to our great advantage is fixed in a place of secure authority, there is no want of ecclesiastical writings, in reading which a man of ability will acquire a tinge of the eloquence with which they are written, even though he does not aim at this, but is solely intent on the matters treated of; especially, of course, if in addition he practice himself in writing, or dictating, and at last also in speaking, the opinions he has formed on grounds of piety and faith. If, however, such ability be wanting, the rules of rhetoric are either not understood, or if, after great labor has been spent in enforcing them, they come to be in some small measure understood, they prove of no service. For even those who have learnt them, and who speak with fluency and elegance, cannot always think of them when they are speaking so as to speak in accordance with them, unless they are discussing the rules themselves. Indeed, I think there are scarcely any who can do both things—that is, speak well, and in order to do this, think of the rules of speaking while they are speaking. For we must be careful that what we have got to say does not escape us whilst we are thinking about saying it according to the rules of art. Nevertheless, in the speeches of eloquent men, we find rules of eloquence carried out which the speakers did not think of as aids to eloquence at the time when they were speaking, whether they had ever learnt them, or whether they had never even met with them. For it is because they are eloquent that they exemplify these rules; it is not that they use them in order to be eloquent.

And, therefore, as infants cannot learn to speak except by learning words and phrases from those who do speak, why should not men become eloquent without being taught any art of speech, simply by reading and learning the speeches of eloquent men, and by imitating them as far as they can? And what do we find from the examples themselves to be the case in this respect? We know numbers who, without acquaintance with rhetorical rules, are more eloquent than many who have learnt these; but we know no one who is eloquent without having read and listened to the speeches and debates of eloquent men. For even the art of grammar, which teaches correctness of speech, need not be learnt by boys, if they have the advantage of growing up and living among men who speak correctly. For without knowing the names of any of the faults, they will, from being accustomed to correct speech, lay hold upon whatever is faulty in the speech of any one they listen to, and avoid it; just as city-bred men, even when illiterate, seize upon the faults of rustics.

It is the duty, then, of the interpreter and teacher of Holy Scripture, the defender of the true faith and the opponent of error, both to teach what is right and to refute what is wrong, and in the performance of this task to conciliate the hostile, to rouse the careless, and to tell the ignorant both what is occurring at present and what is probable in the future. But once that his hearers are friendly, attentive, and ready to learn, whether he has found them so, or has himself made them so, the remaining objects are to be carried out in whatever way the case requires. If the hearers need teaching, the matter treated of must be made fully known by means of narrative. On the other hand, to clear up points that are doubtful requires reasoning and the exhibition of proofs. If, however, the hearers require to be roused rather than instructed, in order that they may be diligent to do what they already know, and to bring their feelings into harmony with the truths they admit, greater vigor of speech is needed. Here entreaties and reproaches, exhortations and upbraidings, and all the other means of rousing the emotions, are necessary.

And all the methods I have mentioned are constantly used by nearly every one in cases where speech is the agency employed.

But as some men employ these coarsely, inelegantly, and frigidly, while others use them with acuteness, elegance, and spirit, the work that I am speaking of ought to be undertaken by one who can argue and speak with wisdom, if not with eloquence, and with profit to his hearers, even though he profit them less than he would if he could speak with eloquence too. But we must beware of the man who abounds in eloquent nonsense, and so much the more if the hearer is pleased with what is not worth listening to, and thinks that because the speaker is eloquent what he says must be true. And this opinion is held even by those who think that the art of rhetoric should be taught: for they confess that "though wisdom without eloquence is of little service to states, yet eloquence without wisdom is frequently a positive injury, and is of service never" [Cicero]. If, then, the men who teach the principles of eloquence have been forced by truth to confess this in the very books which treat of eloquence, though they were ignorant of the true, that is, the heavenly wisdom which comes down from the Father of Lights, how much more ought we to feel it who are the sons and the ministers of this higher wisdom! Now a man speaks with more or less wisdom just as he has made more or less progress in the knowledge of Scripture; I do not mean by reading thém much and commiting them to memory, but by understanding them aright and carefully searching into their meaning. For there are who read and yet neglect them; they read to remember the words, but are careless about knowing the meaning. It is plain we must set far above these the men who are not so retentive of the words, but see with the eyes of the heart into the heart of Scripture. Better than either of these, however, is the man who, when he wishes, can repeat the words, and at the same time correctly apprehends their meaning.

Now it is especially necessary for the man who is bound to speak wisely, even though he cannot speak eloquently, to retain in memory the words of Scripture. For the more he discerns the poverty of his own speech, the more he ought to draw on the riches of Scripture, so that what he says in his own words he may prove by the words of Scripture; and he himself, though small and weak in his own words, may gain strength and power from the confirming testimony of great men. For his proof gives pleasure when he cannot please by his mode of speech. But if a man desire to speak not only with wisdom, but with eloquence also (and assuredly he will prove of greater service if he can do both), I would rather send him to read, and listen to, and exercise himself in imitating, eloquent men, than advise him to spend time with the teachers of rhetoric; especially if the men he reads and listens to are justly praised as having spoken, or as being accustomed to speak, not only with eloquence, but with wisdom also. For eloquent speakers are heard with pleasure; wise speakers with profit. And, therefore, Scripture does not say that the multitude of the eloquent, but "the multitude of the wise is the welfare of the world" [Wisd. 6:24]. . . .

Here, perhaps, some one inquires whether the authors whose divinely-inspired writings constitute the canon, which carries with it a most wholesome authority, are to be considered wise only, or eloquent as well. A question which to me, and to those who think with me, is very easily settled. For where I understand these writers, it seems to me not only that nothing can be wiser, but also that nothing can be more eloquent. And I venture to affirm that all who truly understand what these writers say, perceive at the same time that it could not have been properly said in any other way. For as there is a kind of eloquence that is more becoming in youth, and a kind that is more becoming in old age, and nothing can be called eloquence if it be not suitable to the person of the speaker, so there is a kind of eloquence that is becoming in men who justly claim the highest authority, and who are evidently inspired of God. . . .

But it is not the qualities which these writers have in common with the heathen orators and poets that give me such unspeakable delight in their eloquence; I am more struck with admiration at the way in which, by an eloquence peculiarly their own, they so use this eloquence of ours that it is not conspicuous either by its presence or its absence: for it did not become them either to condemn it or to make an ostentatious display of it; and if they had shunned it, they would have done the former; if they had made it prominent, they might have appeared to be doing the latter. And in those passages where the learned do note its presence, the matters spoken of are such, that the words in which they are put seem not so much to be sought out by the speaker as spontaneously to suggest themselves; as if wisdom were walking out of its house,—that is, the breast of the wise man, and eloquence, like an inseparable attendant, followed it without being called for. . . .

For teaching, of course, true eloquence consists, not in making people like what they disliked, nor in making them do what they shrank from, but in making clear what was obscure; yet if this be done without grace of style, the benefit does not extend beyond the few eager students who are anxious to know whatever is to be learnt, however rude and unpolished the form in which it is put; and who, when they have succeeded in their object, find the plain truth pleasant food enough. And it is one of the distinctive features of good intellects not to love words, but the truth in words. For of what service is a golden key, if it cannot open what we want it to open? Or what objection is there to a wooden one if it can, seeing that to open what is shut is all we want? But as there is a certain analogy between learning and eating, the very food without which it is impossible to live must be flavored to meet the tastes of the majority.

Accordingly a great orator [Cicero] has truly said that "an eloquent man must speak so as to teach, to delight, and to persuade." Then he adds: "To teach is a necessity, to delight is a beauty, to persuade is a triumph." Now of these three, the one first mentioned, the teaching, which is a matter of necessity, depends on what we say; the other two on the way we say it. He, then, who speaks with the purpose of teaching should not suppose that he has said what he has to say as long as he is not understood; for although what he has said be intelligible to himself, it is not said at all to the man who does not understand it. If, however, he is understood, he has said his say, whatever may have been his manner of saying it. But if he wishes to delight or persuade his hearer as well, he will not accomplish that end by putting his thought in any shape no matter what, but for that purpose the style of speaking is a matter of importance. And as the hearer must be pleased in order to secure his attention, so he must be persuaded in order to move him to action. And as he is pleased if you speak with sweetness and elegance, so he is persuaded if he be drawn by your promises, and awed by your threats; if he reject what you condemn, and embrace what you commend; if he grieve when you heap up objects for grief, and rejoice when you point out an object for joy; if he pity those whom you present to him as objects of pity, and shrink from those whom you set before him as men to be feared and shunned. I need not go over all the other things that can be done by powerful eloquence to move the minds of the hearers, not telling them what they ought to do, but urging them to do what they already know ought to be done.

If, however, they do not yet know this, they must of course be instructed before they can be moved. And perhaps the mere knowledge of their duty will have such an effect that there will be no need to move them with greater strength of eloquence. Yet when this is needful, it ought to be done. And it is needful when people, knowing what they ought to do, do it not. Therefore, to teach is a necessity. For what men know, it is in their own hands either to do or not to do. But who would say that it is their duty to do what they do not know? On the same principle, to persuade is not a necessity: for it is not always called for; as, for example, when the hearer yields his assent to one who simply teaches or gives pleasure. For this reason also to persuade is a triumph, because it is possible that a man may be taught and delighted, and yet not give his consent. And what will be the use of gaining the first two ends if we fail in the third? Neither is it a necessity to give pleasure; for when, in the course of an address, the truth is clearly pointed out (and this is the true function of teaching), it is not the fact, nor is it the intention, that the style of speech should make the truth pleasing, or that the style should of itself give pleasure; but the truth itself, when exhibited in its naked simplicity, gives pleasure, because it is the truth. And hence even falsities are frequently a source of pleasure when they are brought to light and exposed. It is not, of course, their falsity that gives pleasure; but as it is true that they are false, the speech which shows this to be true gives pleasure.

He then who, in speaking, aims at enforcing what is good, should not despise any of those three objects, either to teach, or to give pleasure, or to move, and should pray and strive, as we have said above, to be heard with intelligence, with pleasure, and with ready compliance. And when he does this with elegance and propriety, he may justly be called eloquent, even though he do not carry with him the assent of his hearer. For it is these three ends, viz., teaching, giving pleasure, and moving, that the great master of Roman eloquence himself seems to have intended that the following three directions should subserve: "He, then, shall be eloquent, who can say little things in a subdued style, moderate things in a temperate style, and great things in a majestic style:" as if he had taken in also the three ends mentioned above, and had embraced the whole in one sentence thus: "He, then, shall be eloquent, who can say little things in a subdued style, in order to give instruction, moderate things in a temperate style, in order to give pleasure, and great things in a majestic style, in order to sway the mind." . . .

And yet, while our teacher ought to speak of great matters, he ought not always to be speaking of them in a majestic tone, but in a subdued tone when he is teaching, temperately when he is giving praise or blame. When, however, something is to be done, and we are speaking to those who ought, but are not willing, to do it, then great matters must be spoken of with power, and in a manner calculated to sway the mind. And sometimes the same important matter is treated in all these ways at different times, quietly when it is being taught, temperately when its importance is being urged, and powerfully when we are forcing a mind that is averse to the truth to turn and embrace it. For is there anything greater than God himself? Is nothing, then, to be learnt about him? Or ought he who is teaching the Trinity in unity to speak of it otherwise than in the method of calm discussion, so that in regard to a subject which it is not easy to comprehend, we may understand as much as it is given us to understand? Are we in this case to seek out ornaments instead of proofs? Or is the hearer to be moved to do something instead of being instructed so that he may learn something? But when we come to praise God, either in himself, or in his works, what a field for beauty and splendor of language opens up before man, who can task his powers to the utmost in praising him whom no one can adequately praise, though there is no one who does not praise him in some measure! . . .

Now it is a matter of importance to determine what style should be alternated with what other, and the places where it is necessary that any particular style should be used. In the majestic style, for instance, it is always, or almost always, desirable that the introduction should be temperate. And the speaker has it in his discretion to use the subdued style even where the majestic would be allowable, in order that the majestic when it is used may be the more majestic by comparison, and may as it were shine out with greater brilliance from the dark background. Again, whatever may be the style of the speech or writing, when knotty questions turn up for solution, accuracy of distinction is required, and this naturally demands the subdued style. . . .

If frequent and vehement applause follows a speaker, we are not to suppose on that account that he is speaking in the majestic style; for this effect is often produced both by the accurate distinctions of the quiet style, and by the beauties of the temperate. The majestic style, on the other hand, frequently silences the audience by its impressiveness, but calls forth their tears. For example, when at Caesarea in Mauritania I was dissuading the people from that civil, or worse than civil, war which they called *Caterva* (for it was not fellow-citizens merely, but neighbors, brothers, fathers and sons even, who, divided into two factions and armed with stones, fought annually at a certain season of the year for several days continuously, every one killing whomsoever he could), I strove with all the vehemence of speech that I could command to root out and drive from their hearts and lives an evil so cruel and inveterate; it was not, however, when I heard their applause, but when I saw their tears, that I thought I had produced an effect. For the applause showed that they were instructed and delighted, but the tears that they were subdued. And when I saw their tears I was confident, even before the event proved it, that this horrible and barbarous custom (which had been handed down to them from their fathers and their ancestors of generations long gone by and which like an enemy was besieging their hearts, or rather had complete possession of them) was overthrown; and immediately that my sermon was finished I called upon them with heart and voice to give praise and thanks to God. And, lo, with the blessing of Christ, it is now eight years or more since anything of the sort was attempted there. In many other cases besides I have observed that men show the effect made on them by the powerful eloquence of a wise man, not by clamorous applause so much as by groans, sometimes even by tears, finally by change of life.

The quiet style, too, has made a change in many; but it was to teach them what they were ignorant of, or to persuade them of what they thought incredible, not to make them do what they knew they ought to do but were unwilling to do. To break down hardness of this sort, speech needs to be vehement. Praise and censure, too, when they are eloquently expressed, even in the temperate style, produce such an effect on some, that they are not only pleased with the eloquence of the encomiums and censures, but are led to live so as themselves to deserve praise, and to avoid living so as to incur blame. But no one would say that all who are thus delighted change their habits in consequence, whereas all who are moved by the majestic style act accordingly, and all who are taught by the quiet style know or believe a truth which they were previously ignorant of.

From all this we may conclude, that the end arrived at by the two styles last mentioned is the one which it is most essential for those who aspire to speak with wisdom and eloquence to secure. On the other hand, what the temperate style properly aims at, viz., to please by beauty of expression, is not in itself an adequate end; but when what we have to say is good and useful, and when the hearers are both acquainted with it and favorably disposed towards it, so that it is not necessary either to instruct or persuade them, beauty of style may have its influence in securing their prompter compliance, or in making them adhere to it more tenaciously. For as the function of all eloquence, whichever of these three forms it may assume, is to speak persuasively, and its object is to persuade, an eloquent man will speak persuasively, whatever style he may adopt; but unless he succeeds in persuading, his eloquence has not secured its object.

ROBERT OF BASEVORN

Ornamentation

Nothing is known of Robert of Basevorn except that in 1322 he wrote an influential treatise, *The Form of Preaching*. We know Robert's name only because he reveals it in an acrostic combination of letters from the chapter headings of the book. In his treatise he speaks knowledgeably of preaching styles in Paris and Oxford. Robert's work is representative of a highly developed medieval genre, the *ars praedicandi*, a handbook of sermon design and construction. Such manuals appeared in profusion in the 13th and 14th centuries. They describe the "thematic" or "university" sermon whose complex arrangement was probably more directly influenced by scholastic (Aristotelian) logic than by Augustinian (Ciceronian) rhetoric. The typical manual prescribes a sermon in six parts: (1) theme: a scriptural quotation; (2) protheme: introduction of the theme followed by a prayer; (3) repetition of theme with explanation of the sermon's purpose; (4) division or partition of theme (usually into threes) with "authorities" of various sorts to "prove" each division; (5) subdivision of theme; (6) amplification of each division. The rigorous division of theme was a medieval commonplace. Although it was modified by Renaissance classicism and repudiated by the Reformation, the three-point outline has survived as a staple for many preachers.

Robert of Basevorn, *The Form of Preaching*, trans. Leopold Krul O.S.B. in James J. Murphy, ed., *Three Medieval Rhetorical Arts* (Berkeley, Los Angeles, London: University of California Press, 1971), pp. 132–133, 138–139, 145–148. Reprinted by permission.

We must come now to our proposal to discuss the ornamentation which is used in sermons by certain of the careful craftsmen. It must be realized that in the most carefully contrived sermons twenty-two ornaments are especially employed. These are: Invention of the Theme, Winning-over of the Audience, Prayer, Introduction, Division, Statement of the Parts, Proof of the Parts, Amplification, Digression, which is properly called "Transition," Correspondence, Agreement of Correspondence, Circuitous Development, Convolution, Unification, Conclusion, Coloration, Modulation of Voice, Appropriate Gesture, Timely Humor, Allusion, Firm Impression, Weighing of Subject Matter. The first fifteen of these are inserted into their proper places once, or at any rate into a few places; the remaining three, and generally Allusion and Firm Impression, can be placed almost anywhere. The element that follows after these, Humor, ought to be used in a few places and very sparingly. The last must be observed in all places. All these, when concurring, embellish a sermon elegantly, and so can be called the ornaments of a sermon. And if perhaps there are more elements than have been enumerated, they can be reduced to these.

For a good Invention of the Theme the following are required: that it concur with the feast, that it beget full understanding, that it be on a Bible text which is not changed or corrupted, that it contain not more than three statements or convertible to three, that sufficient concordances can be found on these three ideas, even vowel concordances, and that the theme itself can serve in place of the antetheme or protheme. For example, concerning the first, suppose that someone has to preach about Advent and he takes as his theme: *Come, Lord Jesus*, from the Nativity: *the Grace of God has appeared*, from the Epiphany: *A great sign has appeared*; thus he will find the above-mentioned conditions concurrent.

Likewise concerning the saints. He should consider what or which things about the saints or saint about whom he preaches he especially wishes to commend. For example, as I consider St. Andrew, I see much that is especially commendable in him: that he hung on the cross for so long and did not waiver, that in spirit he seemed rather affixed to Christ than corporally to the cross. And thus the saying of his fellow Apostle is seen in his own person: *with Christ I am nailed to the cross* (Gal. 2:19). . . .

Further, in this method of preaching only three statements, or the equivalent of three, are used in the theme—either from respect to the Trinity, or because a threefold cord is not easily broken, or because this method is mostly followed by Bernard, or, as I think more likely, because it is more convenient for the set time of the sermon. A preacher can follow up just so many members without tiring his hearers; and if he should mention fewer, he would occupy too little time.

The reason why a theme may be the equivalent of three statements is that it can happen that some words which cannot be divided and should not be may fall into a theme. Of such kind are prepositions and conjunctions, and also a general word which is included in every other word. Hence if the theme were: *the just is delivered out of distress*, no division would fall upon *out of* nor upon *is*. . . .

No matter how many statements there may be, as long as I can divide them into three, I have a sufficient proposition. Posit that the theme on the Annunciation, on the vigil of Nativity, or on the day, and on the first Sunday within the octave of the Nativity, and on the day of Circumcision: *God sent his Son made of a woman, made under the law, that he might redeem them who were under the law.* Here are seventeen words; yet the whole can be divided into three so that it may be said that in these words three things are touched upon: (1) There is noted in the doctor a generously-expended sublimity because it says *God sent his Son*. (2) There is shown how virtuously-shown humility heals because it says *made of a woman, made under the law*. (3) There is shown how fruitfully-extended utility is derived, because it says *that he might redeem them who were under the law*.

But when the theme is thus divided, one must see that the dividing parts correspond with the parts of that which is divided. For example, here is said that in the doctor is noted a sublimity, etc. when is said *God sent* etc. Notice the correspondence, because *God*: sublimity; because *he sent*: expended; because *his Son*: generously. And thus about the rest. There is no lack of artistry if these three things can be confirmed by one authority in which verbally there are the three: *God*, *sent*, and *Son* and that in the sentence such great nobility is communicated to us. But because such authorities are difficult to find, themes of so many words are not commonly accepted. . . .

Now that we have treated in general the first ornament of preaching, to wit, the Invention of the Theme, the second ornament follows, namely the Winning-over of the Audience. The preacher, as far as he can do so according to God, ought to attract the mind of the listeners in such a way as to render them willing to hear and retain. This can be done in many ways. One way is to place at the beginning something subtle and interesting, as some authentic marvel which can be fittingly drawn in for the purpose of the theme. For instance, suppose that the theme is concerned with the Ascension or the Assumption: *a spring rose from the earth*. One could adduce that marvel which Gerald narrates in his book, *De mirabilibus Hiberniae* about the spring in Scicilia: if anyone approaches it dressed in red clothing, immediately water gushes from the place of the spring

221

though none appeared there before, while it remains unmoved in the presence of all other colors. That spring is Christ, about whom it is written in Eccles. I: *the word of God is the fountain of wisdom,* to whom he "approaches dressed in red" who, devoutly suffering with him and as it were incarnadined with the blood of his Passion, intently and inwardly revolves the thought (of him), and considers the saying of Isaiah: *why is thy apparel red?* Such a one approaching finds living water, viz. graces, because his blood was of such virtue that, when it was shed, the earth quaked and the rocks were torn asunder. Much more ought our hearts to quake and be torn by the cry of God's word, unless they be drier than the earth and harder than rocks.

Likewise if an unknown cause of some saying is used, it is reducible to the same category, for example if a cause is given to explain why the eye does not have a determined color; because if it did have a definite color, it would perceive only that color and there would have to be as many senses as there are colors; and this may be applied to sinners, especially the avaricious and clever ones who do not perceive the word of God or its effect because they are totally determined by its opposite.

Another way is to frighten them by some terrifying tale or example, in the way that Jacques de Vitry [a compiler of popular *exempla*] talks about some one who never willingly wanted to hear the word of God; finally when he died and was brought to the church, and the priest in the presence of the parish began the eulogy which is wont to be spoken over the body of the dead, the image of Christ standing between the choir and the church tore away and pulled his hands from the nails piercing them and from the wood to which they were fixed, and plugged his ears, as if to intimate that he did not wish to hear the prayer for him who once spurned to listen to him in his preachers.

Likewise, pertinent to the same topic are the different stories which teach how Christ appeared to some hardened sinners, extending his palm full of blood taken from his side, saying: This blood which you so obdurately contemn will bear witness against you on the day of judgment. After they lived awhile it was frequently disclosed that the blood could not be washed away and they were buried with it. Some repented and confessed and then easily enough, as it were, it disappeared.

This second example I myself have come upon, in connection with an infamous woman hardened to all sermons. Christ appeared to her and took the woman's hand, putting it into the wound in his side, saying, as she herself had said: the blood which you reject will adhere to you for evil, unless you correct yourself. It is well known that she confessed; still it adhered to her and could not be washed away till finally in some way she confessed a great hidden sin and immediately after that it disappeared. Such terrifying stories have great value in the beginning of a sermon.

The third way is to show by an example or story that the devil always tries to hinder the word of God and the hearing of it.

The fourth way is to show that to hear the word of God is a great sign of predestination. To this are reduced those ways which show that other benefits, earthly or heavenly, such as the fertility of the earth, the disposition to penitence, and the like, accrue to those who listen willingly.

The fifth way is to show that the preacher intends only to convert them, and not immediately after that to start begging. He should draw them to the love of God, to the fear of evil, to the honor of God, lest, if it is a principal feast, it may lack due honor. Then he should put the hearers into the right disposition for the Indulgence, which is granted to those who listen to the word of God, and preach like things by which he rightly deems to win over the hearers according to their condition.

FRANÇOIS FÉNÈLON

Natural Communication

Like Augustine's *On Christian Doctrine*, which was said to "begin rhetoric anew," the *Dialogues* of François Fénèlon (1651–1715) constitute the first modern rhetoric. Following the model of Plato and Cicero, Fénèlon, who was later Archbishop of Cambrai, allows his position on preaching to emerge dialectically through a conversation of characters designated A, B, and C. Character A expresses Fénèlon's opposition to the neo-scholasticism of Peter Ramus. One hundred years earlier Ramus had assigned rhetoric's traditional tasks of *invention* (research) and *disposition* (presentation or arrangement) to dialectic and had restricted rhetoric to ornamental eloquence. Fénèlon decried the effects of Ramism on the French pulpit of the seventeenth century. Mere ingenuity of speech was of no help to preachers like Fénèlon, who were concerned with a persuasive, missionary apostolate to the Huguenots. In an effort to restore the integrity of rhetoric (and preaching with it), he advocated a plain style of discourse and encouraged preachers to interpret and apply the Scripture according to the way in which the hearer most naturally appropriates the truth. The purposes of the gospel, he said, cannot be met by the artificially divided and tiered scholastic sermon. According to Fénèlon's method, the message is logically unfolded rather than displayed. Although his proposal stops short of modern "inductive preaching," it is clearly influenced by the growing pressures of seventeenth century experimental science. Fénèlon's rhetoric was a part of a comprehensive revolution in the relations of experience, thought, and discourse. Reliance on the predetermined structures of reason or on any other "authorities" would no longer do.

François Fénèlon, *Three Dialogues on Pulpit Eloquence*, trans. Samuel J. Eales (London: Thomas Baker, 1901 [1717]), pp. 1–9, 95–102.

A: Good morning, sir! have you then been to hear one of the sermons to which you have so often been desirous to take me? For my part, I am contented with the preacher of our parish.

B: I was charmed with mine; you have lost much, sir, by not having been present to hear him. I have rented a seat, so as not to lose one of the sermons for Lent. He is an admirable preacher, if you had once heard him you would be dissatisfied with every other.

A: I shall be careful, then, not to hear him, for I do not at all wish that one preacher should give me a distaste for all others; on the contrary, I wish for a man who will give me such a taste for and delight in the word of God, that I shall be the more disposed to listen to it whenever I can. But since I have, as you say, lost so much by not hearing this fine sermon, and you are full of it, you can make up to me for part of that loss, if you will be so kind as to repeat to me something of what you remember of it.

B: My account would do injustice to the sermon. There were a hundred beauties in it which I fail to remember. It would require a preacher to give you an account. . . .

A: But still; his plan, his demonstrations, his practical lessons, the chief truths which made up the body of his discourse—do none of these remain in your mind? or were you not attentive?

B: Far from it! I never listened with more attention and pleasure.

A: What then! do you wish me to beg and intreat you? . . .

B: Listen, then! I will repeat to you what I am able to remember. This was the text: "I have eaten ashes as it were bread" (Ps. 102:9). How could you find a more ingenious text for Ash Wednesday? He showed how, according to this passage, ashes ought to be on this day the food of our souls; then he interwove in his introduction, in the most ingenious way in the world, the story of Artemisia and the ashes of her husband. His transition to the "Ave Maria" was full of art. Then his division of his subject was happy; you shall judge of it. "These ashes," he said, "although they are a sign of penitence, are a principle of happiness: although they seem to humble us they are, in reality, a source of glory: although an emblem of death they are a remedy which leads to immortality." This division he repeated in various forms, and each time gave it a new luster by his antitheses. The rest of the discourse was no less polished and brilliant. . . .

A: I am rather afraid to tell you my opinion of that sermon, or to lower the high estimate which you have of it. . . .

B: Do not be afraid of that in the present instance. It is not at all from curiosity that I ask this of you. I have need to have correct ideas upon this matter. I wish to obtain solid information, not only for my own sake, but for that of others, since I too am, by my profession, under the obligation to preach. Speak to me, then, without reserve; do not hesitate to contradict me, nor fear that I shall be shocked.

A: As you wish it I will do so, and even from your report of that sermon I judge that it was exceedingly faulty.

B: In what respect?

A: You will see. Can a sermon be considered good in which the applications of Scripture are false, in which a story out of secular history is related in a puerile and unedifying manner, in which a false affectation of brilliancy is predominant everywhere?

B: Doubtless it cannot, but the sermon of which I have been telling you does not seem to me to be at all of that character.

A: Wait a little, and you will agree with what I say. When a preacher has chosen for his text these words, "I have eaten ashes as it were bread," ought he to have contented himself with tracing out a mere connection of words between the text and the ceremony of this day? Ought he not to have begun by explaining the true sense of his text before applying himself to his subject?

B: No doubt.

A: Would it not also have been desirable to look thoroughly into the circumstances and take the trouble to understand the whole occasion and design of the Psalm? Would it not have been proper to examine if the interpretation about which he was occupied was in accordance with the true sense of the words before giving it to the people as the word of God?

B: Most truly; but in what respect was it otherwise?

A: David, or whoever was the author of Ps. 102, is speaking in that passage of his own misfortune. He says that his enemies cruelly taunted him, seeing him beaten down into the dust, lying at their feet, and reduced (he uses here a poetical metaphor) to feed upon bread made of ashes, and water mixed with tears. What resemblance is there between the complaints of David, when he was driven from his throne and persecuted by his son Absalom, and the humiliation of a Christian who puts ashes upon his head in order to bring himself to think of death, and to withdraw from the pleasures of the world? Was there no other text in the Scripture that he could have taken? Had Jesus Christ, the apostles, the prophets never spoken of death and of the ashes of the tomb to which God brings down our human weakness? Are not the Scriptures full of a thousand touching phrases about this truth? . . .

B: You are growing too warm on this subject, sir. It is true, however, that this text is not used in a literal sense, but the preacher's explication of it may, nevertheless, have been very fine.

A: For my part I like to know if a saying be true before I find any beauty in it. But what as to the remainder?

C: The remainder of the sermon was of the same kind as the text. But what was the advantage of saying pretty things upon a subject so terrible, and of amusing the hearer by the secular story of the grief of Artemisia, when he was bound to speak gravely and solemnly, and to give only terrible ideas of death?

B: I see that you do not love flashes of wit on such occasions. But unless these are allowed, what would become of eloquence? Would you reduce all preachers to the simplicity of missionaries? That is needful for the unlearned people of course, but those who are cultivated have more delicate ears, and it is necessary to adapt our discourses to their taste.

A: Now you are leading me to another subject, but I was endeavoring to show you how ill-conceived this sermon was, and I was just about to speak of the division of it, but I think that you understand what it is that I am obliged to disapprove of. Here is a man who divides the whole subject of his discourse into three points. Now, when a division is made, it ought to be simple and natural; it should be a division which is found ready made in the subject itself, which clears up the details and arranges them in order, which is itself easily remembered, and which helps the hearer to remember other things: finally, a division which displays the greatness of a subject and of its parts. But here, on the contrary, you see a man who endeavors in the first place to dazzle you, who displays before you three epigrams, or three riddles, which he turns round and round with a practiced hand until you think you are looking at the passes of a juggler. Is that such a serious and grave manner of address as is calculated to make you hope for something useful and important? . . .

B: You have already frequently mentioned that *order*: do you mean anything else than a division? Have you upon that subject also some peculiar opinion?

A: You are, as you think, speaking in jest: but the fact is, that I am not less singular in my opinion on that subject than on the others.

B: Are you really serious?

A: Be assured that I am: and since we are on the subject, I am going to show you how defective is the *order* adopted by the greater number of orators.

B: Since you love order so much, *divisions* ought not to displease you.

A: But I am far from approving of them.

B: Why? Do they not render a discourse orderly and methodical?

A: Frequently, and indeed generally, they are put where they should not properly be, and thus they hinder a discourse, and render it uninteresting. They cut it up into two or three parts, which interrupts the action of the orator, and hinders the effect which it ought to produce. There is no longer a true unity in the discourse: it is divided into two or three different discourses, which are united only by an arbitrary bond. The sermon of the day before yesterday, that of yesterday, and that of today, provided that they are according to a plan strictly followed out, like the plans of sermons for Advent, make up just as much the body of a single discourse as the three points of one of those sermons make up together one sermon.

B: But what is order then, according to your views? What confusion there would be in a discourse which was not divided at all!

A: Do you suppose that there was much more confusion in the harangues of Demosthenes and of Cicero, than in the sermons of the preacher of your parish?

B: I do not know: I suppose not.

A: Do not be afraid to concede too much: the harangues of those great men are not divided as are the sermons of the present time. Not only they, but also Isocrates, of whom we have said so much, and the other ancient orators never adopted that method of division at all. The Fathers of the Church did not even know of it. S. Bernard, the last of them, often marks divisions; but he does not follow them, nor does he formally divide his sermons at all. Preaching existed for a long while without sermons having been divided; and it is a very modern invention which comes to us from the scholastic divines.

B: I allow that the schoolmen are but a faulty model for eloquence; but what form was there then anciently given to a discourse?

A: I am about to tell you that. A discourse was not formally divided at all: but all the subjects which it was necessary to distinguish from each other were carefully taken in succession, its own place was assigned to each, and each subject was arranged in proper order, so that it should follow where it would be most likely to make an impression upon the hearer. Often a consideration which, if put forth at first, would have appeared of little importance, becomes decisive when it is reserved for the time when the hearer shall have been prepared by other reasonings to appreciate all the power of it. Often a single word, happily employed in the place to which it belongs and which suits it, brings out an entire truth in all its clearness. Sometimes it is needful to leave a truth veiled and disguised till the very end of the speech: it is Cicero who asserts

228

this. In every case there ought to be an orderly succession of proofs; the first should prepare the way for the second, and the second should strengthen the first. It is needful to give a general view of the whole subject to begin with, and to dispose the mind of the hearer favorably towards it, by a modest and winning opening, by order of probity and candor. Then the preacher should go on to lay down his *general principles*; after that to state the *facts* he is engaged upon in a simple, clear, and telling manner, laying special stress upon those of which he means to make use afterwards. First *principles*; then *facts*; and from these draw the *conclusions* which you desire to reach; taking care to arrange the reasoning in such a manner as that the proofs will admit of being borne in mind easily. All this ought to be done in such a manner that the discourse should be continually growing; and that the hearer should feel more and more the growing weight of truth. Then is the time to throw out vivid and striking metaphors, and transitions of rhetoric calculated to excite the feelings. For that purpose it is needful to be acquainted with the interconnections of the feelings; to know which of them may be aroused most easily at first, and may then serve to arouse the others; and finally, which of them are able to produce the greatest effects; for with these latter the discourse should be brought to a close. It is often useful to make at the end a recapitulation or summary, which gathers up in a few sentences all the power of the orator, and sets anew before the hearers all that he has said which is most winning and persuasive. At the same time, it is not absolutely necessary always to follow that order in a uniform manner; each subject has its fitnesses and its exceptions. But even in this order a variety may be found almost infinite. This method, which is almost marked out for us by Cicero, cannot, as you see, be followed in a discourse which is cut invariably into three parts, nor observed absolutely in every point. An order is needful, but not an order that is expressly stated and shown from the commencement of the discourse. Cicero says that the best course, almost always, is to conceal it; and to lead on the hearer without his perceiving it. He goes so far as to state distinctly (I remember it well) that a speaker ought to conceal even the number of his arguments, so that they may not be counted, although they may be distinct in themselves, and in his own mind: and that a discourse ought not to have any clearly marked divisions. But the lack of discernment of late has gone so far that people do not recognize at all the order of a discourse, unless the speaker warns them of it at the commencement, and makes a pause at each point.

C: But do not divisions serve as an assistance to the mind and memory of the hearer? It is for this practical purpose they are made.

A: Divisions help the memory of the *speaker*. But the observance of a natural and consecutive order in subjects would effect that object still better, and that without being specially marked: since the true-connection of subjects best guides the mind. But as for divisions, the only people whom they help are those who have studied it, and whom their course of instruction has rendered familiar with that method; and if the great body of hearers remember the divisions better than the rest of the discourse, it is because they have been repeated more frequently. Generally speaking, things which are plain and practical will be best remembered.

JOHN BROADUS

Rhetoric and Homiletics

John Broadus (1827–1895) was a Baptist preacher, chaplain to Confederate forces in Virginia, church leader, and for many years professor of homiletics at Southern Baptist Seminary in Louisville. His textbook in homiletics first appeared in 1870 and remained the authoritative work for more than fifty years. (By 1889 the book was in its fourteenth edition.) In 1889 Broadus became the first Southern Baptist to give the Beecher Lectures at Yale. Although he warned against "the dangers of rhetoric," Broadus' homiletics is informed by the rhetorical works of Aristotle, Longinus, Cicero, and Horace, and he perpetuated the durable misconception: "homiletics may be called a branch of rhetoric, or a kindred art." Such a view reflected Ramus' restriction of rhetoric to style and delivery and, more seriously, prolonged the separation of homiletics from biblical studies, theology, and liturgics.

John Broadus, *A Treatise on the Preparation and Delivery of Sermons* (New York: A. C. Armstrong & Son, 1889 [1870]), pp. 25–31.

Now in respect of skill, preaching is an *art*; and while art cannot create the requisite powers of mind or body, nor supply their place if really absent, it can develop and improve them, and aid in using them to the best advantage. To gain skill, then, is the object of rhetorical studies, skill in the construction and in the delivery of discourse.

The rules of rhetoric are properly the result of induction. They are sometimes spoken of as if they had been drawn up by would-be wise men, who undertook to tell, on general principles, how one *ought* to speak. But they simply result from much thoughtful observation of the way in which men *do* speak, when they speak really well. Every one will sometimes see occasion to depart from these rules; but he ought to

231

understand that in disregarding the "rules of rhetoric," he is not nobly spurning artificial fetters and barriers, but simply turning aside, for the time, and for good reason, from the path in which it is usually found best to walk. And to do this will be wise or not wise, according as there is real occasion for it, and it is well managed. So too, we notice, men of sense often exactly conform to these rules, without knowing anything about them; for this is only saying that they speak exactly as men of sense usually do.

What we call rules are but the convenient expression of a principle. They put the principle into a compact form, so as to be easily remembered and readily applied. But the rule, however judiciously framed, can never be as flexible as the principle it represents. There will therefore be cases, and as regards some rules many cases, in which one *may violate the rule and yet be really conforming to the principle*, these being cases in which the principle would bend, and adapt itself to peculiar conditions, while the rule cannot bend. This consideration explains many of the instances in which a speaker produces a powerful effect though utterly violating the rules of rhetoric. Other such instances are explained by the sort of shock produced by a departure from what is usual, as the sleeping miller will wake when the mill stops. And in still other cases the effect is produced by a man's power in other respects, *in spite of* the particular violation of rule.

Rhetoric has to do with the use we make of material, the choice, adaptation, arrangement, expression. But after all, the material itself is more important. We hold that Demosthenes did not mean to contradict this, when he said (if he ever did in fact say it), that the first thing, second thing, third thing in speaking is delivery. He took the other for granted. No man has ever surpassed Demosthenes, in thorough mastery of the subjects upon which he spoke. But delivery had been with him a matter of peculiar difficulty, his deficiencies in that respect had defeated his early attempts, and his subsequent excellence had been gained only by enormous labor; it was natural that he should lay stress upon its importance, supposing that no man of sense could overlook the necessity of being fully acquainted with his subject. Now the things which ought *most* to be thought of by the preacher, are piety and knowledge, and the blessing of God. Skill, however valuable, is far less important than these; and there is danger that rhetorical studies will cause men to forget that such is the case. It is lamentable to see how often the remarks upon preaching made by preachers themselves, in conversation and in newspaper critiques, are confined to a discussion of the performance and the performer. Unsympathizing listeners or readers have, in such cases, too much ground for concluding that preachers are anxious only to display skill and gain oratorical reputation.

All are aware that there is both a conscious and an unconscious imitation. That which is unconscious is of course not so blameworthy, but it cannot fail to be injurious, and it is a subtle evil which should be guarded against with the sharpest self-inspection. Every one observes, too, that imitators are especially apt to imitate a man's faults. The reason is easily seen. The excellencies of a good speaker are apt to be symmetrical, while his faults are salient, prominent. The latter, therefore, will most readily attract unconscious imitation. As to the conscious imitator, he is sure to be a superficial observer, who will think that what he notices most in some admired speaker is the secret of his power, and will go to imitating that. Besides, it is *easier* to ape the single, salient fault, than the symmetrical combination of many excellencies.

Is the danger of imitation increased by attendance upon institutions of learning? Hardly. He who is so susceptible on the one hand, or on the other hand so silly, as to fall readily into it, will find some one to imitate, wherever he may be. Every country district has some favorite preacher, whom others around may be seen to imitate. When many of these imitators are gathered at a public institution, the men they imitate are fewer and more generally known, and therefore the fact attracts more attention. On the other hand, they are more likely to have pointed out to them the danger and the evils of imitation, so as utterly to eschew that which is conscious, and promptly to correct the unconscious, when made aware of it. Nor is there any greater danger of such imitation at a theological institution than at a college or university. Still, some men are very liable to this fault, and when about to hear the same speaker several times a week for many months, all ought to be on their guard against imitating his peculiarities.

There is much artificiality which ought not to be called by the odious name of affectation. The speaker's motives are good; he merely errs in judgment and taste. But a great error it is. In all speaking, especially in preaching, naturalness, genuineness, even though awkward, is really more effective for all the highest ends, than the most elegant artificiality. "But it is the highest art to conceal art." Nay, no art *can* conceal art. We may not perceive it, but we dimly, instinctively feel that there is something the matter, and perhaps wonder what it is; somehow, the preacher's well-meant efforts are failing to reach their aim. The danger of artificiality in speaking is very great. When one begins, he is apt to feel awkward to the new and strange situation. As one unaccustomed to riding on horseback must *learn* to sit naturally, and feel at ease, in the saddle, so very many speakers, perhaps all, have to *learn to be natural.* They must not only reject all intentional artificiality, but must carefully guard against that which is undesigned and unconscious. To forget self, because full of living desire to do men good, is the great means of being natural. It follows that a preacher ought never to preach merely for practice; this will inevitably tend to encourage artificiality. The first few efforts of a young man—which will often go much farther than he is at the time aware to form his habits for life—ought to be genuine, *bona fide* preaching. If he ever preaches in the presence of none but his fellow students and instructors, it ought to be only upon a subject thoroughly suited to *their* religious wants, and with a most earnest and prayerful effort to do them good. (It is believed that the plan of causing students to preach before the class results, upon the whole, in more harm than good, and that it ought to be avoided. Let them preach where it can be real preaching, or not at all. Even the debating society proposes a present end to be gained, and awakens some living interest.)

As regards all that pertains to preaching, and especially delivery, our efforts at rhetorical improvement must be *mainly negative.* We endeavor to gain correct general principles, and some idea of the errors and faults to which speakers are generally liable. We then speak, aiming to be guided by these principles, and to correct our faults as they may arise. It is unwise to set up at the outset some standard of excellence, and aim to conform to that. If one should take a fancy that cedar trees are more beautiful than oaks, and attempt to trim his oaks into the shape, and color them into the hue, of cedars, the result could only be ridiculous. Let the young cedar grow as a cedar, and the young oak as an oak, but straighten, prune, improve each of them into the best possible tree of its kind. And so as to speaking, be always yourself, your actual, natural self, but yourself developed, corrected, improved into the very best you are by nature capable of becoming.

The Greek word *homilia* signifies conversation, mutual talk, and so familiar discourse. The Greek writer Photius (9th century) says of Chrysostom's expository sermons on Genesis, that he finds the book bearing the name of discourses, but that they are much more like homilies (talks) because he so often speaks as if seeing the hearers before him, asks questions, and answers, and makes promises, and because they have not the formal arrangement of discourses. The Latin word *sermo* (from which we get *sermon*) has the same sense, of conversation, talk, discussion. It is instructive to observe that the early Christians did not apply to their public teachings the names given to the orations of Demosthenes and Cicero, but called them *talks*, familiar discourses.

From this word *homily* has been derived the term *homiletics*, as denoting the science or art of Christian discourse, or a treatise on that subject, embracing all that pertains to the preparation and delivery of sermons. Homiletics may be called a branch of rhetoric, or a kindred art. Those fundamental principles, which have their basis in human nature, are of course the same in both cases, and this being so, it seems clear that we must regard homiletics as rhetoric applied to this particular kind of speaking. Still, preaching is properly very different from secular discourse, as to the primary source of its materials, as to the directness and simplicity of style which become the preacher, and the unworldly motives by which he ought to be influenced. And while these and other peculiarities do not render it proper to treat homiletics as entirely distinct from rhetoric, they ought to be constantly borne in mind by the student of homiletics and by the working preacher.

AMOS N. WILDER

The New Utterance

The contribution of Amos N. Wilder (1895–) to homiletics is indirect but seminal. Wilder, who until his retirement in 1963 was Hollis Professor of Divinity at the Harvard Divinity School, is best known for his studies in ethics, eschatology, and aesthetics, and for his poetry, including the volume, *Grace Confounding*. His studies in Christianity and rhetoric transcend the older Bible-as-literature approaches by demonstrating the indissoluble connection between the content of the Christian message and its literary form. Wilder taught New Testament scholars (and preachers) that the question of *how* is as important to understanding a text as *what*. In many ways his work is most suggestive for preaching. Preaching does not require an esoteric or other-worldly vocabulary. The New Testament language, he says, is both common, ordinary, *Kleinliteratur*—a kind of folk art—and at the same time uncommonly tilted toward the future and the eschatological. One of its marks is brevity born of apocalyptic urgency. Focusing on the dialogue, story, and poem in the New Testament, Wilder reminds preachers of the oral-aural basis of the gospel and challenges the church to recover the potency of its earliest preaching.

Amos N. Wilder, *Early Christian Rhetoric* (Cambridge, MA: Harvard University Press, 1964, reissue, 1971), pp. 1–2, 9–15. Copyright © President and Fellows of Harvard College 1964, 1971. Reprinted by permission.

   Men of our time have inevitably had their attention called to the problem of language, and in various aspects. As modern devices make the world smaller and smaller, and throw us ever closer to peoples we had thought of as alien and remote, we find ourselves under the necessity of mastering more foreign tongues. But it is not only a matter of diverse

236

languages. We are now more conscious of the problem of communication itself even in our own language. Familiar words have lost their meaning for many; or the same word means different things to different people. Jargon and clichés usurp the place of discriminating speech in many areas of life. It is not only in the modern arts that we wrestle with the problem of meaning. It is not surprising that philosophy is today occupied above all with language, or that social science interests itself in the rhetoric of propaganda, or the church with the task of communication. In a situation like ours any use of language that aspires to a wide audience, as with mass-entertainment or advertising, has perforce to sink to a very low common denominator of what is not so much language as elementary stimuli by verbal gags, pictures and rhythms.

No doubt we are going through a period of the death and birth of language, one of the primordial features of human nature and culture. We have to become dumb before we can learn to use names and words faithfully again. It is in modern poetry that one sees this struggle most revealingly. In view of all this it is again not surprising that a main concern of the Christian church today is that of communication. The preacher, we are told, is like a man speaking into a dead microphone. We hear on all sides about the need for the modernization of the Christian message, translation of the ancient ideas and images, rediscovery of effective media of discourse. It has seemed worth while, therefore, to study the speech-forms and utterance of the Early Church and see what we can learn from it.

We are concerned first of all, therefore, not so much with what the early Christians said as how they said it. Yet this is a false distinction. The two cannot really be separated, but they can be looked at separately. We are interested here in all that has to do with the form and style of the New Testament writings. In this sense we are taking a literary approach. One could call it a study of the literary forms and genres of the Early Church. However, we must deal here not only with the writings as such but with the oral speech that lies behind them. It is not only a question of how the first Christians wrote but how they spoke and talked. It is better, therefore, to call our topic, "early Christian rhetoric." It is true that the term "rhetoric" has unfortunate connotations. But it has the advantage of covering both written and oral discourse. . . .

Jesus of Nazareth and his first followers broke into the world of speech and writing of their time, and, indeed, into its silence, with a novel and powerful utterance, that is, with a word, and the word of a layman. Ignatius of Antioch states the matter in his own surrealist style: "Jesus Christ, his son, who is his word proceeding from silence," (*Ad Magn.*

8:2); "he is the mouth which cannot lie, by which the Father has spoken truly," (*Ad Rom.* 8:2).

Just on the secular level note how significant this was and has been. At least there was here a new dynamics in human speech. One thinks of what John Keats said about "the indescribable gusto of the Elizabethan voice." But one searches for more significant analogies. It is a question of a word from the depths, with power. One analogy would be that of the man who stands up when a panic is spreading in a theater or a riot in the streets and recalls men to their true selves by a compelling word of authority. But this new word in Israel initiated a new world of meaning that went on spreading through ancient society. Here an analogy would be that of the impact of Dante's use of his vernacular dialect rather than Latin upon the spiritual culture of Europe. One can think also of the train of consequences that ensued upon the writing by the teenager Arthur Rimbaud of his *Bateau ivre*. This new spring of symbolist incantation determined much of the history of modern poetic utterance.

Thus we can understand the sense in which Ernst Fuchs has called the rise of the gospel a "speech-event" (*Sprachereignis*). By this he means a new departure, not just in the sense of a new religious teaching, but rather the opening up of a new dimension of man's awareness, a new breakthrough in language and symbolization. He can also say that the gospel represented a renewal of myth in Israel and the ancient world. The new enlargement of language took on ever new articulation in the course of the Apostolic Age.

To quote Professor Fuchs further: "Primitive Christianity is itself a speech-phenomenon. It is for that very reason that it established a monument in the new style-form which we call a 'gospel'. The Johannine apocalypse and, indeed, in the first instance the apostolic epistle-literature, these are creations of a new utterance which changes everything that it touches." [*Zur Frage nach dem historischen Jesus*, p. 261].

He adds that it is only on the margin of the New Testament that one can observe direct assimilation of pagan rhetoric, as for example in the Pastoral Epistles and in post-canonical writings; at a time, that is, when ecclesiastical patterns had begun to solidify.

Early Christianity, of course, brought forth new forms not only in language but in life itself, not only in writing but in ritual. One could say the same thing about other religions. But the spoken and written word have a basic role in the Christian faith. We note the background for this in the Old Testament. The religion of Israel is very much a matter of hearing rather than of seeing. Even God's actions are spoken of by the prophets as his word. No man can see God and live, but he is known in his speaking. By contrast it is the gods of the nations that are mute, and their visible images are dumb. As we read in Psalm 115:7, "They do not make a sound in their throat." Throughout Scripture, revelation is identified above all with speaking and hearing, with writing and reading, with colloquies and recitals, with tablets and scrolls and parchments, rather than with the imagery of the visual arts. Even visions are converted into writing: "Write the vision," we read in Hab. 2:2; and "write what you see in a book" in Rev. 1:11. The seer, indeed, seems to confuse the senses when he speaks of seeing the voice or of the "little scroll" which he was bidden to eat which was "as sweet as honey" in his mouth (10:10). Of course, like all religions Christianity has its sacred actions and spectacles, sacred places and times, sacred arts and objects, but it is in connection with God speaking that they are sacred.

It is intriguing to classify religions or even Christian groups according as they assign priority to auditory or visual images. On the one hand we have religion identified with word and answer; on the other with vision and ecstasy or metamorphosis. The New Testament speaks of the divine apprehension in terms of all the senses, not only hearing and sight but touch and smell (this last in the form of incense and fragrant odors). Yet the hearing mode is primary. The spirit may be rapt in vision, but it is with the heart that man hears the word of faith and with his mouth that he confesses and is saved (Rom. 10:8-10). Language, then, is more fundamental than graphic representation, except where the latter is itself a transcript in some sense of the word of God. . . .

In this light it is significant that the emotional dynamics of the gospel were always controlled by the meaningfulness of speech. To this, visionary and psychic phenomena were subordinated. And the language in question was not only the spoken word but personal address; it was not only in the indicative mode but in the imperative; it was not only in the third person but in the second and the first; it was not only a matter of declaration but a dialogue.

We can, therefore, appreciate the special incentives to the literary arts that Christianity has always provided, just as other faiths have provided special incentives to the visual arts or to music and dancing. Christianity is a religion of the Book and this has had its corollaries for its total cultural thrust. It is true that when the church took over the heritage of classical culture—ancient rhetoric, architecture, painting and sculpture—it related itself to all the arts and has exploited them all every since in changing situations. But the thesis still holds that the faith identifies itself fundamentally with the arts of hearing as against those of sight and touch. Even when the Christian paints or carves or dances or sings he does so to a text, and identifies himself with an archetypal dialogue between God and man.

Even so far as the literary arts themselves are in view – arts which have, of course, come to consummate expression in many religious traditions – one could argue that particular genres are at home both in the church and in particular Christian cultures of different periods. Erich Auerbach has studied the peculiar forms and styles of biblical and post-biblical Christian narrative forms as compared with classical. Martin Jarrett-Kerr has presented illustrations in different periods of Western literature of the special morphology of writings of Christian inspiration. One can also say that the novel as it has evolved in the modern period is a form which is only possible in a world whose view of man and society has been shaped by Christian presupposition.

Throughout our analysis we shall find ourselves recurring to one feature of the *earliest* Christian speech including that of Jesus. It is naïve, it is not studied; it is *extempore* and directed to the occasion, it is not calculated to serve some future hour. This utterance is dynamic, actual, immediate, reckless of posterity; not coded for catechists or repeaters. It is only one aspect of this that it is oral and not written. We find ourselves at first and for a rather long time in the presence of oral and live face-to-face communication. The gospel meant freedom of speech in this deeper sense. One did not hoard its formulas, since when occasion arose the Spirit would teach one what to say and how to witness and what defense to make. The earliest Christians lived on the free bounty of God in this sense also. The speech of the gospel was thus fresh and its forms novel and fluid; it came and went, as Ernst Fuchs says, with the freedom of sunshine, wind and rain.

Even the writing forms of the Early Church are better understood if we keep in mind the primal role of oral speech in the beginning. *Viva voce* communication is more malleable, more personal and more searching. These qualities were to distinguish Christian discourse even when it was obliged to take on written form. So far as we know Jesus never wrote a word, except on that occasion when, in the presence of the woman taken in adultery, "he bent down and wrote with his finger on the ground." In secular terms we could say that Jesus spoke as the birds sing, oblivious of any concern for transcription. Less romantically we can say that Jesus' use of the spoken word alone has its own theological significance. For one thing speaking is more direct than writing, and we would expect this in him through whom God openly staged his greatest controversy with his people. This transaction in which Jesus was involved was neither more nor less than a trial, and the parties in a trial confront each other in direct confrontation, as in Jesus' parables of the talents and the sheep and the goats. Jesus was a voice not a penman, a herald not a scribe, a watchman with his call in the market-place and the Temple, and not a cry of alarm in the wilderness like John the Baptist. This deportment of Jesus is a sign. We are reminded of the acted parables of certain of the prophets of earlier times: one of whom went naked as a token of slavery to come; and one of whom was eloquently dumb for a period. In Israel's tradition God's servants the prophets did not write unless they were ordered to, however it might be with the scribes.

That Jesus confined himself to the spoken and precarious word is of a piece with his renunciation of all cultural bonds such as home and trade and property; and with his instruction to his disciples to "take nothing for their journey except a staff; no bread, no bag, no money in their belts; but to wear sandals and not to put on two tunics" (Mark 6:8–9). This deportment has its true significance in the crisis with which Jesus was identified. For him and his generation history was fractured, time's course was in dissolution, continuities were broken. The act of writing presupposes continuities and a future. Jesus' word was for the present, the last hour. Indeed, his whole manifestation was a presence. This observation agrees with Günther Bornkamm's thesis in his *Jesus of Nazareth*. The Judaism of the time looked back to the Lawgiver and the covenants, and forward to the time of salvation. In so doing, the contemporaries of Jesus forfeited the present. Jesus brought both the will of God and the promises of God into the present with inexorable sharpness and actuality. Only the living voice can serve such an occasion.

Professor Fuchs makes this observation that Jesus wrote nothing and adds that even Paul wrote reluctantly. When he and other authors of our New Testament writings *did* write or dictate, their speech still has a special character, since the new depth and freedom of speech perpetuated itself even in the written productions. The voice of the writer is the voice of the speaker to a remarkable degree.

Paul wrote reluctantly and in any case without an extended historical perspective. He saw himself in the situation of harvester of the last days (Rom. 1:18), and as vocal herald of a world-crisis, as is suggested in the passage he cites from Psalm 16: "Their voice has gone out to all the earth, and their words to the ends of the world." [Rom. 10:18]

Paul writes always as one thwarted by absence and eagerly anticipating meeting or reunion. He is distressed by circumstances which prevent face-to-face address: "I could wish to be present with you now," he writes to the Galatians, "and change my tone, for I am perplexed about you" (4:20). Even in writing he falls into the style of direct oral plea and challenge. The very nature of the gospel imposes upon him ways of expression that suggest dramatic immediacy: devices and rhythms of the speaker rather than the writer; imagined dialogue; the situation of a court hearing or church trial with its accusations and defenses; the use of direct discourse; challenges not so much to understand the written words but to listen and behold; queries, exclamations and oaths.

To return to the sayings of Jesus. It is true that we do have evidence that his words and deeds were carried in memory and reported. We find such statements in the Gospels as the following: "At that time Herod the tetrarch heard about the fame of Jesus" (Matt. 14:1); or, "so his fame spread throughout all Syria" (Matt. 4:24). But we should make a distinction between an inevitable live diffusion of Jesus' words, on the one hand, and formal memorization or writing down of what he said, on the other. Some scholars hold that Jesus taught much as the scribes did with a view to the learning by heart of his words and deeds as though for catechetical use among his disciples. They have a plausible argument in the poetic and formal structure of much of his utterance. They even speak of mnemonic devices employed: parallelism, assonance, chiasmus and various scribal patterns of pronouncement. But all this ignores the radical difference between Jesus and the Jewish teachers, the eschatological outlook of Jesus, who was not schooling his followers in a learned mode for new generations to come, and the intense urging with which he spoke to the immediate crisis and the face-to-face hearer. The incomparable felicity and patterning of his sayings is indeed evident, but this formal perfection is not a matter of mnemonics; it is the countersign of the most effective communication of the moment. Naturally his words and parables were remembered and retold, often with great accuracy, so lucid and inevitable was his phrasing. But here as always the new speech of the gospel was not a matter of words on a tablet but a word in the heart, not a copybook for recitation but winged words for life.

JOSEPH SITTLER

The Role of the Imagination

One of the most neglected dimensions of preaching, that of the imagination, is addressed by Joseph Sittler (1904–　) in his Beecher Lectures of 1959. For Sittler the imagination is much more than a twister of texts or a turner of phrases. One of its functions is to fuse the theological *what* and the rhetorical *how* of each text, indeed, to show the inevitability of the *how*. Sittler's work on the rhetoric of preaching reflects the concerns of Amos Wilder, though Sittler approaches his task from a theological rather than a biblical and literary perspective. Theologically, he pioneered this generation's passion for the created order and ecology. Because humanity lives fully in the overlap of nature and grace, the religious imagination must be true to both, even if that fidelity means the loss of symmetry and polished assurance. Sittler offers preachers a succinct definition of the imagination: "Imagination is the process by which there is reenacted in the reader the salvatory immediacy of the word of God as this word is witnessed to by the speaker." Speaking from the vantage of hermeneutics, Ebeling makes a similar point when he says that the preacher "executes the text"–allows it to work its original will on the hearer. Sittler models an approach to preaching begun by Augustine. He uses Paul as a rhetorical paradigm. But instead of enjoining us to *imitate* Paul's *style* as it is revealed in selected passages, Sittler would have the preacher *imagine* Paul's *faith* as it is given shape, tonality, and style in language.

Joseph Sittler, *The Ecology of Faith* (Philadelphia: Fortress Press, 1961), pp. 46–48, 53–59. Copyright © by Fortress Press, 1961. Used by permission.

Imagination is not used here to designate that mere vivacity of the mind whereby unlikely juxtaposition of things or notions imparts startling cleverness to discourse; it is not a quality produced by the accidental endowment of the temperament with whimsicality. Contemporary preaching is full of dramatic and piquant turnings of the text, irresponsible arbitrariness in strained if ever so personable interpretations of biblical figures, events, and statements. That these practices are indulged in does not define imagination; one might be so unkind as to suggest that they define the preacher.

Imagination in its proper meaning is never an addition, it is an evocation. It is perception, not piquancy. Its work is not cosmetical or decorative; it is a function of percipiency. It is exercised not only in the perception of new qualities in things, but also in the discovery of hitherto unseen relationships between things. . . .

We move even closer to the definition of the role of imagination in preaching when we proceed from that judicious statement about general religious discourse to affirm that specifically Christian discourse is intrinsically needful of the same thing. For the central revelation of God in an Incarnation of grace in a world of nature inwardly requires that all discourse inclusive of these two magnitudes is of necessity dialectical. And imagination is the name for that category-transcending and fusing vision and speech which is proper to the given character of God's self-disclosure. The problem of proper Christian statement may be put in another way.

The "power and the truth" of the Christian gospel is in the level and the dimensions of its assault upon the hurt God-man relationship. When once it is acknowledged that man is a creature of nature who nevertheless cannot settle for the natural and that he is an object of grace who nevertheless must celebrate grace *in* the natural—it is at the same time settled that any adequate theological explication must forever be two sided; that is, dialectical. Its statements will always have to walk the knife edge at the frontier or fuse together the magnitudes of nature and grace.

This double character of Christian communication, if lost or blurred by oversimplification, banalization, or moralization, can perhaps achieve a hearing—but usually at the cost of the truth. Every simple term of the faith must be set forth in such a way that the multiple dimensions of its own content are exposed. . . .

Suppose that the substance of the sermon is a section from one of the Epistles of St. Paul. The substance and the style are here so wedded that the full-blooded personal substance of what the man is saying cannot be apprehended if the imagination has not been quickened and informed by the style of the utterance. There are ways of saying this, but we shall be better instructed if we test [Richard] Kroner's statement that "Imagination maintains the original unity of elements separated by abstract thought" by testing it against a concrete instance of the Pauline style.

In the whole of Scripture there is perhaps no passage in which is so tightly compressed and interwoven a various company of massive ideas as in the eighth chapter of Romans. To make a unity out of that complexity, a symphony out of that baffling polyphony of powerful voices is a task before which the dissecting intelligence feels its incompetence. And yet one has to know little of Paul to know that he, who wrote this, was in no confusion. His mind, though intricate in its matter and process, was no chaotic jumble of high epigrams. The task then is to seek from the inside of that passage its vital motif, its invisible cohesive element. And it is in this task that the imagination, if it has been informed by acquaintanceship with the ways of men as immemorially they have uttered in speech their turgid and passionate hearts, may silently and in strange ways come to an apprehension of what otherwise eludes the mind.

With the character of that passage in Romans in your memory, consider this: That there is here exhibited a quality of the mind in its working which is not permeable to the merely analytical intelligence. Here is a quality that inheres as much in the *how* of a man's speech as in the *what* of it. The prose is forward leaning, eager, exuberant—a manifestation of that end-over-end precipitousness that Deissmann remarked in Paul's writing, and caught in the phrase "his words come as water jets in uneven spurts from a bottle held upside down!" By imaginative association of this peculiarity of Paul's prose with other evidences of this quality in experience we can come closer to knowing what it was that made him write so. And when we know that, we shall perceive in this particular instance the value claimed for the imagination in our first proposition— perceptive clarity. For is not this exuberance precisely what nature regularly exhibits at every moment of arriving at something? A horse runs with a new rhythmic vitality when he turns the last curve and straightens out on the home stretch. This vitality is due not only to the drive to win but arises out of something elemental—the combination of joy and release, the sudden realization of a long and burdening task almost done. An intricate piece of music draws its diffuse parts together in its last pages and in a muscular and positive *coda* resolves its far-wandering voices. Mighty Burke, when he "arrives" at the end of his persuasive paragraphs, gathers together his powers of thought and language for coalescence into final words of authoritative eloquence.

To have "gotten through," to have come to the end, to sense the laborious process of "working toward" about to break through into an "end achieved," is a feeling we all know. I once worked in a shop where it was my job to operate an electric drill, boring holes at marked intervals in four-by-four timbers. For the first three and half inches, it goes its way with a steady, dull growl. And then the sound becomes more open, the machine gains speed, small splinters fly as the bit bites through the last solid stuff and spins and whines with singing ease. All "arriving," all completion has this quality, whether it be a four-inch timber, a symphony, a running horse, or a work of the mind. Can you, I wonder, have failed to observe that our minds have this quality in their working? — or can we fail to catch the tempo of "arriving" in these paragraphs of the apostle? For thirty-four verses Paul's powerful mind twists and turns and torments with as mighty a complex of ideas, actions, heavenly wonders as ever lived together in a sane man's mind. His language, like thought, is muscular, contorted, and tense — but always leaning forward . . . boring . . . boring into the hard deeps of his great subject. And then, at the thirty-fifth verse, "at last he beats his music out" in the amazing march of affirmations: "What shall we say to these things? . . . . If God be for us, who shall be against us. . . . " and passes into that song of intolerable joy that ends the chapter.

Here is imagination operating exegetically to do for a passage what studious mastery of its individual parts could never accomplish. For the imagination understands that this chapter is not only argument but adoration, not a series but a sequence, not an order but an organism. Meanings "by the way" are only to be understood from the peak of spiritual song which is the brave conclusion. The ideas here are not unrelated equals pitched into a rhetorical concatenation by enthusiasm; here is, rather, the sovereignty of grace battering its way to victory through all the torments and doubts and opacities of this man's embattled soul. . . .

It is possible to state how the imagination, immersed in the Pauline substance and peculiar style, works to prepare the preacher for more lively and fuller utterance of the writer's intention. The proposition is this: Imagination is the process by which there is reenacted in the reader the salvatory immediacy of the word of God as this word is witnessed to by the speaker.

The peculiarity of the style mirrors the fierce dialectic set up in the psyche by the invasive word. The strange jump, the quick, unself-conscious corrections, the contradictions — these, which bring pain to the teacher of composition, bring theological light to the preacher. The natural-religious man can make a clean explication of his case; and the beatified child of grace could, presumably, write untroubled prose descriptive of his life in God. But the Epistles of Paul stand at the intersection of nature and grace. They are the utterances of a man drawn taut between the huge repose of "a man in Christ" and the huge realism of a man of flesh and earth. It's the same man at the same time bearing witness to an inseparable movement of faith who can say: "Wretched man that I am. . . . There is therefore now no condemnation." "I don't care what you think of me. . . . I am troubled about what you think of me." Work out your own salvation in fear and trembling because no man can work out his own salvation and does not have to, for God is at work in you!

Preaching dare not put into unbroken propositions what the tormented peace of simultaneous existence in nature and grace can utter only in broken sentences. What God has riven asunder let no preacher too suavely join together. When we find, as we regularly do, that Paul stops the forward rush of active-voice statements to crack the integral structure of the affirmation with a joyous and devout regrounding of everything he is saying in the ultimacy of the passive voice, then we are obliged to stop with him. The salvatory power of the word of God is eloquent precisely at the embarrassed halt. Where grammar cracks, grace erupts.

"I know," says Paul. And then he reflects upon what he knows, how he came to know it, and what kind of a religious confidence it was within which such knowledge occurred. The reflection stops the assertion cold, and he writes, "I mean, rather, that I have been known."

"I love," says Paul. And then he reflects upon how he came to the point where he can say that, by virtue of what startling and reconstitutive convulsion it has been made possible, and he stops the active voice in the remembrance of ". . . this Son of God who loved me, and gave himself. . . ."

"I accept," says Paul. And then the reflection! And in the course of it the remembrance of the forgiving madness of the Holy which is the creator of all sanity, the huge and obliterating acceptance by God which powers all acceptances among men. The passive both destroys and recreates the active in its own image; and the Christian life is spun on the axis of this holy freedom whose one end is sunk in the accepting mercy of God, its other end in the need of man for an ultimate acceptance.

This transformation of the realm of the active by the power of the passive is a key not only to isolated fragments of Paul's witness, but also to an understanding of the man's total bearing within the world of nature and history. A peculiarly illuminating instance of this transformation is the memorable passage near the end of the Philippian letter. "Finally, brethren, whatever is true, whatever is honorable, whatever is just, whatever is pure, whatever is lovely, whatever is gracious, if there is any excellence, if there is anything worthy of praise, think about these things."

This paragraph, occurring as the summary of the argument of the entire Epistle, is strange. It's almost as if Paul had forgotten what he had written, or taken back what he had so passionately affirmed, or suddenly replaced his intense and consecrated gaze by a genial and relaxed smile. For three chapters he has hacked away at the adequacy of all the confidences and solidities of religion, morality, culture. I count everything as loss. . . even as refuse, he says—and drills through to the "surpassing worth of knowing Christ Jesus my Lord. . . . that I may know him and the power of his resurrection, and may share his sufferings, becoming like him in his death, that if possible I may attain the resurrection from the dead."

And then the shift. From the packed and intense inwardness of that statement, which locates the dynamics of the faith-full life of the Christian within the enacted morphology of the Incarnation and resurrection, he passes, after sundry personal and admonitory asides, to the blithe and humane: "Finally, brethren, whatever is true, whatever is honorable, whatever is just, whatever is pure, whatever is lovely. . . ."

This change in tone is not a shift in center. It is, in fact, not a shift at all. It is simply the language of a man who raises his eyes from the center to the circumference. It is the maturation of centered faith into a kind of evangelical humanism. It is rhetorical celebration of a basic Christian paradox: The way to breadth is by the road of narrow concentration; the road to beauty, graciousness, justice is a road that begins with the beauty of holiness, the graciousness of grace, the justice of judgment. The really humane is a function of the fully human; the fully human is beheld and bestowed in the new man who is the second Adam who, obedient in Gethsemane, restores to God and to himself the first Adam, faithless in Eden.

These too brief samplings of the Pauline style, while sufficient perhaps to make our formal point, suggest further and more subtle things to be learned from the Apostle to the Gentiles. To these we shall give some attention in the next. But these do suffice to bring under question the venerable practice of preaching from isolated texts, or even brief pericopes. This practice, perilous enough when exercised upon the Gospels, is intrinsically disastrous when applied to the Epistles of Paul. For to a degree unmatched in the world's literature, anything the man wrote has to be made luminous in the glow of everything he wrote. The apparent unsystematic of his language must be inwardly controlled and ordered by the central systematic of his passion. And he is the first to protest that this passion is a passive; that it is God's before it is his, and that it is his only because God's passion became a historical fact in a locatable garden.

FRED B. CRADDOCK

Narrative: Distance and Participation

Fred B. Craddock (1928–   ) is Professor of Preaching and New Testament at Candler School of Theology in Atlanta, Georgia. His book *Overhearing the Gospel* originated as the Beecher Lectures for 1978. Craddock's homiletical method incorporates the traditional concerns of rhetoric: subject matter, speech-design, and analysis of the hearer. By beginning with the last element, Craddock shows the necessity of the inductive approach to preaching which, he believes, more accurately conforms to the ordinary, human dialectic of search and discovery. The three-point deductive sermon violates the fundamental movement of thought and conversation. It tells too much too soon. Moreover, in a culture desensitized to the Christian message, the announcement of propositions will not communicate. Our contemporaries can no longer hear the gospel; they must overhear it. Intimations of these concerns are present in the rhetorician Fénelon, the pietist Spener, and the problem-solver Fosdick. But in terms of communication, the most profound modern theorist of indirect discourse is Kierkegaard whose comment Craddock takes as the epigraph to *Overhearing the Gospel*: "There is no lack of information in a Christian land; something else is lacking, and this is a something which the one man cannot directly communicate to the other."

The modest proposal being offered here is that the listener's experience of overhearing is a natural, effective, and at times life-changing dynamic that belongs in the church's classroom and sanctuary. And since it is also appropriate to the study, the transition from desk to pulpit or lectern is made less awkward and difficult. The discussion began with the perspective of the listener, not with the speaker's preparation or with the format of the content to be communicated. The reason was simple: with the listener is the place to begin. This has not always been the case. As we have observed, in the community of critical scholarship, the fear of the loss of objectivity and historical honesty made it seem essential that research and the reporting of that research be done with no consciousness of the existence of listener or reader. Otherwise, the listener's own needs and circumstances would add a variable to the investigations and color the results. The point is, in a laboratory or in a library the gathering of listeners would be an intrusion, an interruption of the proper business conducted in those settings. But in a classroom or sanctuary, listeners are not intruders; they are as ingredient to the proper business of these settings as equipment and formulae in the laboratory or books in the library. And the proper business in classroom and sanctuary is communication. To that end the teacher or preacher is servant and instrument; to that end, the subject matter is shaped and aimed.

It is so vital to our task that we be aware that the experience of listening is not a secondary consideration after we have done our exegesis of the texts and theological exploration. The listener is present from the beginning. The Christian tradition, biblical and extrabiblical, came to us from those who *heard* it and we *hear* it and pass it on to other *hearers*. The stamp of listening and the listenability of the message is on it when we get it, and in telling it, we confirm that it is listenable. To give such attention to the listener is not a concession to "what they want to hear," playing to the balcony or to the groundlings, nor is it an introduction to how to succeed as a speaker; it is no more or less than to describe the shape of the subject matter (it came from listeners) and the nature of the occasion (to effect a hearing).

Having begun with the experience of listening as the governing consideration in a communicative event and as the preoccupation that harnesses the imaginative, emotive, and cognitive powers of the speaker, I characterized that posture of listening called overhearing as consisting of two elements: distance and participation. Because the term and idea of distance may need rehabilitation I have urged that we think of distance as that quality in a communicative event that preserves invaluable benefits for the message and for the listener. For the message, distance preserves its objectivity as history, its continuity as tradition, and its integrity as a word that has existence prior to and apart from me as a listener. In other words, the distance between the message and the listener conveys the sense of the substantive nature and independence of the message, qualities that add to rather than detract from the persuasive and attention-drawing power of the message. I am much more inclined toward a message that has its own intrinsic life and force and that was prepared with no *apparent* awareness of me than toward a message that obviously did not come into being until I as a listener appeared and then was hastily improvised with desire for relevance offered as reason for the sloppy form and shallow content. These didactic and hortatory pieces are usually offered by well-meaning speakers who so highly prize relevance that they prepare their messages during the delivery. I do not wish to be sarcastic. My students who resist the lectionary and advanced planning for preaching with the retort "Who can know in January what will be relevant in June?" have a point, a good point, but a point that has its value only when held in tension with the *extra nos* of the gospel: the word does not have its source in the listener. This I am calling distance, a necessary dimension of the experience of overhearing that says to the listener, "You are sitting in on something that is of such significance that it could have gone on without you."

As for the benefit distance provides the listener, we have talked of the room the listener has, room in which to reflect, accept, reject, decide. As a listener, I must have that freedom, all the more so if the matter before me is of ultimate importance. As a listener who is also a teacher and preacher, I am aware that being armed with Holy Writ and the word of God tempts the communicator to think the urgency and weight of the message call for pressing in and pressing down, leaving the hearer no room for lateral movement. But the listener worth his salt will soon, against this assault, launch a silent but effective counterattack: find flaws in the speaker's grammar or voice or logic or dress; raise questions about the speaker's real motives; wonder imaginatively if the speaker has a dark past or even at this moment is entangled in affairs illicit; make distracting body movements; count things, such as light bulbs, knots in wood, number of persons present wearing glasses, etc. I need go no further; your list of things to do when surrounded by such a speaker probably is longer than mine.

The other element in the experience of overhearing is participation: free participation on the part of the hearer in the issues, the crises, the decisions, the judgment, and the promise of the message. Participation means the listener overcomes the distance, not because the speaker "applied" everything, but because the listener identified with experiences and thoughts related in the message that were analogous to his own. The fundamental presupposition operative here is the general similarity of human experiences. It is this which makes communication possible, but it is surprising how many speakers do not trust this to be the case and feel it incumbent on themselves to supply descriptions of experiences as though they were foreign to the hearer. If both speaker and listener have observed an old man asleep in church, lengthy description is unnecessary; if not, lengthy description evokes nothing. The story the speaker is telling and the personal story of the hearer must intersect at points or the hearer will despair; however, if they are exactly the same, the hearer will be bored or suspicious or defensive. Of course, the speaker who wants the listeners to overhear will preserve distance in narration, but the vocabulary, idiom, imagery, and descriptive detail will be such as will allow points or moments in the process at which the listener can "enter," identify, be enrolled. Otherwise, the listener cannot overcome the distance, and the communication, if attended to, becomes nothing more than shared information or a speech on a certain topic. . . .

There is a way of presenting a message that can be "consumed by the listener," a desirable goal if one is convinced that the meaning for a listener is not a product at the end of the event but rather that meaning is coextensive with the process of listening. We may be helped in understanding by the distinction between rhetoric and dialectic in Plato.

Rhetoric satisfies the listener, and at the end of a rhetorical presentation, the listener says, "That was a good speech." As a speech it is an identifiable entity, it has form and substance and can be repeated as is or printed and published. Dialectic, however, disturbs a listener toward a kind of conversion of thought or values or life direction, but it proceeds *at its own expense*. As it effects an experience in the listener, the presentation itself is used up. The early part of it moves you on to the next part, which may cause you to lose interest in or abandon the earlier part. And so the entire presentation proceeds. If effectively done, the listener could hear the earlier portions of the message repeated and be uninterested or even reject them. Why? Because the words and sentences and images moved the listener along in changing views or values; as those words did their work, they died. They were not framed to carry a truth statement or a position on a doctrine, but they were in the service of the listeners, to the end that what remained after the occasion would not be "a good speech" but a listener modified or changed or at least beginning to experience anew old notions fast asleep in the soul. . . .

Among the aids for generating listener experience, perhaps none is more effective than the metaphor. A metaphor is not simply a way of prettifying what is already known but a "medium of riper fuller knowing" [Phillip Wheelwright]. "A metaphor after all is the verbal recognition of a similarity between the apparently dissimilar" [Brian Wicker, *The Story-Shaped World*, p. 15]. The metaphor thus sets up a tension that can give a fresh new vision of that which had become familiar. Of course, some object to metaphors as imprecise, dishonest, and self-indulgent. For instance, why not clearly and directly say "the clouds are gray" instead of describing the clouds as *sad*? "To use metaphors, for example to speak of 'capricious' weather, 'majestic' mountains, or the 'merciless' sun, is to taint a mere object with illicitly anthropomorphic and moral meaning" [Wicker, p. 2]. The objection, however, presupposes that the only proper and valid use of language is positivistic, measured, and accurately descriptive, and forgets that a major function of language is to evoke, to draw the mind to the limits of the known, to hold the world before the eye at a new angle, to offer new configurations that shatter old calculations. The use of metaphor is for the communicator an act of creative imagination that has its completion in the equally creative and imaginative act of hearing the metaphor. At the heart of the parables of Jesus is the metaphor.

But imaginative language without a carefully chosen structure that it serves may be little more than teasing and dancing before the listeners. The shape of the communication is paramount in the business of effecting listener experience, and if the experience being sought is overhearing, the structure most congenial and with greatest potential for effectiveness is narrative. Before a narrative the hearer's posture is naturally that of the overhearer. A narrative is told with distance and sustains it in that the story unfolds on its own, seemingly only casually aware of the hearer, and yet all the while the narrative is inviting and beckoning the listener to participation in its anticipation, struggle, and resolution.

However, so much has been written and said in recent years about "narrative" and "story" in theological discourse that I feel it important to clarify what I do *not* mean and what I *do* mean by narrative structure for generating the dynamic of overhearing. First, I do not mean that narrative is to replace rational argument in Christian discourse. Rational argument serves to keep the communication self-critical, athletically trim, and free of a sloppy sentimentality that can take over in the absence of critical activity. We need always to be warned against the use of narratives and stories to avoid the issues of doctrine, history, and theological reflection. In the church we are doing more than telling anecdotes and sharing illustrations. Some readers of SK [Kierkegaard] become enamored of his stories and forget his insistence that Christianity can be conceptualized, and there are times and arenas in which that is the proper business. Nevertheless, it would be fatal for the cause of the gospel to allow logos (argument, proof) to discredit the story simply because "telling stories, even listening to stories, counts in our society as an unscientific occupation." Wherever the narrative is outlawed by theology as precritical, then theology becomes an exercise in trading symbols and terms, no longer nourished by experience. And if theology does not reflect critically upon human experiences with a view to changing or modifying them, what then does it do?

Second, I do not mean by proposing narrative form that the communicator is to do exegesis and interpretation in the texts of secular literature, ferreting out religious meanings that would justify using these pieces as the substance of Christian communications. There is, no doubt, great value in exploring the explicit and implicit dialogues between the Christian tradition and the secular literature of a given period, but there is something second-rate about combing through this literature for Christian meanings. It often represents a reaction against or an early abandoning of the texts of the Christian faith in favor of impoverishing and depleting the rich world of literature for "relevant" ideas. Many of us are weary of "meanings" and interpretation that tames art by reducing it to content and then applying the content. Just leave me alone with the narratives, to overhear them and to allow them and me room to maneuver. And this includes the narratives of the Bible.

Third, I do not mean by narrative structure that the lecture or sermon consists merely of reading or reciting long narrative portions of Scripture verbatim, as though the ancient texts can be thus simply and uncritically transferred from one language, land, culture, century, to another. The biblical text is always carried through history on the lap of the church, and it is her task, through the Holy Spirit, to keep the voice of Scripture a living voice through her teaching and preaching. But having said that, let me urge the irreplaceable value, for speaker and listener, of direct exposure to the text. Paul Ricoeur has written perceptively of the value of a naïve reading of the text, allowing the text to touch all our faculties and instincts. Such a reading should be followed by critical examination of the text without fear or reservation. Finally, the student returns to the text with a second naïveté, recovering again the narrative and discourse nature of the text. And even before Ricoeur, SK had urged a threefold method: spontaneity—reflection—spontaneity.

Finally, by narrative structure I am not proposing that the lecture or sermon be a long story or a series of stories or illustrations. While such may actually be the form used for a given message, it is not necessary in order to be narrative. Communication may be narrativelike and yet contain a rich variety of materials: poetry, polemic, anecdote, humor, exegetical analysis, commentary. To be narrativelike means to have the scope that ties it to the life of a larger community; it means the message has memory and hope; it means to be life-size in the sense of touching all the keys on the board rather than only intellectual or emotional or volitional; it means conveying the sense of movement *from* one place *to* another; it means having this movement on its own, as though the presence of the listeners were not essential to its process; it means thinking alongside the hearers. .

Narratives do not summarize events and relationships with commentary and application following. No listeners overhear that. Narratives reproduce and recreate events, with characters developing and events unfolding, and the teller reexperiencing while narrating. This reexperiencing is the source of the emotive and imaginative power in the telling. Emotion and imagination are not added as though options on the part of the speaker. In addition, narratives move from beginning to end, not vice versa for the benefit of lazy ears that want to be sure of the speaker's position, that want to be secure about "where he comes out," but that do not want to have to listen to the message to ascertain it. And finally, narratives move at a pace that most accurately recreates the pace of that which is narrated, sometimes slow, sometimes fast, now meandering, now running.

I pause here to remind myself how difficult it is to do what I have described in the last few sentences. For example, it is not easy to share with listeners the story of Abraham's offering of Isaac without rushing to the part about the ram caught in the bush. SK often complained that preachers would hurry to the happy fact of the ram in the bush or begin with it to assure the anxious or interrupt themselves often to promise the hearers that there will be a ram in the bush soon! Of course we know the story thus ended, but if the ending is allowed to scatter its smile back over the long and tortuous path of Abraham, then his faith is no longer seen as faith; it has been robbed of fear and trembling and is far removed from the pilgrimage of the hearer. A narrative that reproduces the painful journey up Mount Moriah reexperiences all the churning chemistry of a faith that is absolute in its obedience. And those who overhear the story begin to wish for and to despair of, to want and to dread, to seek and to fear, finding such faith. These can then enter into Abraham's profound joy and gratitude when the ram appears in the story.

In the same fashion, Easter can abort genuine appreciation of the pilgrimage of Jesus or any real grasp of what it means to follow Jesus. Of course, Easter is there and from that experience early Christians remembered and anticipated. But introduced too soon into the narrative, and

256

too easily, Easter can make Jesus' ministry a walk-through rehearsal, script in hand, and can make discipleship a real winner. I have heard pastors at funerals make the bereaved feel guilty for their tears. "Don't you believe in the resurrection?" Unfeeling chatter! Easter is *for* the tearful. The Christian faith insists the resurrection perpetuated the nail prints, it did not erase them. Easter has been put too soon in the story from many pulpits with the result that the tomb was not a cave, it was a short tunnel. In many churches Easter celebrations are empty of meaning because no one really was dead. The problem? The narrative is lost. In her wisdom the historic church insisted on the narrative: suffering, Good Friday, Easter, waiting, Pentecost. But what if Good Friday services are dropped because they are not successful, and Pentecost is dropped because it comes so late school is out and vacations have begun? I know; we can make up for it by having three services on Easter. No—the story has been lost. I go a-fishing.

Probably one reason people will overhear a story with more sustained attention than they will give to many lectures and sermons obviously prepared for them and addressed to them is that a narrative is of the nature of life itself. The form fits. "We dream in narrative, daydream in narrative, remember, anticipate, hope, despair, believe, doubt, plan, revise, criticize, construct, gossip, learn, hate, and love by narrative" [Wicker, p. 47]. All traditional societies have community stories in which the people live and by which they explain to themselves and to each other their social and metaphysical relationships. The chronology of a narrative locates the participants in time and place. Stories are read and heard because the experience of movement through time, common to the story and all its hearers, reassures that we are alive and can enlarge our living by identifying, participating, appropriating, the experiences of others. This is true even if the narrative disturbs and shocks. And if someone tells me a story large enough, with enough memory and enough hope to provide a context for my own personal narrative, then I am interested.

And this is the story Christians tell. It is very important that the structure of the message be a narrative. A narrative, by its structure, provides order and meaning, and therefore I cannot stress too heavily the indispensability of narrative shape and sequence. Change the shape, for instance, into a logical syllogism, and the question of whether the *content* of the message is altered is a moot one; the important point is the *function* of the message as narrative is now lost. The movement from chaos to order, from origin to destiny is broken and in its place are some ideas, well argued.

257

Again, let the Scriptures provide some models. Treat yourself to the experience of reading Mark in a single sitting. Let the narrative form of the Gospel move you along through meaningful activity, to crisis, through death, into an open future. Or the book of Acts: its impact is not solely in its message but in the form of its message. Casting the message as history puts the reader in touch with purposeful struggle toward a future which is God's. In fact, a narrative tends to *do* what it *tells*, mediating suffering and healing and salvation. These values accrue, not in a discussion about the story outside the narrative process, but in the actual telling.

VI
THE HEARER

GREGORY THE GREAT

Catalogue of Hearers

The ancient rhetorical arts were not concerned with audience analysis. It was the occasion—forensic, political, or ceremonial—that determined the quality of the speech. Although Aristotle examined the stimulation of various emotions in the hearer in Book II of the *Rhetoric*, neither he nor Augustine after him addressed the problem of a mixed audience. Indeed, it was a uniquely Christian problem created by the intellectual, social, and economic diversity represented at any given worship service. To this heterogeneity Gregory the Great (c. 540–604) spoke as no one had before him. He wrote the *Pastoral Rule* in 591 shortly after his election to the episcopacy of Rome. Like Chrysostom's *On the Priesthood*, it deals with the responsibilities of the bishop, especially preaching and pastoral care. His treatise reflects less rhetorical theory and more the pragmatic, administrative concerns of a pastor for his huge flock. Under the rubric of "one doctrine—many exhortations" Gregory first enumerates thirty-six pairs of opposite characters and then proceeds with a sermonette appropriate to each pairing. Thus this section of the *Pastoral Rule* is a series of sermon helps designed, in Gregory's words, "to suit all and each for their several needs."

Gregory the Great, *The Book of Pastoral Rule*, Part III, 1–3, 8, trans. James Barmby, *A Select Library of Nicene and Post-Nicene Fathers of the Christian Church*, Vol. XII (New York: The Christian Literature Company, 1894), pp. 24–29.

Since, then, we have shown what manner of man the pastor ought to be, let us now set forth after what manner he should teach. For, as long before us Gregory Nazianzen of reverend memory has taught, one and the same exhortation does not suit all, inasmuch as neither are all bound together by similarity of character. For the things that profit some often hurt others; seeing that also for the most part herbs which nourish some animals are fatal to others; and the gentle hissing that quiets horses incites whelps; and the medicine which abates one disease aggravates another; and the bread which invigorates the life of the strong kills little children. Therefore according to the quality of the hearers ought the discourse of teachers to be fashioned, so as to suit all and each for their several needs, and yet never deviate from the art of common edification. For what are the intent minds of hearers but, so to speak, a kind of tight tensions of strings in a harp, which the skillful player, that he may produce a tune not at variance with itself, strikes variously? And for this reason the strings render back a consonant modulation, that they are struck indeed with one quill, but not with one kind of stroke. Whence every teacher also, that he may edify all in the one virtue of charity, ought to touch the hearts of his hearers out of one doctrine, but not with one and the same exhortation.

What diversity there ought to be in the art of preaching

Differently to be admonished are these that follow:
Men and women.
The poor and the rich.
The joyful and the sad.
Prelates and subordinates.
Servants and masters.
The wise of this world and the dull.
The impudent and the bashful.
The forward and the fainthearted.
The impatient and the patient.
The kindly disposed and the envious.
The simple and the insincere.
The whole and the sick.
Those who fear scourges, and therefore live innocently; and those who have grown so hard in iniquity as not to be corrected even by scourges.
The too silent, and those who spend time in much speaking.
The slothful and the hasty.
The meek and the passionate.
The humble and the haughty.
The obstinate and the fickle.

The gluttonous and the abstinent.

Those who mercifully give of their own, and those who would fain seize what belongs to others.

Those who neither seize the things of others nor are bountiful with their own; and those who both give away the things they have, and yet cease not to seize the things of others.

Those that are at variance, and those that are at peace.

Lovers of strife and peacemakers.

Those that understand not aright the words of sacred law; and those who understand them indeed aright, but speak them without humility.

Those who, though able to preach worthily, are afraid through excessive humility; and those whom imperfection or age debars from preaching, and yet rashness impels to it.

Those who prosper in what they desire in temporal matters; and those who covet indeed the things that are of the world, and yet are wearied with the toils of adversity.

Those who are bound by wedlock, and those who are free from the ties of wedlock.

Those who have had experience of carnal intercourse, and those who are ignorant of it.

Those who deplore sins of deed, and those who deplore sins of thought.

Those who bewail misdeeds, yet forsake them not; and those who forsake them, yet bewail them not.

Those who even praise the unlawful things they do; and those who censure what is wrong, yet avoid it not.

Those who are overcome by sudden passion, and those who are bound in guilt of set purpose.

Those who, though their unlawful deeds are trivial, yet do them frequently; and those who keep themselves from small sins, but are occasionally whelmed in graver ones.

Those who do not even begin what is good, and those who fail entirely to complete the good begun.

Those who do evil secretly and good publicly; and those who conceal the good they do, and yet in some things done publicly allow evil to be thought of them.

But of what profit is it for us to run through all these things collected together in a list, unless we also set forth, with all possible brevity, the modes of admonition for each?

Differently, then, to be admonished are men and women; because on the former heavier injunctions, on the latter lighter are to be laid, that those may be exercised by great things, but these winningly converted by light ones.

Differently to be admonished are young men and old; because for the most part severity of admonition directs the former to improvement, while kind remonstance disposes the latter to better deeds. For it is written, "Rebuke not an elder, but entreat him as a father" (I Tim. 5:1).

How the poor and the rich should be admonished

Differently to be admonished are the poor and the rich: for to the former we ought to offer the solace of comfort against tribulation, but in the latter to induce fear as against elation. For to the poor one it is said by the Lord through the prophet, "Fear not, for thou shall not be confounded" (Isa. 54:4). And not long after, soothing her, he says, "O thou poor little one, tossed with tempest." And again he comforts her, saying, "I have chosen thee in the furnace of poverty." But, on the other hand, Paul says to his disciple concerning the rich, "Charge the rich of this world, that they be not high-minded nor trust in the uncertainty of their riches" (I Tim. 6:17); where it is to be particularly noted that the teacher of humility in making mention of the rich, says not "Entreat," but "Charge"; because, though pity is to be bestowed on infirmity, yet to elation no honor is due. To such, therefore, the right thing that is said is the more rightly commanded, according as they are puffed up with loftiness of thought in transitory things. Of them the Lord says in the Gospel, "Woe unto you that are rich, which have your consolation" (Luke 6:24). For, since they know not what eternal joys are, they are consoled out of the abundance of the present life. Therefore consolation is to be offered to those who are tried in the furnace of poverty; and fear is to be induced in those whom the consolation of temporal glory lifts up; that both those may learn that they possess riches which they see not, and these become aware that they can by no means keep the riches that they see. Yet for the most part the character of persons changes the order in which they stand; so that the rich man may be humble and the poor man proud. Hence the tongue of the preacher ought soon to be adapted to the life of the hearer so as to smite elation in a poor man all the more sharply as not even the poverty that has come upon him brings it down, and to cheer all the more gently the humility of the rich as even the abundance which elevates them does not elate them. . . .

But sometimes, when the powerful of this world are taken to task, they are first to be searched by certain similitudes, as on a matter not concerning them; and, when they have pronounced a right sentence as against another man, then in fitting ways they are to be smitten with regard to their own guilt; so that the mind puffed with temporal power may in no wise lift itself up against the reprover, having by its own judgment trodden on the neck of pride, and may not try to defend itself, being bound by the sentence of its own mouth. For hence it was that Nathan the prophet, having come to take the king to task, asked his judgment as if concerning the cause of a poor man against a rich one (II Sam. 12:4–5 ff.), that the king might first pronounce sentence, and afterwards hear of his own guilt, to the end that he might by no means contradict the righteous doom that he had uttered against himself. Thus the holy man, considering both the sinner and the king, studied in a wonderful order first to bind the daring culprit by confession, and afterwards to cut him to the heart by rebuke. He concealed for a while whom he aimed at, but smote him suddenly when he had him. For the blow would perchance have fallen with less force had he purposed to smite the sin openly from the beginning of his discourse; but by first introducing the similitude he sharpened the rebuke which he concealed. He had come as a physician to a sick man; he saw that the sore must be cut; but he doubted of the sick man's patience. Therefore he hid the medicinal steel under his robe, which he suddenly drew out and plunged into the sore, that the patient might feel the cutting blade before he saw it, lest, seeing it first, he should refuse to feel it.

How the joyful and the sad are to be admonished

Differently to be admonished are the joyful and the sad. That is, before the joyful are to be set the sad things that follow upon punishment; but before the sad the promised glad things of the kingdom. Let the joyful learn by the asperity of threatenings what to be afraid of; let the sad hear what joys of reward they may look forward to. For to the former it is said, "Woe unto you that laugh now! For ye shall weep" (Luke 6:25); but the latter hear from the teaching of the same Master, "I will see you again, and your heart shall rejoice, and your joy no man shall take from you" (John 16:22). But some are not made joyful or sad by circumstances, but are so by temperament. And to such it should be intimated that certain defects are connected with certain temperaments; that the joyful have lechery close at hand, and the sad wrath. Hence it is necessary for every one to consider not only what he suffers from his peculiar temperament, but also what worse thing presses on him in connection with it; lest, while he fights not at all against that which he has, he succumb also to that from which he supposes himself free.

How subjects and prelates are to be admonished

Differently to be admonished are subjects and prelates: the former that subjection crush them not, the latter that superior place elate them not; the former that they fail not to fulfill what is commanded them, the latter that they command not more to be fulfilled than is just; the former that they submit humbly, the latter that they preside temperately. For this, which may be understood also figuratively, is said to the former, "Children, obey your parents in the Lord:" but to the latter it is enjoined, "And ye, fathers, provoke not your children to wrath" (Col. 3:20–21). Let the former learn how to order their inward thoughts before the eyes of the hidden judge; the latter how also to those that are committed to them to afford outwardly examples of good living. For prelates ought to know that, if they ever perpetrate what is wrong, they are worthy of as many deaths as they transmit examples of perdition to their subjects. Wherefore it is necessary that they guard themselves so much the more cautiously from sin as by the bad things they do they die not alone, but are guilty of the souls of others, which by their bad example they have destroyed. Wherefore the former are to be admonished, lest they should be strictly punished, if merely on their own account they should be unable to stand acquitted; the latter, lest they should be judged for the errors of their subjects, even though on their own account they find themselves secure. Those are to be admonished that they live with all the more anxiety about themselves as they are not entangled by care for others; but these that they accomplish their charge of others in such wise as not to desist from charge of themselves, and so to be ardent in anxiety about themselves, as not to grow sluggish in the custody of those committed to them. To the one, who is at leisure for his own concerns, it is said, "Go to the ant, thou sluggard, and consider her ways, and learn wisdom" (Prov. 6:6): but the other is terribly admonished, when it is said, "My son, if thou be surety for thy friend, thou hast stricken thy hand with a stranger, and art snared with the words of thy mouth, and art taken with thine own speeches." For to be surety for a friend is to take charge of the soul of another on the surety of one's own behavior. Whence also the hand is stricken with a stranger, because the mind is bound with the care of a responsibility which before was not. But he is snared with the words of his mouth, and taken with his own speeches, because, while he is compelled to speak good things to those who are committed to him, he must needs himself in the first place observe the things that he speaks. He is therefore snared with the words of his mouth, being constrained by the requirement of reason not to let his life be relaxed to what agrees not with his teaching. Hence before the strict judge he is compelled to accomplish as much in deed as it is plain he has enjoined on others with his voice. . . .

Wherefore those who are over others are to be admonished, that through earnestness of circumspection they have eyes watchful within and round about, and strive to become living creatures of heaven. For the living creatures of heaven are described as full of eyes round about and within. And so it is meet that those who are over others should have eyes within and round about, so as both in themselves to study to please the inward judge, and also, affording outwardly examples of life, to detect the things that should be corrected in others.

Subjects are to be admonished that they judge not rashly the lives of their superiors, if perchance they see them act blamably in anything, lest whence they rightly find fault with evil they thence be sunk by the impulse of elation to lower depths. They are to be admonished that, when they consider the faults of their superiors, they grow not too bold against them, but, if any of their deeds are exceedingly bad, so judge of them within themselves that, constrained by the fear of God, they still refuse not to bear the yoke of reverence under them. . . .

How the forward and the faint-hearted are to be admonished

Differently to be admonished are the forward and the faint-hearted. . . .

For we then best correct the forward, when what they believe themselves to have done well we show to have been ill done; that whence glory is believed to have been gained, thence wholesome confusion may ensue. But sometimes, when they are not at all aware of being guilty of the vice of forwardness, they more speedily come to correction if they are confounded by the infamy of some other person's more manifest guilt, sought out from a side quarter; that from that which they cannot defend, they may be made conscious of wrongly holding to what they do defend. . . .

But on the other hand we more fitly bring back the faint-hearted to the way of well-doing, if we search collaterally for some good points about them, so that, while some things in them we attack with our reproof, others we may embrace with our praise; to the end that the hearing of praise may nourish their tenderness, which the rebuking of their fault chastises. And for the most part we make more way with them for their profit, if we also make mention of their good deeds; and, in case of some wrong things having been done by them, if we find not fault with them as though they were already perpetrated, but, as it were, prohibit them as what ought not to be perpetrated; that so both the favor shown may increase the things which we approve, and our modest exhortation avail more with the faint-hearted against the things which we blame.

JONATHAN EDWARDS

The Inner Turmoil of the Awakened

Jonathan Edwards (1703–1758) wrote his *Narrative of the Surprising Work of God in Northampton, Mass., 1735*, to explain and defend the revival known as the Great Awakening. In the course of the narrative he draws a composite psychological portrait of the person "being wrought upon." His account includes the story of a woman who declared that it was pleasant to think of lying in the dust all the days of her life, mourning for sin, and the famous case study of four-year-old Phoebe Bartlett who spent a part of each day in her closet contemplating hell. The narrative concludes with the "Gradual Withdrawing of the Spirit" instanced first by a townsman who slit his own throat. Edwards' psychology focused on the "affections" or emotions as the source of all behavior. In genuine cases of revival the affections were influenced and augmented by a supernatural sense given by the Holy Spirit. But because the affections are so crucial to religious behavior, they are also the workshop in which Satan creates false images and religious delusions. Although Edwards is aware of some "impure" elements in the awakening, he judges it on the whole to be a "work of God." The question of the listener's emotional response and its validity as a measurement of conversion is one that has persisted in contemporary discussions of preaching. What is the most appropriate *form* — liturgical, psychological, and otherwise — of the listener's response to the word? While the *Narrative* does not answer the question, it says much about the inner turmoil and the pressures of the social environment that weighed upon those to whom Jonathan Edwards preached and ministered.

Jonathan Edwards, *Thoughts on the Revival of Religion in New England, 1740, to which is prefixed a Narrative of the Surprising Work of God in Northampton, Mass., 1735* (New York: American Tract Society, n.d.), pp. 28–34.

269

I therefore proceed to give an account of the manner of persons being wrought upon; and here there is a vast variety, perhaps as manifold as the subjects of the operation; but yet in many things there is a great analogy in all.

Persons are first awakened with a sense of their miserable condition by nature, the danger they are in of perishing eternally, and that it is of great importance to them that they speedily escape and get into a better state. Those that before were secure and senseless, are made sensible how much they were in the way to ruin in their former courses. Some are more suddenly seized with convictions; it may be, by the news of others' conversion, or something they hear in public or in private conference, their consciences are suddenly smitten, as if their hearts were pierced through with a dart; others have awakenings that come upon them more gradually; they begin at first to be more thoughtful and considerate, so as to come to a conclusion in their minds that it is their best and wisest way to delay no longer, but to improve the present opportunity; and have accordingly set themselves seriously to meditate on those things that have the most awakening tendency, on purpose to obtain convictions; and so their awakenings have increased, till a sense of their misery, by God's Spirit setting in therewith, has had fast hold of them. Others that, before this wonderful time, had been something religious and concerned for their salvation, have been awakened in a new manner, and made sensible that their slack and dull way of seeking was never like to attain their purpose, and so have been roused up to a greater violence for the kingdom of heaven.

These awakenings, when they have first seized on persons, have had two effects: one was, that they have brought them immediately to quit their sinful practices, and the looser sort have been brought to forsake and dread their former vices and extravagancies. When once the Spirit of God began to be so wonderfully poured out in a general way through the town, people had soon done with their old quarrels, backbitings, and intermeddling with other men's matters; the tavern was soon left empty, and persons kept very much at home; none went abroad unless on necessary business, or on some religious account, and every day seemed, in many respects, like a Sabbath day. And the other effect was, that it put them on earnest application to the means of salvation, reading, prayer, meditation, the ordinances of God's house, and private conference; their cry was, "What shall we do to be saved?" The place of resort was now changed—it was no longer the tavern, but the minister's house; and that was thronged far more than ever the tavern had been wont to be.

270

There is a very great variety as to the degree of fear and trouble that persons are exercised with before they obtain any comfortable evidences of pardon and acceptance with God: some are from the beginning carried on with abundantly more encouragement and hope than others; some have had ten times less trouble of mind than others, in whom yet the issue seems to be the same. Some have had such a sense of the displeasure of God, and the great danger they were in of damnation, that they could not sleep at night; and many have said that when they have lain down, the thoughts of sleeping in such a condition have been frightful to them, and they have scarcely been free from terror while they have been asleep, and they have awaked with fear, heaviness, and distress still abiding on their spirits. It has been very common that the deep and fixed concern that has been on persons' minds, has had a painful influence on their bodies, and given disturbance to animal nature.

The awful apprehensions persons have had of their misery have, for the most part, been increasing the nearer they have approached to deliverance, though they often pass through many changes in the frame and circumstances of their minds. Sometimes they think themselves wholly senseless, and fear that the Spirit of God has left them, and that they are given up to judicial hardness; yet they appear very deeply exercised about that fear, and are in great earnest to obtain convictions again.

Together with those fears, and that exercise of mind which is rational, and which they have just ground for, they have often suffered many needless distresses of thought, in which Satan probably has a great hand to entangle them and block up their way; and sometimes the disease of melancholy has been evidently mixed; of which, when it happens, the tempter seems to make great advantage, and puts an unhappy bar in the way of any good effect. One knows not how to deal with such persons; they turn everything that is said to them the wrong way, and most to their own disadvantage. And there is nothing that the devil seems to make so great a handle of as a melancholy humor, unless it be the real corruption of the heart.

But it has been very remarkable that there has been far less of this mixture in this time of extraordinary blessing, than there was wont to be in persons under awakenings at other times; for it is evident that many that before had been exceedingly involved in such difficulties, seemed now strangely to be set at liberty. Some persons that had before for a long time been exceedingly entangled with peculiar temptations of one sort or other, and unprofitable and hurtful distresses, were soon helped over former stumbling-blocks that hindered any progress towards saving good, and convictions have wrought more kindly, and they have been successfully carried on in the way to life. And thus Satan seemed to be restrained till towards the latter end of this wonderful time, when God's Spirit was about to withdraw.

Many times persons under great awakenings were concerned because they thought they were not awakened, but miserable, hard-hearted, senseless creatures still, and sleeping upon the brink of hell. The sense of the need they have to be awakened, and of their comparative hardness, grows upon them with their awakenings, so that they seem to themselves to be very senseless, when indeed most sensible. There have been some instances of persons that have had as great a sense of their danger and misery as their natures could well subsist under, so that a little more would probably have destroyed them; and yet they have expressed themselves much amazed at their own insensibility and dullness in such an extraordinary time as it then was.

Persons are sometimes brought to the borders of despair, and it looks as black as midnight to them a little before the day dawns in their souls. Some few instances there have been of persons who have had such a sense of God's wrath for sin, that they have been overborne and made to cry out under an astonishing sense of their guilt, wondering that God suffers such guilty wretches to live upon the earth, and that he doth not immediately send them to hell; and sometimes their guilt does so glare them in the face, that they are in exceeding terror for fear that God will instantly do it; but more commonly the distresses under legal awakenings have not been to such a degree. In some these terrors do not seem to be so sharp, when near comfort, as before; their convictions have not seemed to work so much that way, but they seem to be led further down into their own hearts to a further sense of their own universal depravity, and deadness in sin.

The corruption of the heart has discovered itself in various exercises in the time of legal convictions. Sometimes it appears in a great struggle like something roused by an enemy, and Satan, the old inhabitant, seems to exert himself like a serpent disturbed and enraged. Many, in such circumstances, have felt a great spirit of envy towards the godly, especially towards those that are thought to have been lately converted, and most of all towards acquaintances and companions when they are thought to be converted: indeed some have felt many heart-risings against God, and murmurings at his ways of dealing with mankind, and his dealings with themselves in particular. It has been much insisted on, both in public and private, that persons should have the utmost dread of such envious thoughts, which, if allowed, tend exceedingly to quench the Spirit of God, if not to provoke him finally to forsake them. And when such a spirit has much prevailed, and persons have not so earnestly strove against it as they ought to have done, it has seemed to be exceedingly to the hinderance of the good of their souls, but in some other instances where persons have been much terrified at the sight of such wickedness in their hearts, God has brought good to them out of evil, and made it a means of convincing them of their own desperate sinfulness, and bringing them off from all self-confidence. The drift of the Spirit of God in his legal strivings with persons, has seemed most evidently to be to make way for and to bring to a conviction of, *their absolute* dependence on his sovereign power and grace, and the universal necessity of a mediator, by leading them more and more to a sense of their exceeding wickedness and guiltiness in his sight; the pollution and insufficiency of their own righteousness, that they can in no wise help themselves, and that God would be wholly just and righteous in rejecting them and all that they do, and in casting them off for ever, though there be a vast variety as to the manner and distinctness of persons' convictions of these things.

As they are gradually more and more convinced of the corruption and wickedness of their hearts, they seem to themselves to grow worse and worse, harder and blinder, and more desperately wicked, instead of growing better. They are ready to be discouraged by it, and oftentimes never think themselves so far off from good, as when they are nearest. Under the sense which the Spirit of God gives them of their sinfulness, they often think that they differ from all others; their hearts are ready to sink with the thought, that they are the worst of all, and that none ever obtained mercy who were so wicked as they.

PHILLIPS BROOKS

The Congregation

In several ways the homiletical theory of Phillips Brooks (1835–1893) exemplifies the liberal tradition in America, especially liberalism's optimistic view of human nature. Yale theologian Lewis Brastow, writing at the turn of the century, observes that "[Brooks] was the consummate flower of nine generations of cultured Puritan stock. . . . [O]n the one side he inherited the Puritan's high sense of the worth of humanity, his large estimate of its possibilities of development, his recognition of the sacredness of the individual soul, and his enthusiastic devotion to its highest welfare. This was the spring of that lofty idealism that passed into an optimism that was unmatched in his generation." (*Representative Modern Preachers*, p. 195). The loftiness of perspective in Brooks is always tempered by common sense and the working pastor's eye for reality. After heralding the "ideal and heroic" qualities of the assembled congregation, Brooks adds soberly, "It may be a delusion." His view of the congregation as a microcosm of humanity adds balance and breadth to the parochialism of much preaching. His counter-insistence on the preacher's rootedness and sense of place derives ultimately from his liberal understanding of the Incarnation: just as Jesus assumed human nature in order to lead it to its highest attainable level, so preaching strives to elevate its audience by helping it recognize and capitalize on its higher nature.

Phillips Brooks, *Lectures on Preaching* (New York: E. P. Dutton & Company, 1907 [1877]), pp. 180–190.

I have said what I had to say about the preacher and about the sermon. Today I want to speak to you about the congregation. There is something remarkable in the way in which a minister talks about "my congregation." They evidently come to seem to him different from the rest of humankind. There is the rest of our race, in Europe, Asia, Africa, and America, and the Islands of the Sea, and then there is "my congregation." A man begins the habit the moment he is settled in a parish. However young, however inexperienced he may be, he at once takes possession of that fraction of the human family and holds it with a sense of ownership. He immediately assumes certain fictions concerning them. He takes it for granted that they listen to his words with a deference quite irrespective of the value of the words themselves. He talks majestically about "what I tell my congregation," as if there were some basis upon which they received his teachings quite different from that upon which other intelligent men listen to one who takes his place before them as their teacher. He supposes them to be subject to emotions which he expects of no one else. He thinks that, in some mysterious way, their property as well as their intelligence is subject to his demand, to be handed over to him when he shall tell them that he has found a good use to which to put it. He imagines that, though they are as clear-sighted as other people, little devices of his which are perfectly plain to everybody else impose upon them perfectly. He talks about them so unnaturally that we are almost surprised when we ask their names and find that they are men and women whom we know, men and women who are living ordinary lives and judging people and things by ordinary standards, with all the varieties of character and ways which any such group must have, whom he has separated from the rest of humanity and distinguished by their relation to himself and calls "my congregation."

I think that a good deal of the unreality of clerical life comes from this feeling of ministers about their congregations. I have known many ministers who were frank and simple and unreserved with other people for whom they did not feel a responsibility, but who threw around themselves a cloak of fictions and reserves the moment that they met a parishioner. They were willing to let the stranger clearly see that there were many things in religion and theology which they did not know at all, many other questions on which they were in doubt, points of their church's faith which they thought unimportant to salvation, methods of their church's policy which they thought injudicious. All this they would say freely as they talked with the wolf over the sheepfold wall, or with some sheep in the next flock; but in their own flock they held their peace, or said that everything was right, and never dreamed that their flock saw through their feeble cautiousness. The result of all this has sometimes been that parishioners have trusted other men more than their minister just because he was their minister, and have gone with their troublesome questions and dark experiences to some one who should speak of them freely because he should not feel that he was speaking to a member of his congregation.

It is easy to point out what are the causes of this feeling which we thus see has its dangers. The bad part in it is a love of power. The better part is an anxious sense of responsibility, made more anxious by the true affection which grows up in the preacher's heart. It is almost a parental feeling in its worse as in its better features, in its partialness and jealousy as well as in its devotion and love. But besides these there is another element in the view which the preacher takes of his congregation which I beg you to observe and think about. It is the way in which he assumes a difference in the character of people when they are massed together from any which they had when they were looked at separately. This is the real meaning of the tone which is in that phrase "my congregation." It is to the minister a unit of a wholly novel sort. There is something in the congregation which is not in the men and women as he knows them in their separate humanities, something in the aggregate which was not in the individuals, a character in the whole which was not in the parts. This is the reason why he can group them in his thought as a peculiar people, hold them in his hand as a new human unity, his congregation.

And no doubt he is partly right. There is a principle underneath the feeling by which he vaguely works. A multitude of people gathered for a special purpose and absorbed for the time into a common interest has a new character which is not in any of the individuals which compose it. If you are a speaker addressing a crowd you feel that. You say things to them without hesitation that would seem either too bold or too simple to say to any man among them if you talked with him face to face. If you are a spectator and watch a crowd while some one else is speaking to it, you can feel the same thing. You can see emotions run through the mass that no one man there would have deigned to show or submitted to feel if he could have helped it. The crowd will laugh at jokes which every man in the crowd would have despised, and be melted by mawkish pathos that would not have extorted a tear from the weakest of them by himself. Imagine Peter the Hermit sitting down alone with a man to fire him up for a crusade. Probably all this is less true of one of our New England audiences than of any other that is ever collected in our land. In it every man keeps guard over his individuality and does not easily let it sink in the character of the multitude. And yet we are men and women even here, and the universal laws of human nature do work even among us. And this is a law of nature which all men have observed. "It is a strange thing to say," says Arthur Helps in "Realmah," "but when the

276

number of any public body exceeds that of forty or fifty, the whole assembly has an element of joyous childhood in it, and each member revives at times the glad, mischievous nature of his schoolboy days." Canning used to say that the House of Commons as a body had better taste than the man of the best taste in it, and Macaulay was much inclined to think that Canning was right.

What are the elements of this new character which belongs to a congregation, a company of men? Two of them have been suggested in the two instances which I have just quoted,—the spontaneousness and liberty, and the higher standard of thought and taste. It is not hard to see what some of the other elements are. There is no doubt greater receptivity than there is in the individual. Many of the sources of antagonism are removed. The tendency to irritation is put to rest. The pride of argument is not there; or is modified by the fact that no other man can hear the argument, because it cannot speak a word, but must go on in a man's own silent soul. It is easier to give way when you sit undistinguished in an audience, and your next neighbor cannot see the moment when you yield. The surrender loses half its hardness when you have no sword to surrender and no flag to run down. And besides this, we have all felt how the silent multitude in the midst of which we sit or stand becomes ideal and heroic to us. We feel as if it were listening without prejudice, and responding unselfishly and nobly. So we are lifted up to our best by the buoyancy of the mass in which we have been merged. It may be a delusion. Each of these silent men may be thinking and feeling meanly, but probably each of them has felt the elevation of the mass about him of which we are one particle, and so is lifting and lifted just as we are. Who can say which drops in the great sweep of the tide are borne, and which bear others toward the shore, on which they all rise together?

This, then, is the good quality in the character of the congregation. It produces what in general we call responsiveness. The compensating quality which takes away part of the value of this one is its irresponsibility. The audience is quick to feel, but slow to decide. The men who make up the audience, taken one by one, are slower to feel an argument or an appeal to their higher nature, but when they are convinced or touched, it is comparatively easy to waken the conscience, and make them see the necessity of action. . . .

The result of all this is that in the congregation you have something very near the general humanity. You have human nature as it appears in its largest contemplation. Personal peculiarities have disappeared and man simply as man is before you. This is a great advantage to the preacher. "It is more easy to know man in general than to know a man

277

in particular," said La Rochefoucauld. If in the crowd to whom you preach you saw every man not merely in general but in particular, if each sat there with his idiosyncrasies bristling all over him, how could you preach? There are some preachers, I think, who are ineffective from a certain incapacity of this larger general sight of humanity which a congregation ought to inspire. . . .

I think that it is almost necessary for a man to preach sometimes to congregations which he does not know, in order to keep this impression of preaching to humanity, and so to keep the truth which he preaches as large as it ought to be. He who ministers to the same people always, knowing them minutely, is apt to let his preaching grow minute, to forget the world, and to make the same mistakes about the gospel that one would make about the force of gravitation if he came to consider it a special arrangement made for these few operations which it accomplishes within his own house. I think there are few inspirations, few tonics for a minister's life better than, when he is fretted and disheartened with a hundred little worries, to go and preach to a congregation in which he does not know a face. As he stands up and looks across them before he begins his sermon, it is like looking the race in the face. All the nobleness and responsibility of his vocation comes to him. It is the feeling which one has had sometimes in travelling when he has passed through a great town whose name he did not even learn. There were men, but not one man he knew; houses, shops, churches, bank, post-office, business and pleasure, but none of them individualized to him by any personal interest. It is human life in general, and often has a solemnity for him which the human lives which he knows in particular have lost. And this is what we often find in some strange pulpit, facing some congregation wholly made up of strangers.

But this should be occasional. A constant travelling among unknown towns would no doubt weaken and perhaps destroy our sense of humanity altogether. There can be no doubt that it is good for a man that his knowledge of a congregation should be primarily and principally the knowledge of his own congregation, certain dangers of a too exclusive relationship being obviated by preaching sometimes where the people are all strange. It is remarkable how many of the great preachers of the world are inseparably associated with the places where their work was done, where perhaps all their life was lived. In many cases their place has passed into their name as if it were a true part of themselves. Chrysostom of Constantinople, Augustine of Hippo, Savonarola of Florence, Baxter of Kidderminster, Arnold of Rugby, Robertson of Brighton, Chalmers of Glasgow, and in our New England a multitude of such associations which have become historic and compel us always to think of the man with the place and of the place with the man. Everywhere a man must have his place. The disciples are sometimes set before us as if our pastoral life of modern times were an entire departure from their methods; and yet they had their pastorates. Think of St. Paul at Ephesus. Think of St. John in the same city. Think of St. James at Jerusalem. The same necessity, may we not say, which required that the Incarnation should bring divinity, not into humanity in general, but into some special human circle, into a nation, a tribe, a family, requires that he who would bear fruit everywhere for humanity should root himself into some special plot of human life and draw out the richness of the earth by which he is to live at some one special point. There is nothing better in a clergyman's life than to feel constantly that through his congregation he is getting at his race. Certainly the long pastorates of other days were rich in the knowledge of human nature, in a very intimate relation with humanity. These three rules seem to have in them the practical sum of the whole matter. I beg you to remember them and apply them with all the wisdom that God gives you. First. Have as few congregations as you can. Second. Know your congregation as thoroughly as you can. Third. Know your congregation so largely and deeply that in knowing it you shall know humanity.

W. E. B. DU BOIS

The Faith of Black Folk

The overriding reality for the black congregation in America is its heritage of enslavement and the continuing problem of alienation in a white society. William Edward Burghardt Du Bois (1868–1963) described that alienation as "the Veil" and devoted a lifetime of scholarship to removing the Veil that separates the races. Du Bois studied at Fisk, Berlin, and Harvard, where he earned a Ph.D. For many years he taught sociology at Atlanta University. His breadth of learning, long life, and enduring passion for justice and truth made Du Bois the presiding intellectual in the black awakening in the late nineteenth and early twentieth centuries. He wrote numerous studies on black history and civilization, including works on black religion, but the series of "sketches" he was at first hesitant to publish, *The Souls of Black Folk*, was the work that established his international reputation. Since its appearance in 1903, the book has gone through more than twenty-five editions. Although later in his life Du Bois rejected the organized church, he appreciated black folk religion and spirituality, and well understood the religious matrix of contemporary black culture and institutions in America. He also wearied of racism in the United States and moved to Ghana, where he died on the day of the March on Washington in August, 1963. The following selection does not describe a religious "audience" as much as it evokes several atmospheres: the rural milieu in which preaching first thrived and the modern, urban ambiguities with which it now struggles. In a few paragraphs he captures the aura of black folk worship, which he summarizes under three headings: the preacher, the music, and the frenzy. His later analysis of the plight of the modern black, torn between conformity and radicalism, still illumines the contemporary black church.

W. E. B. Du Bois, *The Souls of Black Folk* (Chicago: A. C. McClurg and Company, 1903), pp. 189–206.

280

It was out in the country, far from home, far from my foster home, on a dark Sunday night. The road wandered from our rambling log-house up the stony bed of a creek, past wheat and corn, until we could hear dimly across the fields a rhythmic cadence of song,—soft, thrilling, powerful, that swelled and died sorrowfully in our ears. I was a country school-teacher then, fresh from the East, and had never seen a Southern Negro revival. To be sure, we in Berkshire were not perhaps as stiff and formal as they in Suffolk of olden times; yet we were very quiet and subdued, and I know not what would have happened those clear Sabbath mornings had some one punctuated the sermon with a wild scream, or interrupted the long prayer with a loud Amen! And so most striking to me, as I approached the village and the little plain church perched aloft, was the air of intense excitement that possessed that mass of black folk. A sort of suppressed terror hung in the air and seemed to seize us,—a pythian madness, a demoniac possession, that lent terrible reality to song and word. The black and massive form of the preacher swayed and quivered as the words crowded to his lips and flew at us in singular eloquence. The people moaned and fluttered, and then the gaunt-cheeked brown woman beside me suddenly leaped straight into the air and shrieked like a lost soul, while round about came wail and groan and outcry, and a scene of human passion such as I had never conceived before.

Those who have not thus witnessed the frenzy of a Negro revival in the untouched backwoods of the South can but dimly realize the religious feeling of the slave; as described, such scenes appear grotesque and funny, but as seen they are awful. Three things characterized this religion of the slave,—the Preacher, the Music, and the Frenzy. The Preacher is the most unique personality developed by the Negro on American soil. A leader, a politician, an orator, a "boss," an intriguer, an idealist,—all these he is, and ever, too, the center of a group of men, now twenty, now a thousand in number. The combination of a certain adroitness with deep-seated earnestness, of tact with consummate ability, gave him his preeminence, and helps him maintain it. The type, of course, varies according to time and place, from the West Indies in the sixteenth century to New England in the nineteenth, and from Mississippi bottoms to cities like New Orleans or New York.

The Music of Negro religion is that plaintive rhythmic melody, with its touching minor cadences, which, despite caricature and defilement, still remains the most original and beautiful expression of human life and longing yet born on American soil. Sprung from the African forests, where its counterpart can still be heard, it was adapted, changed, and intensified by the tragic soul-life of the slave, until, under the stress of law and whip, it became the one true expression of a people's sorrow, despair, and hope.

Finally the Frenzy or "Shouting," when the Spirit of the Lord passed by, and, seizing the devotee, made him mad with supernatural joy, was the last essential of Negro religion and the one more devoutly believed in than all the rest. It varied in expression from the silent rapt countenance or the low murmur and moan to the mad abandon of physical fervor,—the stamping, shrieking, and shouting, the rushing to and fro and wild waving of arms, the weeping and laughing, the vision and the trance. All this is nothing new in the world, but old as religion, a Delphi and Endor. And so firm a hold did it have on the Negro, that many generations firmly believed that without this visible manifestation of the God there could be no true communion with the Invisible.

These were the characteristics of Negro religious life as developed up to the time of Emancipation. Since under the peculiar circumstances of the black man's environment they were the one expression of his higher life, they are of deep interest to the student of his development, both socially and psychologically. Numerous are the attractive lines of inquiry that here group themselves. What did slavery mean to the African savage? What was his attitude toward the world and life? What seemed to him good and evil,—God and Devil? Whither went his longings and strivings, and wherefore were his heart-burnings and disappointments? Answer to such questions can come only from a study of Negro religion as a development, through its gradual changes from the heathenism of the Gold Coast to the institutional Negro church of Chicago.

Moreover, the religious growth of millions of men, even though they be slaves, cannot be without potent influence upon their contemporaries. The Methodists and Baptists of America owe much of their condition to the silent but potent influence of their millions of Negro converts. Especially is this noticeable in the South, where theology and religious philosophy are on this account a long way behind the North, and where the religion of the poor whites is a plain copy of Negro thought and methods. The mass of "gospel" hymns which has swept through American churches and well-nigh ruined our sense of song consists largely of debased imitations of Negro melodies made by ears that caught the jingle but not the music, the body but not the soul, of the Jubilee songs. It is thus clear that the study of Negro religion is not only a vital part of the history of the Negro in America, but an interesting part of American history.

The Negro church of today is the social center of Negro life in the

United States, and the most characteristic expression of African character. Take a typical church in a small Virginia town: it is the "First Baptist"—a roomy brick edifice seating five hundred or more persons, taste-
fully finished in Georgia pine, with a carpet, a small organ, and stained-
glass windows. Underneath is a large assembly room with benches. This
building is the central club-house of a community of a thousand or more
Negroes. Various organizations meet here,—the church proper, the
Sunday-school, two or three insurance societies, women's societies,
secret societies, and mass meetings of various kinds. Entertainments,
suppers, and lectures are held beside the five or six regular weekly religious services. Considerable sums of money are collected and expended
here, employment is found for the idle, strangers are introduced, news
is disseminated and charity distributed. At the same time this social,
intellectual, and economic center is a religious center of great power.
Depravity, Sin, Redemption, Heaven, Hell, and Damnation are preached
twice a Sunday with much fervor, and revivals take place every year after
the crops are laid by; and few indeed of the community have the hardi-
hood to withstand conversion. Back of this more formal religion, the
church often stands as a real conserver of morals, a strengthener of
family life, and the final authority on what is good and right.

Thus one can see in the Negro church today, reproduced in microcosm, all that great world from which the Negro is cut off by color-
prejudice and social condition. In the great city churches the same
tendency is noticeable and in many respects emphasized. A great church
like the Bethel of Philadelphia has over eleven hundred members, an
edifice seating fifteen hundred persons and valued at one hundred
thousand dollars, an annual budget of five thousand dollars, and a
government consisting of a pastor with several assisting local preachers,
an executive and legislative board, financial boards and tax collectors;
general church meetings for making laws; subdivided groups led by class
leaders, a company of militia, and twenty-four auxiliary societies. The
activity of a church like this is immense and far-reaching, and the
bishops who preside over these organizations throughout the land are
among the most powerful Negro rulers in the world.

Such churches are really governments of men, and consequently a
little investigation reveals the curious fact that, in the South, at least,
practically every American Negro is a church member. Some, to be sure,
are not regularly enrolled, and a few do not habitually attend services;
but, practically, a proscribed people must have a social center, and that
center for this people is the Negro church. The census of 1890 showed
nearly twenty-four thousand Negro churches in the country, with a total

enrolled membership of over two and a half millions, or ten actual church members to every twenty-eight persons, and in some southern states one in every two persons. Besides these there is the large number who, while not enrolled as members, attend and take part in many of the activities of the church. There is an organized Negro church for every sixty black families in the nation, and in some states for every forty families, owning, on an average, a thousand dollars' worth of property each, or nearly twenty-six million dollars in all.

Such, then, is the large development of the Negro church since Emancipation. The question now is, What have been the successive steps of this social history and what are the present tendencies? First, we must realize that no such institution as the Negro church could rear itself without definite historical foundations. These foundations we can find if we remember that the social history of the Negro did not start in America. He was brought from a definite social environment,—the polygamous clan life under the headship of the chief and the potent influence of the priest. His religion was nature-worship, with profound belief in invisible surrounding influences, good and bad, and his worship was through incantation and sacrifice. The first rude change in this life was the slave ship and the West Indian sugar-fields. The plantation organization replaced the clan and tribe, and the white master replaced the chief with far greater and more despotic powers. Forced and long-continued toil became the rule of life, the old ties of blood relationship and kinship disappeared, and instead of the family appeared a new polygamy and polyandry, which, in some cases, almost reached promiscuity. It was a terrific social revolution, and yet some traces were retained of the former group life, and the chief remaining institution was the priest or medicine-man. He early appeared on the plantation and found his function as the healer of the sick, the interpreter of the Unknown, the comforter of the sorrowing, the supernatural avenger of wrong, and the one who rudely but picturesquely expressed the longing, disappointment, and resentment of a stolen and oppressed people. Thus, as bard, physician, judge, and priest, within the narrow limits allowed by the slave system, rose the Negro preacher, and under him the first Afro-American institution, the Negro church. This church was not at first by any means Christian nor definitely organized; rather it was an adaptation and mingling of heathen rites among the members of each plantation, and roughly designated as Voodooism. Association with the masters, missionary effort and motives of expediency gave these rites an early veneer of Christianity, and after the lapse of many generations the Negro church became Christian.

Two characteristic things must be noticed in regard to this church. First, it became almost entirely Baptist and Methodist in faith; secondly, as a social institution it antedated by many decades the monogamic Negro home. From the very circumstances of its beginning, the church was confined to the plantation, and consisted primarily of a series of disconnected units; although, later on, some freedom of movement was allowed, still this geographical limitation was always important and was one cause of the spread of the decentralized and democratic Baptist faith among the slaves. At the same time, the visible rite of baptism appealed strongly to their mystic temperament. Today the Baptist Church is still largest in membership among Negroes and has a million and a half communicants. Next in popularity came the churches organized in connection with the white neighboring churches, chiefly Baptist and Methodist, with a few Episcopalian and others. The Methodists still form the second greatest denomination, with nearly a million members. The faith of these two leading denominations was more suited to the slave church from the prominence they gave to religious feeling and fervor. The Negro membership in other denominations has always been small and relatively unimportant, although the Episcopalians and Presbyterians are gaining among the more intelligent classes today, and the Catholic Church is making headway in certain sections. After Emancipation, and still earlier in the North, the Negro churches largely severed such affiliations as they had had with the white churches, either by choice or by compulsion. The Baptist churches became independent, but the Methodists were compelled early to unite for purposes of episcopal government. This gave rise to the great African Methodist Church, the greatest Negro organization in the world, to the Zion Church and the Colored Methodist, and to the black conferences and churches in this and other denominations.

The second fact noted, namely, that the Negro church antedates the Negro home, leads to an explanation of much that is paradoxical in this communistic institution and in the morals of its members. But especially it leads us to regard this institution as peculiarly the expression of the inner ethical life of a people in a sense seldom true elsewhere. Let us turn, then, from the outer physical development of the church to the more important inner ethical life of the people who compose it. The Negro has already been pointed out many times as a religious animal,—a being of that deep emotional nature which turns instinctively toward the supernatural. Endowed with a rich tropical imagination and a keen, delicate appreciation of Nature, the transplanted African lived in a world animate with gods and devils, elves and witches; full of strange influences,—of good to be implored, of evil to be propitiated. Slavery, then, was to him the dark triumph of evil over him. All the hateful powers of the underworld were striving against him, and a spirit of revolt and revenge filled his heart. He called up all the resources of heathenism to aid,—exorcism and witchcraft, the mysterious Obi worship with its barbarous rites, spells, and blood-sacrifice even, now and then, of human victims. Weird midnight orgies and mystic conjurations were invoked, the witch-woman and the voodoo-priest became the center of Negro group life, and that vein of vague superstition which characterizes the unlettered Negro even today was deepened and strengthened.

In spite, however, of such success as that of the fierce Maroons, the Danish blacks, and others, the spirit of revolt gradually died away under the untiring energy and superior strength of the slave masters. By the middle of the eighteenth century the black slave had sunk, with hushed murmurs, to his place at the bottom of a new economic system, and was unconsciously ripe for a new philosophy of life. Nothing suited his condition then better than the doctrines of passive submission embodied in the newly learned Christianity. Slave masters early realized this, and cheerfully aided religious propaganda within certain bounds. The long system of repression and degradation of the Negro tended to emphasize the elements in his character which made him a valuable chattel: courtesy became humility, moral strength degenerated into submission, and the exquisite native appreciation of the beautiful became an infinite capacity for dumb suffering. The Negro, losing the joy of this world, eagerly seized upon the offered conceptions of the next; the avenging Spirit of the Lord enjoining patience in this world, under sorrow and tribulation until the Great Day when he should lead his dark children home,—this became his comforting dream. His preacher repeated the prophecy, and his bards sang,—

"Children, we all shall be free
When the Lord shall appear!"

With the beginning of the abolition movement and the gradual growth of a class of free Negroes came a change. We often neglect the influence of the freedman before the war, because of the paucity of his numbers and the small weight he had in the history of the nation. But we must not forget that his chief influence was internal,—was exerted on the black world; and that there he was the ethical and social leader. Huddled as he was in a few centers like Philadelphia, New York, and New Orleans, the masses of the freedmen sank into poverty and listlessness; but not all of them. The free Negro leader early arose and his chief characteristic was intense earnestness and deep feeling on the slavery question. Freedom became to him a real thing and not a dream. His religion became darker and more intense, and into his ethics crept a note of revenge, into his songs a day of reckoning close at hand. The "Coming of the Lord" swept this side of death, and came to be a thing to be hoped for in this day. Through fugitive slaves and irrepressible discussion this desire for freedom seized the black millions still in bondage, and became their one ideal of life. The black bards caught new notes, and sometimes even dared to sing.—

> "O Freedom, O Freedom, O Freedom over me!
> Before I'll be a slave
> I'll be buried in my grave,
> And go home to my Lord
> And be free."

For fifty years Negro religion thus transformed itself and identified itself with the dream of Abolition, until that which was a radical fad in the white North and an anarchistic plot in the white South had become a religion to the black world. Thus, when Emancipation finally came, it seemed to the freedman a literal Coming of the Lord. His fervid imagination was stirred as never before, by the tramp of armies, the blood and dust of battle, and the wail and whirl of social upheaval. He stood dumb and motionless before the whirlwind: what had he to do with it? Was it not the Lord's doing, and marvellous in his eyes? Joyed and bewildered with what came, he stood awaiting new wonders till the inevitable Age of Reaction swept over the nation and brought the crisis of today.

It is difficult to explain clearly the present critical stage of Negro religion. First, we must remember that living as the blacks do in close contact with a great modern nation, and sharing, although imperfectly, the soul-life of that nation, they must necessarily be affected more or less directly by all the religions and ethical forces that are today moving the United States. These questions and movements are, however, overshadowed and dwarfed by the (to them) all-important question of their civil, political, and economic status. They must perpetually discuss the "Negro Problem,"—must live, move, and have their being in it, and interpret all else in its light or darkness. With this come, too, peculiar problems of their inner life,—of the status of women, the maintenance of home, the training of children, the accumulation of wealth, and the prevention of crime. All this must mean a time of intense ethical ferment, of religious heart-searching and intellectual unrest. From the double life every American Negro must live, as a Negro and as an American, as swept on by the current of the nineteenth while yet struggling in the eddies of the fifteenth century,—from this must arise a painful self-consciousness, an almost morbid sense of personality and a moral hesitancy which is fatal to self-confidence. The worlds within and without the Veil of Color are changing, and changing rapidly, but not at the same rate, not in the same way; and this must produce a peculiar wrenching of the soul, a peculiar sense of doubt and bewilderment. Such a double life, with double thoughts, double duties, and double social classes, must give rise to double words and double ideals, and tempt the mind to pretense or revolt, to hypocrisy or radicalism.

In some such doubtful words and phrases can one perhaps most clearly picture the peculiar ethical paradox that faces the Negro of today and is tingeing and changing his religious life. Feeling that his rights and his dearest ideals are being trampled upon, that the public conscience is ever more deaf to his righteous appeal, and that all the reactionary forces of prejudice, greed, and revenge are daily gaining new strength and fresh allies, the Negro faces no enviable dilemma. Conscious of his impotence, and pessimistic; he often becomes bitter and vindictive; and his religion, instead of a worship, is a complaint and a curse, a wail rather than a hope, a sneer rather than a faith. On the other hand, another type of mind, shrewder and keener and more tortuous too, sees in the very strength of the anti-Negro movement its patent weaknesses, and with Jesuitic casuistry is deterred by no ethical considerations in the endeavor to turn his weakness to the black man's strength. Thus we have two great and hardly reconcilable streams of thought and ethical strivings; the danger of the one lies in anarchy, that of the other in hypocrisy. The one type of Negro stands almost ready to curse God and die, and the other is too often found a traitor to right and a coward before force; the one is wedded to ideals remote, whimsical, perhaps impossible of realization; the other forgets that life is more than meat and the body more than raiment. But, after all, does not this imply the writhing of the age translated into black,—the triumph of the Lie which today, with its false culture, faces the hideousness of the anarchist assassin?

Today the two groups of Negroes, the one in the North, the other in the South, represent these divergent ethical tendencies, the first tending toward radicalism, the other toward hypocritical compromise. It is no idle regret with which the white South mourns the loss of the old-time Negro,—the frank, honest, simple old servant who stood for the earlier religious age of submission and humility. With all his laziness and lack of many elements of true manhood, he was at least open-hearted, faithful and sincere. Today he is gone, but who is to blame for his going? Is it not those very persons who mourn for him? Is it not the tendency, born of Reconstruction and Reaction, to found a society of lawlessness and deception, to tamper with the moral fiber of a naturally honest and straightforward people until the whites threaten to become ungovernable tyrants and the blacks criminal and hypocrites? Deception is the natural defense of the weak against the strong, and the South used it for many years against its conquerors; today it must be prepared to see its black proletariat turn that same two-edged weapon against itself. And how natural this is! The death of Denmark Vesey and Nat Turner proved long since to the Negro the present hopelessness of physical defense. Political defense is becoming less and less available, and economic defense is still only partially effective. But there is a patent defense at hand,—the defense of deception and flattery, of cajoling and lying. It is the same defense which peasants of the Middle Age used and which left its stamp on their character for centuries. Today the young Negro of the South who would succeed cannot be frank and outspoken, honest and self-assertive, but rather he is daily tempted to be silent and wary, politic and sly; he must flatter and be pleasant, endure petty insults with a smile, shut his eyes to wrong; in too many cases he sees positive personal advantage in deception and lying. His real thoughts, his real aspirations, must be guarded in whispers; he must not criticize, he must not complain. Patience, humility, and adroitness must, in these growing black youth, replace impulse, manliness, and courage. With this sacrifice there is an economic opening, and perhaps peace and some prosperity. Without this there is riot, migration, or crime. Nor is this situation peculiar to the southern United States, is it not rather the only method by which undeveloped races have gained the right to share modern culture? The price of culture is a lie.

On the other hand, in the North the tendency is to emphasize the radicalism of the Negro. Driven from his birthright in the South by a situation at which every fiber of his more outspoken and assertive nature revolts, he finds himself in a land where he can scarcely earn a decent living amid the harsh competition and the color discrimination. At the same time, through schools and periodicals, discussions and lectures, he is intellectually quickened and awakened. The soul, long pent up and dwarfed, suddenly expands in new-found freedom. What wonder that every tendency is to excess,—radical complaint, radical remedies, bitter denunciation or angry silence. Some sink, some rise. The criminal and the sensualist leave the church for the gambling-hall and the brothel, and fill the slums of Chicago and Baltimore; the better classes segregate themselves from the group-life of both white and black, and form an aristocracy, cultured but pessimistic, whose bitter criticism stings while it points out no way of escape. They despise the submission and subserviency of the southern Negroes, but offer no other means by which a poor and oppressed minority can exist side by side with its masters. Feeling deeply and keenly the tendencies and opportunities of the age in which they live, their souls are bitter at the fate which drops the Veil between; and the very fact that this bitterness is natural and justifiable only serves to intensify it and make it more maddening.

Between the two extreme types of ethical attitude which I have thus sought to make clear wavers the mass of the millions of Negroes, North and South; and their religious life and activity partake of this social conflict within their ranks. Their churches are differentiating,—now into groups of cold, fashionable devotees, in no way distinguishable from similar white groups save in color of skin; now into large social and business institutions catering to the desire for information and amusement of their members, warily avoiding unpleasant questions both within and without the black world, and preaching in effect if not in word: *Dum vivimus, vivamus.*

But back of this still broods silently the deep religious feeling of the real Negro heart, the stirring, unguided might of powerful human souls who have lost the guiding star of the past and seek in the great night a new religious ideal. Some day the Awakening will come, when the pentup vigor of ten million souls shall sweep irresistibly toward the Goal, out of the Valley of the Shadow of Death, where all that makes life worth living—Liberty, Justice, and Right—is marked "For White People Only."

HARRY EMERSON FOSDICK

Preaching as Personal Counseling

Harry Emerson Fosdick (1878–1969) is recognized by many as the greatest American preacher in the twentieth century. He was pastor of Riverside Church in New York City from 1926 to 1946 and professor of practical theology at Union Seminary from 1915 to 1946. From his platform at Riverside and in more than twenty books he established himself as the popular voice of liberalism in America. Although he never wrote a book on preaching, his method can be pieced together from several articles on homiletics and from his sermons. Fosdick rejected both expository preaching and topical preaching. The former tends toward biblical anti-quarianism, the latter toward subjectivism. He proposed the "project method" of preaching by which he joined preaching with pastoral counseling. He writes, "A good sermon is an engineering operation by which a chasm is bridged so that spiritual goods on one side — the 'unsearchable riches of Christ'— are actually transported into personal lives upon the other." In the language of the Aristotelian triangle of speaker, message, and audience, Fosdick's method always begins with the experience and situation of the audience. Like Brooks, Fosdick was a keen student of human nature and, like Brooks, Fosdick imagines an audience of individuals whose trials are the "presenting problem" of each sermon. A sampling of his sermon titles suggests the practical orientation of his preaching: "Handicapped Lives," "Handling Life's Second Bests," "On Catching the Wrong Bus," "The Sacred and the Secular are Inseparable."

Harry Emerson Fosdick, "Personal Counseling and Preaching," *Pastoral Psychology* (March 1952), pp. 11–15. Reprinted in *Harry Emerson Fosdick's Art of Preaching*, ed. Lionel Crocker, 1971. Courtesy of Charles C. Thomas, Publisher, Springfield, Illinois.

The relationship between personal counseling and preaching is a two-way street. Any preacher who in his sermons speaks to the real condition of his people, making evident that he knows what questions they are asking and where their problems lie, is bound to be sought out by individuals, wanting his intimate advice. And any pastor who, with intelligence and clairvoyance, practices such personal counseling, is bound to find his sermons, in content and form, insight and impact, profoundly affected. The right kind of preacher is coerced to become a personal counselor, and the right kind of personal counselor gains some of the most necessary ingredients of preaching.

One does not mean to say that a man cannot be an excellent preacher without being an excellent personal counselor, and vice versa. Gifts differ. Certainly there are expert counselors who cannot preach, and I suppose that there are powerful preachers who do little or no individual counseling—although how that latter thing can be true I only with difficulty see. Our statement about this relationship, however, is not negative but positive. For some of us, at least, the two functions of the ministry are mutually indispensable to each other.

The only way I see to make this statement vital is to make it autobiographical, and I may as well be frankly that. When I began my ministry I did not know how to preach. I had been trained to stand up and talk in public, so that, however little I had to say, I could at least say it, but how my first parishioners endured those early sermons I do not see. In reminiscence I can discern several factors which helped me out of that morass of homiletical frustration and bewilderment, but one factor is primary. Perhaps I now over-emphasize my first victorious experience in personal counseling, but it certainly was crucial.

A young man from one of the church's finest families, falling victim to alcoholism, sought my help. I recall my desperate feeling that if the gospel of Christ did not have in it available power to save that youth, of what use was it? When months of conference and inward struggle ended in triumph, when that young man said to me, "If you ever find anyone who doesn't believe in God, send him to me—I know!" something happened to my preaching that courses in homiletics do not teach. *This* was the kind of effect that a *sermon* ought to have. It could deal with real problems, speak directly to individual needs, and because of it transforming consequences could happen to some person then and there. From that day on, the secret prayer which I have offered, as I stood up to preach, has run like this: Somewhere in this congregation is one person who desperately needs what I am going to say: O God, help me to get at him!

Personal counseling has its routine aspects, its drudgeries and bore-doms, but ever and again it becomes thrilling. A real problem is presented and a real victory gained. The gospel works. One sees a miracle take place before one's eyes. A life is made over, a family is saved, a valuable youth turns about in his tracks and heads right, a potential suicide becomes a happy and useful member of society, a skeptic who had thought that life comes from nowhere, means nothing and goes nowhither, accepts the Christian faith and is "transformed by the renew-ing of his mind." Such experiences in the consultation room—indubi-table experiences of sometimes almost incredible regeneration—must have a profound effect when the counselor steps into the pulpit.

For one thing, personal counseling deepens the preacher's clairvoy-ance. He learns a lot about human nature which otherwise he could not have known. Books on nervous disorders are useful, but now he has *seen* what the books talk about. Newspapers tell him the news, but now he has confronted at first hand what the news is doing to real people inside. He gains that elemental factor without which all preaching is futile—insight into what actually is going on in the lives of those he preaches to.

For another thing, personal counseling deepens the preacher's confi-dence in the gospel of Christ, and in the power which it makes available. He intimately faces frustration, despair about the world, abysmal sin, fear, and the endless disasters of egocentricity, and he actually watches the miracle of transformation wrought. *It can happen*—not just because the Bible says so, or because it is orthodox to think it, but because he has seen it, and has helped to mediate the truth and power that did it. Noth-ing so much as this experience, I suspect, can send a man into the pulpit, sure that preaching can be personal consultation on a group scale, and that someone's life that morning can be made all over.

For another thing, personal counseling tends to shift the preacher's mind from obsession with his sermon's subject to a purposeful concern about its object. A famous Scotch preacher was once greeted after service by an admiring friend who exclaimed, "That was a wonderful sermon"; and the preacher turned on him. "What did it *do*?" he said; "What did it *do*?" Far too many sermons are harmless discussions of a subject, intel-ligent it may be, well thought out and well delivered, but lacking any purposeful drive to achieve an object. I do not see how a pastor, experi-enced in counseling, can preach like that. When he goes into the pulpit he is after something, with definite, deliberate intent. When he lifts a great truth, he intends, like a pile-driver, to drop it on something. He has a subject, of course, but when he chose his subject, he had an object. He proposed that somebody that morning should face his Damascus Road.

We are not saying that personal counseling, by itself, can make a good preacher. Obviously it cannot. But it can give tone and direction and significance to preaching which our generation critically needs.

During a long ministry I have watched with interest two familiar types of sermon. The first is the expository model—elucidation of a scriptural text, its historic occasion, its logical meaning in the context, its setting in the theology and ethic of the ancient writer; and then, at long last, application to the auditors of the truth involved. That a vital preacher can use that model with excellent effect goes without saying; but is there not something the matter with the model? To start with a biblical passage, and spend nearly all the sermon on its historic explanation and exposition, presupposes the assumption that the congregation came to church that morning primarily concerned about the meaning of those venerable texts—which, in my experience, is a condition contrary to fact. Long ago I wrote petulantly: "Only the preacher proceeds still upon the idea that folk come to church desperately anxious to discover what happened to the Jebusites."

In revolt against the expository model the topical preachers arose. They searched contemporary life in general and the newspapers in particular for subjects. Instead of concentrating on textual analysis, they dealt with present-day themes about which everyone was thinking. I watched those topical preachers with a dubious mind. Week after week, turning their pulpits into platforms and their sermons into lectures, they strained after new intriguing subjects, and one knew that in private they were straining even more strenuously after new intriguing ideas about them. Instead of launching out from a great text, they started with their own opinions on some matter of current interest, often much farther away than a good biblical text would be from the congregation's vital concerns and needs. Indeed, the fact that history had thought it worth while to preserve the text for centuries would cause a wise gambler to venture confidently on the text's superior vitality. If people do not come to church to learn what happened to the Jebusites, neither do they come yearning to hear a lecturer express his personal opinion on themes which editors, columnists, and radio commentators have been discussing all the week.

Jesus dealt primarily with individuals and, after that, he spoke to the multitude. Does not that indicate a third approach to preaching which our generation needs? At any rate, it has been a godsend to me. People come to church with every kind of difficulty and problem flesh is heir to. A sermon is meant to meet such needs—the sins and shames, the doubts and anxieties that fill the pews. This is the place to start, with the real problems of the people. This is a sermon's specialty, which makes it a sermon—not an essay, an exposition, a lecture. Every sermon should have for its main business the head-on, constructive meeting of some problem which is puzzling minds, burdening consciences, distracting lives, and no sermon which so meets real human difficulty, with light to throw on it and power to win victory over it, can possibly be futile. Any preacher who, with even moderate skill, is thus helping people, is functioning, delivering the goods which the community has a right to expect from him. Even when he addresses a multitude he speaks to them as individuals, and is still a personal counselor.

Of course, these three approaches to preaching are not mutually exclusive. When one tries to bring the truth of the gospel to bear on personal needs, the great texts of the Bible beg to be used, and their exposition can be the backbone of the sermon. And when one deals seriously with personal perplexities, one runs straight into social, economic, international problems which loom in the background and penetrate the foreground of every life. Nevertheless, the orientation of a sermon is profoundly affected, when one approaches the pulpit as though one were beginning a personal consultation.

To plead for such an approach, without pointing out its dangers would be unfair. I once presented this approach in a group of experienced ministers and collected a galaxy of warnings about its possible perversions. They had endeavored so precisely to deal with a real problem that Mr. Smith has vexaciously waked up to the fact that they were talking about him; or they had been so practical in dealing with some definite problem that they had become trivial, failing to bring the eternal gospel to bear on the issue; or they had been so anxious to deal with felt needs in the congregation that they had forgotten still deeper needs, unfelt, but real; or they had so limited the difficulties they preached about to private, psychological maladjustments that they became merely amateur pulpit psychiatrists; or they had been so concerned to help people that they had become soft nursemaids of sick souls and had omitted all the stern, thunderous, prophetic affirmations of God's truth which our generation ought to hear. Unskilled mishandling of any homiletical method can wreck it.

The most familiar and deplorable danger in attempting to make sermons personal consultations on a group scale is, I think, the limitation of the preacher's scope. If his field of private counseling is confined pretty much to neurotic disorders, his pulpit may all too easily reflect the fact. Every Sunday he will be telling people how to overcome anxiety and fear, and achieve peace of mind. He rides a hobby, attracts an audience of nervous patients, and in the pulpit becomes a homiletical neurologist.

This is a pathetic perversion of what we are trying to say. We are supposed to preach to "all sorts and conditions of men," and no minister's private consultations include them all. His insight must run beyond his individual experience in the consultation room. He has other ways of gaining clairvoyance into human need, and he should use them all. His scope, like the Bible's, should include all human life, personal and social, and the whole message of the gospel.

Nevertheless—while any approach to preaching can be misused—it is a great day in a minister's life when, having seen what miracles can be wrought by Christ's truth and power brought to bear on individual souls, he mounts his pulpit sure that a sermon, too, can be thus a medium of creative and transforming effects. No longer on Sunday is he merely making a speech about religion; he is engaged in an engineering operation, building a bridge by which a chasm is spanned so that spiritual goods on one side—the "unsearchable riches of Christ"—are actually transported into personal lives on the other.

At this point the old preachers have much to teach us. At their best they did achieve results. Their sermons were appeals to the jury, and they got decisions. They knew where the powerful motives were and appealed to them with conclusive effect. While we modern preachers talk about psychology much more than our predecessors did, we commonly use it a good deal less ably.

As the experience involved in personal counseling can thus minister to a preacher's power, so preaching can open up to the pastor hitherto unguessed opportunities for individual usefulness. One of the best tests of a sermon is the number of people who afterwards wish to see the preacher alone. It was a notable day in my own experience when, feeling that pastoral calling from house to house was not filling the bill, I announced a consultation hour for those who wished privately to talk with me. That first day I found myself facing a suicidal case, with fourteen others awaiting their turn. That was a generation ago, before the development of personal counseling clinics in Protestant churches had begun. Our churches are on their way now to meet that kind of need, which by many of our ministers had been long unguessed. Unfortunately some ministers who did not see that need were right; they did not evoke the need in their parishes; their sermons were not of a kind to make hungry and distracted souls want to see them alone. One of the most hopeful movements in Protestantism today is the growing tie-up between preaching and personal counseling—the first so directed that it leads inevitably to the second, and the second so used that it gives individual force and impact to the first.

John Wesley is known as a preacher who customarily addressed audiences of twenty thousand people. He certainly spoke to the multitude. But Wesley was always a tireless personal counselor, and his whole "Society" was organized with a view to the care and supervision of individuals. Surely this factor in Wesley's habit and experience is basic in any explanation of his preaching power. How else can one account for John Nelson's statement concerning the first sermon he heard Wesley preach, before a great audience at Moorfields? "When he did speak," wrote Nelson, "I thought his whole discourse was aimed at me."

HELMUT THIELICKE

The Worldliness of Spurgeon's Preaching

It is fitting that Helmut Thielicke (1908–1986) should write a commentary on the homiletics of C. H. Spurgeon. For the genius of Thielicke's preaching, like Spurgeon's, lies in its "worldliness," that is, in its daring willingness to speak the language of its hearers. Like Spurgeon, Thielicke regularly filled a vast metropolitan church (in Hamburg) with worshippers drawn from all classes of society. Thielicke also has much in common with an earlier Lutheran preacher, church official, and seeker of renewal, Philip Jacob Spener. Both addressed a German society devastated by war, and both were sharply critical of the church and its prevailing theology, whether orthodox or existentialist, for its disregard of the practical, evangelical nature of the Christian faith. Thielicke has established himself as a leading evangelical theologian in Europe with the publication of his multi-volumed ethics, *Theological Ethics*, and his dogmatics, *The Evangelical Faith*. To Americans, however, he is best known as a preacher who brings to his sermons theological discrimination and vividness of expression. In Thielicke's preaching the traditional Lutheran emphasis on law and gospel is not imposed on the text in a heavy-handed way. Rather, the judgment and grace of God emerge from the preacher's lively and personal dialogue with the scriptural word. Thielicke's most popular works include *Our Heavenly Father, The Waiting Father, Nihilism, How the World Began,* and *The Trouble with the Church.*

Helmut Thielicke, *Encounter with Spurgeon,* trans. John W. Doberstein (Philadelphia: Fortress Press, 1963), pp. 29–41. Copyright © Fortress Press. Used by permission.

There are three points which seem to me to be important in a theological evaluation of the worldliness of Spurgeon's preaching.

First, by plunging with his message into the world and emerging in its climate, Spurgeon was fulfilling the original intention of the gospel to meet man where he is. For, after all, the meaning and intent of the Incarnation of Jesus Christ is, as Paul Tillich once expressed it, that God emerges "within the conditions of historical reality" and subjects himself to its pressure in solidarity with "his" people: that God is on man's side. These, his people, no longer need to resort to a temple, a sacred place reserved for God; they have no need for special ascetic disciplines, flights of spiritual feeling, purgings and cleansings, and other methods of spiritual training in order to come to him. Rather they meet their Lord in *their* marketplaces, *their* highways and hedges; in short, God comes to meet them. To be sure, in all this, God also remains the "totally other," who cannot be imprisoned in any human formula. And if there is anything in the history of Christianity that bears witness to this inaccessibility of God, it is the failure of every form of the doctrine of the "two natures" which attempts to "think together" the divine and the human natures in one system of thought. . . .

It is true, of course, that when Spurgeon articulates in words, sounds, and sentences that side of the gospel which is oriented toward man, thus emphasizing only the "human nature" which is involved, he is being quite as one-sided as the pure liturgiologists who, at least in the "how" of their proclamation, are just definitely oriented toward the *theiotes*, the deity. I deliberately mention this one-sidedness of Spurgeon in order to avoid the impression that I wish to make him in too direct a sense an exemplary pattern of evangelical preaching. The paradox of the unity of deity and humanity in Christ must, in my opinion, have as its counterpart a corresponding tension involving the juxtaposition and coexistence of a liturgical adherence to tradition on the one hand and a historical immediacy in preaching on the other. Historically speaking, however, the balance between the two will never be something given and perfect, any more than the balance between the divine and the human has been in the doctrine of the two natures. Historically speaking, it will rather always be true that we shall be able to express in words this mystery of the divine and the human only by an interplay of statements which correct each other.

With this in mind, then, I would certainly think that we are in special need of the corrective which is provided for us in Spurgeon's "worldly" preaching. For the one-sidedness of *our* generation is the *liturgical* component,the possible withdrawal from the present of which we spoke above. Despite the immense concern with homiletical questions, we have forgotten the worldliness of preaching. And even where we have recognized that it is part of our task—how else could the universal respect for Dietrich Bonhoeffer's theological principles be explained?—we still have not succeeded.

The fact that this program for worldly preaching has repeatedly failed certainly has deeper causes than a mere mechanical failure to employ the proper kind of language. For even when this language is used—and here and there we have heard sermons and meditations in which the parlance of back-slapping brassiness and the tabloid press has been employed— we have hardly ever been stirred to say that here somebody has hit upon what could really be called worldly preaching. On the contrary, we have the somewhat painful feeling that what we are hearing is a calculated, tactical effort to be chummily familar, that this is the very thing that is *not* appropriate to the subject, and that the substance of what is said is compromised by the very way in which it is said.

Here again it is evident that one cannot make up for theological deficiencies by means of artistic techniques, and that the techniques have to be "baptized" and made servants if they are to become trustworthy instruments. These theological deficiencies may consist in the fact that we have lost sight of the gospel as God's coming to meet man. We have forgotten the Christmas miracle and therefore foolishly devote ourselves to a useless attempt to recover what has been lost by means of popularizing the "Christian religion" and beating secularization with its own weapons. All efforts to arrive at a language for preaching that is close to life will remain illusory as long as we have not spelled out theologically the "what" of the Miracle of Bethlehem. And the worldly "how" of preaching will be "added to us" only when we have first learned about the worldliness of God and heard anew the words "God *so* loved the world."

Spurgeon can teach us something about this dogma of the worldliness of God, not only by what he says about it, but also by the way he deals with his congregation. For he not only spoke in a worldly way, he also went out into the world with his people. He actually went with his students from the Pastor's College into the highways and hedges and marketplaces. He turned up in the most dubious quarters and slums of London and gathered together the children from the streets. As far as I have been able to determine, when he did this he never preached a special sermon beamed at the particular situation of his hearers, but always preached in the same style, no matter whether he was speaking to the students in the Pastor's College, to a "mature" congregation in some church, or in the great forum of his Tabernacle where he had a mixed audience of proletarians and businessmen, aristocrats and middle-class people. Genuine worldliness can always remain the same, for the hedges and highways, the cellars and hovels, are the same in every life, and the powers of sin, suffering, and death pose the same questions everywhere. All of them who are gathered there we hear on Pentecost, praising the mighty works of God *"in their own tongues."*

Second, the worldly style of speaking has witnessing power in still another respect. Only he who is very familiar with and close to what he is saying can talk about it quite naturally and in a conversational tone. Only because the message here emerges as something that is almost tangibly a part of the person is its effect credible and trustworthy and, even for the skeptic, worth listening to. For here is a person, like ourselves, who lives with this message and has obviously tried it and found that one *can* live with it. The casual testimony of a man of the world, included in some incidental comment, often has more influence than the reasoned, carefully prepared speech of the "professional" witness.

Here I must go out of my way to correct a possible misunderstanding. Some may think that the worldliness of this speech with its natural flow represents an "accommodation" to the world and thus evades the necessary offense and scandal of the message. Just the opposite is true. One can shout from the pulpit in traditional academic language the most tremendous things—even that Christ rose from the dead!—without eliciting anything more than bored assent to the routine ecclesiastical vocabulary. Linguistic Docetism never offends anybody, because it never gets under anyone's skin. Its effect is merely that of a report that "in far-off Turkey the nations are clashing," while I, withdrawn from all that, can bless my lucky stars for "peace and peaceful times" and "quaff my ale" in comfort [*Faust*, I, ii]. This is no fateful encounter in which I hear *my* death sentence or *my* pardon. And even the refrain—added perhaps with some emotion—"This concerns *you*!" makes no impact at all, if the explosive is not already inherent in the message itself and brought to the kindling point.

The converse is true also: he who tells nothing more than a parable of Jesus, but tells it in the same way that one would speak of the weather or a hospital visit or the next election, evokes a shock because what he has said is now in the familiar realm of the ordinary; it gets at people where they are. So only he who accommodates and goes out to meet people in *this* way gets a confirmation of his faithful witness in a response of genuine resistance.

This, of course, is a different kind of accommodation from that which conforms to the *substantive* expectations of the hearers. The "German Christians" under Hitler performed this kind of substantive, and therefore disavowing, accommodation by fabricating a painless and innocuous synthesis of Christianity and contemporary ideologies. The genuine accommodation which is motivated by the purpose of reaching people where they are would have been quite different. It might be illustrated in this way:

Imagine one of the great mass meetings in the Berlin Sportpalast at that time, in which a Nazi orator allows himself to be carried away in violent tirades against Christianity. If someone had leaped to his feet and shouted out his counter-confession, "Christ is the Messiah!" the people sitting next to him would probably have looked up with some astonishment; but not much more would have happened. But if another had cried out, "Jesus Christ is the only Lord, and all who make themselves into gods by their own power will go to hell along with the pseudo-savior Adolf Hitler," he would probably have been torn to pieces by the crowd.

In reality both were saying the same thing. The one who declared that Christ is the Messiah was implicitly saying that all earthly entities are relative, and thus pronouncing judgment upon Hitler and his cohorts. But he was doing so in a veiled and cryptic way, for he was speaking in esoteric, churchly terminology. But the other said it in terms that were accommodated to the language and consciousness of those who were present. He spoke in clear terms. For this reason, and this reason *alone*, did it create disturbance and offense. Offense is not a sign that one has *not* understood, but a symptom of the fact that one *has* understood all too well, or at least is afraid he will *have* to understand. . . .

Third, the worldly way of speaking is credible because it gives to the hearer what is the speaker's own. I hardly need to add that what is the speaker's own is not something he has gained himself, but rather the reservoir of talents bestowed upon him. But as such the *alienum* (the gift that comes from outside of him) has now become a *proprium* (his own). And this is what gives legitimacy to worldly preaching as the very opposite of that which often makes people today so skeptical of public speech, namely, propaganda.

The person who promotes propaganda is generally a professional advertising man who speaks his piece no matter which margarine or soft drink is being sold; and the deep tone of conviction in which he commends these products does not alter the skepticism of those who listen to his television utterances and read his ads. They know very well that he has to talk this way, because he is paid to do so; they know that the deep tone of conviction is no natural product, but a synthetic, very carefully and purposefully mixed cocktail designed to affect the nervous system.

But the professional advertising man is only the extreme example of a type that haunts us in many variations. One of these variations is the functionary who represents and advocates a group decision, even though his "private" views may be totally different. Another species is the manager, who does not act for himself but represents the stockholders. . . .

Because this type of speech, which is typical of professional advertising men, functionaries, and managers, is more than an isolated phenomenon of the moment, and because for many reasons it has now grown to immeasurable proportions compared with Spurgeon's time, our contemporaries have understandably come to distrust *all* forms of public speech, *every* kind of "speaking on someone else's orders"– and hence what the *church* says too. "The minister has to talk that way": this is the dreadful phrase by which men seek to defend themselves and keep the demanding summons of the message at arm's length.

Why do people seek out the consulting room of the psychotherapist and hardly ever the pastor's study? Why do people not entrust themselves to the minister but write instead to the editor of the "worry column" in our newspapers and magazines? Obviously because they think they know beforehand what the minister "has" to say; for, after all, he is an employee of that institution whose dogmatic stipulations stand, or at least *seem* to stand, like silent monuments in full view of everybody. Naturally, he has to be "against sin"; so it would hardly be worth his while, once he has diagnosed the problem as "sin," to consider impartially the matters confided to him. Naturally, he is against divorce, against love affairs on the part of married men, against disrespect for parents. Therefore he is incapable of evaluating exceptional cases; therefore he cannot recognize genuine crises, real conflict and borderline situations. As a "human being" he might perhaps understand, but he dare not let me know what he thinks about it personally. For his job is simply to carry out the collective will of his institution – and that is dogmatically fixed. "The minister has to talk that way."

We can hardly measure the extent to which this misguided prejudice – for, of course, that is what it is! – curbs people's willingness to listen and come to grips with Christianity. And if we examine this attitude more carefully it becomes clear that, strictly speaking, it is not a matter of their taking offense at the message itself, because they have not yet come even within earshot of it. Rather here again this offense springs from a reaction to the "how" of preaching. Distrust of the message increases to the extent to which it is presented in terms of formulas and expressed – even as regards the tone of voice – impersonally. For this only suggests the more strongly that here it is not the man himself who is speaking, but that he is a ventriloquist regurgitating voices other than his own.

And here again it is all too easy to put forward the parsonical self-justification and say that after all it is the task of the witness, not to present himself, but rather to retire behind the testimony and therefore to present it in a tone of aloof objectivity.

But this is quite wrong. The fact is that the witness does not withdraw; he comes forward. (If he puts himself in the foreground like a prima donna and misuses the message merely as a means to play up himself, then this is something quite different and has absolutely nothing to do with what is meant here.) The witness does not merely recite a confession; he confesses. He confesses that this is "his" confession; that he personally has made it his own and therefore that he himself is in it. Otherwise we should have to credit the remark of Alexander Schweizer (1808–88) that whereas the fathers once "confessed their beliefs," our modern Christian generation struggles largely just to "believe their confessions"—and hence to keep aloof from the matter itself. Only as the witness himself comes forward will men regard him as credible and worth listening to.

This coming forward of the witness, of course, need not by any means manifest itself in the use of the first person singular or an autobiographical tone of speech. Nevertheless the individuality of the preacher will undoubtedly make itself felt, or more cautiously stated, dare not fight shy of letting itself be known. The witness' own individual tone is itself a part of the witness. . . .

This indicates why it is that the term "instrument" is only an imperfect and halting metaphor of what witnessing means. If one takes this image in its literal, absolute sense—which is the very thing one dare not do—then there would be no difference at all between the witness and the functionary, since he too is an instrument. The witness, however, discloses himself in his own tone and individuality; for what characterizes him is not only that he testifies to *something*, but also that *he* is the one who is testifying and "standing up" for it. The mere instrument knows nothing of the one who is using it; nor does it know the purpose it is serving. But the witnessing person is so constituted that he consciously and purposely grasps and understands both who it is that is using him and the purpose he is serving. Therefore he must confess himself as the one who accepts responsibility for his testimony (cf. I Pet. 3:15).

If I see aright, it was precisely this instinct for the personal character of witnessing that set Spurgeon so strongly against "formalism." It made him go out of his way to guard against the misunderstanding that it was not he but merely an institution that was speaking, and that his personal position might be something different from what he was saying.

But how does this "individual tone," which is itself witness, come into being? It comes into being through the worldliness of a man's speech and the immediate naturalness of his diction. For in order to be able to speak in this way I cannot simply declaim or recite a given statement, even if it is a passage from the Bible or a creed. Every statement requires translation, recasting, actualizing. Simply by going through these acts of assimilation and appropriation, preaching causes the medium of the message, namely, the preacher, to become a part of itself; it puts its stamp upon him, and also imparts to him his own individual stamp. . . .

Only he who runs the risk of heresy can gain the truth. Only he who risks good form and ventures to go even to the limits of good taste (so long as this is only a sign and remains an exceptional thing and does not itself become merely a routine!) can allow substance and content to break through. The man who will not utter anything that is not guarded and "safe" is not reckoning with him who is able from "stones to raise up children to Abraham." This passion to safeguard ourselves is not inspired by the Holy Spirit; it is based merely upon fleshly anxiety. The witness must venture something and dare not be afraid of the chips that fly as he hews. The discipline and the hard application must be taken care of *before* the witness begins to speak. But once he begins to speak, he must be free to venture and expose himself without defense. There is no real witness that is not utterly defenseless.

All this should be taken into account when one considers the homiletical risks that Spurgeon took. The dogmatician, the exegete, and also the professor of practical theology (the preceptor of the homiletical nursery) may often be impelled to wield their blue pencils; the aesthete may often see red and the liturgiologist turn purple when they read his sermons and hear what he did. For the priests and the Levites always have the hardest time listening with simplicity and without bias. Not only that; they also find it all too easy to pass by those who have fallen among thieves, those who can no longer hear because they have been corroded by distrust—and in this way too become as sheep without a shepherd.

Such critics ought to see in this man Spurgeon the shepherd who was content to allow his robe—including his clerical robe—to be torn to tatters by thorns and sharp stones as he clambered after the lost sheep, at times seemingly to be engaged more in training for a cross-country race than in liturgical exercises. Worldly preaching is impossible without having the earth leave its traces on a man's wardrobe. Here there are no robes that look as if they had just come out of a bandbox. And sometimes the voice is rough and hoarse from much calling. The shepherds of the New Testament too were rough and ready fellows.

VII
THE HOLY SPIRIT

JOHN CALVIN

The Internal Testimony of the Spirit

Few have written extensively of the work of the Holy Spirit in preaching. The doctrine of inspiration affirms the Spirit's role in the production of the Scriptures, and preachers have long relied on the Spirit for both the "inspiration" and the delivery of their sermons. Helmut Thielicke assigns a mediating role to the Spirit in the task of hermeneutics. The Spirit, he says, is the "great Hermeneut" who enables the interpreter to move from what is alien in the past to the contemporary situation. The mighty preacher, theologian, and renewer of the church, John Calvin (1509–1564) stresses the importance of the Holy Spirit both in the interpretation of Scripture and in the "manner of receiving the grace of Christ." In matters of biblical authority, the inward testimony of the Holy Spirit transcends the authority of the church and overrules the arguments of reason. Only by the working of the Holy Spirit can the Scripture be understood as self-authenticating (*Institutes*, I, vii). In the following selection Calvin first establishes the significance of the word for faith. But the word, he says, meets with such unbelief that the only way it can achieve God's purpose in our hearts is through the illuminating power of the Holy Spirit. The Spirit seals the mystery of election which, says Calvin alluding to Augustine, is "a depth of the cross." For Calvin the tasks of biblical interpretation and preaching are closely linked. His description of the Spirit's testimony in both serves to set the whole cycle of sermon preparation, delivery, *and* reception into the context of the ongoing activity of God the Holy Spirit.

John Calvin, *Institutes of the Christian Religion*, trans. John Allen (Philadelphia: Presbyterian Board of Christian Education, n.d. [1813]), Vol. I, Bk. III, 33–36, pp. 636–640.

309

This simple and external demonstration of the divine word ought, indeed, to be fully sufficient for the production of faith, if it were not obstructed by our blindness and perverseness. But such is our propensity to error, that our mind can never adhere to divine truth; such is our dulness, that we can never discern the light of it. Therefore nothing is effected by the word, without illumination of the Holy Spirit. Whence it appears, that faith is far superior to human intelligence. Nor is it enough for the mind to be illuminated by the Spirit of God, unless the heart also be strengthened and supported by his power. On this point, the schoolmen are altogether erroneous, who, in the discussion of faith, regard it as simple assent of the understanding, entirely neglecting the confidence and assurance of the heart. Faith, therefore, is a singular gift of God in two respects; both as the mind is enlightened to understanding the truth of God, and as the heart is established in it. For the Holy Spirit not only originates faith, but increases it by degrees, till he conducts us by it all the way to the heavenly kingdom. "That good thing," says Paul, "which was committed unto thee, keep, by the Holy Ghost which dwelleth in us" (II Tim. 1:14). If it be urged, that Paul declares the Spirit to be given to us "by the hearing of faith," this objection is easily answered. If there were only one gift of the Spirit, it would be absurd to represent the Spirit as the effect of faith, of which he is the author and cause. But when the apostle is treating of the gifts with which God adorns his church, to lead it, by advancements in faith, forwards to perfection, we need not wonder that he ascribes those gifts to faith, which prepares us for their reception. It is accounted by the world exceedingly paradoxical, when it is affirmed, that no one can believe in Christ, but he to whom it is given. But this is partly for want of considering the depth and sublimity of heavenly wisdom, and the extreme dulness of man in apprehending the mysteries of God, and partly from not regarding that firm and steadfast constancy of heart, which is the principal branch of faith.

But if, as Paul tells us, no one is acquainted with the will of a man but "the spirit of a man which is in him," how could man be certain of the will of God? And if we are uncertain respecting the truth of God in those things which are the subjects of our present contemplation, how should we have a greater certainty of it, when the Lord promises such things as no eye sees and no heart conceives? Human sagacity is here so completely lost, that the first step to improvement, in the divine school, is to forsake it. For, like an interposing veil, it prevents us from discovering the mysteries of God, which are revealed only to babes. "For flesh and blood hath not revealed," and "the natural man receiveth not the things of the Spirit of God; for they are foolishness unto him; neither can he know them, because they are spiritually discerned" (I Cor. 2:14). The aids of the Spirit therefore are necessary, or rather it is his influence alone that is efficacious here. "Who hath known the mind of the Lord? or who hath been his counsellor?" (Rom. 11:34) but "the Spirit searcheth all things, yea, the deep things of God"; (I Cor. 2:10) and through him, "we have the mind of Christ" (I Cor. 2:16). "No man can come to me (says he) except the Father, which hath sent me, draw him. Every man therefore that hath heard and hath learned of the Father, cometh unto me. Not that any man hath seen the Father, save he which is of God." Therefore, as we can never come to Christ, unless we are drawn by the Spirit of God, so when we are drawn, we are raised both in mind and in heart above the reach of our own understanding. For illuminated by him, the soul receives, as it were, new eyes for the contemplation of heavenly mysteries, by the splendor of which it was before dazzled. And thus the human intellect, irradiated by the light of the Holy Spirit, then begins to relish those things which pertain to the kingdom of God, for which before it had not the smallest taste. Wherefore Christ's two disciples receive no benefit from his excellent discourse to them on the mysteries of his kingdom, till he opens their understanding that they may understand the Scriptures. Thus, though the apostles were taught by his divine mouth, yet the Spirit of Truth must be sent to them, to instil into their minds the doctrine which they had heard with their ears. The word of God is like the sun shining on all to whom it is preached, but without any benefit to the blind. But in this respect we are all blind by nature. Therefore it cannot penetrate into our minds, unless the internal teacher, the Spirit, make way for it by his illumination.

In a former part of this work, relating to the corruption of nature, we have shown more at large the inability of men to believe; therefore I shall not fatigue the reader by a repetition of the same things. Let it suffice that faith itself, which we possess not by nature, but which is given us by the Spirit, is called by Paul "the spirit of faith" (II Cor. 4:13). Therefore he prays "that God would fulfil," in the Thessalonians, "all the good pleasure of his goodness, and the work of faith with power" (II Thess. 1:11). By calling faith "the work" of God, and "the good pleasure of his goodness," he denies it to be the proper effect of human exertion; and not content with that, he adds that it is a specimen of the divine power. When he says to the Corinthians, that faith stands "not in the wisdom of men, but in the power of God" (I Cor. 2:5), he speaks indeed of external miracles; but because the reprobate have no eyes to behold them, he comprehends also the inward seal which he elsewhere mentions. And that he may more illustriously display his liberality in so eminent a gift, God deigns not to bestow it promiscuously on all, but by a singular privilege imparts it to whom he will. We have already cited testimonies to prove this point. Augustine, who is a faithful expositor of them, says, "It was in order to teach us that the act of believing is owing to the divine gift, not to human merit, that our Savior declared, 'No man can come to me, except the Father which hath sent me draw him, and except it were given unto him of my Father.' It is wonderful, that two persons hear; one despises, the other ascends. Let him who despises, impute it to himself; let him who ascends, not arrogate it to himself." In another place he says, "Wherefore is it given to one, not to another? I am not ashamed to reply, This is a depth of the cross. From I know not what depth of the divine judgments, which we cannot scrutinize, proceeds all our ability. That I can, I see; whence I can, I see not; unless that I see thus far, that it is of God. But why one, and not another? It is too much for me; it is an abyss, a depth of the cross. I can exclaim with admiration, but not demonstrate it in disputation." The sum of the whole is this—that Christ, when he illuminates us with faith by the power of his Spirit, at the same time ingrafts us into his body, that we may become partakers of all his benefits.

It next remains, that what the mind has imbibed, be transfused into the heart. For the word of God is not received by faith, if it floats on the surface of the brain; but when it has taken deep root in the heart, so as to become an impregnable fortress to sustain and repel all the assaults of temptation. But if it be true that the right apprehension of the mind proceeds from the illumination of the Spirit, his energy is far more conspicuous in such a confirmation of the heart; the diffidence of the heart being greater than the blindness of the mind, and the furnishing of the heart with assurance being more difficult than the communication of knowledge to the understanding. Therefore the Spirit acts as a seal, to seal on our hearts those very promises, the certainty of which he has previously impressed on our minds, and serves as an earnest to confirm and establish them. "After that ye believed," says the apostle, "ye were sealed with that Holy Spirit of promise, which is the earnest of our inheritance" (Eph. 1:13). Do you see how he shows that the hearts of believers are impressed by the Spirit, as by a seal? How, for this reason, he calls him "the Spirit of promise," because he ratifies the gospel to us?

CHARLES HADDON SPURGEON

The Holy Spirit and the Ministry of Preaching

For more than thirty years the self-educated Baptist preacher Charles Haddon Spurgeon (1834–1892) captivated a weekly congregation of 6,000 people in his Metropolitan Tabernacle in London. He was the foremost of the "princes of the pulpit" in what has been called The Age of Preaching. For many years he also taught homiletics at the Pastors' College which he founded in 1857. He published a multitude of books of helps for preachers and a commentary on the Psalms, *The Treasury of David*, his major work. His sermons teem with story, anecdote, illustration from nature, simile, pathos, humor, caricature, and all other rhetorical techniques, of which he was past master. Despite both his fame and his enormous homiletical talent—to say nothing of his instinct for sheer joy in the pulpit—Spurgeon seems to have retained a sense of awe toward the task of preaching. He is one of the few great preachers in whose printed sermons one can still divine something of the man. Although Spurgeon himself is "the compleat preacher," he does not contribute the following selection on the Holy Spirit for the sake of theological completeness. The Holy Spirit is not a pious footnote to this preacher's prowess. Spurgeon believed that between the hard work of preparation and the exhilaration (as he confessed it) of delivery lies the stillness of the Spirit's presence. It is the presence of the Holy Spirit that changes preaching from performance to ministry and the preacher from actor to servant of the word.

Charles Haddon Spurgeon, *Lectures to My Students*, 2nd series (London: Passmore and Alabaster, 1887), pp. 3–10.

We will now come to the core of our subject. To us, as ministers, the Holy Spirit is absolutely essential. Without him our office is a mere name. We claim no priesthood over and above that which belongs to every child of God; but we are the successors of those who, in olden times, were moved of God to declare his word, to testify against transgression, and to plead his cause. Unless we have the spirit of the prophets resting upon us, the mantle which we wear is nothing but a rough garment to deceive. We ought to be driven forth with abhorrence from the society of honest men for daring to speak in the name of the Lord if the Spirit of God rests not upon us. We believe ourselves to be spokesmen for Jesus Christ, appointed to continue his witness upon earth; but upon him and his testimony the Spirit of God always rested, and if it does not rest upon us, we are evidently not sent forth into the world as he was. At Pentecost the commencement of the great work of converting the world was with flaming tongues and a rushing mighty wind, symbols of the presence of the Spirit; if, therefore, we think to succeed without the Spirit, we are not after the Pentecostal order. If we have not the Spirit which Jesus promised, we cannot perform the commission which Jesus gave.

I need scarcely warn any brother here against falling into the delusion that we may have the Spirit so as to become inspired. Yet the members of a certain litigious modern sect need to be warned against folly. They hold that their meetings are under "the presidency of the Holy Spirit": concerning which notion I can only say that I have been unable to discover in holy Scripture either the term or the idea. I do find in the New Testament a body of Corinthians eminently gifted, fond of speaking, and given to party strifes—true representatives of those to whom I allude, but as Paul said of them, "I thank God I baptized none of you," so also do I thank the Lord that few of that school have ever been found in our midst. It would seem that their assemblies possess a peculiar gift of inspiration, not quite perhaps amounting to infallibility, but nearly approximating thereto. If you have mingled in their gatherings, I greatly question whether you have been more edified by the prelections produced under celestial presidency, than you have been by those of ordinary preachers of the word, who only consider themselves to be under the influence of the Holy Spirit, as one spirit is under the influence of another spirit, or one mind under the influence of another mind. . . .

Wherein may we look for the aid of the Holy Spirit? I should reply—in seven or eight ways.

First, he is the Spirit of knowledge,—"He shall guide you into all truth." In this character we need his teaching.

We have urgent need to study, for the teacher of others must himself be instructed. Habitually to come into the pulpit unprepared is unpardonable presumption: nothing can more effectually lower ourselves and

our office. After a visitation discourse by the Bishop of Lichfield upon
the necessity of earnestly studying the word, a certain vicar told his
lordship that he could not believe his doctrine, "for," said he, "often
when I am in the vestry I do not know what I am going to talk about;
but I go into the pulpit and preach, and think nothing of it." His lordship
replied, "And you are quite right in thinking nothing of it, for your
churchwardens have told me that they share your opinion." If we are not
instructed, how can we instruct? If we have not thought, how shall we
lead others to think? It is in our study-work, in that blessed labor when
we are alone with the Book before us, that we need the help of the Holy
Spirit. He holds the key of the heavenly treasury, and can enrich us
beyond conception; he has the clue of the most labyrinthine doctrine,
and can lead us in the way of truth. He can break in pieces the gates of
brass, and cut in sunder the bars of iron, and give to us the treasures of
darkness, and hidden riches of secret places. If you study the original,
consult the commentaries, and meditate deeply, yet if you neglect to cry
mightily unto the Spirit of God your study will not profit you; but even
if you are debarred the use of helps (which I trust you will not be), if you
wait upon the Holy Ghost in simple dependence upon his teaching, you
will lay hold of very much of the divine meaning.

The Spirit of God is peculiarly precious to us, because he especially
instructs us as to the person and work of our Lord Jesus Christ; and that
is the main point of our preaching. He takes of the things of Christ, and
shows them unto us. If he had taken of the things of doctrine or precept,
we should have been glad of such gracious assistance; but since
he especially delights in the things of Christ, and focuses his sacred light
upon the cross, we rejoice to see the center of our testimony so divinely
illuminated, and we are sure that the light will be diffused over all
the rest of our ministry. Let us wait upon the Spirit of God with this
cry—"O Holy Spirit, reveal to us the Son of God, and thus show us
the Father." . . .

In the second place, the Spirit is called the Spirit of wisdom, and we
greatly need him in that capacity; for knowledge may be dangerous if
unaccompanied with wisdom, which is the art of rightly using what we
know. Rightly to divide the word of God is as important as fully to
understand it, for some who have evidently understood a part of the
gospel have given undue prominence to that one portion of it, and have
therefore exhibited a distorted Christianity, to the injury of those who
have received it, since they in their turn have exhibited a distorted character in consequence thereof. A man's nose is a prominent feature in his
face, but it is possible to make it so large that eyes and mouth, and every-

thing else are thrown into insignificance, and the drawing is a caricature and not a portrait: so certain important doctrines of the gospel can be so proclaimed in excess as to throw the rest of truth into the shade, and the preaching is no longer the gospel in its natural beauty, but a caricature of the truth, of which caricature, however, let me say, some people seem to be mightily fond. The Spirit of God will teach you the use of the sacrificial knife to divide the offerings; and he will show you how to use the balances of the sanctuary so as to weigh out and mix the precious spices in their proper quantities. Every experienced preacher feels this to be of the utmost moment, and it is well if he is able to resist all temptation to neglect it. Alas, some of our hearers do not desire to hear the whole counsel of God. They have their favorite doctrines, and would have us silent on all besides. Many are like the Scotchwoman, who, after hearing a sermon, said, "It was very well if it hadna been for the trash of duties at the *hinner* end." There are brethren of that kind; they enjoy the comforting part—the promises and the doctrines, but practical holiness must scarcely be touched upon. Faithfulness requires us to give them a foursquare gospel, from which nothing is omitted, and in which nothing is exaggerated, and for this much wisdom is requisite. I gravely question whether any of us have so much of this wisdom as we need. We are probably afflicted by some inexcusable partialities and unjustifiable leanings; let us search them out and have done with them. We may be conscious of having passed by certain texts, not because we do not understand them (which might be justifiable), but because we do understand them, and hardly like to say what they have taught us, or because there may be some imperfection in ourselves, or some prejudice among our hearers which those texts would reveal too clearly for our comfort. Such sinful silence must be ended forthwith. To be wise stewards and bring forth the right portions of meat for our Master's household we need thy teaching, O Spirit of the Lord!

Nor is this all, for even if we know how rightly to divide the word of God, we want wisdom in the selection of the particular part of truth which is most applicable to the season and to the people assembled; and equal discretion in the tone and manner in which the doctrine shall be presented. I believe that many brethren who preach human responsibility deliver themselves in so legal a manner as to disgust all those who love the doctrines of grace. On the other hand, I fear that many have preached the sovereignty of God in such a way as to drive all persons who believe in man's free agency entirely away from the Calvinistic side. We should not hide truth for a moment, but we should have wisdom so to preach it that there shall be no needless jarring or offending, but a gradual enlightenment of those who cannot see it at all, and a leading of weaker brethren into the full circle of gospel doctrine. . . .

Thirdly, we need the Spirit in another manner, namely, as the live coal from off the altar, touching our lips, so that when we have knowledge and wisdom to select the fitting portion of truth, we may enjoy freedom of utterance when we come to deliver it. "Lo, this hath touched thy lips." Oh, how gloriously a man speaks when his lips are blistered with the live coal from the altar—feeling the burning power of the truth, not only in his inmost soul, but on the very lip with which he is speaking! Mark at such times how his very utterance quivers. Did you not notice in the prayer-meeting just now, in two of the suppliant brethren, how their tones were tremulous, and their bodily frames were quivering, because not only were their hearts touched, as I hope all our hearts were, but their lips were touched, and their speech was thereby affected. Brethren, we need the Spirit of God to open our mouths that we may show forth the praises of the Lord, or else we shall not speak with power.

We need the divine influence to keep us back from saying many things which, if they actually left our tongue, would mar our message. Those of us who are endowed with the dangerous gift of humor have need, sometimes, to stop and take the word out of our mouth and look at it, and see whether it is quite to edification; and those whose previous lives have borne them among the coarse and the rough had need watch with lynx eyes against indelicacy. Brethren, far be it from us to utter a syllable which would suggest an impure thought, or raise a questionable memory. We need the Spirit of God to put bit and bridle upon us to keep us from saying that which would take the minds of our hearers away from Christ and eternal realities, and set them thinking upon the grovelling things of earth.

Brethren, we require the Holy Spirit also to incite us in our utterance. I doubt not you are all conscious of different states of mind in preaching. Some of those states arise from your body being in different conditions. A bad cold will not only spoil the clearness of the voice, but freeze the flow of the thoughts. For my own part if I cannot speak clearly I am unable to think clearly, and the matter becomes hoarse as well as the voice. The stomach, also, and all the other organs of the body, affect the mind; but it is not to these things that I allude. Are you not conscious of changes altogether independent of the body? When you are in robust health do you not find yourselves one day as heavy as Pharaoh's chariots with the wheels taken off, and at another time as much at liberty as "a hind let loose"? Today your branch glitters with the dew, yesterday it was parched with drought. Who knoweth not that the Spirit of God is in all this? The divine Spirit will sometimes work upon us so as to bear us completely out of ourselves. From the beginning of the sermon to the end we might at such times say, "Whether in the body or out of the body I cannot tell: God knoweth." Everything has been forgotten but the one all-engrossing subject in hand. If I were forbidden to enter heaven, but were permitted to select my state for all eternity, I should choose to be as I sometimes feel in preaching the gospel. Heaven is foreshadowed in such a state: the mind shut out from all disturbing influences, adoring the majestic and consciously present God, every faculty aroused and joyously excited to its utmost capability, all the thoughts and powers of the soul joyously occupied in contemplating the glory of the Lord, and extolling to listening crowds the Beloved of our soul; and all the while the purest conceivable benevolence towards one's fellow creatures urging the heart to plead with them on God's behalf—what state of mind can rival this? Alas, we have reached this ideal, but we cannot always maintain it, for we know also what it is to preach in chains, or beat the air. We may not attribute holy and happy changes in our ministry to anything less than the action of the Holy Spirit upon our souls. I am sure the Spirit does so work. Often and often, when I have had doubts suggested by the infidel, I have been able to fling them to the winds with utter scorn, because I am distinctly conscious of a power working upon me when I am speaking in the name of the Lord, infinitely transcending any personal power of fluency, and far surpassing any energy derived from excitement such as I have felt when delivering a secular lecture or making a speech—so utterly distinct from such power that I am quite certain it is not of the same order or class as the enthusiasm of the politician or the glow of the orator. May we full often feel the divine energy, and speak with power.

But then, fourthly, the Spirit of God acts also as an anointing oil, and this relates to the entire delivery—not to the utterance merely from the mouth, but to the whole delivery of the discourse. He can make you feel your subject till it thrills you, and you become depressed by it so as to be crushed into the earth, or elevated by it so as to be borne upon its eagle wings; making you feel, besides your subject, your object, till you yearn for the conversion of men, and for the uplifting of Christians to something nobler than they have known as yet. At the same time another feeling is with you, namely, an intense desire that God may be glorified through the truth which you are delivering. You are conscious of a deep sympathy with the people to whom you are speaking, making you mourn over some of them because they know so little, and over others because they have known much but have rejected it. You look into

318

some faces, and your heart silently says, "The dew is dropping there"; and, turning to others, you sorrowfully perceive that they are as Gilboa's dewless mountain. All this will be going on during the discourse. We cannot tell how many thoughts can traverse the mind at once. I once counted eight sets of thoughts which were going on in my brain simultaneously, or at least within the space of the same second. I was preaching the gospel with all my might, but could not help feeling for a lady who was evidently about to faint, and also looking out for our brother who opens the windows that he might give us more air. I was thinking of that illustration which I omitted under the first head, casting the form of the second division, wondering if A felt my rebuke, and praying that B might get comfort from the consoling observation, and at the same time praising God for my own personal enjoyment of the truth I was proclaiming. Some interpreters consider the cherubim with their four faces to be emblems of ministers, and assuredly I see no difficulty in the quadruple form, for the sacred Spirit can multiply our mental states, and make us many times the men we are by nature. How much he can make of us, and how grandly he can elevate us, I will not dare to surmise: certainly, he can do exceeding abundantly above what we ask or even think.

FRANK BARTLEMAN

Pentecostal Preaching

Calvin, Edwards, and their successors identified a discrete role for the Holy Spirit in biblical interpretation, preaching, and conversion. It was Wesley's emphasis on spiritual perfection, however, that gave birth to holiness movements in Europe and America. The holiness groups stressed the "second blessing" of sanctification. A child of the holiness movement, American Pentecostalism, insisted on glossalalia or "speaking in tongues" as the third and definitive mark of the true Christian. Modern American Pentecostalism was born in a three-year revival from 1906 to 1909 at the Azusa Street Mission in downtown Los Angeles. City newspapers gave the revival a bad press under such headlines as "Weird Babel of Tongues," and many were offended at Pentecostalism's mixing of races. Yet "Azusa" became a lively shrine for holiness and pentecostalist Christians from around the world. The Azusa Street revival was chronicled by Frank Bartleman (1871–1935), an itinerant holiness preacher and reporter for religious magazines. His eye-witness reports of the infectious power and hysteria of the movement, fueled as it was by the California earthquake of 1906, are among the classic documents of American religious history. Pentecostalism relies on the immediacy of the Holy Spirit in preaching and, as the following comments indicate, describes spiritual power in terms of a variety of physical manifestations.

Frank Bartleman, *How Pentecost Came to Los Angeles—As It Was in the Beginning* [1925], pp. 26–27, 48–49, 60, 71–73, 75–76, 121–122.

One evening [in Los Angeles] I went to Brother Manley's tent meeting, without a thought of taking part in the service. I sat in the rear. Soon the Spirit came mightily upon me. I rose and spoke and the power of God fell upon the congregation. The whole company fell on their faces. For three hours the whole tent was an altar service and prayer continued. A number were saved and everybody seemed to get help from God. It was a wonderful visitation of the Spirit. The people were not as rebellious in those days as they are now. They were more willing to have the program broken into, and there were not so many fanatical spirits to hinder. There was a real hunger for God. Almost every night found me taking part in some meeting. The Lord continued to pour out his Spirit. . . .

One evening at the Holiness camp the Lord told me he wanted me to preach. I went out in the woods and tried to pray for the meeting. But he said, I want you to preach. I told him they would not let me. They had a dozen of their own itching for the opportunity. Besides they were half afraid of me. I did not belong to their particular branch of religion. But he said preach! I told him if he would close every other mouth that night I would obey him. Throwing the responsibility thus on him I went to the meeting. It was time for the message. They looked at one another but every tongue was tied. No one looked at me. The Spirit came upon me and I sprang to my feet. God flooded my soul with power. The message came straight from him and went like an arrow to the mark. It shook the camp. . . .

I gave a message at my first meeting at "Azusa." Two of the saints spoke in "tongues." Much blessing seemed to attend the utterance. It was soon noised abroad that God was working at "Azusa." All classes began to flock to the meetings. Many were curious and unbelieving, but others were hungry for God. The newspapers began to ridicule and abuse the meetings, thus giving us much free advertising. This brought the crowds. The devil overdid himself again. Outside persecution never hurt the work. We had the most to fear from the working of evil spirits within. Even spiritualists and hypnotists came to investigate, and to try their influence. Then all the religious sore-heads and crooks and cranks came, seeking a place in the work. We had the most to fear from these. But this is always the danger to every new work. They have no place elsewhere. This condition cast a fear over many which was hard to overcome. It hindered the Spirit much. Many were afraid to seek God, for fear the devil might get them.

We found early in the "Azusa" work that when we attempted to steady the Ark the Lord stopped working. We dared not call the attention of the people too much to the working of the evil. Fear would follow. We could only pray. Then God gave victory. There was a presence of God with us, through prayer, we could depend on. The leaders had a limited experience, and the wonder is the work survived at all against its powerful adversaries. But it was of God. That was the secret. . . .

[At the Azusa Street Mission] some one might be speaking. Suddenly the Spirit would fall upon the congregation. God himself would give the altar call. Men would fall all over the house, like the slain in battle, or rush for the altar enmasse, to seek God. The scene often resembled a forest of fallen trees. Such a scene cannot be imitated. I never saw an altar call given in those early days. God himself would call them. And the preacher knew when to quit. When he spoke we all obeyed. It seemed a fearful thing to hinder or grieve the Spirit. The whole place was steeped in prayer. God was in his holy temple. It was for man to keep silent. The shekinah glory rested there. In fact some claim to have seen the glory by night over the building. I do not doubt it. I have stopped more than once within two blocks of the place and prayed for strength before I dared go on. The presence of the Lord was so real. . . .

On the afternoon of August 16, at Eighth and Maple, the Spirit manifested himself through me in "tongues." There were seven of us present at the time. It was a week day. After a time of testimony and praise, with everything quiet, I was softly walking the floor, praising God in my spirit. All at once I seemed to hear in my soul (not with my natural ears), a rich voice speaking in a language I did not know. I have later heard something similar to it in India. It seemed to ravish and fully satisfy the pent up praises in my being. In a few moments I found myself, seemingly without volition on my part, enunciating the same sounds with my own vocal organs. It was an exact continuation of the same expressions that I had heard in my soul a few moments before. It seemed a perfect language. I was almost like an outside listener. I was fully yielded to God, and simply carried by his will, as on a divine stream. I could have hindered the expression but would not have done so for worlds. A heaven of conscious bliss accompanied it. It is impossible to describe the experience accurately. It must be experienced to be appreciated. There was no effort made to speak on my part, and not the least possible struggle. The experience was most sacred, the Holy Spirit playing on my vocal cords, as on an Aeolian harp. The whole utterance was a complete surprise to me. I had never really been solicitous to speak in "tongues." Because I could not understand it with my natural mind I had rather feared it.

I had no desire at the time to even know what I was saying. It seemed a soul expression purely, outside the realm of the natural mind or understanding. I was truly "sealed in the forehead," ceasing from the works of my own natural mind fully. I wrote my experience for publication later, in the following words: "The Spirit had gradually prepared me for this culmination in my experience, both in prayer for myself, and others. I had thus drawn nigh to God, my spirit greatly subdued. A place of utter abandonment of will had been reached, in absolute consciousness of helplessness, purified from natural self-activity.". . .

In the experience of "speaking in tongues" I had reached the climax in abandonment. This opened the channel for a new ministry of the Spirit in service. From that time the Spirit began to flow through me in a new way. Messages would come, with anointings, in a way I had never known before, with a spontaneous inspiration and illumination that was truly wonderful. This was attended with convincing power. The Pentecostal baptism spells complete abandonment, possession by the Holy Ghost, of the whole man, with a spirit of instant obedience. I had known much of the power of God for service for many years before this, but I now realized a sensitiveness to the Spirit, a yieldedness, that made it possible for God to possess and work in new ways and channels, with far more powerful, direct results. I also received a new revelation of his sovereignty, both in purpose and action, such as I had never known before. I found I had often charged God with seeming lack of interest, or tardiness of action, when I should have yielded to him, in faith, that he might be able to work through me his sovereign mighty will. I went into the dust of humility at this revelation of my own stupidity, and his sovereign care and desire. I saw that the little bit of desire I possessed for his service was only the little bit that he had been able to get to me of his great desire and interest and purpose. His word declares it. All there was of good in me, in thought or action, had come from him. Like Hudson Taylor I now felt that he was asking me simply to go with him to help in that which he alone had purposed and desired. I felt very small at this revelation, and my past misunderstanding. He had existed, and had been working out his eternal purpose, long before I had ever been thought of, and would be long after I would be gone. . . .

The early church lived in this, as its normal atmosphere. Hence its abandonment to the working of the Spirit, its supernatural gifts, and its power. Our wiseacres cannot reach this. Oh, to become a fool, to know nothing in ourselves, that we might receive the mind of Christ fully, have the Holy Ghost teach and lead us only, and at all times. We do not mean to say we must talk in "tongues" continually. The "baptism" is not all "tongues." We can live in this place of illumination and abandonment and still speak in our own language. The Bible was not written in "tongues." But we may surely live in the Spirit at all times, though possibly few, if any, always do. Oh, the depth of abandonment, all self gone! Conscious of knowing nothing, of having nothing, except as the Spirit shall teach and impart to us. This is the true place of power, of God's power, in the ministry of service. There is nothing left but God, the pure Spirit. Every hope or sense of capability in the natural is gone. We live by his breath, as it were. The wind on the day of Pentecost was the breath of God.—Acts 2:2. But what more can we say? It must be experienced to be understood. It cannot be explained. We have certainly had a measure of the Spirit before without this. To this fact all history testifies. The church has been abnormal since its fall. But we cannot have the Pentecostal baptism without it, as the early church had it. The Apostles received it suddenly, and in full. Only simple faith and abandonment can receive it. Human reason can find all kinds of flaws and apparent foolishness in it.

I spoke in "tongues" possibly for about fifteen minutes on this first occasion. Then the immediate inspiration passed away, for the time. I have spoken at times since, also. But I never try to reproduce it. The act must be sovereign with God. It would be foolishness and sacrilege to try to imitate it. The experience left behind it the consciousness of a state of utter abandonment to the Lord, a place of perfect rest from my own works and activity of mind. It left with me a consciousness of utter God-control, and of his presence naturally in corresponding measure. It was a most sacred experience. Many have trifled most foolishly with this principle and possession. They have failed to continue in the Spirit and have stumbled many. This has wrought great harm. But the experience still remains a fact, both in history and present day realization. The greater part of most Christians' knowledge of God is and has always been, since the loss of the Spirit by the early church, an intellectual knowledge. Their knowledge of the word and principles of God is an intellectual one, through natural reasoning and understanding largely. They have little revelation, illumination or inspiration direct from the Spirit of God. . . .

[Later, on tour in Indianapolis] the Lord gave me a number of messages. We had a wonderful time. In fact I had not felt the power of God in such measure for a long time. There was tremendous opposition also, but God gave the victory. The work had been split into two factions. They came together in the meeting but were not reconciled. At one meeting the Spirit was so mightily on me in the message that the opposing faction held on to their seats and stiffened their backs to keep from yielding. I have seldom seen such resistance to the Spirit of God, and by Pentecostal saints, at that. It was simply awful. One night they had arranged for foot-washing. I gave the message that night and by the time I got through I think they had forgotten all about the foot-washing. They were too busy getting right with God, and with one another. Their souls needed washing more.

The Lord blessed me much at Indianapolis. I was so glad I had obeyed him and gone there. I was there by his invitation purely. But I seldom if ever had felt such a wonderful flow of the Spirit before. The message seemed to be fairly drawn out of me in preaching. I felt almost drawn off the platform by the hungry desire of the people. I could not talk as rapidly as the thoughts came to me and almost fell over myself trying to speak fast enough. At one meeting when I was through the slain of the Lord lay all over the floor. I looked for the preachers behind me and they lay stretched out on the floor too. One of them had his feet tangled up in a chair, so I knew they had gone down under the power of God. I stepped over near the piano, among the people. My body began to rock under the power of God and I fell over onto the piano and lay there. It was a cyclonic manifestation of the power of God. We left the convention with great victory. I had not received a penny since leaving home and the devil was tempting me much over the matter. But the Lord kept assuring me he would make it up to me later on. I had to take his word for it, for I could not understand the situation. It was a new one to me. But I knew God had spoken.

RUDOLF BOHREN

The Spirit as Giver and Gift of the Word

Rudolf Bohren (1920–) is Professor of Practical Theology at the University of Heidelberg. His *Predigtlehre* is the last great systematic theology of preaching in Germany, and its four editions have exerted enormous influence among Protestant preachers in that country. In it Bohren attempts a comprehensive framework for both the theory and the practice of preaching, ranging from theological definition to communications theory. Bohren's roots are in Calvin, the Blumhardts, Bonhoeffer, and Barth, and in years of experience as a pastor and preacher. Against Bonhoeffer's Christological approach to preaching, Bohren situates preaching in pneumatology, the doctrine of the Holy Spirit. Christological homiletics leads to Christ-mysticism, but the Holy Spirit is the Spirit of the church and thereby rules out preaching as a mystical or individualistic activity. Bohren understands spirit as life-force and therefore shows the necessity of distinguishing the Holy Spirit's activity in preaching from the various spirits of the age. He has little difficulty juxtaposing discussions of communications theory and pneumatology and retaining the concept of miracle in connection with the sermon. The Holy Spirit's relation with the other persons of the Trinity informs Bohren's notion of "theonomic reciprocity" by which the Holy Spirit "works with" human language and culture. An important part of the following discussion is the word *Begeisterung*, which has been rendered "in-spiration" in an effort to set it off from its English connotation of general enthusiasm.

Rudolf Bohren, *Predigtlehre* (München: Chr. Kaiser Verlag, 1971), pp. 82–88. Selection translated by Susan Harsh. Used by permission.

I call the Spirit the giver of the word, which is to say at the beginning that I as a preacher do not possess the word in myself. First the Spirit

326

speaks, then I speak. "Theonomic reciprocity" [which is the relation of human and divine agency in preaching] occurs first in the give and take of language.

One encounters this reality in the New Testament on many levels and in many ways. Jesus himself begins to preach only after his baptism with the Spirit (Mark 1:9). In the commissioning of the disciples the Spirit is promised as an advocate before judges and kings: "When they deliver you up, do not be anxious how you are to speak or what you are to say; for what you are to say will be given to you in that hour; for it is not you who speak, but the Spirit of your Father speaking through you" (Matt. 10:19-20). Paul claims to have the Spirit of God, to speak "with words taught by the Spirit" (I Cor. 2:12) as one who has his ability from God (II Cor. 3:5). The manifestation of the Holy Spirit on Pentecost has as its consequence a language-miracle (Acts 2:4). . . . When Paul lays hands upon the disciples of Apollos in Ephesus and the Spirit comes, they speak in tongues and preach from inspiration (Acts 19:6). It is reported about Paul himself — and Jesus as well — that he preaches after receiving the Spirit and baptism. The Paraclete promised in the Gospel of John makes Jesus' word a present word (14:26), and Jesus' breath, which mediates the Holy Spirit to the disciples, empowers them to proclaim the forgiveness or the retention of sin (John 20:22f.).

If in keeping with the New Testament we maintain that the Spirit gives the word, it follows that the Spirit himself is, so to speak, nothing without that which he gives, namely, the word. It is remarkable that the giving of the Spirit, according to both Luke and John, is not in and of itself sufficient. The language-miracle of Pentecost evidently needs expansion by Peter's sermon, to which we have already referred. A text is introduced to explain the event; the event does not explain itself. In John the giving of the Spirit is framed by a preceding and a following word — the sending of the disciples into the world and the authority for absolution and retention — while the gift of the Spirit itself is accompanied by a gift-formula: "Receive the Holy Spirit" (John 21:21-23). The agreement of the two New Testament authors on the relationship of the giving of the Spirit and the word is all the more amazing given the great differences in their reporting. The Spirit is not only the giver of the word; he apparently *requires* the word of interpretation. The Spirit's need for the word might be called the *kenosis* (emptying) of the Spirit. . . . Only what we call the kenosis of the Spirit makes the notion of "theonomic reciprocity" finally understandable.

The Spirit becomes the speech teacher of the disciple, and the disciple the mouthpiece of the Spirit. It is not the disciple who speaks, but the

Spirit. But the Spirit needs the mouth of the disciple, and the disciple himself must speak. If the disciple brings the Spirit into language, the Spirit also helps the disciple to speak. The Spirit gives not only the word but its articulation. The Spirit determines not only the word's advent and presence but also its future. For preaching this means first of all that the preacher receives the word from the Holy Spirit. The prospective speaker's speechlessness is overcome by the reciprocal give and take of speech between Spirit and preacher. . . .

Accordingly, the Spirit's presence in the preacher does not mean a linguistic facility or wit, as we generally understand them, but rather a gift. This gift is the certainty of a relationship and the designation of a special time; in short, it is the discovery of a new self in a new relationship. . . . In the relationship to the Spirit the preacher is able to say "I." There is a passive and an active dimension of this relationship between Spirit and preacher. One has to do with what the Spirit does with the preacher, the other of what the preacher does for himself. In the active and the passive there is also a question of what the preacher does with the Spirit (notice the verbs used in connection with the Holy Spirit, e.g., Acts 1:8, "receive" or Acts 7:51, "resist"). Because the Spirit's presence does not exclude but rather includes the human presence, the question of sermon method cannot be set aside. . . .

We confine ourselves to references to the Spirit as giver and gift of the word and do not speak about what the Spirit does with the word or how the Spirit accompanies the word. Since we have already alluded to the Spirit's need of the word, we turn now to another dimension. The Spirit not only gives the word, and the word not only explains the Spirit, it *mediates* the Spirit. But then "in-spiration" or "spiritualization" [*Begeisterung*] becomes the goal of the sermon.

If one wished to speak manneristically, one could here speak of "spiritualism." The offensiveness of the word "in-spiration" would be avoided, much to the liking of the spiritualists. However, since docetism represents the greatest danger in pneumatology, I will stay with the offensive manner of speaking by using "in-spiration." But this is misleading. In colloquial language we use the word synonymously with an unreflective idealism, also with ecstasy and staggering. In this case "in-spiration" [*Begeisterung*] as the goal of the sermon would be "opium for the people," and preaching has been this time and time again: food for illusions. The offensive concept "in-spiration" nevertheless seems absolutely necessary to me, precisely because it demands critical understanding, in that it clearly shows the necessity of testing the spirits. I would like to be strictly literalistic also. Preaching that inspires is preaching that enlivens. For further clarification of the concept, consult first of all the New Testament. . . .

Because all speaking contains spirit, it also in some way mediates some kind of spirit. In this regard it can be said that all speaking inspires. Therefore there is also no preaching which does not in some way communicate some kind of spirit. Every sermon transmits the spirit in which and out of which it is preached. A preacher may have a suggestive effect and fill the hearers with his own life-spirit. The "in-spiration" of the speaker may carry the audience along, working contagiously. The value of this kind of "in-spiration" is a separate question, but "in-spiration" as such should not be distrusted. It should be remembered that the weary preacher is also contagious and can impart to the congregation the sense of his own weariness. The preacher who has given up can convey that. Even with his powerlessness the preacher "inspires" his hearers. Boredom is also a kind of "in-spiration," the reverse of enthusiasm. It has a spontaneity all its own—yawning! Finally, we should consider the spirit of the milieu from which the preacher emerges and which also exerts influence on the hearers.

Thus understood, "in-spiration" has a rich range and as such is neither to be praised nor criticized, but tested. However, if one wishes to overlook the function of "spirit" as it has been described, one will also deny the coming of the Spirit into the human sphere and will most certainly think about the Spirit in docetic terms. Such thinking encourages and insures the widespread and, for the most part, unconscious error, that preaching is infallible and does not require examination and critique by the listening congregation.

The disregard of "in-spiration" reveals a lack of common sense and the sense of reality. The actual repression of enthusiasm in our churches and the absence of any critique of preaching are two sides of one piece of evidence. If at the outset enthusiasm is disparaged, the necessity of testing the spirits slips from our hand—practically, if not theoretically. . . . "There is no Christian freedom without a shot of enthusiasm," says Ernst Käsemann (*Der Ruf der Freiheit*, p. 78). Sermon-critique, congregational maturity, an active laity—without freedom there are none of these. Spirit-giving preaching truly inspires by giving freedom. In the giving of freedom it always inspires to something. It sets an end and a beginning; thus it animates.

Because "in-spiration" is variously evaluated and because its rich range necessitates testing, it may be postulated that preaching does not offer just any spirit but precisely the Holy Spirit. Preaching should communicate the Spirit who creates the world anew. It inspires by means of the

Creator-Spirit. No more and no less is expected from preaching than this—that it gives this Spirit who is the Spirit of freedom. But the preacher cannot give this Spirit from himself, even though he is always giving something of himself. For this Spirit proceeds from the Father and the Son, not from the preacher. The preacher certainly may hope that in transmitting a word given by the Spirit that the Spirit will give himself. Therefore I insist on the concept of miracle with regard to the sermon because everything depends on this, namely, that the Spirit from the Father and Son imparts himself through our preaching. The miracle of preaching is pentecostal, and the preacher may hope that in speaking the Spirit-given word the Spirit will communicate himself. Therefore the preacher will take care that his individuality does not spoil everything for the Spirit. Preparing and delivering a sermon involve creativity which leads to a process of dying. To preach is to experience death. It only becomes "in-spiration for life" because of the dominance of the resurrection. But whoever enters the pulpit as a little paradise will first pass through deserts and will discover that paradise is the ultimate place of the temptation to be like God and to confuse our spirit with the Holy Spirit.

This is not the place to describe the purpose of the Holy Spirit's inspiration. Nevertheless, two types of "in-spiration" in the context of the new creation should be pointed out. The Holy Spirit is a Spirit of joy. Wherever he gives himself there is joy. In giving joy, he inspires praise and awakens the spirit for singing. In bringing in the future, the Spirit gives praise with joy. Preaching inspired by the Spirit looses the tongue not only to praise but also to protest and lament. The Holy Spirit is not a Spirit of joy in the sense that he deludes himself about things. He knows very well about sadness; he can waken the ability to mourn since he teaches not only the exaltation of Pentecost but also lamentation and even perhaps the psalms of vengeance. He teaches us to cry out. He himself raises worship's cry for freedom! The Spirit raises up accusations against the injustice of the world, laments the sorrows of the world, and brings misery to articulation. This is his way to initiate the transformation of the world. Joy and sorrow are named here as two forms of "in-spiration" with which the Spirit opposes the new against the most widespread Anti-spirit—indifference. The new establishes itself as freedom and brings itself to articulation in laments and praise.

We have spoken here about the goal of preaching in order to better understand the origin of preaching. From the perspective of the goal it becomes quite clear how important it is that not just any spirit whispers in the ear of the preacher, but that the Holy Spirit himself is the Inspirer of preaching.

330

VIII
THEOLOGY, WORD AND SACRAMENT

P. T. FORSYTH

Positive Theology and Preaching

Theology and preaching are both the church's language. But what is their relationship? For Barth, dogmatic theology is the monitor of the church's proclamation, while for Barth's successor at Basel, Heinrich Ott, theology and preaching are functional equals. Early in the twentieth century P. T. Forsyth (1848–1921) assessed the relation of theology to preaching by establishing the theological principle of grace as the substantive core of all preaching. It is the theological principle that gives the preacher his or her staying power. It is important to note that for Forsyth the principle of grace is the expression of a living and holy Christ by whose cross the world is changed forever. The objectivity of the Atonement and the necessity of its proclamation lie at the center of Forsyth's "positive theology", by which he meant "evangelical theology." He opposed the liberal, evolutionary drift of his day, especially as it was manifest in R. G. Campbell's *The New Theology*, which, to Forsyth's mind, blurred all distinctions between God and the human spirit. Forsyth was the first great evangelical of this century. In his Beecher Lectures he offered a prophetic critique of evangelical theology "which has not really escaped from the idea of orthodoxy, a theology not only elaborate and final, irrevisable, and therefore obscurantist, and therefore robbed of public power." Forsyth challenges the preacher to examine the theological *principle* rather than the effects of his or her preaching and, having done so, to discover the personal God within it.

P. T. Forsyth, *Positive Preaching and Modern Mind* (New York: A. C. Armstrong, 1907), pp. 199–205.

The first requisite for a Christian man is faith. That is what makes a soul a member of Christ and of the true church—the faith that works and blossoms out into love. Being faith in Christ, how could it but work and flower out into love? The fact that so often it does not must mean that in so many cases it is not really faith, or not faith in Christ. It is not personal contact and commerce with him. This faith it is that is the greatest thing in the world, having in it all the promise and potency of love, godliness, peace, and joy in the Holy Ghost. It is such living faith that makes a man a Christian.

But among Christians the preacher stands out in a special place and work. And the first requisite for the ministry of a church is a theology, a faith which knows what it is about, a positive faith, faith with not only an experience but a content, not glow only but grasp, and mass, and measure. The preacher who is but feeling his way to a theology is but preparing to be a preacher, however eloquent he may have become. He may be no more than "the hierophant of an unapprehended inspiration." And that kind of inspiration may be mantic or romantic, but it is neither prophetic nor apostolic. The faith which makes a man a Christian must go on in the preacher to be a theology. He cannot afford to live on in a *fides non formata*. A viscous unreflecting faith is for the preacher a faith without footing and therefore without authority. In special cases it may have a certain infection about it, but it has not authority. Yet it is authority that the world chiefly needs and the preaching of the hour lacks—an authoritative gospel in a humble personality. And for authority, for weight, we need experience indeed, but, still more, positive faith.

It is but a little way that experience will carry the herald of the gospel. He has to expound a message which, because it is eternal, far transcends his experience. He has to do more than set to his own personal seal. Every Christian has to do that. The preacher has to be sure of a knowledge that creates experience, and does not rise out of it. His burden is something given, something that reports a world beyond experience, a world that is not of experience, though always in its shape. Experience is but in part, yet he has to dogmatize about the whole. He has to be sure of what ever is, and evermore shall be. Experience is in time, and he has to be positive about eternity. His experience covers but his own soul, or at most a few besides that he touches; yet he has to declare a certainty about the eternal destiny of the whole world, and the eternal will of the whole God. That is a knowledge far beyond experience. It is not realizable except in experience, but experience could not reach it, could not assure it. It is a knowledge that comes by faith. Wherever you have a universe you have something beyond experience, and accessible only to faith. Experience is not the only organ of knowledge, however it may be a condition. Experience deals with but the one, or the several; faith deals with a whole; for it deals with God, eternity and the world; it deals with a reality of the whole, which we experience but in a measure. There is a knowledge by faith as sound of its kind as the knowledge by experience, by science; and its kind is much higher, deeper, more momentous. It is the knowledge of a person in his purpose, not of a thing and its features, not of a force and its laws. It is not simply faith as a personal experience that is the burden of the preacher, but faith as a knowledge, the inner objective content of faith, the thing in faith which always creates the experience of it; in a word, the person, will, and action of God in Christ. It is there, in the objective personal content of faith, and not in the subjective personal experience, that the authority of the preacher lies. His experience may make him impressive at times, but it is his faith that gives him permanent power. That power really lies not in the preacher but in his gospel, in his theology. For the preacher it is most true that his theology is an essential, perhaps the essential, part of his religion. He may be quite unfit to lecture in theology as a science, but he is the less of a preacher, however fine a speaker, if he have not a theology at the root of his preaching and its sap circulating in it. And if he is a pastor, producing his effect not by a few addresses but by a cumulative ministry, all this is still more true.

The first requirement of the ministry, then, is a positive theology. But by that I do not mean a highly systematic theology, nor an orthodox theology. For a systematic theology easily becomes doctrinaire, and an orthodoxy soon becomes obsolete. It were well to banish antiquated words like orthodoxy and heterodoxy as anything but historical terms. . . . Let us consider the words, therefore, as archaic and defunct for faith. And instead of speaking or thinking about an orthodox theology, which is canned theology gone stale, let us think of a positive theology which is theology alive, alert, and in power.

Again, by a positive theology I mean naturally the opposite of a negative. But when is a theology negative? Negative of what? Negative of a tradition? No, of a power. Negative of the gospel. A positive theology is an evangelical theology. Positivity in this connection has a chief reference to what I have often to describe as the primacy of the will. It is moral; but moral in a far higher sense than a mere imperative—moral as being not diffused in an idea or organized in thought, but concentrated in a personal act, in redemption. The love manifested by Christ in his life was positive in the sense that it was not merely affectional but rational and moral. That is to say its great features were first that it understood the total situation—so far as it was rational—and second that it condensed into one definite practical purpose—it was saving and moral. It understood God uniquely; no man knoweth the Father but the Son. It understood man to his moral center, and needed that no man should tell it what was in man. And it was concentrated into crucial action both on God and on man. It was decisive and redemptive. Positive means moral in the great evangelical sense. That is to say, in the first place, it means that the supreme form of God's love was a real act, central in history and critical for eternity. It was a holy life not simply in the sense of being spotless but in the sense of being one vast moral deed, one absolute achievement of conscience, affecting the being both of God and man and the whole spiritual world. It was not merely impressionist. It was not an influence but an act, not a fresh stimulus but a new creation, not a career opened for the race but a finished thing. Holiness has no meaning apart from an act into which is put a whole moral person; and if there be an eternal person it is an eternal act, and not merely a past event, or the attribute of an eternal being, or an infinite presence, as the mystics dream. Accordingly, in the second place, God's gift was an eternal life, something beyond natural goodness, however good, and however refined. For what is morality, when we are at the height to which we have now come? It is not a mere obedience. That were in the end but some kind of Pharisaism, of which indeed Protestantism has been greatly the victim. No compliance with a mere law or creed, however good or fine, makes a moral action. Morality is the expression of our personality; and to grow moral means to grow in personality, and not merely in a certain exercise of personality. It is our creative action. It is the soul co-operating with the holy energy of God and fulfilling its redeemed destiny. To live in the Spirit is not simply to walk in the light. The Spirit is creative energy; and to live in the Spirit is to exercise this energy. It is eternal life in its countless concrete forms of actuality, experience, and history—in worship, art, science, politics, in church, state, or family. Positive Christianity then is Christianity which recognizes the primacy of the moral in the shape of life, and of holy life. It is Christianity which first adjusts man to the holy and then creates the holy in man, and does both through the Cross with its atoning gift of eternal life. It is evangelical Christianity—Christianity not as a creed nor as a process but as a Holy Spirit's energy and act, issuing always from the central act and achievement of God and of history in the Cross of Christ.

But the name of evangelical theology has often been monopolized by a theology which has not really escaped from the idea of orthodoxy, a theology not only elaborate but final, irrevisable, and therefore obscurantist, and therefore robbed of public power. By an evangelical theology

I mean any theology which does full justice to the one creative principle of grace. Any theology is evangelical which does that. A theology is not evangelical by its conclusions but by its principles, not by its clauses and statements, not by its spirit or temper, but by the Holy Spirit of grace and power.

KARL BARTH

Revelation, Sacrament, and Doctrine

For Karl Barth (1886–1968) preaching may not be restricted to a particular locus of Christian doctrine, be it Christology, pneumatology, or ecclesiology. According to the *Church Dogmatics*, preaching is "the attempt by someone called thereto in the church, in the form of an exposition of some portion of the biblical witness to revelation, to express in his own words and to make intelligible to the men of his own generation the promise of the revelation, reconciliation and vocation of God as they are to be expected here and now" (I, 1, p. 56). The greatest part of Barth's discussion of preaching occurs under the heading, Word of God. That word is threefold: the revealed Word made flesh; the written word of Scripture; and the preached word. The latter word, and the sacraments, make up the church's proclamation. It is not the task of dogmatic theology to provide the content of sermons. "This content must be found each time in the middle space between the particular text in the context of the whole Bible and the particular situation of the changing moment." Dogmatics can only be a "guide" for preaching to help it choose what must be said in a given circumstance or what must not be said under any circumstance (I, 1, p. 79). Ultimately, dogmatics aims to insure that the church's talk conforms to the church's being, which is the richness of its life given to it by God. The centrality of revelation in Barth's theology means that preaching is a divine activity. True preaching does not add to or embellish the revelation with "vain images" or "outpourings of sentimental eloquence." Preaching is a human activity that becomes the word of God where and whenever it witnesses and attests to the primary revelation of God in Jesus Christ. Barth held a high view of preaching to which, as he said of his own preaching, his *Dogmatics* was a "footnote." The following selection from his lectures on preaching is based on notes recorded by his students.

KARL BARTH

Karl Barth, *The Preaching of the Gospel*, trans. B. E. Hooke. English translation © S.C.M. Press Ltd. 1963, pp. 12–19, 20, 22–26, 28–32. Reprinted and used by permission of The Westminster Press, Philadelphia, Pennsylvania.

Preaching and Revelation

The relation of preaching to revelation may be considered first in its negative aspect. It is not the function of the preacher to reveal God or to act as his intermediary. When the gospel is preached, God speaks: there is no question of the preacher revealing anything or of a revelation being conveyed through him. It is necessary, in all circumstances, to have regard to the fact that God has revealed himself (Epiphany) and will reveal himself (Parousia). Whatever happens by means of preaching—in the interval between the first and the second coming—is due to its divine subject. Revelation is a closed system in which God is the subject, the object, and the middle term.

The practical consequences of this are as follows:

Preaching cannot claim to convey the truth of God; neither can its aim be to provide a rational demonstration of the existence of God by expounding briefly or at length certain theoretical propositions. There is no proof that God exists except that which he himself provides. Nor are we required to display the truth of God in an artistic form by the use of vain images or by presenting Jesus Christ in outpourings of sentimental eloquence. When Paul told the Galatians that he had portrayed before their eyes Jesus Christ crucified, he was not referring to speeches in which he had used every device of artistry to capture the imagination of his hearers. For him, to portray Christ was to show him forth in plain truth without embellishments. We are under orders to "make no image or likeness." Since God wills to utter his own truth, his word, the preacher must not adulterate that truth by adding his own knowledge or art. From this point of view, the representation of the figure of Christ in art, the crucifix in churches, as well as symbolic images of God, may be of doubtful value.

Neither must the preacher seek to establish the reality of God. His task is to build God's kingdom and he must work toward a decision. His message must be authentic and alive; he must lay bare man's actual situation and confront him with God. But he is going too far if he thinks of this confrontation as "a sickness which leads to death" (Kierkegaard). This phrase no doubt presupposes things which are implicit in preach-

339

ing, but it concerns the action of God and no man ought to intrude in what is not his province.

If it is maintained that a preacher ought to convert others and cause his hearers to share his own faith, this can only be understood in the sense that he should be aware of what is happening when he is bearing witness. The preacher who believes in Christ will never present himself to his congregation in such a way that they will suppose him able to bestow on them Christ and the Spirit, or think that the initiative in what is done is his. God is not a *Deus otiosus*; he is the author of what is done. We can act only in obedience to the task given to us; neither our aims nor our methods are of our own devising.

Our preaching does not differ in essence from that of the prophets and apostles who "saw and touched"; the difference is due to the different historical setting in which it takes place. The prophets and apostles lived during that moment of the historical revelation of which Scripture is the record. We, on the other hand, bear witness to the revelation.

But if God speaks through our words, then in fact that same situation is produced: the prophets and apostles are present even though the words are spoken by an ordinary minister. But we must not think of ourselves as uttering prophecies; if Christ deigns to be present when we are speaking, it is precisely because the action is God's, not ours. Since this is the way things happen, the preacher can make no claims for his own program.

Thus any independent undertaking that is attempted, whether with the intention of developing a theoretical subject or with the practical purpose of leading one's hearers into a certain frame of mind, can in fact be nothing else but a waiting on God, so that he may do with it what he will. If the preacher sets himself to expound a particular idea, in some form or another—even if the idea is derived from a serious and well-informed exegesis—then the Scripture is not allowed to speak for itself; the preacher is discoursing on it. To put it more positively, preaching should be an explanation of Scripture; the preacher does not have to speak "on" but "from" (*ex*), drawing from the Scriptures whatever he says. He does not have to invent, but rather to repeat something. No thesis, no purpose derived from his own resources, must be allowed to intervene: God alone must speak. Perhaps, afterward, he will have to ask himself whether he has allowed himself to be influenced by an idea of his own or has attempted to arrive at a unity which only God could create. He must follow the special trend of his text, and keep to it wherever it may lead him, not raising questions about a subject which may, as it seems to him, arise from the text.

340

KARL BARTH

In this connection it may be pointed out that the choice of a text may present dangers, in that one may choose a text because it bears on a subject one would like to discuss; one may even turn to the Bible in order to find in it something which fits in with one's own thoughts! To have to speak from a particular text to a particular congregation in an actual situation is in itself a dangerous undertaking. It may be that in that situation God will speak and work a miracle, but we must not build on that miracle in advance. Otherwise it would be easy for a preacher to become a sort of pope and indoctrinate his congregation with his own ideas by presenting them as the word of God.

The positive aspect of this matter must now be considered. The starting point is the fact that God wills to reveal himself; he himself bears witness to his revelation; he has effected it and will effect it. Thus preaching takes place in obedience, by listening to the will of God. This is the process in which the preacher is involved, which constitutes part of his life and controls the content as well as the form of his preaching. Preaching is not a neutral activity, nor yet a joint action by two collaborators. It is the exercise of sovereign power on the part of God and obedience on the part of man.

Only when preaching is controlled by this relationship can it be regarded as "kerygma," that is, as news proclaimed by a herald who thereby fulfills his function. Then the preacher is omnipotent, but only because of the omnipotence of the one who has commissioned him. The kerygma means therefore to start from the Epiphany of Christ in order to move toward the Day of the Lord. Thus New Testament preaching consists in a dual movement: God has revealed himself, God will reveal himself.

From these considerations certain consequences follow:

The fixed point from which all preaching starts is the fact that God has revealed himself, and this means that the Word has become flesh; God has assumed human nature; in Christ he has taken on himself fallen man. Man, who is lost, is called back to his home. The death of Christ is the final term of the Incarnation. In him our sins and our punishment are put away, they no longer exist; in him man has been redeemed once for all; in him God has been reconciled with us. To believe means to see and know and recognize that this is so.

If then preaching is dominated by this starting point, the preacher can adopt no attitude other than that of a man to whom everything is given. He knows, without any possible doubt, that everything has been restored by God himself. He is, however, constantly beset by the temptation to denounce man's sin or to attack his errors. Certainly it is

341

necessary to speak of human sin and error, but only in order to show that sin is annihilated and error destroyed. For either it is true that man is forgiven or else there is no forgiveness whatever. Sin cannot be spoken of except as borne by the Lamb of God.

At the same time, to separate the gospel from the law in preaching is not Christian. How is it possible to proclaim the gospel without also hearing the law which says: "Thou shalt fear and love God"? This danger is particularly noticeable in Calvinism.

Moreover, from its first to its last word, preaching follows a movement. This has nothing to do with the preacher's convictions, or his earnestness, or his zeal. The movement starts from the fact that the Word became flesh, and the preacher must abandon himself to its guidance. If this rule were observed, how many introductory remarks would become quite unnecessary! The movement does not consist so much in going toward men as in coming from Christ to meet them. Preaching therefore proceeds downward; it should never attempt to reach up to a summit. Has not everything been done already?

It has already been pointed out that preaching has one single point of departure, which is that God has revealed himself. It should also be recognized that it has one unique end: the fulfillment of the revelation, the redemption which awaits us.

From beginning to end the New Testament looks toward the achievement of salvation. This, however, is not to deny that all has been accomplished once for all. The Christ who has come is the one who will return. The life of faith is orientated toward the day of the Parousia. The point of departure and the point to which everything tends are summed up in the declaration: "Christ the same yesterday, today, and forever." And assuming that we await the whole Christ, Christology and eschatology may be said to be one. Revelation, therefore, is before as well as behind us.

It follows, then, that preaching moves in an atmosphere of expectation. There is no settling down comfortably in faith and the assurance of salvation, as if divine grace manifested in the past allowed us now to take our rest in tranquillity. Without doubt there is a profound and joyful assurance, but there is also the solemn and earnest concern of one who watches because the end is near. Preaching, like all Christian life, grows to its fullness between the first advent and the second. . . .

KARL BARTH

Preaching and the Church

Preaching has its place within the context of what is called the church; it is bound up with the church's existence and its mission. . . .

The true church is characterized by the fact that "*Evangelium pure docetur et recta administrantur sacramenta*" (Augsburg Confession, VII). These two concepts, sacraments and preaching the gospel, throw light on the connection between the church and conformity to revelation.

The sacrament, with all its wealth of meaning, may first be considered, for it is impossible to understand what preaching is without understanding what the sacrament is. There is indeed no preaching, in the precise meaning of the term, except when it is accompanied and illuminated by the sacrament. What is the sacrament? Unlike preaching or any other ecclesiastical activity, the sacrament goes back to that action of the revelation which founded the church and constitutes her promise, for the sacrament is not merely a word but an action, physically and visibly performed.

Baptism confers on a man the seal of belonging to the church, for his life begins not with his birth but with his baptism. To be baptized means that a relationship between the revelation and a man has been established and is made actual in a specific situation (Rom. 6:3). If baptism represents the event which is the point of departure, the Lord's Supper, on the other hand, is the sign of the same event but turned toward the future which we all await (I Cor. 11:26).

Preaching, then, is given within that church where the sacrament of grace and the sacrament of hope are operative, but each partakes at once of the character of grace and hope, for neither sacrament nor preaching has significance except within the church, where each is authenticated by its relation to the other. Preaching, in fact, derives its substance from the sacrament which itself refers to an action in the total event of revelation. Preaching is a commentary on and an interpretation of the sacrament, having the same meaning but in words. If this fact be recognized, it will be clear that preaching is impossible except within the territory of the church, in that setting where, in baptism and the Lord's Supper, man is chosen by God himself to belong to the body of Christ, to be nourished and protected during his journey to eternal life. And we should know that all those who hear are baptized and called to partake of grace, and what has been thus begun in them will be fulfilled.

In this way, by reference to baptism and the Lord's Supper, the origin and the aim of preaching, and the course it pursues, are more clearly defined and the place of the messenger of the word is more plainly seen.

Having discussed these theoretical questions, let us consider what goes on in the evangelical church. At the outset something appears to be lacking. In those circles which embraced the Reformation, the sacramental Church of Rome was replaced by a church of the word. Very soon, preaching became the center of worship and the celebration of the sacrament came to occupy a more restricted place, so that today in the Roman Church, the church of the sacrament, preaching has little significance, while in the Reformed Church the sacrament, while it exists, does not form an integral and necessary element of worship. These two positions are in effect a destruction of the church. What meaning can there be in preaching which exalts itself at the expense of the sacrament, and does not look back to the sacrament which it should interpret? Our life does not depend on what the minister may be able to say, but on the fact that we are baptized, that God has called us. This lack has indeed been recognized, and attempts have been made to fill it by various means (reform of the liturgy, beautifying worship with music, etc.). But these palliative measures are bound to fail because they do not touch the real issue.

Those who advocate such methods of renewing the forms of worship take their stand — mistakenly — on Luther. But he, seeking to retain all that was of value in the Roman liturgy, gave first place to the Lord's Supper. Calvin, also, constantly emphasized the necessity for a service of Communion at every Sunday worship. And this is precisely what we lack today: the sacrament every Sunday. The order of worship should be as follows: at the beginning of the service, public baptism; at the end, the Lord's Supper; between the two sacraments, the sermon, which in this way would be given its full significance. This would indeed be *"recte administrare sacramentum et pure docere evangelium."* So long as the true significance of evangelical worship in its totality is not understood, no theological efforts or liturgical moments will be efficacious. Only when worship is rightly ordered, with preaching and sacrament, will the liturgy come into its own, for it is only in this way that it can fulfill its office, which is to lead to the sacrament. The administration of the sacraments must not be separated from the preaching of the gospel, because the church is a physical and historical organism, a real and visible body as well as the invisible, mystical body of Christ, and because she is both these at once.

There is no doubt that we should be better Protestants if we allow ourselves to be instructed in this matter by Roman Catholicism; not to neglect preaching, as it so often does, but to restore the sacrament to its rightful place. It is open to question whether the motive for our liturgical efforts is anything more than a desire to approach nearer to the "beautiful services" of the Church of Rome. But what is rightly to be sought is not an elaboration of the liturgy but the true significance of the sacrament in the church. A good Protestant will allow himself to admit this, and at the same time will insist on good preaching.

In preaching, all that is necessary is to recount again what concerns the prior event of revelation. And in order to distinguish the two actions to which revelation refers, the preacher may point to the sacrament on the one hand and the Holy Scripture on the other; the one looks back to the act of revelation which God accomplished, the other refers to the nature of the revelation. It is idle to oppose sacrament to preaching; they cannot be separated, since they are two aspects of the same thing. . . .

Preaching and Doctrine

It has already been shown that preaching is subject to an order; it is a mission and a command, and therefore has a relation to doctrine.

In setting out to educate men, it is possible to follow a scheme and determine one's aim. This method could be applied by the preacher also if it were the church's task to educate humanity and make human beings into real men. But if the true function of the church be understood, it cannot proceed thus. The church is not an institution intended to keep the world on the right path, nor is it dedicated to the service of progress. It is not an ambulance on the battlefields of life. On the other hand, it must not seek to establish an ideal community, whether of souls, hearts, or spirits. No doubt all these things have their value and should engage one's attention. They can, moreover, be accessories to preaching and can play a part in it, as they do in ordinary life. The preacher, like other Christians, lives in the world and cannot avoid these things. But the moment he makes them his chief object, the preacher ceases to have any justification for preaching. This is becoming more and more obvious today when all the various civilizing agencies have been taken over by organizations other than the church. If the church were to disappear—a point of view expressed by Richard Rothe, for example, who advocated the progressive fusion of church and state—the press, the radio, social welfare schemes, psychology, and politics would suffice to care for the life of the family and of the soul. As regards public morals and similar preoccupations, the children of this world know more about them than the church does and have access to more efficient methods. In these circumstances the church is merely the fifth wheel of the carriage—and not even a spare wheel!

It is necessary, therefore, to consider seriously the mission laid upon the church. What is needed are men who are obedient to an order given to them from outside themselves, to a necessity prior to everything which determines our earthly existence, such as birth or death. The church is obliged to recognize precisely that an order has been given which must be carried out. The church can justify her existence only insofar as she understands that she is founded on a call. Therefore, she has no plan—for the plan is God's—but only a task to fulfill. Preaching, set within the frame of worship, should be the proclamation of the church's obedience to the task committed to her by Christ.

From all this the following considerations emerge:

Preaching must faithfully adhere to doctrine, that is, to the confession of our faith, which is not a summary of the religious ideas drawn from our own inner consciousness but a statement of what we believe and confess because we have received it and have heard the word of revelation. The confession is man's response to what God has said, and every sermon is a response for which the preacher is responsible.

Preaching, therefore, has nothing to do with any scheme or notion which the preacher has wrought out in his own mind. Here only obedience is required; in other words, having heard the word of God he responds in accordance with the confession of faith. Naturally one is not required to preach confessions of faith, but to have as the purpose and limit of one's message the confession of one's church, taking one's stand where the church stands.

A second, practical consequence concerns the element of edification: What is to be built up? Clearly, the church itself. But building up the church is not to be understood in the sense given to it in the *Shepherd of Hermas*, where it means "to go on building," "to build upon an edifice in course of construction." To build up the church means to rebuild each time from foundation to roof. The church has to be remaking itself continually; continually the orders given have to be accepted, obedience has constantly to be learned again. "By obedience to obedience" is the journey of the Christian. The church is a community placed under revelation and built up by hearing the word of God, built up by the grace of God in order that it may live. In this context then, but only there, can one speak of educating men, of giving moral and spiritual help to humanity; there is a place for such secondary structures in the shadow of the main building. "Seek ye first the kingdom of God and his righteousness"; "one thing is needful."

R. E. C. BROWNE

The Exposition of Doctrine

Another view of doctrine, quite unlike Barth's, is present in the thought of R. E. C. Browne (1906–1975), an Irish-born priest and theologian who concluded his ministry as Rector of St. Chrysostom, Manchester, England. Browne is not well known as a theologian, and his published output is slight, but his collection of essays, *The Ministry of the Word*, has been called "a classic of British twentieth-century divinity." In it Browne's concern for preaching leads him into literate and nuanced discussions of revelation and its authority and communication. A poet himself, Browne might have taken as his "text" for the following essay the lines from George Herbert: "Doctrine and life, colors and light, in one, when they combine and mingle. . . ," for the revelation of doctrine, in Browne's vocabulary, is not sharp and segregated from all that is human, but *includes* every human correlative, implicate, or analogue of the divine life. His analogical theology of preaching is the antithesis of Barth's "preaching from above." Preaching that arises from a matrix of pastoral care will never cease to probe the human expressions of doctrine, not in order to create a theological system for the hearer, but to help the hearer interpret and apply doctrine in life. Because *analogy* is central to its theological task, preaching will be attentive to image, metaphor, and all other forms by which language serves doctrine.

R. E. C. Browne, *The Ministry of the Word* (Philadelphia: Fortress Press, 1976 [1958]), pp. 41–50. Copyright © Fortress Press. Used by permission.

Simple people recognize the complexity of life without resentment. They think, mindful that their thinking must do justice to this complexity, and they attempt to speak to others in language that neither minimizes nor overestimates the extent of human knowledge. Simplicity of speech is most nearly achieved in the frank acceptance of the mystery of reality and of the mysterious nature of words as parts of the reality they are used to describe. Added to this the speaker must constantly remember that he is part of the reality he discusses; in fact when he speaks of anything he is inevitably talking about himself, for he is not a spectator of the complexity of life but a factor in it, because he partly makes the complexity he seeks to understand. Religion is not a way of mastering this complexity but of bearing it. Christian doctrine does not offer a complete interpretation of human experience but suggests a way toward its interpretation, nor does Christian doctrine claim that examination of human experience will provide a final satisfactory way of checking the truths of the Christian revelation. But where there can be no exact disclosure of the meaningfulness of human experience or literal statement of doctrine it is nevertheless possible to talk significantly about each in terms of the other. For instance, it is not given to a minister of the word to state the exact meaning of the corporate experiences shared by members of the body of Christ, yet he can say a great deal that is pertinent about church membership.

Ministers of the word are always being led to reflect on the nature of Christian doctrine as well as on its content in their work to achieve the coherency necessary for intelligible speech in the pulpit, in the confessional and on all the manifold occasions of their ministry. To proclaim sound doctrine means that it must be firmly held through the ups and downs of moods, in disasters, in disappointments, in achievements and in triumphs. The way to hold it is largely found through reflections on its nature and its content. There is an old saying that the monk who knows he is praying is not praying. It could be said that a minister of the word who is consciously aware of himself as doctrinally sound is not doctrinally sound. Doctrinal soundness would be to think the truth and do the truth and pray the truth in that full state of self-affirmation which is that self-forgetfulness which no direct conscious efforts can create. That is the aim; to know it is not the same as having achieved it, to travel is not to arrive but in the journeying we are vouchsafed some knowledge of our journey's end. This chapter suggests the sort of reflections which might be made by a minister of the word in the hope that it will be given him to speak boldly as he ought to speak.

If Christian doctrine were the formulation of a complete knowledge of reality or if it presented the principle of interpretation through which every experience could be completely explained, then the holding of doctrine would be determined accordingly, and so would its exposition. But Christian doctrine does not claim to tell exactly why and exactly how God creates; it does not claim to tell exactly why and exactly how God became man without ceasing to be God. Christian doctrine does not offer a full explanation of the birth, life, death, resurrection and ascension of the Lord whereby we are saved from the bondage of sin and death and time and the order of this world. It does not offer a man the definition of his identity or of what constitutes his differences from and likenesses to all other human beings. Christian doctrine does not enable a man to see the reason for earthquake, tornado, typhoon, for pain, war, death and treachery. A neat doctrinal system rounded and conclusive could only be built with the support of extra axioms brought in to supplement those that revelation gives. The mind when left to itself plays tricks and scrupulous theologians must be quick to detect the introduction of unwarranted axioms in an attempt to make complete what must be left incomplete. To hold sound doctrine always means the maintenance of a system of thought through which every new fact of experience can be interpreted to the degree that interpretation is possible. A false doctrinal system is one that dismisses awkward experiences as irrelevant or imposes an interpretation which is convenient rather than truthful. A true system safeguards the reality of partial human knowledge and so orders this knowledge that a man may realize that the totality of his experiences makes sense even if he cannot fully see it. . . .

Fear of error is the greatest enemy of truth. The minister of the word needs to be fearless in his thinking if he is to be truthful and humble in his speaking. Ministers of the word sometimes encourage one another to dread error rather than reverence truth. Those who dread error talk in a pattern of qualified statements where each qualifying statement drains the meaning out of the statement it qualifies. Fear of error also leads to such carefully balanced utterances that the force of a sermon is lost in an array of citations from theologians who are given opposing positions and seem to struggle against one another on the fringes of the sermon, and the struggle is gradually brought into such a position of prominence that the rest of the sermon is hidden. Sometimes a sermon is spoiled by unresolved conflicts in the preacher's mind which show themselves by broken sentences, by paragraphs unfinished or artificially finished and by excessive speed over unmade roads in the course of the sermon's journey. Christian doctrine is not given that we may avoid mistakes in our thought and utterance. Christian doctrine is given so that we can think and talk positively in full recognition that no minister of the word is the sole agent, that his is not the only sermon that people listening will ever have the opportunity to hear. To think positively is to discover that the minister of the word's true doctrinal position is always on the fringes of error. We can only think our clearest thoughts and speak our most authoritative words from the frontiers of error; for example, our clearest statements of the omnipotence of God almost deny the freedom of man. But there is a more apt metaphor from modern warfare where battles are fought in zones rather than from behind fixed lines; mental operations are better considered as the movement and counter-movement of thoughts and feelings in zones, and the thing is to control the movement not by restricting its range but by paying attention to its purpose; thus he who moves freely in the zones will have eloquence. Eloquence is the art of putting into words that which is extremely difficult to put into words. It is the minister of the word's vocation to be eloquent in this sense. That eloquence cannot be without the adventure of holding doctrine in such a way that one is always in danger of losing one's grip of it. Our religion rests on the foundation of theism which can only be made real to the mind by continual meditation on the doctrine of creation, which puts one in danger of pantheism and a denial of the necessity of the Incarnation. It is only by reflection on the creative activity of God that the full glory of the Incarnation can be seen, for when every creative act is recognized as an act of revelation then it can be seen how the one act that is the revelation of revelations illuminates and is illuminated by all other acts of God. It is only by thinking emphatically about the humanity of our Lord that one can realize his divinity, while it is only by concentrated reflection on his divinity that the reality of his manhood is apprehended. In other words, meditation on his being must always be concerned both with his earthly ministry and his eternal sovereignty, because meditation is not part of a process that ends in a finished conclusion, it is the prelude to adoration of the mystery that is God. All theology begins in adoration and ends in adoration, but it can only end in adoration if emotion, imagination, intelligence are not stifled but used by the preacher in the pursuit of his calling, which may be described as an attempt to master words sufficiently to expound the truth which in mastering men frees them from the errors born in sin and from the errors that give birth to sins. And at this point one is led to remember that it is only by considering the power of God's grace that one begins to understand the nature of the human effort required in individual man's salvation; it is only by seriously considering the nature of this human effort that one begins to know the ceaseless activity of God in which all human action has its beginning. It is by devotion to Christ in the Blessed Sacrament that one discovers most fully that where the word is not spoken the bread will not be broken. It is only through diligent attention to the necessity for the spoken word that the essential nature of the sacraments is realized—where the bread is not broken soon

350

the word will not be spoken. The importance of the ministry is most clearly seen when one is at the point of denying it; the significance of the church's corporate life can best be seen at the point where one is about to deny it in emphasizing the value of the individual; the value of each individual is most clearly seen when one is about to deny it in affirming the value of the corporate. A truth is often capable of being most clearly seen when it is about to be denied.

The minister of the word does his clearest thinking on the edges of error, he is most orthodox when on the point of coming to heretical conclusions. In a sense thinking means submitting to the movement of the mind, not blindly or mechanically but maintaining a remote control over the movement. This remote control is maintained by the Christian through constant reflection on the limits of his creatureliness in the light of his doctrine. The image for thinking is not movement within a square marked by firm thick lines but rather that of movement in a space bounded by distant but discernible boundaries. Doctrine is not held by supression of thoughts that challenge its truth but by their proper development. . . .

To expound doctrine is not to teach a system of thought and then demonstrate that no experience can disturb it. It is not that doctrine is supremely important and that life proves its importance; it is that life is supremely important and doctrine illuminates it. The minister of the word is called to be an expert in living rather than an expert in doctrine. At the command of the Lord he studies doctrine, he teaches it that people may have life and that they may have it more abundantly. As this chapter is showing, the way doctrine is held shapes the way it is expounded and the way it is held is determined by what a man thinks about its nature and content. Christian doctrine does not provide the answer to every question but the way to begin answering; doctrine does not tell a man what to think but how to think. Revelation is not a huge gift which makes man's work unnecessary and takes away from him all need of initiative. We are given sufficient knowledge to make the life of faith possible, but to live faithfully does not mean that one is given all knowledge, but rather the ability to live the full human life, being reconciled to and rejoicing in the reality of partial human knowledge. . . .

No one lectures abstractly on doctrine; one talks it to people who are fellow human beings if not also fellow church members; always there is a common tie which makes conversation possible and has much to do with its form. Relationships are living, changing things which make it impossible for any minister of the word to depend on a few invariable forms for his use in saying what he has to say. The mental and psychic

351

atmosphere of the day decides the pattern of his secret reflections about doctrine. The more compassionate a pastor is, the more he is in danger of speaking heretically, but that danger is inevitable if he is to discover a way of making himself clear to the men and women of his generation with that degree of clarity which his subject permits. But who can be entirely coherent about the whole of life? That is the size of the preacher's subject, but he can hope that doctrinal integrity will sharpen the edges of his intelligibility sufficiently for it to cut through the traffic that blocks the minds of so many who listen.

Perhaps the most significant consideration of doctrine for the minister of the word is that which is concerned with all that the doctrine of creation implies. This has a direct effect on his whole conception of preaching and it also enables him to speak in the pulpit and out of the pulpit in the ways that are most expedient for this generation. To take the first point: belief in preaching, or indeed in meaningful conversation, has doctrinal roots or else it has no roots. To go on believing in the value of human speech and the possibility of communication can only be justified by what one believes about the nature of reality. More than that, human speech is not fully appreciated till it is recognized as a part of creation just as much as landscapes and shifting clouds. That is, no poem or sermon comes into being without the divine initiation. A poem or sermon is made in much the same way as bread is made. Bread ultimately consists of the energy of the sun, the sustenance given by rain and soil and the mysterious energy of life within the seeds sown by men. The loaf on the table is there because God ceaselessly provides all the raw materials necessary including the psychic energy which enables men to work and co-operate with one another. The making of bread is a significant human action which we proclaim every time we reverently place the common bread on the altar; this common unconsecrated bread is only less wonderful than the consecrated bread. Before the altar we are reminded that man does not live by bread alone. He needs the things that are made by human speech which are nourishment for his mind. Music and the visual arts have their place in life, but whenever speech is absent or deficient the human spirit dwindles and the human mind is bewildered and becomes brutal. The utterances of men are possible because God ceaselessly brings into being the raw materials necessary for their making: we can neither contemplate fulness of human life nor the possibility of our religion bringing that fulness to perfection without the arts, and in particular without the art of ordered speech. . . . Human speech is never fruitless; they use it best who most frequently ponder its origin and its end.

GEOFFREY WAINWRIGHT

Preaching as Worship

In some Protestant traditions preaching plays so dominant a role in worship that liturgy and sacraments appear as preface or appendix to the sermon. Barth criticized the lack of proportion in Protestant worship, insisting that preaching derives its substance from the sacrament and means the same as the sacrament "but in words." Geoffrey Wainwright (1939–   ), a British Methodist, Professor of Systematic Theology at Duke Divinity School and author of *Doxology* (1980), underscores Barth's point and draws an even closer parallel between preaching and sacramental worship. In the following selection Wainwright uses the language of the eucharist to demonstrate that the homily is not merely located in the *context* of worship, but that it is a liturgical act itself. Such preaching is doxological, for it understands itself as a "reasonable service" to God, its primary "audience." In its concern to hear the Scripture, preaching is an exercise in anamnesis, or remembering. Just as the eucharistic anamnesis recites the mighty acts of God culminating in the resurrection, so preaching never forgets the story that shapes the church's life and hope. In the epiclesis the celebrant (and preacher) invoke the power of the Holy Spirit on that which is to be enacted and said. Like Thielicke and others, Wainwright assigns to the Holy Spirit the task of joining the remembered word to the present situation. Throughout his analysis Wainwright draws on the thought of John Chrysostom, the Eastern Church's greatest exegete and preacher. The following is taken from the St. John Chrysostom Lectures delivered at the Holy Cross Greek Orthodox School of Theology, Brookline, Massachusetts in November 1982.

Geoffrey Wainwright, "Preaching as Worship," *The Greek Orthodox Theological Review*, Vol. 28, No. 4 (Winter 1983), 325–336. Used by permission.

The Second Vatican Council, in its Constitution on the Sacred Liturgy, restated what had always been in principle true: the homily is part of the liturgy itself. The Easter narrative of the Emmaus pilgrims may already reflect a regular Sunday liturgy of the primitive church, in which the presence of the risen Lord is experienced through the reading and exposition of the Scriptures and the divine Stranger is known in the breaking of the mysterious bread. In my own Methodist tradition, the Wesley brothers took St. Luke's story in that way and made a present liturgical application in their *Hymns on the Lord's Supper*:

> O Thou who this mysterious bread
> Didst in Emmaus break,
> Return herewith our souls to feed,
> And to Thy followers speak.
>
> Unseal the volume of Thy grace,
> Apply the gospel word,
> Open our eyes to see Thy face,
> Our hearts to know the Lord.

Certainly word and sacrament belonged together in the Sunday assembly of the Christians by the time of St. Justin Martyr in the middle of the second century:

> And on the day called Sun-day an assembly is held in one place of all who live in town or country, and the records of the apostles or writings of the prophets are read for as long as time allows.
> Then, when the reader has finished, the president in a discourse admonishes and exhorts us to imitate these good things.
> Then we all stand up together and offer prayers; and as we said before, when we have finished praying, bread and wine and water are brought up, and the president likewise offers prayers and thanksgivings to the best of his ability, and the people assent, saying the Amen; and there is a distribution, and everyone participates in the elements over which thanks have been given; and they are sent through the deacons to those who are not present [Apol. I, 67].

In the vicissitudes of Christian history, the sermon has sometimes been shifted from its proper place within the liturgy and may even, in certain degenerate periods and places, have disappeared altogether from use, while in Protestantism the service of the word has often been robbed of its sacramental counterpart and context. But since the teaching and practice of the early church indicate that the homily is an integral component of the liturgy, it will be appropriate for us to consider preaching in the same theological categories as we use for Christian worship as such; and it may in return be the case that the sermon sheds light on the whole enterprise of Christian worship. Let us, therefore, try to examine preaching under four aspects which characterize the church's liturgy but which modern writers rarely bring to bear on the sermon. I want to suggest that preaching is, first, doxological; second, anamnetic; third, epicletic; and fourth, eschatological. In the first case, the most explicit divine reference will be to God the Father; in the second case, to the incarnate word; in the third case, to the Holy Spirit; and the fourth and final part of this first lecture will unite these various hypostatic accounts in a suitable trinitarian harmony which will have been implicitly present throughout to sensitive ears. At all stages we shall seek help from the Eastern Church's greatest preacher, John Chrysostom.

The Doxological Character of Preaching

In his treatise *On the Priesthood* [6,5], St. John Chrysostom declares that "all these various [duties of the priest] have one goal in view: the glory of God and the upbuilding of the church." Elsewhere this twin aim is ascribed by him to the preacher in particular, who as God's servant must have his mouth opened, and the word supplied, "for his glory and your edification." Such texts find their broad ecclesiological grounding in the liturgically framed passage of I Peter 2:4-10: By the very fact of being "built into a spiritual house, to be a holy priesthood, to offer spiritual sacrifices acceptable to God through Jesus Christ," Christians are "declaring the excellencies of Him who called you out of darkness into His marvellous light." And contrariwise, by proclaiming the mighty acts of God we are constituting a living temple for the worship of God. It is, however, not to St. Peter but to St. Paul that the preacher of Antioch and Constantinople looks for an example in his own priestly duty of preaching; and we may go with John Chrysostom to his apostolic instructor.

The Apostle to the Gentiles several times envisages his evangelism in liturgical terms. At the very end, he wrote to Timothy: "I am already on the point of being sacrificed; the time of my departure has come" (II Tim. 4:6). The martyrdom which St. Paul expected was but the culmination of an apostolate marked by "afflictions, hardships, calamities, beatings,

355

imprisonments, tumults, labors, watching, hunger" (II Cor. 6:4f). He bore on his body the marks of Jesus (Gal. 6:17). In the trials of apostleship Paul believed that he was "carrying in the body the death of Jesus": "While we live we are always being given up to death for Jesus' sake, so that the life of Jesus may be manifested in our mortal flesh. So death is at work in us, but life in you" (II Cor. 4:7–12). The cultic roots of this sacrificial language become unmistakable when the Apostle writes to the Philippians: "Even if I am to be poured out as a libation upon the sacrificial offering of your faith, I am glad and rejoice with you all" (Phil. 2:17). The self-spending of the gospel-preacher is part of the larger offering that includes the converts' faith. . . .

The Apostle's personal sacrifice finds its verbal counterpart in his preaching. To the Romans St. Paul says: "On some points I have written to you very boldly, by way of reminder, because of the grace given me by God to be a minister (*leitourgón*) of Christ Jesus to the Gentiles in the priestly service of the gospel of God, so that the offering of the Gentiles may be acceptable, sanctified by the Holy Spirit" (Rom. 15:15f). In interpreting that text, Chrysostom places these words in the Apostle's mouth: "My priesthood consists in preaching and proclaiming; this is the sacrifice I offer"; and he develops the image by borrowing from Ephesians 6:17 "the sword of the Spirit, which is the word of God." The offering of the Gentiles—it matters little exegetically whether the genetive is objective or subjective—is their "obedience," which is "the obedience of faith" (Rom. 1:5). When, in response to the preacher's message, conversions are made, the eucharistic chorus is thereby augmented (see II Cor. 4:13–15).

John Chrysostom rightly concludes from the presence of the verb *latreuo* that St. Paul in Romans 1:9 conceives of his evangelizing activity as itself the worship of God: "For God is my witness, to whom I render spiritual worship in proclaiming the gospel of his Son, that without ceasing I mention you always in my prayers . . ." In the sermon he preached at his ordination to the presbyterate, it is not on his prayers for the congregation that Chrysostom concentrates; and the future "doctor of the eucharist" does not so much as mention the sacrament. Rather the sermon itself, which God has put into his mouth, is returned to God as "an offering of firstfruits," "a sacred hymn of praise": "What kind of a sacrifice is the word, someone may ask. It is a great and august sacrifice, better than all others." Elsewhere he calls the closing doxology of the sermon a "fitting end." It is so because it recalls the direction of the whole sermon toward God.

No more than the Apostle is the later preacher alone in his sacrifice. Just as St. Paul's sacrificial evangelism drew the Gentiles into the obedient offering of themselves to God, so it would be fair to see John Chrysostom — by now preaching to the at least half converted — as leading the congregation in and into the "sacrifice of praise, the tribute of lips that acknowledge God's name" (Heb. 13:15). The *sacrificium laudis* is traditionally identified with the eucharist proper, but it may also be appropriate to notice here some words of Chrysostom concerning the Psalms as used in Israel's and the Church's worship: "At one and the same time, God receives praise and the singers receive an instruction to guide their life and lead them to exact knowledge of the truths of faith." Just so with preaching. Not only are the sermons of Chrysostom hymns of praise; they are constantly concerned to help his hearers confess the true faith in the face of heretics and unbelievers and, perhaps above all, to lead a Christian life.

In this last way, preaching is also indirectly doxological in that it is an encouragement to doxological living. Immediately after speaking of the sacrifice of praise, the Letter to the Hebrews continues: "Do not neglect to do good and to share what you have, for such sacrifices are pleasing to God" (13:16). According to St. Paul, "your body is a temple of the Holy Spirit within you, which you have from God. You are not your own; you were bought with a price. So glorify God in your body" (I Cor. 6:18–20; cf. II Cor. 6:16–7:1). Conversely, the Apostle identifies sin with idolatry in Romans 1:18–32, Colossians 3:5, and Ephesians 5:5. The most classical of the texts on ethical sacrifice, however, is probably Romans 12:1f: "I appeal to you therefore, brethren, by the mercies of God, to present your bodies as a living sacrifice, holy and acceptable to God, which is your spiritual worship (*logikan latreian*). Do not be conformed to this world but be transformed by the renewal of your mind, that you may prove what is the will of God, what is good and acceptable and perfect." Preaching has its part to play in the renewing of minds to discern the will of God for the living of lives acceptable to God. The transformation of the believer means an end to conformity with this world. Ethically distinguishable behavior contributes to the Christian witness in a pagan environment. John Chrysostom, who often exhorted his hearers to works of charity, would doubtless have approved of the use of Matthew 5:16 at the almsgiving in the communion office of the English Book of Common Prayer: "Let your light so shine before men, that they may see your good works, and glorify your Father which is in heaven." There we move into the area of what contemporary Orthodox theology has started to call "the liturgy after the Liturgy."

For the moment, however, we must return to the Liturgy itself and consider the anamnetic moment of preaching.

357

The Anamnetic Character of Preaching

The earthly church needs constantly to be reminded of the gospel on which it is founded and which continues to shape its life. That gospel is embodied in the teaching, person, and work of Jesus Christ, the incarnate Word of God and now the exalted Lord; and the definitive written testimony to the gospel is contained in the prophetic books of the Old Testament and the apostolic books of the New. The Scriptures continue to be read in church; and in and through their reading, as Chrysostom recognizes, the Lord makes himself present. But just as the Incarnation itself and the provision of the Scriptures represent a divine condescension and accommodation to the human condition, so a further *sunkatabasis* takes place in the preaching. For while the Scriptures are, Chrysostom holds, in themselves perspicuous, yet human slowness to understand requires the Lord to speak even through the interpretive words of the preacher [see R. Kaczynski, *Das Wort Gottes in Liturgie und Alltag der Gemeinden des Johannes Chrysostomos*, pp. 283–286].

The first task of the preacher, as far as his human audience is concerned, is to expound the Scriptures in their witness to Christ. Modern people will sympathize with Chrysostom's stress—typical of the Antiochene school of exegesis—on the historical sense of the text. Postmodernists will perhaps welcome his recognition, from time to time, that the historical sense may itself have been metaphorical from the first. What will scare our critical scholars in their concern for a narrowly conceived academic integrity is the patristic insistence that faith, prayer, and conversion, as well as careful study, are necessary for the understanding of the Scriptures: "Both a thorough search and persistent prayer are needed," Chrysostom tells the expositor [*Homilia* 21 (20), 1 *in Joannem*]; and he requires of the congregation that they first confess their sins, for otherwise their eyes of faith will be dimmed and their ears blocked for the hearing of the Word of God. Certainly the preacher himself must go on learning from the Scriptures, just as Timothy needed to continue learning from St. Paul. But he will not do this in an isolated way. Doubtless the preacher will spend time in private preparation of his sermon; but it will be as one who participates regularly in the liturgy and is steeped in its spirit, and as one who must deliver the sermon precisely in the framework of the liturgy. The liturgy is the connatural context for the interpretation of the Scriptures [*Doxology*, ch. 5]. So much of the Bible originated in the worship of Israel and of the primitive church. It was, above all, their reading in church which secured the recognition of these particular writings as canonical. It is only by their continued use in the worship of the church that the Scriptures have retained their status as holy books rather than now being treated, if at all, as more or less interesting pieces of ancient literature. The worshipping community supplies a living continuity down the centuries for transmitting the great images and themes of the Scriptures which might otherwise have become unintelligible through external cultural changes. The constant features and qualitative wholeness of the liturgy also provide the stability and unity within which to come to terms with the highly diverse material of the Bible.

John Chrysostom was in fact deeply concerned for the integrity of the Bible. Selective exegesis was the mark of heretics. He himself delighted in drawing instruction from the seemingly most unlikely passages of Scripture. He aimed at making his hearers familiar with the biblical material. He complained that some of them knew the names of the horses at the local race-track better than the names of the churches to which St. Paul wrote his epistles. In discovering the riches of the Scriptures the congregation needed to cooperate with the preacher. The preacher digs for the hidden treasures, draws the water from the well, prepares the table and offers the food and drink, sows the seed. The congregation must come hungering and thirsting, must prepare the ground and allow the fruit to grow in their lives, must put what they have acquired to work with interest.

This devotion to the entirety of Scripture and the determination to exploit it in every part nevertheless raises certain questions. By Chrysostom's time it appears that certain biblical passages or books had become traditional reading at appropriate feasts or seasons; but at other periods of the year and on other occasions it was the preacher's choice of text which determined the public lessons. This latter responsibility has been much prized in some Protestant circles; but while the circumstances of a congregation or an event in its life can call for an appropriate text from Scripture, there is a real danger that the congregation's exposure to the Bible will be limited to a particular preacher's preferred passages, perhaps idiosyncratically interpreted. Protestant moves towards the long-standing practice in the more catholic churches of following a lectionary cycle are therefore welcome. Lectionaries themselves, however, do not drop down directly from heaven, and their choice of texts is not immutable. Luther's key to the Scriptures—"was Christum treibt [that which promotes Christ]—has not only an objective side to it but also a more subjective: it appears that in different times and places, different parts of Scripture serve better than others to advance Christ. After the thoroughgoing revisions of the lectionaries in the Roman and other

Western churches in the past two decades, which were much influenced by the biblical theology movement of the 1950's, it is interesting that the 1977 Prague consultation on "The Role and Place of the Bible in the Liturgical and Spiritual Life of the Orthodox Church" should declare an openness to the "examination of possible changes in the pericope of evangelical and apostolic readings prescribed for Sundays and feasts of the year. For in these days multitudes of God's people assemble who, because of the incompleteness and monotony of the pericope, are deprived of the possibility to listen to the Word of God and its interpretation in its fullness," [Ion Bria, ed., *Martyria/Mission*, p. 235f]. It is not only a question of the amount of Scripture that can be absorbed over a recurring cycle of time. It is also — if I may say so as a preacher — a matter of the *combination* of the readings from the various parts of Scripture; for new juxtapositions can cause freshly illuminating sparks to fly among the appointed texts.

In this second section of the lecture we have been concentrating on the preacher's business with the Scriptures in their witness to the historic self-revelation of God in Jesus Christ; but this irreversible given is only one pole in the hermeneutical ellipse. The preacher must interpret the gospel *in the present situation*. The Word needs the vivifying Spirit. Anamnesis requires elaboration.

The Epicletic Character of Preaching

The preacher's connection with the Scriptures and his connection with the present situation are different in kind and quality. He is *bound* to the Scriptures but he need only *refer* to the present situation. . . . If, as Karl Barth hinted, one almost has to preach with the Bible in one hand and the newspaper in the other, yet there is no doubt that the Bible weighs heavier than even an American Sunday newspaper. No single sermon can conceivably count as much as the definitive witness to Christ in the Scriptures. No human situation has the permanence of the word of God. Nevertheless the same Holy Spirit who rested upon the incarnate Son and who presided over the composition of the Scriptures is appropriately invoked upon the preacher and his sermon.

St. John Chrysostom more than once recalls the gift of the Holy Spirit which the preacher presbyter has received through the laying on of hands at his ordination. He takes the exchange of greetings between preacher and people at the start of the sermon to echo that gift: "The Lord be with you"/ "And with thy spirit." Chrysostom frequently begs his congregation to pray for their preacher. The people's prayer for the preacher is finally to their own advantage, since his words are intended for them. The Holy Spirit's help is needed in order to discern *which* word from Scripture needs to be proclaimed at a particular time, and in order that it may be preached with a power that transcends human words (cf. I Thess. 1:5).

Effective preaching to a concrete situation demands a "reading" of that situation. Here the cooperation between preacher and people is most valuable. Since Pentecost, there is a sense in which all the Lord's people have indeed become prophets (cf. Num. 11:29). The faithful have the responsibility to read "the signs of the times." Through their very multiplicity and variety, believers have the opportunity to penetrate to levels and areas of human society which cannot be reached by the individual preacher or even by a whole college of preachers. By a service of information and discussion, all the members of the church can help their preacher to see the straws in the wind, the smoke that betokens a fire. The preacher then has the responsibility of bringing the word of God to bear on the great issues of the age, particularly as they affect the company of believers. John Chrysostom's series of sermons after the storming of the statues by the turbulent population of Antioch in 387 may serve as an example of sound pastoral advice in a difficult political situation. He was later removed from the see of Constantinople when he incurred the displeasure of the Empress Eudoxia by rebuking her imperial conduct.

Times may change, but the joys and sorrows, the hopes and fears of human beings remain fairly constant. Like many less important figures in the history of the church, Chrysostom was subjected to the complaint that, though he was a fine preacher, he failed to visit his people. What a preacher lacks in rhetorical skills may often be made up in sensitive pastoral care. That experience, in which the Holy Spirit is also present, will likely enhance the preacher's power to touch hearts and minds with a simple statement of the gospel. To interpret a difficult world for a troubled soul is often to change that world by the transfiguring light of God's kingdom.

The Eschatological Character of Preaching

In an essay "Towards a Catholic Use of Hermeneutics," Edward Schillebeeckx has criticized Bultmann for treating the Bible as simply a text, a closed "deposit," on which we draw again and again in the narrow point of the present for the existential possibilities it expresses. The Flemish Dominican writes:

> Everything to which the Bible bears witness is directed towards the fulfillment in the future of God's promise, the history of which has been narrated in faith in the Bible. It is possible to express our understanding of the Bible in this way: we should not look back at the Bible, but rather look forward, with the Bible, to a future which is given us to be achieved—to be achieved, but also *given us* to be achieved. . . . What biblical interpretation "points to" . . . must be orthodoxy (the correct interpretation of the promise insofar as it has already been realized in the past) as the basis of orthopraxis whereby the promise realizes a new future in us. It is only in the sphere of action—of doing in the faith—that orthodox interpretation can be inwardly fulfilled. . . . There certainly is a "deposit of faith," but its content still remains, on the basis of the promise already realized in Christ (realized in fact, but nonetheless still really a *promise*), a promise-for-us, with the result that interpretation becomes orientated to praxis. The Bible reminds us of God's faithfulness in the past, precisely in order to arouse our confidence in God's faithfulness in the future [*God the Future of Man*, pp. 1–49, esp. p. 36f].

In the anaphora of St. John Chrysostom, the *anamnesis* opens out to the final advent of Christ and the fullness of the divine kingdom:

> We therefore, remembering this saving commandment and all the things that were done for us: the cross, the tomb, the resurrection on the third day, the ascension into heaven, the session at the right hand, the second and glorious coming again; offering you your own from your own, in all and through all: we offer you also this reasonable and bloodless sacrifice, and we beseech and pray and entreat you, send down your Holy Spirit on us and on these gifts set forth; and make this bread the precious body of your Christ, changing it by your Holy Spirit, and that which is in this cup the precious blood of your Christ, changing it by your Holy Spirit, so that they may become to those who partake for vigilance of soul, for forgiveness of sins, for fellowship with the Holy Spirit, for the fulness of the kingdom, for boldness towards you, and not for judgment or for condemnation.

John Chrysostom the preacher was well aware of the trinitarian origins of the teaching office. The preacher is called by God to a ministry stemming from Christ, into which one is set by the Holy Ghost. As the herald and ambassador of God, the preacher has the task of building up the faith of the eucharistic community to the glory of God. Through the eucharist, believers are sacramentally maintained in the communion of the Holy Spirit whom they received in their baptisms as the *arabōn* of their promised inheritance. In the eucharistic communion they experience by anticipation the final *parousia* of Christ and enjoy a foretaste of the messianic banquet in the kingdom. In the anaphora they join with the whole company of heaven in worship before the throne of God.

At the last judgment, the preacher, priest and pastor will be called to account for their ministry. Who is sufficient for these things? The preacher stands under the same word as his hearers. He must dare to hope that the grace of which he has been the unworthy minister will not be denied him either.

INDEX